BUDAPEST'S CHILDREN

WORLDS IN CRISIS: REFUGEES, ASYLUM,
AND FORCED MIGRATION

Elizabeth Cullen Dunn and Georgina Ramsay, *editors*

BUDAPEST'S CHILDREN

Humanitarian Relief in the Aftermath of the Great War

Friederike Kind-Kovács

INDIANA UNIVERSITY PRESS

This book is a publication of

Indiana University Press
Office of Scholarly Publishing
Herman B Wells Library 350
1320 East 10th Street
Bloomington, Indiana 47405 USA

iupress.org

© 2022 by Friederike Kind-Kovács

All rights reserved

No part of this book may be reproduced or utilized in any form or by any means, electronic or mechanical, including photocopying and recording, or by any information storage and retrieval system, without permission in writing from the publisher. The paper used in this publication meets the minimum requirements of the American National Standard for Information Sciences—Permanence of Paper for Printed Library Materials, ANSI Z39.48-1992.

Cover image: School kitchen of the SCIU in Budapest (February 1921), image by Frank-Henrie Julien, Archives Privées 92.105.79 (3), CH Archives d'Etat de Genève, Geneva.

All efforts have been made to obtain permissions for use of images. The use of media here is solely for educational purposes. Parts of the work appeared in slightly different form in the following articles:

Kind-Kovács, Friederike. "Compassion for the Distant Other: Children's Hunger and Humanitarian Relief in Budapest in the Aftermath of WWI." In *Rescuing the Vulnerable: Poverty, Welfare and Social Ties in Nineteenth- and Twentieth-Century Europe*, edited by Beate Althammer, Lutz Raphael, and Tamara Stazic-Wendt, 129–59. New York: Berghahn Books, 2016. Reproduced with permission of Berghahn Books.

Kind-Kovács, Friederike. "The Great War, the Child's Body and the American Red Cross." *European Review of History* 23, no. 1–2 (2016): 33–62. Reproduced with permission of Taylor & Francis Online.

Kind-Kovács, Friederike. "The 'Other' Child Transports: World War I and the Temporary Displacement of Needy Children from Central Europe." *La Revue d'histoire de l'enfance "irrégulière"* 15 (2013): 75–95. Reproduced with permission of *La Revue d'histoire de l'enfance "irrégulière."*

Manufactured in the United States of America

First printing 2022

Cataloging information is available from the Library of Congress
ISBN 978-0-253-06215-4 (hardcover)
ISBN 978-0-253-06216-1 (paperback)
ISBN 978-0-253-06217-8 (e-book)

To Gyula, Laura, and Lotte

CONTENTS

Acknowledgments ix

Introduction *1*

1. Migration: Life in a Displacement Hub *25*
2. Hunger: Starving in the Capital City *60*
3. Degeneration: Embodying Postwar Suffering *91*
4. Institutions: The Genesis of Child Protection *121*
5. Infrastructures: Materializing "Glocal" Relief *153*
6. Bodies: Feeding Budapest's Hungry Children *184*
7. (Inter)Nationalism: The Politics of Material Aid *210*
8. Displacement: The Ambiguity of the Children's Trains *246*
9. Education: Workrooms to Teach the Children *273*

    Conclusion: Transformation: From Aid to Self-Help *304*

Bibliography 315

Index 341

ACKNOWLEDGMENTS

THIS BOOK COULD NOT HAVE BEEN WRITTEN WITHOUT the immense support I received in the past decade of my academic career. I would like to express my gratitude for the institutional and financial support of the Department of Southeast and East European History at Regensburg University, the Graduate School of Southeast and East European Studies (Regensburg/Munich), and the Hannah Arendt Institute for Totalitarianism Studies at TU Dresden. I would like to particularly thank Professor Ulf Brunnbauer, who has been immensely supportive since I started the research for this book in 2010, as well as Professor Catriona Kelly, Professor Paul Hanebrink, Professor Heide Fehrenbach, and the external reviewers who all gave me substantial feedback on the original manuscript. A substantial part of the work was written during my stay at the Imre Kertész Kolleg in Jena during the 2017–18 academic year and a semester at the Institute for Advanced Studies at Central European University in Budapest in 2019, supported through a Botstiber Fellowship in Transatlantic Austrian and Central European Relationships, for which I am very grateful. Thank you to the various parties that worked on the publication process, including the staff and anonymous reviewers at Indiana University Press. I would like to also thank Kristina E. Poznan and Jon Ashby for their help with revising the manuscript in various stages and Enikő Zöller for assistance with images. I am thankful for the 2019 Regensburg Prize for Women in Academia and the Arts from the city of Regensburg, which provided me with substantial financial support to finalize this volume for publication.

The work would have not been possible without the support of many archives and individuals. Combining an extensive body of Hungarian sources with a great diversity of written and visual sources from international archives, the text that follows has a genuinely transnational perspective. The monograph draws on Hungarian primary sources that reconstruct the historical legacy of Hungarian child protection before and after World War I. These sources have been gathered from the Hungarian state archives and several denominational archives (Episcopal Archive, Archive of the Evangelical Church, Hungarian Jewish Archive, Hungarian Jewish Congregation of Belief). Other important sources were found at the Semmelweis Library and Museum, Ethnographic Museum, Kiscelli Museum, Hungarian Pedagogical Museum and Library, Hungarian National Museum, Metropolitan

Ervin Szabó Library, and National Széchényi Library. To gain knowledge of Austro-Hungarian imperial child relief activities, I consulted the Austrian state archives in Vienna. To reconstruct the international humanitarian relief activities in Budapest, the book incorporates archival sources from Austria, the United States, Great Britain, and Switzerland. Contemporary British publications were gathered from the British National Archives in Kew and the British Library in London.

To demonstrate the involvement of the Save the Children Fund (London) and its International Union (Geneva), I conducted research at the Save the Children Fund Archive at the Cadbury Research Library in Birmingham. I also conducted research at the state archives in Geneva, which holds the collections of the Save the Children International Union. In Geneva, I also researched the archival collections of the League of Nations and the Archives du Comité International de la Croix-Rouge. To trace the involvement of the American National Red Cross, the US Food Administration, and the American Relief Administration, I conducted research at the National Archives and Records Administration at College Park, Washington, and the Hoover Institution Library & Archives at Stanford University. For insight into the ethnic dimension of relief, I consulted records in the archive of the Jewish Joint Distribution Committee in New York. The Library of Congress in Washington, DC, provided a useful body of US and international contemporary publications. Thank you to the archivists and librarians at each of these locations for their assistance. Finally, I have conducted life-story interviews with some individuals who participated in the "children's trains" to foreign countries. The accounts of the child evacuees, whom I would like to thank here, tell us what it meant to them to live a destitute life in postwar Budapest and to be sent away.

Most important, I would like to thank my husband, Gyula Kovács, and our two daughters, Laura and Lotte, for their support, understanding, and patience over the past decade, when I traveled for various research trips and international conferences abroad. Without them I would have never finished writing this book. I also would like to thank my parents, Gisela and Christian Kind, and my sisters, Ulrike and Sophie, for their continuous support. As the travel that was necessary to research this book and the time to write it were substantial, I feel blessed that I could rely on their helping hands and support throughout the years. And last, I thank all the loving caretakers at the various nurseries, kindergartens, afternoon care facilities, and schools in Regensburg, Budapest, and Weimar—as well as our various au pairs, among them Magdolna György, Csenge Molnár, Borbála Méry, and Sofía Ríos—for spending beautiful hours with our children while I was working on this book.

BUDAPEST'S CHILDREN

INTRODUCTION

A Capital City in the Aftermath of War

"They brought the children away from Budapest, because in the villages people could somehow still survive, but Budapest was a hell hole, it was terrible. The children were starving." This is how Piroska, a ninety-nine-year-old Hungarian woman, remembered her childhood.[1] In 1922, as an eight-year-old, malnourished and nearly starving, she was sent along with thousands of other children from Budapest to a foster family in Holland, where she stayed for several months. Her recollection of Hungary's capital is one of the few oral testimonies of a child's life in Budapest in the aftermath of the Great War. Most people of this generation are no longer alive. To flesh out Piroska's story, written sources and visuals of the period provide a vivid picture of children's experiences in Budapest in the early 1920s, unveiling the two intertwined historical topics that lie at the core of this book: children's destitution and relief.

To understand the particularly pressing condition of children in postwar Hungary, *Budapest's Children* elaborates on how the city and its children were affected by the social consequences of war and imperial dissolution, addressing the largely overlooked civilian dimension of postwar suffering.[2] "War was never a unifying global experience,"[3] as Mischa Honeck and James Marten put it; children's specific experiences in the aftermath of war were dependent on their place of upbringing and belonging, social and ethnic class, gender, and religion. Indeed, "the history of childhood tells a real story," but "it is not [a] uniform and it is not [a] fair" story.[4] Children's lives in the postwar period were greatly contingent on their families' socioeconomic standing and always embedded in their social environment, which influenced how the children experienced, interpreted, and remembered those years of destitution.[5] Because children are shaped and influenced by their families and communities, the history of childhood always relates to general history. Children's history is never just a sidenote; it is a quintessential reflection of the larger historical developments of the twentieth century. While Sarah Maza argues that "children obviously don't make history," I rather agree with Meike Baader, who emphasizes that children in the past were, and still are today, urged to make "their voices heard precisely because they represent the promise of an alternative modernity or society."[6] Their survival and care lie at the heart of every society.

Exploring Budapest's condition through the lens of children's forced displacement and migration, hunger, destitution, and finally relief, this book provides a glimpse into the social turmoil of the aftermath of war and the "afterlife of imperial rule" in Central Europe.[7] The lens of childhood allows us to draw broader conclusions about the period under consideration. Analysis of the ways in which the war affected children's lives, their bodies, and their care sheds light on the relationship between violent conflicts, children in need, and humanitarian intervention. This book's particular focus is on reconstructing how the massive migration to the capital of hundreds of thousands of Hungarians from territories occupied by enemy armies and ceded to neighboring states in the postwar peace process altered life in the capital city and how their destitution was used to push both for international relief and for a revision of Hungary's new truncated borders.

"Starving Budapest: Capital of Human Misery," a 1920 *New York Times* article, judged the situation in Budapest to be the most disastrous anywhere. In public debates, Hungary was represented as the country most affected by the war: "All Central Europe is a bleeding wound, but nowhere, perhaps, is life so poor a gift as in Austria and in Hungary."[8] The capital, which had "taken the lead in all of Hungary's political developments" and where the two postwar revolutions were centered, was hit hardest by the political and economic postwar developments.[9] Colonel S. A. Moffat, the head of the American Red Cross commission to Hungary, observed in October 1919 that, especially due to interrupted transportation networks, Budapest was suffering from the lack of food, whereas "the country outside the city is rich in food supplies."[10] In January 1920, the activist Julia Vajkai, on the other hand, complained that the circumstances of other Hungarian towns and villages differed from those of the capital only in that Budapest "absorbs all the assistance from abroad" and that "nothing has yet been done outside Budapest to relieve the utter misery of five years of war, and blockade followed by Bolshevism and occupation by a rapacious enemy."[11] In fact, sympathy toward the capital's suffering population was even more narrowly focused on Budapest's children. It was not without reason that these children became objects of transnational humanitarian discourse and relief; unlike former enemy combatants, they could be cast as innocent victims of the war. While it is indeed true that humanitarian organizations attempted to "'depoliticize' both aid itself and its recipients, through the construction of the ideal humanitarian subject: the inherently valuable and innately innocent child," the relief of Budapest's children served specific national and international agendas.[12]

An examination of the history of Budapest shows that misery was nothing new to this metropolis. In the late nineteenth century, Budapest experienced increasing problems of overpopulation, insanitary conditions, squalid housing, and rampant industrialization. Due to the "rapid rate of modernization and industrialization," Central Europe's cities witnessed the exploitation of workers, overpopulation, the spread of diseases, and the emergence of urban slums, revealing the many ambiguities and "contradictions of modernity."[13] In the era of urbanization, cities experienced intense political, cultural, ethnic, religious, and social change and negotiated struggles over diversity.[14] But the war and its severely troublesome aftermath intensified these urban afflictions and added new ones, as this book demonstrates. Massive wartime and postwar migration, the absence of men as both fathers and laborers, crowded housing, lack of food, and spreading diseases—all of these brought down the morale of the respective populations and ruined their bodies and their health. Central and East European cities turned into sites where new nation-states were challenged to demonstrate their proper and immediate handling of metropolitan social crises.

In these turbulent conditions, it was not just the displaced, disabled, elderly, and poor who suffered illness and hunger; the economic hardships and disastrous societal transformations had a disproportionate impact on children's wellbeing. A Hungarian girl named Etelka captured how postwar destitution manifested itself in the lives of Budapest's children: "I and my five brothers are exposed to the greatest misery. We have neither clothes nor boots. We are entirely ragged, our food is scarce and, the last week in the moth, we cannot even get bread."[15] Budapest's children were by no means alone in their starvation and suffering. People elsewhere in Hungary, but also throughout Austria, Czechoslovakia, Poland, and Yugoslavia, as well as in Armenia, Lithuania, Estonia, Latvia, Germany, and Crimea—and especially the younger generation—all suffered from displacement, disease, and a terrible scarcity of food.[16] Throughout the entire region, "masses of unsupervised children" were fending for their lives, and infants died in droves.[17] Yet very little is known about children's permanent displacement, hunger, and destitution in postwar Central Europe.[18] Their story is deeply embedded in the general history of the aftermath of war, enabling us to draw broader historical conclusions. As Budapest's suffering children gained the attention of local and international agents, who wanted to "rescue them, redeem them, punish them or provide for them," children's relief reveals, as Nick Baron has argued, how states "conceived and strove to project their own role, their legitimating principles, their visions for the future, their organizational capacities and their relationship with citizens."[19] Furthermore, "children . . . were rarely targeted for protection or relief because of their presumed equality"; rather, they were targeted mostly "because of their perceived vulnerability and innocence."[20] This made children objects of attention in times of disaster and political change.

While engaging with broader questions concerning the history of children's humanitarian relief, this book centers on the case of Budapest, a city described at the Paris Peace Conference in 1919 "to be a small particle of the pending world-problem" while nevertheless being "illustrative of the whole" and on which "depends to a large extent the future of eastern Europe."[21] In times of peace and economic prosperity, capital cities are normally "hubs of communication, powerhouses of industry and commerce, nerve centers of administrative and political power, and/or sites of cultural production and exchange that are bound within (trans-)national networks,"[22] but war and the turmoil that followed substantially changed the outlook and social dynamic of the capital city of Budapest. While in the early twentieth century, poverty in the capital was mostly limited to certain districts and specific ramshackle buildings, contemporary witnesses argued that the postwar situation erased the clear dividing line between the city's haves and have-nots: "In the barracks you can see what is hidden in the city, but this struggle, trouble, suffering and poverty is no longer just a characteristic of the world of barracks, but of Budapest itself."[23]

Budapest did not suffer from extensive physical wartime destruction in World War I, but it experienced massive political and social troubles in the years following the conflict and after the signing of the Treaty of Trianon in 1920. "Budapest, our capital, . . . would be too large for a crippled Hungary," one official complained in a document prepared for the 1919 Paris Peace Conference. "It would become the monstrous head of a dwarf," and "uncounted families would face their ruin."[24] With these words, Hungary pleaded in vain for a restoration of its occupied territories.

Numerous factors were responsible for this challenging situation. The Great War, its aftermath, and the dissolution of the Central and Eastern European empires together brought about a historical caesura in the region's multiethnic, multilingual, and multireligious society. Beyond their long-term political impact, these historical upheavals fundamentally affected the everyday lives of the region's civilian populations, as they brought displacement, famine, and disease to those who survived. On top of this, Hungary had to tackle an ongoing naval food blockade, which restricted the supply of imported foodstuffs even after the Armistice of November 11, 1918.[25] The region's postimperial struggle over territories, political ideologies, and populations crystallized in postwar Hungary. The vacuum that imperial dissolution left behind gave room for a fundamental struggle over the political and ideological outlook of the future Hungarian state. The rapid sequence of political events turned the war's aftermath into a condensed period of historical change. In Hungary, as Eliza Ablovatski observes, it was especially in the year 1919 when "it seemed to many observers not only that the 'old world' could be remade, reimagined, and reformed, but also that it must be."[26] Most vital changes were reflected by the establishment of the Hungarian Soviet Republic between March 21 and August 1, 1919, under the leadership of Béla Kun; an occupation of large parts of Hungary and its capital city until March 28, 1920; the dissolution of the Austro-Hungarian monarchy on June 4, 1920; the inauguration of an ultra-right-wing government under Regent Miklós Horthy on March 1, 1920; and the ravages of a White Terror against Jews in Hungary, organized by the Union of the Awakening Hungarians (Ébredő Magyarok Egyesülete), between November 1919 and January 1922.

Regional networks for supplying food were obliterated by new international borders carving up the former Austro-Hungarian Empire, including the funnel of wheat from the countryside to Budapest for milling. Before the war, the empire had been "an economic unit and self-sustaining in the essentials of life," but the war "sank the birth-rate below the death-rate, spread disease, disrupted transportation, paralyzed industry and brought agricultural production to a dangerous level," as an American Relief Administration report observed.[27] Hungary's distressed population—especially in Budapest—also had to cope with the absence of men who had not returned from captivity and the presence of Russian prisoners of war, along with massive flows of refugees from lost territories. Anti-Jewish pogroms in Galicia resulted in the massive flight of Jews toward cities such as Vienna and Budapest. The swirling population movement created a severe housing shortage and the establishment of emergency dwellings in railcars for displaced families, where infectious diseases spread easily. And to cap it all, there was near famine. Although the scarcity of food had already been an everyday reality during the war, the blockade against Hungary continued, and shortages became critical.

Beyond these tangible crises were psychological ones. For many Hungarians, the loss of territories and their self-image as people of a major imperial power fed into a postwar mental crisis, as *Budapest's Children* demonstrates. The civilian population of postwar Hungary, and particularly of its capital, became actors in a key arena of Europe's postwar transformation process, navigating geographic displacement, social uprootedness, and ethnic violence.[28] Local health and welfare systems were severely damaged and barely able to provide the support that destitute individuals, families, and institutions so urgently needed. Hence, the story of postwar childhood in Budapest is a story not of the war itself but of the social consequences of its aftermath.[29] And it is in this postwar chaos that this book begins.

Clearly, the social implications of the postwar transformation affected not only Hungary but most postimperial, and often new, nation-states in Central and Eastern Europe. During the war, civilians in the region had started to suffer from "malnutrition and disease, physical attack, psychological trauma, and emotional distress."[30] These stress factors did not stop with the war's end. Instead, they were accompanied by migration, hunger, and political turmoil, which drastically altered the social fabric and people's everyday lives. Postimperial capital cities such as Vienna, Budapest, Warsaw, Berlin, and Prague were particularly condensed spaces of postwar turmoil and transformation. They had already turned into "special cases," as historian Jay Winter points out, being "'nerve centers' of the war," where key political players made decisions and where the "the war was actually lived."[31]

Already during the war, inhabitants of larger cities suffered severe food shortages as distribution networks were either discontinued or collapsing, the labor force was missing, and peasants preferred to consume their food instead of selling it for useless money.[32] But the capitals' suffering did not end when the fighting ended. As *Budapest's Children* argues, in the postwar era, capital cities, especially those of the defeated nations, continued to be nexuses of the economic, social, and geopolitical transformations taking place. Existing studies have almost exclusively explored the "hunger crisis" and its relief in Vienna, suggesting that economic desperation was "most apparent in the new Austrian republic."[33] But this book shifts the perspective to the neighboring capital, the city of Budapest, which not only experienced a hunger crisis of huge proportions but was simultaneously the site of some of the most volcanic ideological and political conflicts and challenges of postwar Europe. In a bilingual booklet from 1920 titled *From the Horrors of a Country Condemned to Death*, the Hungarian social photographer and police reporter Kornél Tábori compares the situation in Budapest with that of Vienna, which had not experienced these horrors yet "made its well-deserved claim for pity known throughout the world."[34]

In these troublesome circumstances, children were especially vulnerable and neglected amid the disruption war and its aftermath brought to their physical well-being and family life. They mirrored the city's radical transformation. While once Budapest had been a great European capital "famed for its magnificence and its learning," according to Save the Children, by 1920, Budapest had become the "scene of some of the blackest misery in the areas of distress."[35] Not only had their city changed but also their lives. Many children were displaced, half orphaned, or orphaned. Fathers who returned from the war often came back wounded, mothers had to take over as breadwinners for families, and children suffered. Historically, children have been among the weakest subjects in society, perceived as family property and not as self-determined agents. It was children's role to be cared for, kept clean, adequately fed and dressed, educated, and socially integrated. During and after World War I, children were subordinated to both family and increasingly robust state structures, largely dependent on delivered food and clothing, provided housing, and education.

While childhood poverty and suffering were by no means new in the final years of the war, the sheer intensity of these scourges gained a new dimension in the postwar period. Distress among Budapest's children was compounded by hunger, compromised living conditions, contagious diseases, displacement, and neglect. Parents and local childcare institutions faced massive obstacles in carrying out even basic care. Food shortages threatened children's —especially infants'—very survival'—and stunted their physical and mental development. The child mortality rate was about 20 percent, among the highest rates in Europe.[36] Contemporaries started to worry about the future of the young Hungarian nation. Another consideration was that suffering children, innocent victims of war, had done nothing to deserve their fate. There was a massive presence of starving, orphaned, and sick children in Budapest for all to see. The situation cried out for immediate relief.[37] As life remained austere and grim, the special vulnerability and suffering of children were ever more visible in everyday life in Central Europe's capital cities.[38] Their physical wretchedness became a highly emotive and publicized symbol of Europe's postwar misery, supporting calls for transatlantic humanitarian intervention. This book argues that Budapest was a particularly telling historical laboratory of how Western humanitarianism reached out to one of the former enemy countries. The term *laboratory* is useful in describing the representative yet experimental character of specific historical places, spaces, and constellations. Because capital cities often serve "as national testing grounds for urban planning, policy and design because of their role representing the state" and mirror "international concepts and practices,"[39] I approach Budapest as a historical laboratory of postwar transnational humanitarian aid.[40] I ask why and how Budapest's destitute children came to attract this level of international attention and trigger humanitarian sentiments and initiatives throughout the United States and Western Europe.

Capturing Children's Suffering: The Visual Language of the Postwar Era

In Budapest, the poor, starving, and diseased child became the focus of so-called social photographers employed by Hungarian journals such as *Új Idők*

(New times) and *Az Érdekes Újság* (The interesting journal) so that pictures could be added to reports on the condition of the civilian population. Before delivering any form of aid, Hungarian social photographers, often accompanied by international relief workers, visited displaced families. The idea was to capture the city's misery in pictures and words and present the substandard living conditions to the outside world. These investigators, as this book discusses, reported in detail and relayed their personal impressions, publishing accounts in the United States, Britain, Switzerland, and elsewhere.

The increase in visual representations of children was part of a new public focus on "the social question" of how the deprived classes lived. The images of children gained mass publicity.[41] Photographs were recycled, reframed, annotated, published, and printed multiple times for different uses. This dissemination of photos was the result of the many contacts between the local relief workers and the international organizations active in Budapest. The circulating pictures mirrored the internationalization of relief organizations and further contributed to the creation of a transnational humanitarian community and identity. Those involved in the relief undertaking were able to use photography, as well as caricatures and drawings, to document their international project and adapt it to particular viewing habits in the recipient and donor countries. Pictures provided a more emotionally charged articulation of destitute people's misery than mere texts. Visual representations of the physical impact of the war and its aftermath on children's bodies, which make up a major set of sources in this book, served as a potent means of producing a transnational "revolution in seeing and hearing."[42]

Building on an extensive visual repository of photographs, caricatures, posters, and children's drawings, this book explores how local and international print media linked the plight of starving children with the ideological and national agendas of the relief organizations. This approach offers new insights into the visual language and the moral iconography of transatlantic humanitarianism.[43] The visual language of international relief reflected social patterns of inequality between the destitute Central European children and the donating Western relief workers. As humanitarian relief to Budapest's children was closely linked to modes of seeing and documenting, a very particular visual language emerged, able to appeal to both local and distant audiences. The "pictorial representation of humanitarian suffering" focused on the figure of the child and served as "'ammunition' . . . to convince people" that they should care for distant others.[44]

"One of the essential features of wartime" was and remains "the weight . . . of the dead on the living."[45] Alongside this burden, children's suffering from neglect, hunger, and disrupted social ties weighed heavily on survivors in the aftermath of war. Whereas images of dying soldiers have at times been "considered capable to end a war," images of starving or destitute children in so-called peacetime were used to evoke feelings of solidarity with the victims and to alter international relations.[46] In this way, "photographs," as Annette Vowinkel suggests, "have agency" in that they "transmit information, evoke emotions, support evidence, prompt us to act, offer arguments and illustrate the written and spoken word."[47]

Images of suffering children were used to persuade better-off societies to donate money and to publicize the humanitarian relief offered by organizations such as Save the Children. They were internationally and widely used to elicit tender emotions, which are not mere "bodily reactions" but are "on the level of their articulation culturally coded and discursively embedded."[48] As "emotions and emotional recommendations form a significant part of the history of childhood,"[49] it is telling how children's bodies were depicted and for what purpose certain emotions were meant to be triggered. The masses of images that accompanied the relief endeavor reflect well how press photography, film, and advertisements competed with and complemented one another in capturing Budapest's unfortunate children.[50] Relief organizations not only communicated via reports, letters, and newspaper articles; they relied heavily on photography. The new connections and the simultaneous professionalization of photography made possible a massive international circulation of humanitarian images, passing from the local relief workers to local newspapers, then to international organizations, and on to international media outlets.

The Paradox of War: From Warfare to Humanitarian Relief

Whereas the main endeavor of war had been to kill and harm human bodies, this goal was reversed once the scale and gravity of suffering surfaced, especially once the war had ended. Calls abounded for the "protection of all the war victims, civilians and soldiers alike."[51] As Rob Skinner and Alan Lester discuss, a new vein of humanitarianism surfaced during World War I, mostly as "a response to the techniques of inhumanity, in particular those associated with industrialized war," and "focused on the suffering of individual bodies."[52] In response to the enormous physical and psychological damage that had just taken place, the postwar period witnessed comprehensive efforts to reconstruct Europe with its harmed, dismembered, disabled, starving, and sick bodies.[53] Then, from the fall of 1919 onward, "unexpected help came from overseas, the United States of America."[54] Other organizations followed once the American Relief Administration (ARA) was involved.

Against this backdrop, this book reconstructs the case of Budapest's children as a case study to understand how the children of one particular city could trigger that much international attention and massive intervention. The postwar period saw the rise of a series of local and international humanitarian efforts on the "metropolitan level," which were not only "an important part of the story of victory and defeat in the Great War" but also an important dimension in the (re)making of postwar Europe.[55] Children's impaired bodies were now to be rehabilitated, reconstructed, and healed by the most modern nutritional means, emphasizing body weight, examinations, breastfeeding, milk consumption, honest labor, and even healthful vacations in the countryside or at the seashore.

Exploring the humanitarian discourse around the suffering body helps us identify the humanitarian response to the unforeseen social consequences of wartime confrontation. Budapest's children became iconic victims of the war's aftermath. The visual representation of them was used to activate humanitarian sentiments throughout the United States and Western Europe. Especially in the field of medical and orthopedic rehabilitation, the war stimulated "extraordinary advances in the dissemination of therapeutic, rehabilitative, and surgical technologies for all cripples—male and female, adult and child, soldier and civilian."[56] Such humanitarian behavior shows the extraordinary paradox of the Great War: on the one hand, it created intense suffering; on the other, it ultimately fostered a new sensitivity for the care of the stricken civilian populations and a sense of transnational solidarity. This book tests the provocative conclusion of Deborah Dwork, according to whom, in some twisted ways, "war is good for babies."[57] The book advances our knowledge about how the war and humanitarian relief had long-term implications for the professionalization and expansion of children's welfare. As James Marten notes, "wars can enhance the lives of children in certain ways," especially through the impulse to create child welfare programs that help children cope with the particular challenges posed by wars and their aftermaths.[58] Hugo Slim has drawn attention to "the paradox of human nature that humanitarian values can be present in war."[59]

The fact that humanitarian relief, both then and now, lived off war and disaster is intrinsically problematic. Organizations such as the Red Cross, it has been claimed, "actually needed the war which had become its raison d'être."[60] A contemporary social worker of the American Red Cross in Austria observed in 1921 that emergency relief, "however necessary in times of great distress," is "always demoralizing both to the agencies using them and the people they are trying to serve."[61] Furthermore, the quality and nature of humanitarian relief in postwar Europe must be understood as a direct consequence of the unparalleled destructiveness unleashed through technological advances in weaponry and national separatism. Without the profound trauma of the war and the deeply troublesome circumstances of its aftermath in Europe, there would have been no necessity for massive international efforts at relief and rehabilitation.

Alongside the reciprocal relationship between war-related destruction and postwar reconstruction, the international character of World War I found its correlation in the international dimension of the relief efforts. *Budapest's Children* demonstrates how the need to care for the stricken populations both generated and relied on the transnationalization of aid. While the centennial of World War I generated innovative research on humanitarianism and children's relief, recent scholarship, with a few exceptions, tends to write the history of humanitarianism still mostly "out of the West."[62] *Budapest's Children* departs from this bias and offers a reciprocal gaze, exploring the entanglements between international humanitarianism and one subgroup of Central Europe's relief recipients: Budapest children. Although some recent scholarship deals with humanitarian aid to children, research tends to overlook former "enemy" children.[63]

This book advances our understanding of the development of a transnational infrastructure and the everyday business of humanitarian relief in this Central European laboratory created by extraordinary conditions. Evolving practices of cross-border cooperation not only generated a space of transnational encounter and debate but also affected the "identity and the life paths" of international agents involved and helped broaden their knowledge, communication lines, and expertise.[64] In her study of Austrian children's trains Isabella Matauschek explains the inherent paradox of World War I as an international conflict: once the international humanitarian catastrophe had ended, sympathy for "people's misery" could cross "regional, supra-regional, national, international and even continental borders."[65]

While nationalist sentiments and ideological bias had dominated people's mentalities during the conflict, afterward international philanthropy slowly emerged as a transnational movement with a new approach to child protection and relief extending beyond the nation-state. The postwar years were indeed a time of "rising ethnic nationalism, of closing borders and anxious protectionist sentiment," yet they were also, "paradoxically, the heyday of a vigorous internationalism, and one that reached further than ever before, across the world."[66] Already during the war, which had "uprooted families, disrupted food supplies, destroyed homes and communities, and impaired

Fig. 0.1. Christmas gifts from abroad. Drawing by József Vanek, *Az Érdekes Újság* 7, no. 48 (December 25, 1919): 12.

mental and physical health," visuals in the United States and elsewhere were striving to "demonstrate their compassion as well as their military might."⁶⁷ On December 25, 1919, a year after World War I had ended, the Hungarian journal *Az Érdekes Újság* published a caricature (fig. 0.1) that presents an iconic image of the intertwined relationship between war, destitute children, and international humanitarian relief.

The drawing depicts three Hungarian children and a representative of the Hungarian "better class" receiving Christmas presents offered by representatives from the United States, Britain, Switzerland, and Italy. America's Uncle Sam brings clothes; Britain's John Bull brings money and a toy ship; a Swiss Red Cross worker offers "humanitarian donations," and Italian King Emmanuel gives oranges and lemons. The tree is hung with packages of sugar, salt, and rice, and behind it sits a large basket of victuals. The donors depicted in the cartoon represent the nations engaged in the emerging humanitarian mission to bring relief to Europe's children in the aftermath of the war. The recipients are Hungarian children of the former enemy. The image renders visible the international dimension of children's relief, the importance of material commodities in the mission, and the underlying economic inequalities.

The cartoon takes us straight to the central theme of this book: how a new, transnational philanthropic attitude toward Budapest's children came about. It was not only local Hungarian institutions that concerned themselves with these unfortunates. Though "old hatreds and resentments did not evaporate" after the war, nevertheless, comprehensive efforts were made to achieve rapprochement.[68] This is what the cartoon celebrates. It seizes on the war's function as a trigger for international cooperation and humanitarianism, personifying this as the spirit of Christmas. As a "truly global conflagration," the Great War did "not simply pit peoples against each other"; it later fostered "a growing sense of interconnectedness."[69] Out of this new mentality, the international relief organizations extended their mission to help Budapest and its children. The temporary, transatlantic migration of relief workers to Budapest allowed for close cooperation between local and international aid workers.

The incoming transnational and transatlantic humanitarianism proposed an alternative approach toward the former enemy, challenging the logic of war. Focusing on large sectors of the involved but unarmed civilian populations who suffered from war atrocities, international humanitarian organizations kept "advocating neutrality and peace" even while war was raging and the "mentality of war" was at its height.[70] Internationalist and humanitarian ideas often merged. Those who held these ideas shared a vision of a new peaceful international order, no longer troubled by imperial ambitions. Noting the depth of compassion evoked by the plight of children across Europe, Eglantyne Jebb, head of the British Save the Children Fund, saw the potential of international child relief work to "foster reconciliation between nations and promote a new internationalism—'supranationalism.'"[71] Initially a preoccupation of her own, Jebb's advocacy of internationalism became increasingly accepted and publicly propagated. The relief organizations had general aims of promoting "humanity, neutrality and impartiality, and solidarity."[72] They invested knowledge, money, science, and materials into furthering these ideals, but before this could happen, the suffering in capital cities like Budapest had to touch a nerve so that international humanitarian intervention could win public backing.

Envisioning Europe's Future: Providing Relief to the Enemy's Children

As embodiments of the destitution and hunger that stalked postwar Europe, Budapest's children were able to touch this nerve. Though they had been largely deprived of free agency, their great societal value as future citizens had always been recognized. Throughout the twentieth century, children "as human beings [were] expected to be molded into fully human adult beings through the process of political socialization" in order to create a good "future society."[73] This has made children's well-being a central public undertaking.

As Martina Winkler states, children have "wide-reaching, in some respects even revolutionary potential."[74] Children's visible misery in postwar Budapest was the catalyst for growing international and humanitarian intervention.[75] Children's suffering attracted the attention not only of local philanthropists and social workers but also of relief organizations and initiatives in Britain, the United States, and Western Europe. As Jewish communities in Central and Eastern Europe suffered from poverty, hunger, persecution, and social marginalization, the plight of Jewish children called for immediate relief and sparked humanitarian responses, especially in the United States. The scale of the deprivation that had fallen on Central European children called for broad humanitarian relief on an international basis.[76] Even before the peace treaties were signed, fears were being voiced about the war's long-term impact on Europe's future generation. This, too, was an argument for the ending of economic warfare and the provision of assistance. Hence, the disproportionate suffering that children faced led to new philanthropic visions. Building on somewhat limited experiences accumulated during the Balkan wars in 1912 and 1913, various initiatives merged into what has been called the "first international effort to 'reclaim' and rehabilitate children uprooted by wartime displacement," ethnic cleansing, poverty, and neglect.[77] Geneva, Switzerland, became the international crucible for many of those ideas.

The League of Nations' 1924 Declaration of the Rights of the Child embodied many of the ideas circulating at the time among philanthropists and social workers. The League of Nations, founded in 1920, was an arena for "lobbying of all kinds," not only by politicians trying to get recognition of nationhood but also by those eager to secure the "rights of women, children, slaves, and minority groups."[78] A dynamic and versatile development "from treaties and conventions between nation states to the establishment of a brave new world of international organization"[79] found its reflection in the field of children's relief. The conviction that armed conflicts had deprived young people of their childhoods inspired many social workers, throughout Europe and beyond, to institutionalize child relief organizations on an international scale.[80] In Hungary, as I demonstrate, this conviction was particularly important in prompting the professionalization and modernization of the services.

Childcare had mostly been a family matter before World War I, but a range of local child protection and child welfare organizations and initiatives emerged prior to and during the conflict, creating a new form of modern child welfare. But local activism was not enough. The defeated nations in Central Europe were not in a position to carry out reconstruction and any thorough development of child protection systems without external support, and they were dependent on material, financial, medical, and humanitarian intervention from the victorious nations. The scale of children's starvation and suffering required fast, large-scale international responses. Before the war, imperial and local child protection and philanthropy in Hungary had already undergone some expansion and professionalization, but the conflict had taken its toll and prewar child protection services were entirely inadequate for the task of tackling the huge humanitarian crisis.

After so many years of fierce enmity and ongoing mutual atrocities, how could the victors be persuaded to help their former enemy? How could humanitarian relief become possible for children whose parents had fought on the opposite side? Notably in France, "punishment and delegitimization of the enemy's war" remained at the heart of jingoistic rhetoric, and the war's "defenseless victims were quickly forgotten." This made the idea of relief for enemy children unimaginable to some.[81] Many French women had been raped by the German occupying forces and had immediately chosen to abort the children of the *"barbares."* Their "German blood," it was believed, would prevent them from assimilating into the French nation. The outrage "justified and even legitimized abortion or infanticide."[82] Conceived through violent intrusion and enemy aggression, these unwanted beings did not deserve life.[83] Scenarios like this illustrate the deep divides remaining between the populations of the Allied and the Central powers, with the victors often only wanting revenge for the cruelties they had suffered.

Due to this postwar mentality, the enemy's children were initially not regarded as beings that should be fed or relieved. For instance, the feeding of Russian children who had been left to starve during and after the Great Russian Famine of 1921 was thought to aid and abet Bolshevism.[84] Immediately after the war, the British media tended to oppose relief to enemy countries. It was against this backdrop that some child relief activists started to urge help for Budapest's children. Eglantyne Jebb stated that it was the aim of Save the Children to champion those children "whose parents, country, government or religion happened to be unpopular."[85] Sentiment toward the population notwithstanding, Hungary's postwar Bolshevist government was profoundly unpopular. In August 1919, the *Manchester Guardian* reminded readers in Britain that "the population of Budapest is sincerely friendly to Great Britain, and we are now treating as allies people who fought against the Entente with far greater energy than did the Hungarians proper."[86] The change of heart of Herbert Hoover, who headed the American Relief Administration, was typical of this trend: Initially he was reluctant to assist the former enemy's children, but when he saw the children's bodies, wrecked by hunger and malnutrition, he felt obliged to acknowledge their "biological immaturity." As "growing creatures," they would suffer "more lastingly from malnutrition" than adults, and they needed help to secure the future.[87] In his memoirs from 1951, Hoover recalled that he saw, in the universal love of children and in parents' devotion to their young, a path toward a European "renaissance of unity and of hope."[88]

Just as Hoover came to focus on children, so did a number of European and especially British figures become active as lobbyists on the children's behalf.[89] Eglantyne Jebb (1876–1928) and her sister Dorothy Buxton founded the British Save the Children Fund (SCF) in 1919.[90] In 1920, they laid the foundation for the Save the Children International Union in Geneva and drafted the Declaration of the Rights of the Child, which was prompted by the experiences of children during the recent war and disaster.[91] Jebb thought it right to concentrate on the innocent child.[92] "It was children's hunger . . . that was her first priority," and the child's first right to relief was to receive food before the adults.[93] She combined the modern study of child welfare with the "aim of influencing individuals and governments to promote scientific child welfare."[94]

Jebb actively contributed to the establishment of national SCF societies in the target countries and included former enemy countries in this venture. Hoover and Jebb managed to promote children and childhood as a "zone of peace," in which only the humanitarian cause counted and opposition was not to factor.[95] Advancing this concept of children and childhood, they ignored the "friend-enemy" scheme, which had been stoked by the violent conflict, and included the children of Budapest in their benevolence. As children were seen as "the future of Europe," feeding this new generation could be regarded as an investment, a way to guarantee a renovated society for the future. With the support of sympathetic leaders and growing awareness of the fact that the children had been noncombatants, hesitant publics were encouraged to overcome their initial prejudices and doubts.[96] From 1919 onward, international humanitarian aid flooded into Budapest.

Glocal Relief: International Humanitarianism in the Capital

The managing of children's relief in Budapest was a genuinely glocal undertaking, combining the efforts of global and local relief workers. This collaboration was possible because globalization was turning the world into a more connected "sphere of exchange." This trend was accompanied by the emergence of international associations and civil society initiatives, which "translated, debated and discussed" new concepts of "freedom, political representation and equality, reform and moral amelioration."[97] Analysis of the relief discourses and practices based around the displaced, neglected, and hungry children in one precise social melting pot sheds light on how relief organizations and the international political community became locally involved. By simultaneously centering the analysis on the humanitarian donor nations and the Hungarian recipients, this book highlights the dynamic interplay between local child welfare organizations and international humanitarian relief organizations that were active in Hungary.

I argue that the relief operation was not solely Western largesse to a "backward" East, but rather a space of transatlantic and transnational interaction.[98] Humanitarian organizations would provide an emergency supplement to overwhelmed domestic organizations, partner with local venues for relief and with each other to offer food and care, and in short order transfer the administration of longer-term child protection measures to Hungarian entities and leave. In this space of encounter, local Hungarian welfare workers, international humanitarian workers, and the children at the receiving end of relief actively shaped American, British, and international humanitarianism. In this process, local welfare agents affected global history, and vice versa. Here the book deals with the question of how discourses over the destitute child and everyday encounters, discussions, and collaboration between the local and international relief workers served equally to transform a mentality of violent confrontation into one of emerging international and global humanitarianism. An examination of the public discourse and imagery enables us to understand how instrumental the unsuspecting children were in re-creating links between previously hostile camps. Because humanitarian intervention was heavily dependent on a whole army of relief workers, this volume engages with the question of humanitarian agency in the early twentieth century.[99] I track key relief workers, their duties and responsibilities, their textual and visual representations, and their impact on the relief work itself. Of particular interest is Hungarian child relief worker Julia Vajkai, who headed the Hungarian National Child Protection League and worked for the SCF in Budapest. She was also the delegate of the Hungarian Red Cross (HRC) in Geneva and secretary to the delegate of the International Committee of the Red Cross (ICRC) in Budapest. Her local efforts were quickly supplemented with new arrivals from abroad. Activists like Captain James Pedlow, the representative of the American Red Cross (ARC) in Hungary, took up the challenge of intervening directly in the destitute children's everyday lives, striving to meet their most basic needs. Feeding Budapest's hungry children became one of their primary aims.

Pedlow and Vajkai were Budapest's key humanitarians, but they were joined by various international relief organizations. Significant among them were the American Red Cross, the International Committee of the Red Cross, the Rockefeller Foundation, the British Save the Children Fund and its international union, and the Jewish Joint Distribution Committee. The best-known organizational initiative was Herbert Hoover's American Relief Administration, created on February 24, 1919, under the European Famine Bill, as the successor organization to the United States Food Administration. The ARA was one of the first organizations to respond to the postwar food crisis by initiating a food mission that included children of the former enemy. Local child welfare organizations included the Hungarian National Child Protection League (Országos Gyermekvédő Liga), National Stefánia Association for the Protection of Mothers and Infants (Stefánia Szövetség az Anyák és Csecsemők Védelmére), Hungarian Red Cross, and other smaller initiatives. These local associations administered orphanages, provided free health care through sanitary institutions, ran soup and milk kitchens and children's hospitals, and organized the integration of children into foster families.

Budapest's Children centers its attention on the immediate postwar years—the period between the Armistice in November 1918 and the mid-1920s—because these were the years when the hunger and destitution of the capital's children prompted an immense glocal humanitarian response, calling for a joint effort to halt the children's suffering. The ARA, for instance, sent a first official shipment of 250 tons of food relief from Vienna to Hungary in August 1919,[100] and it closed its work in Hungary on May 30–31, 1922.[101] The book also advances into the late 1920s and 1930s to touch on the legacies of the postwar relief endeavor. Contrasting the postwar emergency relief to sustained relief initiatives, such as the workrooms of Save the Children, which lasted into the 1930s, serves to uncover how the character of aid to children changed over time. No organization could compete with the American endeavor in its immediate postwar scope of aid. British relief organizations, especially the SCF, in contrast, provided a different kind of relief, which focused on children's self-help and thus had perhaps a longer-lasting impact on Budapest's children. Irrespective of which international organizations provided the most aid and which were most successful, Budapest and its destitute children gained immense international attention, and this was translated into a great diversity of relief initiatives. The book shifts back to the prewar and war years to shed light on the causes of children's distress and the making of local Hungarian child protection before international intervention.

At times, competition arose between the local and international relief organizations, in which there might be debates over morality, humanity, and modernity. A 1919 article by a British author argued that any "ordinary sane Englishman" should get involved in relieving Central Europe "not only, or mainly, [as] a matter of checking Bolshevism" but also out of a "common humanity" toward the enemy's children, who were "'dying like flies,' [or living] in an apathy of feebleness with starved bodies and silent ape-like faces." A major incitement was that "the Americans out of their abundance have given with splendid generosity," and even "the Swiss out of their meagre and stinted rations have given with a diligent self-sacrifice." The writer did not want other nations to "believe that we British are less generous than either the Swiss or the Americans."[102]

Focusing especially on the humanitarian practices of feeding, clothing, healing, and educating Budapest's children and their employment in so-called workrooms, the book highlights the problematic ramifications of relief. Among them was the practice of "saving" hundreds of thousands of children by taking them out of their birth families and sending them to foster families in foreign countries. Children's international displacement or "evacuation" to foreign countries, such as Britain, Switzerland, Holland, and Belgium, was meant to be short-term. Yet in reality this was not always the case, and children's removal from their birth families had long-term implications for their upbringing, their identities, and their relationships to their birth families. Analyzing a handful of personal accounts of children who had participated in the children's trains and whom I could still interview allows us to better understand the biographical ruptures that were caused by humanitarian relief interventions. These rare primary sources help us realize how comprehensively humanitarian child relief organizations not only "saved" but objectified children as alarming symbols of Hungary's postwar collapse, as bodies to feed and heal and as future citizens to raise and educate.

The Politics of Humanitarian Aid

Exploring these and other relief initiatives, I offer a critical reading of transatlantic and transnational humanitarianism in Budapest, stressing the ambiguity of the transnationalism that emerged. *Budapest's Children* approaches humanitarianism as a movement closely linked to postwar politics and provides evidence of how the relief operation in the city enabled the involved organizations and states to stir overtly national and patriotic sentiments among home audiences and to pursue their own national agendas. Humanitarianism was far from a neutral undertaking; it served clear political goals. Throwing light on this issue, the book contributes to a critical reading of post–World War I internationalism.[103] The relief of Budapest's children took place in a global "enabling space" with close connections to patriotism and nationalism. "Interwar Central Europe arguable offers an unparalleled testing ground," as

Peter Becker and Natasha Wheatley observe, insofar as this European region experienced simultaneously diverse and paradox processes of "revolutionary nationalization *and* internationalization."[104] Their intertwined and complex relationship expressed itself in myriad ways, forcing us to rethink the "traditional binary between nationalism and internationalism."[105]

Within this entangled competition over nationalization and internationalization, the discourse over children's hunger and food relief clearly demonstrates how the provision of food played its part in the struggle for postwar economic, scientific, and moral hegemony. In the postwar capital city of Budapest, it was the hunger and destitution of children that enabled competition over who was entitled to relieve the war's victims and how this type of aid could be used for the providers' own political agendas. This book uncovers the ways in which humanitarian relief served to create social and economic structural inequality between the donating West and the receiving East. Saving and healing the body of the Central European child in need, through food relief, material items, and medical donations, provided Western humanitarian organizations with an opportunity to alter a collective body of distant children in need.

I argue that the transnational encounters that revolved around children's relief, while a truly international endeavor, were simultaneously a deeply national undertaking. Melanie Tanielian argues in her research on relief in Lebanon that "famine opened a space for local, national and international actors to reshape the ... postwar political landscape."[106] *Budapest's Children* engages with this reflection and tackles the question of how much the relief of the child victims was, at its core, a highly politicized and fundamentally national undertaking—though the mission and its implementation formed an undeniably transnational endeavor.[107] Surveying the interconnections between transnationalism and nationalism contributes to a better understanding of how these two missions were intertwined. While the relief goods crossed physical borders and overcame national boundaries, some of the transnational humanitarian encounters also fostered the circulation of Hungarian territorial revisionist ideas and nationalistic discourse. The book expands the ideas expressed by Paul Betts, according to whom international humanitarian relief work and charity work were "nationalized" in the Great War.[108]

Through providing relief to children in distant Budapest, the United States could manifest its global power by presenting itself as a winner of not only the war but also the humanitarian war against hunger. Furthermore, driven by a deep-rooted anti-Bolshevism, American relief organizations such as the ARA and the ARC provided food relief to Hungary only once Béla Kun left the stage in the summer of 1919. Humanitarian aid was used to prevent revolution and instability. In Hungary, on the other hand, transnational attention was partly used to foster nationalistic sentiments and politics, with intended international appeal. Winning international attention for efforts to help Budapest's children, and thus also the Hungarian state, was highly convenient to those pursuing a revisionist agenda. In the transnational community of humanitarianism, Hungary could evoke widespread feelings of compassion for its "humiliation" at Trianon and could legitimate its "revisionist nationalism" in the eyes of other nations.[109] Hence, transnationalization, I argue, helped produce negative currents, allowing us to identify some of the causes that led to the partial failure of postwar internationalism and the instability of the new international order. Furthermore, in tracing the ways Hungary attempted to rewrite its international reputation from enemy to victim nation, this book offers a better understanding of how this European state codified its revisionist claims, which still reverberate there today.

In all these ways, *Budapest's Children* shows us how the city's displaced, neglected, and impoverished children gained—despite their obvious material, economic, and social powerlessness—a specific form of historical agency in generating a new brand of humanitarianism and internationalism in postwar Europe. The history of Budapest's children serves as a prism illuminating the interdependence between international interference into children's lives and the role of their destitution and relief in enabling and shaping the transnational web of relationships in the postwar world.

Notes

1. Piroska, narrative interview with the author, Budapest, November 23, 2012.
2. See Healy, *Vienna and the Fall of the Habsburg Empire*.
3. Marten and Honeck, "More Than Victims," 12.
4. Fass, "Introduction," 7.
5. Sachs, "Children Remember," 21.
6. Maza, "The Kids Aren't All Right," 1268; Baader, "Tracing and Conceptualising Children's Agency," 11.
7. Becker and Wheatley, "Introduction: Central Europe and the New International Order," 4; on migration, see Gatrell and Zhvanko, *Europe on the Move*; Gerwarth, *The Vanquished*; Zahra, *The Great Departure*; on Hunger see Cox, *Hunger in War and Peace* and "Hunger Games"; de Waal, *Mass Starvation*; Vernon, *Hunger: A Modern History*; Kučera, *Rationed Life*; Roehrkohl, *Hungerblockade und Heimatfront*; Thoms, "Hunger—ein Bedürfnis zwischen Politik"; on postimperial capital cities, see Healy, *Vienna and the Fall of the Habsburg Empire*; Winter and Robert, *Capital Cities at War*; Judson, *The Habsburg Empire*, chap. 8; and Cornwall and Neumann, *Sacrifice and Rebirth*. A few studies have delved into the impact of war on childhood; see Marten, *Children and War*; Audoin-Rouzeau, *La guerre des enfants*; Donson, "Children and Youth"; and Hämmerle, *Kindheit im Ersten Weltkrieg*.

8. Chenery, "Starving Budapest."
9. István Deák, "Budapest and the Hungarian Revolutions," 130–31.
10. Maj. S. A. Moffat Budapest Hungary to Col. E. P. Bicknell Paris, October 26, 1919, Sub: Budapest Relief, 953.62/08, Hungary-Relief Other Than Health, RG 200 Records of the American National Red Cross 1917–34, World War I, 953, Hungary, Budapest Unit, Box 878, 4, NARA.
11. Julia Vajkai, "Supplementary Report on the Conditions of Children in Hungary," January 20, 1920, 1–6, 6, Confederatio Helveticae. Archives d'Etat de Genève (hereafter CH AEG), Archives Privées de la Union International de Secours aux Enfants (hereafter AP) 92.21.2 (1), Geneva.
12. Baughan. *Saving the Children*, 36.
13. Schwartz, *Gender and Modernity in Central Europe*, 4.
14. Wendland, "Ostmitteleuropäische Städte," 108.
15. Jebb, "Life Stories of Hungarian Children," 30.
16. "Europe's Need: Save the Children Fund," 41.
17. Schulte, "Conclusions, Reflections and Outlook," 286.
18. The first volume to tackle the Eastern Europe children's displacement was Baron, *Displaced Children in Russia and Eastern Europe*. See also Kelly, *Children's World*; Zahra, *The Lost Children*; and Zahra, *Kidnapped Souls*, as well as Cox, *Hunger in War and Peace*.
19. Baron, *Displaced Children in Russia and Eastern Europe*, 9.
20. Zahra, "'The Psychological Marshall Plan,'" 38.
21. Apponyi, *The American Peace and Hungary*, 2.
22. Goebel and Keene, "Towards a Metropolitan History," 3.
23. "A barakok világából," 3.
24. Hungarian Territorial Integrity League, *The Consequences of the Division of Hungary*, 2.
25. Mahood and Satzewich, "The Save the Children Fund," 56. See also Breen, "Saving Enemy Children."
26. Ablovatski, *Revolution and Political Violence in Central Europe*, 2.
27. American Relief Administration, *Sketch of the Child-Feeding Operations*, 3.
28. For Jewish relief, see Kind-Kovács, "Transatlantic Humanitarianism"; Granick, *International Jewish Humanitarianism*; Lazaroms, "Marked by Violence."
29. For a general introduction to the dissolution of the Habsburg empires, see Wank, "The Habsburg Empire"; see also István Deák, "The Habsburg Empire."
30. Proctor, *Civilians in a World at War*, 110.
31. Winter, "The Practices of Metropolitan Life," 6.
32. Federico, *Feeding the World*, 191.
33. Clavin, "The Austrian Hunger Crisis," 266. See also Adlgasser, *American Individualism Abroad*.
34. Tábori, *Egy halálraítélt ország*, 1.
35. "'Our' Godchildren: Who They Are and Where They Live," 45.
36. Vernon Kellogg, "In Budapest and Vienna," 2.
37. Irwin, "Sauvons les bébés."
38. Chouliaraki and Blaagaard, "The Ethics of Images."
39. Gal, "Borrowing Ideas," 1.
40. Kasianov and Ther approach Ukraine as a laboratory because of the "simultaneous existence of several national and religious movements and empires or, to be even more general, cultures and societies." Kasianov and Ther, *A Laboratory of Transnational History*.
41. Case, *The Age of Questions*, 138ff.
42. Last, "Putting Children First," 195.

43. Fehrenbach and Rodogno, *Humanitarian Photography*; Wilkinson, "The Provocation of the Humanitarian Social Imaginary"; Kurasawa, "The Making of Humanitarian Visual Icons."
44. Wilkinson, "The Provocation of the Humanitarian Social Imaginary," 270.
45. Audoin-Rouzeau and Becker, *1914–1918*, 8.
46. Vowinkel, *Agenten der Bilder*, 18.
47. Ibid., 427.
48. Bösch and Borutta, "Medien und Emotionen," 16.
49. Stearns, "The Emotional Life of Children," 158.
50. Ramsbrock, Vowinkel, and Zierenberg, "Bildagenten und Bildformate," 15.
51. Cabanes, *The Great War*, 1. On veterans as international agents, see Eichenberg and Newman, *The Great War*.
52. Skinner and Lester, "Humanitarianism and Empire," 736.
53. Carden-Coyne, *Reconstructing the Body*; Bourke, *Dismembering the Male*.
54. János Bokay, "History of Infant Protection in Hungary: Inception and Growth of American Red Cross Work in Hungary," National Archives and Records Administration (in the following NARA) at College Park (New York City), Records of the American National Red Cross 1917-1934, RG 200, Box 878, 953.62./08 Commission to Hungary WWI Reports.
55. Winter, "The Practices of Metropolitan Life in Wartime," 24.
56. Koven, "Remembering and Dismemberment," 193, 1200.
57. Dwork, *War Is Good for Babies*.
58. Marten, "Children and War," 152.
59. Slim, "Relief Agencies and Moral Standing," 343.
60. Audoin-Rouzeau, Becker, and Smith, *France and the Great War*, 137–39.
61. Dorothy E. Wysor to George W. Bakeman, Monthly Report for August, August 31, 1921, NARA RG 200, Box 878, Hungary, Budapest Unit, WWI Reports, 953.08.
62. Cabanes, *The Great War*; Tooze, *The Deluge*; Paulmann, *Humanitarianism and Media*; Barnett, *Empire of Humanity*; Klose and Thulin, *Humanity: A History of European Concepts in Practice*; Klose, *The Emergence of Humanitarian Intervention*; Fassin, *Humanitarian Reason*; Druelle, *Feeding Occupied France*; Mahood and Satzewich, "The Save the Children Fund"; Droux, "Life during Wartime"; Baughan, "'Every Citizen of Empire'"; Baughan, *Saving the Children*; Cox, "Hunger Games"; Fehrenbach, "From Aid to Intimacy"; Tanielian, *The Charity of War*; Watenpaugh, *Bread from Stones*; Rodogno, *Against Massacre*. On the American donor perspective, see Irwin, *Making the World Safe*.
63. Among research on relief in the region, the Russian famine has figured most prominently. See Sasson, "From Empire to Humanity"; Patenaude, *The Big Show in Bololand*.
64. Naumann, "Verflechtung durch Internationalisierung," 401.
65. Matauschek, *Lokales Leid-Globale Herausforderung*, 69.
66. Arsan, Lewis, and Richard, "Editorial," 162–63.
67. Irwin, *Making the World Safe*, 71.
68. Sharp and Stibbe, "Introduction: Women's Movements," 6.
69. Arsan, Lewis, and Richard, "Editorial," 162–63.
70. Audoin-Rouzeau, Becker, and Smith, *France and the Great War*, 137–39.
71. Mulley, *The Woman Who Saved the Children*, 274.
72. Slim, "Relief Agencies and Moral Standing."
73. Piattoeva, Silova, and Millei, "Remembering Childhoods," 5.
74. Winkler, *Kindheitsgeschichte: Eine Einführung*, 11.
75. Canning, "The Body as Method?" 500.
76. Jones, "International or Transnational?"
77. Zahra, *The Lost Children*, 30.

78. Clavin, *Securing the World Economy*, 9.
79. Weindling, *International Health Organisations*, 2.
80. Marshall, "Humanitarian Sympathy for Children," 185.
81. Audoin-Rouzeau, Becker, and Smith, *France and the Great War*, 233.
82. Audoin-Rouzeau, *L'enfant de l'ennemi*, 181.
83. Rivière, "'Special Decisions.'"
84. Mahood and Satzewich, "The Save the Children Fund."
85. Jebb, "Cheap Publicity," 67.
86. "Distress in Budapest," *Manchester Guardian*, August 16, 1919, 7.
87. Marshall, "Children's Rights and Children's Action," 355.
88. Hoover, *The Memoirs of Herbert Hoover*, 322.
89. On British relief, see Baughan, "The Imperial War Relief Fund."
90. On the SCF, see Baughan, *Saving the Children*.
91. Mahood, *Feminism and Voluntary Action*.
92. Muckle, "Saving the Russian Children."
93. Last, "Putting Children First," 194.
94. Rooke and Schnell, "'Uncramping Child Life,'" 183.
95. Vittachi, *Between the Guns*.
96. Irwin, "Sauvons les bébés," 38.
97. Arsan, Lewis, and Richard, "Editorial," 158.
98. On the theory of transnational history, see Haupt and Kocka, introduction, chap. 2, chap. 9.
99. See, for instance, Piana, "The Dangers of 'Going Native,'" 272; Piana, "Dr. Ruth A. Parmelee."
100. American Relief Administration European Children's Fund, *Final Report*, 3.
101. Bell, "Final Inspection Trip to Budapest," 54.
102. "The Hungry Sheep."
103. On postwar internationalism, see Sluga and Clavin, *Internationalisms: A Twentieth-Century History*; Sluga, *Internationalism in the Age of Nationalism*; Geyer and Paulmann, *The Mechanics of Internationalism*.
104. Becker and Wheatley, "Introduction," 6.
105. Ibid.
106. Tanielian, *The Charity of War*, 5.
107. Children were frequently used for the creation of national coherence. See Zahra, "Reclaiming Children for the Nation."
108. Betts, "Universalism and Its Discontents," 56.
109. Zimmer, "Nationalism in Europe," 425.

1

MIGRATION

Life in a Displacement Hub

WHEREAS OTHER EUROPEAN COUNTRIES WERE PRIMARILY DAMAGED BY the destruction of the war itself, Hungary's worst time was in the war's aftermath. As the American Relief Administration concluded in its final report in 1920, Hungary "is a country which suffered far more after than during the war."[1] Already in 1918 the pediatrician Ödön Lévai feared that the postwar period was as dangerous as "the bloody war" itself: "The future of the Hungarian state and the Hungarian nation" were again "at stake."[2] Large-scale displacement and migration from the ceded territories to within the new Hungarian boundaries contributed to widespread destitution in Budapest. Examining both the causes of migration and the experience of migration, this chapter explains how displacement fundamentally affected and altered this urban center and everyday life in the capital city. To explore the impact of migration on individuals and on the social conditions in the city, this chapter highlights the public discourse surrounding one specific group of refugees in Budapest at the time—the "railcar dwellers" whose homes were railcars in the sidings of Budapest's major railway stations. That this group of refugees had to be housed for months, and even years, in railcars reveals the dire political and social consequences following the radical shifts of Hungary's territorial boundaries. Through the story of these homeless Hungarians who came to epitomize postwar removal, this first chapter engages with the intertwined discourses of displacement, destitution, and emerging advocacy for political and territorial revisionism, demanding the revocation of the Treaty of Trianon and the return of the lost territories.

Shifting Borders, Lost Homes, and the Displaced

Throughout Central, Eastern, and Southeastern Europe, the Great War and its aftermath led to the denaturalization and denationalization of ethnic minorities and often their abrupt displacement.³ War and postwar society in Central and Eastern Europe, in general, had to cope with large-scale territorial changes and population movements. The conscription of soldiers resulted in "separation from loved ones," which Tammy M. Proctor identifies as the heaviest psychological effect on civilians during the war. The massive migration flows resulted in social disintegration and the fragmentation of families.⁴ Large-scale territorial shifts at the end of World War I brought about the dissolution of the Austro-Hungarian Empire as a geographic and political entity. The successor states were confronted with changed borders and the displacement of entire populations, often leaving their home regions because of ethnic identification, segregation, and persecution.⁵

Budapest also witnessed the arrival of great numbers of Jewish refugees, mostly from Galicia, who had fled the war and persecution. With few resources, these refugees had trouble gaining acceptance among Budapest's more urban Jews, who often treated them with suspicion and dislike. Authorities in Budapest made vigorous attempts to send Galician refugees back "home."⁶ But the refugees stayed, struggling to survive among the better-off Jewish refugees who faced fewer difficulties in their everyday lives. For both Jews and non-Jews, displacement came to represent one of the key challenges of the postwar period. Peter Gatrell writes of refugees as an "unprecedented social problem," defined "in terms of liminality and loss, damage and danger."⁷

When Hungary's new borders were drawn in the postwar period, massive groups of refugees began to arrive seeking the "safe" heartlands. In 1920, the Treaty of Trianon had defined new borders, resulting in one-third of ethnic Hungarians finding themselves outside the political boundaries of the Hungarian state. As a result, 400,000 to 500,000 refugees migrated from formerly Hungarian territories.⁸ The Hungarian minority in Transylvania, land ceded to Romania, "emerged as the largest national minority in Europe."⁹ Large sections of these minority populations relocated within Hungary's new borders.

Hungarian migration from Transylvania and the other ceded territories had not begun with the signing of the Treaty of Trianon, however; rather, it took place in several stages from 1916 until the mid-1920s. One of the earliest waves of migration was spurred by the invasion of Transylvania by Romanian troops in August 1916, after Romania had declared war on the Austro-Hungarian Empire on the twenty-seventh of that month.¹⁰ In war-torn and postwar Hungary, the term *menekült* (refugee) referred to a great variety of people from different religious, linguistic, and ethnic backgrounds who were moving into the heart of Hungary from occupied and later ceded territories now governed by Austria, Czechoslovakia, Romania, or the Kingdom of Croats, Serbs, and Slovenes. As Liisa Malkki has convincingly argued, the term *refugee* is a shorthand description of "a world of different socioeconomic statuses, personal histories, and psychological or spiritual situations."[11] Yet in the case of Hungary, we can observe an especially large exodus of middle-class Hungarians who left their homes in various migration waves.[12]

A large group of these Hungarian refugees ended up in Budapest, where, in addition to new forms of social housing—which offered emergency barracks to displaced, evicted, and unemployed families—major train stations were turned into emergency shelters for streams of families arriving from the ceded territories in the capital.[13] Originally these venues represented nodes of urban mobility, designed to facilitate the smooth flow of people across the country and beyond. However, in the postwar turmoil, Budapest's major train stations became bottlenecks from which no further movement was possible. No one knew how to distribute the massive influx of people, most of whom had no clear destination. Thousands of refugees were stranded at the train stations and hastily accommodated in ramshackle cattle wagons. They became known as *vagonlakók*, or railcar dwellers.[14] Other refugees were temporarily placed in empty classrooms. In November 1919, a diverse mix of thirty refugee families, mostly civil servants and members of the military, from all ceded territories (including the cities of Petrozsény, Kolozsvár, Décs, Brassó, Marosvásárhely, Sepsiszentgyörgy, Nagyszeben, Máramarossziget, and Kassa) were accommodated in a school on Baross Street. Classrooms were equipped with simple iron beds and primitive chairs, and each housed four or five families. In one of the unheated rooms, refugee children were seen "sitting on the beds with their hanging feet in ragged shoes."[15]

Refugees were accommodated throughout the city, but contemporary photographers were particularly drawn to the living conditions of the railcar dwellers. Some of the photographers' images aimed to show the massive scale of the refugee influx; others focused on individual middle- or upper-class families to personalize the fate of these displaced people. The arrival of Hungarian refugees from 1916 onward is closely documented in the 1927 revisionist compilation *A Nagy Vihar Hajótöröttei (Shipwrecked People of the Great Storm)*, which sought to draw attention to the devastating consequences of World War I and the Treaty of Trianon on Hungary.[16] In one chapter in the book, Endre Liber, the metropolitan governmental refugee commissioner, recalled that on the evening of August 30, 1916, "the first refugees from Petrozsény, Brassó and Csíkszereda arrived at Budapest's Eastern train station" after Transylvanian cities had been occupied by Romanian forces. According to him, many of these refugees believed that their exile from the occupied Romanian territories would be temporary and that they would soon be able to return home.[17] Reports from the press revealed the precarious situations of the displaced. A letter published on July 21, 1918, in the popular conservative newspaper *Budapesti Hírlap* (Budapest News) describes the escape of some Hungarians from the city of Csíkszereda in August 1916, unable to return to their former homes throughout several "months of statelessness." When they did return to their hometowns, their dwellings had been stripped bare; most returnees did not even have a cushion on which to lay their tired heads. The situation changed little in the ensuing two years, during which the displaced Hungarians lived in crowded flats in the former homeland. After having "hoped for so long" that their "destiny would change for the better," these Hungarians concluded that no one was interested in changing their miserable situation. For instance, a call was made to the citizens of Budapest, asking them to send any kind of material or financial aid to Csíkszereda to ease the situation of the "homeless" Hungarians there.[18] The capital was seen as both a potential destination for refuge and a potential source for material relief. Yet it was unable to live up to either of these expectations.

Many contemporary articles in Hungarian journals chronicle the stories of individuals who had lost their homes and properties in Transylvania. There were even poems printed bemoaning Hungarian victimhood. One such poem by Minka Czóbel, "The Stateless," describes the return of a stateless girl to her former room. She looks around and wonders "Why can she no longer have her place? / Why is she a foreigner here? / . . . Why do other people occupy the room?" and "Why can she, who is the owner of it all, . . . / no longer live there?"[19] The author's focus on the young girl's bewilderment seeks to evoke the collective experience of loss. The poem is not about the girl's citizenship but rather about her longing for her lost childhood home. Another poem upbraids the "Hungarian motherland," personified as a neglectful parent who "no longer protects her own children" and has turned into a wicked and "merciless stepmother" who has even "hunted her own sons out of the world."[20] The lines refer to those who had remained in the occupied Hungarian territories waiting for their liberation from the Romanian troops and for the return and restoration of their former homes.

The refugees who arrived in Hungary in 1916 were able to be accommodated in and integrated into Budapest, but the streams of refugees increased dramatically after 1918. The declaration of the union of Transylvania with Romania on December 1, 1918, and the resulting war between Romania and the Hungarian Soviet Republic from April to July of the next year considerably worsened the situation of Hungarians in Transylvania. Transylvania's integration into Romania resulted in daily conflict between the Hungarian and Romanian populations. The "Romanian elites always suspected them [the Hungarians] of keeping strong ties with their nation and former country," while the Hungarian minorities "hardly accepted the new minority conditions in Romania and feared slow and painful assimilation."[21] Consequently, increasing numbers of people left for the now-smaller Hungarian state.

Above all, it was the final peace treaties that prompted a mass migration of Hungarians. The Treaty of Versailles, signed in June 1919, formally gave Romania power over Transylvania, triggering a virtual stampede of Hungarian refugees. An article in the popular illustrated weekly *Új Idők* (New Times), which was conservative in its orientation, described the refugees arriving in Budapest as "stateless, sad, scared and sorrowful figures" that were "walking with a limp." The "stream" of these dispossessed wretches had neither "a beginning nor an end."[22] Hannah Arendt rightly observed that the peace treaties prompted the "arrival of the stateless people" as a mass phenomenon. People's "real origin" could no longer be determined, especially if, at the end of the war, they "happened not to reside in the city of their birth" and their nationality had "changed from year to year" due to the "turmoil of postwar disputes." The arrival of masses of stateless people and widespread unwillingness to protect ethnic minorities in the newly formed nation-states brought an end to the illusion that ethnic minorities could be protected without legal intervention.[23] In attempts to ensure protection for refugees, various treaties were signed between the Allied powers (represented by the League of Nations) and the countries of Central and Eastern Europe. The main purpose of these treaties regarding minorities was to prevent violence or the outbreak of war "by removing the protection of minorities from the jurisdiction of individual states to the collectivity of all states."[24]

December 9, 1919, saw the signing of a treaty between Romania and the principal Allied and Associated powers. The treaty stipulated, theoretically, the "full and complete protection of life and liberty to all inhabitants of Roumania without distinction of birth, nationality, language, race or religion." Citizenship was to be granted "*ipso facto* and without the requirement of any formality" to "persons of Austrian or Hungarian nationality who were born in the territory transferred to Roumania by the Treaties of Peace."[25] Compliance with these stipulations proved problematic, however, because the treaty was never codified. Furthermore, serious international controversies arose concerning citizenship regulations throughout the postwar period, because the majority societies were often "not fully aware of international obligations" or were inclined to apply national regulations instead. Consequently, "a large number of persons were left stateless and were not entitled to full civil and political rights."[26] In the Romanian-Hungarian conflict over Transylvania, the grievance of the Hungarian minority became a "means of bringing interstate tensions over transferred territory to the attention of the international community."[27] Before the signing of the Minorities Treaty, on July 19, 1919, Romania had issued a decree stipulating that Hungarians "who had not been born in their current domicile or had taken their residence only after 1st of August 1914" were to be deemed foreigners.[28] The severity behind this rejection of Hungarian speakers was a reaction to the counteroffensive the Hungarian Bolshevist revolutionary Béla Kun had launched against the Romanian army on July 17 in the hope of regaining former Hungarian territories that had been occupied.

On September 20, 1919, another decree was issued stating that Hungarian government officials were to be expelled if they did not declare their loyalty to the new state. The exclusion of Hungarian employees from public administration and state positions led to extensive unemployment among the Hungarian middle class in Transylvania, resulting in a large migration to the new Hungarian state. Though economically motivated, this decree had deeper roots in the Romanian-Hungarian struggle over national ascription, making it harder for Hungarians to feel any sense of belonging in contested Transylvania.[29] Though the "transfer of sovereignty" only became formalized in the Treaty of Trianon, military conflict between Romania and the Austro-Hungarian Empire had been ongoing since 1916, turning Transylvania into an arena of opposing nationalizing projects.[30] If they wanted to remain in a home region there, Hungarians lost not only their jobs but also their Hungarian citizenship. While in the period before 1918 the term *hontalanság* (statelessness) referred primarily to loss of housing and property, it now took on another meaning, describing those who felt unable to submit to unqualified loyalty to the Romanian state. Statelessness now encompassed the whole issue of citizenship in a time when territorial shifts and the demands of peace treaties entailed possible loss of original citizenship and the acquisition of an alternative one.

The Treaty of Trianon, signed on June 4, 1920, again formalized the ceding of some Hungarian territory to several neighboring states and provided a basic legal framework for determining the citizenship status of ethnic and national minorities. Article 61 of the treaty declared that "every person possessing rights of citizenship (*pertinenza*) in territory which formed part of the territories of the former Austro-Hungarian Monarchy" should be allowed to "obtain *ipso facto*" the "nationality of the State exercising sovereignty over such territory."³¹ Hungarians living outside the borders of the new Hungarian state could therefore become temporarily stateless if they did not take up Romanian citizenship and also had not applied for Hungarian citizenship. In such instances, as Miriam Rürüp explains, people could fall into "a state of legal limbo, of mostly temporary *non*-status, of *not* belonging to any of the modern national frameworks." There were also Hungarian refugees, mostly Jewish, who neither wanted to become subjects of the Romanian state nor wanted to settle in the new Hungarian territory and who preferred to be declared legally stateless. These refugees could apply for the Nansen passport, a "highly symbolic document" that "proved that a person did *not* belong to any state entity" and should therefore be "accepted in any state in which he or she produced the document for authorities to examine."³²

Contemporary sources indicate that many Hungarians in Transylvania tried hard to solve the problem of their unclear citizenship status. On June 11, 1922, in *Budapesti Hírlap*, László Sömjén, a judge at the court of appeal assigned to the ministry of justice, reported in detail on "the citizenship option" (*az állampolgársági opció*) after Trianon. Sömjén compared the mass of Hungarians seeking citizenship to an anthill disturbed by a clumsy hand: "Hundreds of thousands of Hungarians were running . . . from office to office" trying to get the right citizenship papers. Sömjén further observed that, due to the highly problematic formulations of the Treaty of Trianon, which based rights of citizenship on proven communal residence, there were bound to be a "great number of stateless people, people with double or multiple citizenship, and people who would change their citizenship for [purely] egoistic reasons."³³

Further confusion arose from a clause in Article 63 of the treaty stipulating that "persons over 18 years of age losing their Hungarian nationality and obtaining *ipso facto* a new nationality [were] entitled within a period of one year . . . to opt for the nationality of the state in which they had possessed rights of citizenship before acquiring such rights in the territory-transferred."³⁴ In other words, people might be able to change their citizenship later on. Overnight, 1.7 million Hungarians became a national minority in Romania.³⁵ Those who decided to remain Hungarian had to "transfer their place of residence to the State for which they [had] opted" within one year, taking with them only "their movable property."³⁶ Similar scenes took place in other ceded Hungarian territories. Those who wanted to remain Hungarian and continue to work in state administrative jobs had no choice but to leave and move to Hungary proper.

However, this was not a feasible option on a wide scale. Sömjén urged Hungarians in the occupied territory "not to look for asylum in our tight home." The Hungarian state was already unable "to help the great majority of those here, already living in chronic poverty." He even argued that Hungarians would "commit a crime against the idea of the eternal homeland if they [opted] for Hungarian citizenship." There was no room in Hungary; "those of our blood" left in the territories outside should assert their right to "stay there, to remain our sentinel of those ideas which rule the soul of every honest Hungarian man."[37] The new Hungarian government furthermore feared "that through large-scale emigration, the Hungarian minorities would be greatly weakened, thereby exposing themselves to rapid assimilation" in their regions. This would dilute the argument being made internationally to have the Treaty of Trianon revised on a more just linguistic basis.[38]

It was not surprising that people—mostly from the better-off classes who had "forfeited the privileged position they enjoyed as landed gentry or as government officials"—preferred to leave and make their way to the reduced Hungarian state. This option, to them, was better than having to suffer "social or political subordination" to the discriminatory policies of the foreign "nationalizing states," with their refusal to "absorb groups of persons whom they did not want as nationals." But their abrupt displacement, social and economic losses, and emotional nostalgia for their lost homes risked forming the "backbone of a reactionary and revanchist politics" and strident nationalist fervor.[39] It was indeed by such processes, as Julie Thorpe has noted, that the tolerance of the Austro-Hungarian Empire "was lost" and "replaced by nationalizing successor states."[40] The minorities issue both reflected and paved the way to an intensification of nationalist sentiments and politics throughout interwar Central Europe. Such were the complicated matters of citizenship in postwar Transylvania and other territories that created the flood of migrants arriving in Budapest in the early 1920s.

Managing the Arriving Refugees

Though migration from the eastern parts of the Kingdom of Hungary toward the western regions had been taking place since 1916, the flow of people after 1918 was on an entirely different scale. In 1918, Országos Menekültügyi Hivatal (OMH), the National Office for Refugees, was established to cope with the problem. In 1924, the OMH listed a total of 350,000 refugees who had left occupied or ceded territories between October 30, 1918, and June 30, 1924, to enter the new state of Hungary. The majority of these displaced persons—197,035 refugees—were recorded as "Eastern Hungary (Romanian)," while

106,841 were listed as "Northern Hungary (Czech)" and 44,903 as "Southern Hungary (Serb)."⁴¹ Migration between 1916 and December 1918 was believed to be a temporary phenomenon, and indeed some of the refugees did return. But the occupation of Transylvania in 1918 and the 1920 Treaty of Trianon provoked a departure of refugees in critical numbers from all directions. Agitation for the restitution of the lost territories and for the refugees' return home was rampant. The new Hungarian refugees represented a "volatile and militant 'inner-diaspora'" of exiles fully "committed to the recovery of 'Greater Hungary.'"⁴² "Lost Transylvania," in particular, became a vanished Eden that refugees and many politicians alike were determined to get back. Even today, a nostalgic memory of Transylvania fuels emotions and right-wing rhetoric.⁴³

During World War I and in its aftermath, refugees poured in mostly by train, arriving in Budapest and other Hungarian cities. Refugees hoped to be rapidly integrated into the bureaucracy of the reconstituted Hungarian state.⁴⁴ The refugees' transfers were organized by the Hungarian government and implemented by the Magyar Állami Vasutak (hereafter MÁV), the Hungarian State Railway. MÁV was deeply involved in the logistics of refugees' travel and in the physical relocation of the refugees within the new Hungarian borders. Because the arrivals were classed as refugees, their transfer was largely a well-organized bureaucratic undertaking. The Hungarian railways worked closely with the OMH, overseeing the organization of the physical transfer. As Hungarian historian István Szűts has explained, "The majority of the Hungarian refugees did not want to travel with [only] hand luggage, but rather with their movable possessions," so MÁV often had to "secure for every family an entire train compartment."⁴⁵

Once the refugees arrived at Budapest, the main task for the OMH was to arrange accommodation and work for them. There were no language barriers to overcome, but it was still a monumentally challenging task amid the dire postwar economic situation. The influx of refugees resulted in the doubling of Budapest's population—from a prewar one million to a postwar two million—creating an immensely high unemployment rate and a serious housing shortage in the capital.⁴⁶ Registered refugees were eligible for relief of various kinds, such as preliminary accommodation, food, groceries, clothing, work placement, health care, legal assistance, and education. However, records contain huge discrepancies between the numbers of refugees arriving in Budapest and the number of relief recipients, indicating an insurmountable gap. While a many as five hundred thousand refugees arrived in Hungary, the OMH lists only a few thousand recipients of relief food and clothing.⁴⁷

Local Hungarian refugee and relief organizations such as the OMH were deeply and often also personally involved in the refugees' cause. Emil Petrichevich-Horváth, the head of the OMH, offered the proceeds from his premiere *Minnesinger* evening at the opera in Budapest as funds "for the benefit of the refugees."[48] This event was in June 1920, the month of the Trianon treaty signing, indicative of how revisionist propaganda and refugee support were closely linked even in culture and literature. The OMH focused its relief provisions on middle-class "public servants who had been expelled from their homeland and had become homeless refugees." For this elite group, the office once arranged "280 rooms in 63 hotels in Budapest at a 50% discount." In addition, five double rooms and thirty-six single rooms were arranged in thirty-four Budapest guest houses.[49]

Some refugees were moved into communal accommodations. In an effort to provide mass housing, the government started to build refugee barracks and colonies on the outskirts of the city. Among these were the Mária Valéria Colony (1914) and the Auguszta Colony and Zita Colony (both 1919). The colonies were named after key figures of the prewar empires and well-known philanthropists.[50] The buildings—very plain barracks—offered rather dire living conditions. Eyewitnesses described their inhabitants as lonely victims with ragged shoes, fringed pants, and wrinkles on their pale faces.[51] After 1923, 60 percent of the refugees who had been accommodated in the hotels received one-room apartments in the Auguszta Colony.[52] There, 351 apartments were provided for 284 families. The Bocskay barracks provided 148 flats for 100 families. Barracks were installed in other suburbs of Budapest, too—for example, in "the poor districts of Tripoli and Tiflis, suburbs of Budapest, where thousands of destitute people were huddled together in army barracks so overcrowded that 20 people frequently lived in a single small room."[53]

However, most refugees did not receive any accommodation and ended up in far less comfortable living situations. As Budapest was unable to house the masses of people arriving, the very same train compartments in which the refugees had traveled were allocated to many of them as preliminary housing facilities. A 1920 report in the *New York Times* described how the refugees had to resort to the railcars, because they could not find any house or single room to lodge in.[54] This is how they became the "railcar dwellers." Contemporary sources described in detail how many highly educated and financially well-off refugees found shelter in idle railcars at train stations in Budapest.[55]

In a 1920 report, Julia Vajkai from the Hungarian National Child Protection League emphasized the social composition of the refugee group. She confirmed that even "Judges, railway and postal officials, state employees of all kinds, the best of the people, were compelled to seek shelter in such territory as was still left to Hungary."[56] The Budapest weekly *Erdélyi Hírek* (News from Transylvania), which provided refugees from there with news about the situation back home (and urged them to "never ever forget" what had happened to their home region),[57] described the refugees as "distinguished families, not only civil servants, but also land owners, industrialists and merchants [who] were forced to evacuate their own houses."[58] Having previously belonged to the upper echelon, many of the displaced Hungarians experienced an abrupt social degradation and often remained dispossessed and unemployed. Indeed, the postwar migration from Transylvania has been characterized as a substantially (though not exclusively) "elite migration."[59] A July 1922 article in *Budapesti Hírlap* distinguishes between those stateless Hungarians who were "real" refugees deserving welcome and the undeserving *patkányok* (rats) who were only out to make "a good profit."[60]

But the capital city was unable to integrate and provide for all the refugees, "deserving" or not. Budapest had already absorbed a large number of refugees, and the new Hungarian state was entirely overwhelmed in its attempts to deal with the immense displacement problem. As István Mócsy has concluded, "Society was no longer capable of absorbing the vast surplus of educated people."[61] Many of the displaced Hungarians had belonged to the state bureaucracy in Transylvania, but, as the new Hungarian state had been reduced to a third of its territorial size and population, it no longer needed the same extensive civil service. Count István Bethlen, the Hungarian representative at the Paris Peace Conference in 1919 and prime minister of the Kingdom of Hungary between 1921 and 1931, pointed out to the Allied Reparation Commission how difficult it was for the Hungarian government to "treat these poor stateless people as superfluous state employees" and "let them die of starvation." Yet there was no way to shed the immense economic burden caused by the influx of more than "322,000 refugees," of whom "a majority had been employed by the state."[62]

On January 25, 1920, *Budapesti Hírlap* recounted an "unbearably sad" letter from the city of Temesvár in the Banat outlining the "harrowing tragedy of the last remnant of its Hungarian intellectual class." One hundred thirty-seven Hungarian families, unwilling to serve the "Romanian empire" and consisting of "judges, teachers, preachers and even a famous Hungarian poet," were forced to leave their homes within fourteen days of January 12. The letter denounces the inhumane character of this decree, which showed no regard for "international law" and was turning the Hungarians into "stateless" beings "in their own home." In emotionally loaded language, the letter accuses

Romanian authorities of chasing the Hungarians out of former Temesvár, in winter no less, and "handing them over to a sure death." The author beseeched the Hungarian government to prevent this catastrophe for "parents, children and wives" who had resided in Transylvania for centuries. "Hungarian brothers and sisters" should show solidarity and help these impoverished, displaced, and "repatriated souls," welcoming them "with warm love" into "our bare kitchens and cold rooms."[63]

Though accommodation in cattle wagons was meant to be short-term, many refugees stayed housed in them for months and even years. This posed a significant slate of challenges for the OMH to overcome. A major problem arising from the displacement and the temporary accommodation arrangements was the dispersal of families whose members lost contact with one another. Thus, from very early on, the OMH collected lists of the railcar dwellers' names and published them in the newspapers to help those with any affiliation to these refugees find them more easily.[64] Help desks assisting those who sought to trace lost family members were set up at the railway stations and were open every day from nine o'clock in the morning until seven in the evening. In 1922, the welfare minister, Nándor Bernolák, admitted that he had been unable to provide all railcar dwellers with flats before the coming of winter, because refugee groups were continuously arriving in Budapest and the construction of new accommodation was progressing too slowly.[65] The displaced families were still waiting for permanent housing and had yet to be integrated into the new Hungarian state. The discourse over the refugees' suffering served to stoke political fury over the loss of former Hungarian territories. Ideas of territorial revision were widely propagated both inside Hungary and to the international community.

The media, even the less conservative outlets, presented the issue of the railcar dwellers as a "national disaster," hotly blaming the "barbarian aggression of the Romanian regime" and holding Romania fully responsible.[66] This only bolstered the Hungarian government's revisionist claims. Throughout the 1920s, Hungarian politicians, public figures, and journalists used every available propaganda channel to rail against the Treaty of Trianon and the "amputation" of "Greater" Hungary's territories, which had left the country a shriveled relic of what it had been. These voices lobbied tirelessly for a revision of the peace treaty.[67] The struggle Hungarian minorities faced in the neighboring countries strengthened "the feeling of belonging to a common nation amongst the Hungarian population both inside and outside the Hungarian state."[68] Foreign minister Pál Teleki founded the Hungarian Revisionist League, commissioned supposedly scientific "research and advocacy," and organized international conferences to further Hungarian calls for territorial revision.[69] Historian Miklós Zeidler describes a "cult" of revisionism overtaking Hungary at this time.[70] As a "strongly, sometimes harshly nationalizing state,"[71] Hungary sought "to mobilize tens of thousands under the banner of nationalistic interwar politics" to regain its lost territories.[72] As physical embodiment of the nation's territorial loss, the Transylvania, Burgenland, Uplands, and Vojvodina refugees became both advocates for their own lost estates and for Hungary's larger territorial claims. Their abject physical presence in Budapest made the loss of the empire impossible to forget.

Seeing the Misery: Inspecting Refugee Dwellings

Budapest's railcar dwellers attracted a fair amount of domestic and international attention. As relief donations were dependent on the continuous observation and identification of local needs, local and international relief organizations invested much effort and time in going to see the suffering and to issue both scientific and eyewitness reports. Such inspection tours of postwar poverty dwellings in Budapest represented, I argue, a form of humanitarian slumming. International relief workers were driven by a slightly voyeuristic curiosity to see the refugees' misery, even if they came to help. This type of humanitarian tourism found its expression in hundreds of reports authored by representatives of the Save the Children International Union (SCIU), Save the Children Fund (SCF), and International Committee of the Red Cross (ICRC), and in the various contemporary publications of the relief agencies. Many of the reports of Hungarian refugees' suffering reached well beyond Hungarian newspapers and humanitarian relief offices in Geneva to larger newspapers in the United States and Britain. The mass circulation of these reports brought international attention to the suffering of Hungary's refugees.

In most relief work, "storytelling is the very nature of their work" as humanitarians, James Dawes contends. He asserts people in need seldom require solely food or medicine; instead, the "hope of being able to tell their story" is sometimes their "only hope." While those in need often require "someone to believe" them, local and international humanitarians in postwar Budapest had to bear witness and tell the refugees' stories.[73] Yet "the authority to represent the suffering of others" always carries the danger, as Michael Barnett suggests, to "(mis)appropriate the pain" of others and deprive the victims of their ability to express their own subjectivity.[74] Despite this, acts of witnessing and testimonial narratives, as Michal Givoni argues, are often the sole means to provide "a face to collective grievances," give a "touch of reality," or mirror "the voice of individuals exposed to or affected personally by violence and persecution."[75]

Through written testimonies, reports, and photographs, humanitarians could convey their eyewitnessed impressions of the refugees' destitution in the railcars to the relief agencies in Geneva and to potential donors. The testimonial character turned the reports into tools to evoke readers' compassion, solidarity, and feelings of guilt. Similar to the statement of the United Nations secretary-general in 2015 that the relief of refugees was a "fundamental common duty of all human beings" that should acknowledge "the true human tragedies involved,"[76] the postwar international call for humanitarian relief used individual stories and human tragedies of Hungary's middle-class refugees to alter Hungary's international reputation and public image. The English novelist and eyewitness Coningsby Dawson was convinced that "misery is best depicted in individual cases."[77]

One of those eyewitnesses was William Andrew MacKenzie, a Catholic priest and treasurer of the SCIU in Geneva, who regularly visited Budapest. It was important for him "to see for himself where urgent help is needed." He visited all the relief organizations that worked on behalf of children and afterward wrote a report for the SCIU. MacKenzie wanted to assure Hungary that the SCIU would do anything it could to relieve the "misery of Hungary's little ones."[78] Kornél Tábori, an important Hungarian social photographer, visually documented in his famous *War Album* not only the suffering of soldiers at the front but also the situation on the home front and the social side effects of the war and the dissolution of the empire.[79] One of his photos (see fig. 1.1) captures the departure and arrival of refugees at a railway station.

Tábori often centered his perspective on the refugee children. Many articles and photographs documenting the plight of the railcar dwellers were published in papers and journals, stressing the social decline refugees had experienced. Reports emphasized the injustice of forcing people of such social standing to "live in railway freight and cattle cars."[80] They documented the appalling living conditions the refugees had to endure, thereby underlining their victimhood. Individuals of former high social standing became icons of Hungary's territorial loss and its impact on the people. Reporters described "conditions of previously unimaginable misery, starving and freezing, without warm clothes or a roof over their head."[81]

Hungarian child relief worker Julia Vajkai wrote an English-language report about the living conditions of the railcar dwellers in Budapest. Vajkai and a Mrs. Schoch from Zürich were invited by Theodor Bärtle to visit the

Menekülők egy határszéli állomáson

Fig. 1.1. Refugees at a train station near the border. Photo by Kornél Tábori, in Tábori, *Háborús Album*, 84.

train stations in Budapest in January 1920. Bärtle was the municipal secretary of Budapest, commissioner for the fugitives, and one of the few local representatives at the recently established meetings of the so-called foreign missions in Budapest. Bärtle brought Vajkai and Schoch to the Western Railway Station, where he showed them long lines of cars that were usually used "for the transport of animals and cargo."[82] A local employee informed Bärtle that a total of 127 railway coaches were present at the station that day, all populated by Hungarian refugees from the ceded territories. In her report, Vajkai took meticulous care in describing the refugees' living conditions and their physical and mental constitution. She recalls how she and her colleagues knocked at the closed door of a wagon car, then "climbed on a little ladder into the dim interior," where they were stricken by a "filthy gust of air." She observed that the cars had no proper windows, "only the usual little latticed openings" that were "covered with rags or paper" to keep the cold out and the heat in. She described the absence of any furniture and the use of dirty straw for beds. Twenty-two men, women, and children had lived in the car since April 1919 "in the most repulsive promiscuity," she observed.

Vajkai portrayed the mental and moral state of the cars' inhabitants. She described the railway-car dwellers as "perfectly apathetic"; they would "steal wood here and there" to keep the wagon warm. She noticed the physical degeneration of the great number of children from Transylvania who looked "very pale and thin with their bones sticking out" and whom nobody would recognize as the children of the Székely (Transylvania Hungarians), whom she usually considered a "strong and healthy race." A week-old child, she stated, was only "wrapped in a petticoat of the young mother"; the foreign missions could only give relief gifts to destitute individuals once the asylums and children's hospitals were adequately provided for, so there was neither linen nor baby cloth available. Vajkai wondered when "those poor car-dwellers can get their share." "God knows," was her resigned answer.

Naturally, railcar dwellers did not always openly welcome inspectors. Heading toward a line of cars occupied by middle-class teachers and judges from Slovakia and Transylvania, Bärtle cautioned Vajkai that she might not get to see them, because these refugees were ashamed of their misery and would "rather die than exhibit it." An aid worker knocked on the door, and a "very thin and white" woman opened it. "I peep into the interior," Vajkai stated, and felt that it was miserably cold, because there was no fire. When asked if she would be able to get more wood, the woman shrugged her shoulders and declared that she would not steal. "They are all like her, the better people I mean," an aid worker explained, referring to the many impoverished former Hungarian state employees.[83]

Vajkai's report tackles the psychological impact on refugees of homelessness, uprootedness, and the loss of a "place which stands fixed upon the earth and which is their home." She was told that the refugees at first tried to integrate, but then lost all their energy and finally became "quite apathetic. She expressed her indignation that "the very best of a nation, the bravest, the most honest and most faithful" were now "compelled to live as no animal would bear it," only because they "had lost the war." She judged it a "criminal indifference of humanity" and the "most outrageous medieval way," while US president Woodrow Wilson was preaching the protection of the minorities.[84]

Many humanitarian reports stressed the refugees' physical and moral degeneration, supposedly evidenced by the car dwellers' lack of cleanliness, growing indifference, "promiscuity," and inability to maintain a morally civilized life. Novelist Coningsby Dawson confirmed many of Vajkai's findings. When he visited the railcar dwellers, he noticed their presence "by a smell not unlike an open sewer." Children "lay dying in those boxes while the living slept beside them." Dawson commented on the lack of any "attempt of decency," noting that "women bore children in the publicity of their families" and that "all the intimate details of married life were witnessed by the most innocent and the youngest."[85]

The "mob of refugees without work and uprooted from their homelands" was believed to be not only a heavy burden on the Hungarian state but also a "danger in the center of Europe."[86] In a supplementary report about the condition of children's life in Hungary from January 20, 1920, Vajkai again addressed the issue of the refugees' improper (and therefore immoral) housing and its impact on children's lives. She observed with concern that it was not the wealthy class that was anxious to have children but the poor. While understanding those "young couples who are hungry for the joy of life after the physical and moral suffering of the war" and for whom love formed "the one moment of oblivion in their dreadful existence," Vajkai considered the improper social circumstances responsible for excess births and the inappropriate upbringing of "most of these unfortunate little creatures."[87]

Vajkai's similarly renowned sister, Rose Vajkai, also mediated her knowledge of the refugees in Budapest to Western social workers and a general audience. She culturally translated her firsthand experiences of the refugees' living conditions to Western readers. In one report, she described the condition of the babies of the middle-class judges and teachers. Even if the children were "wasted and underfed," their parents' class anxieties made them unwilling "to exhibit their misery and get the generous foreigners to help them."[88] In a 1927 article for *The World's Children*, the official publication of the British Save the Children Fund, Rose Vajkai recalled the postwar transformation of the Budapest cityscape, with "long lines of emergency huts, big colonies of small buildings of wood or cement with unpaved roads" that were created when the city could no longer handle the pressure of necessity. She was commenting on the "appalling promiscuity" that could be witnessed in these overcrowded rooms, where the refugees were forced to mix with the "poorest of the poor," who also had been forced out of the "real," central Budapest. In her work for the Save the Children International Union, she felt obliged to "go into their very midst" to save the refugees' children.[89]

Witnessing refugee conditions in Budapest spurred significant involvement from local welfare workers and foreign sympathizers. An "Account on Circumstances of Subsistence in Budapest" by Endre Liber from October 1921 described an "investigation/razzie," a common practice by the children's police tribunal to expose the misery of the capital's young refugees. The investigation was this time accompanied by Hedwig Lotter Corroven, a Swiss journalist for a Bern newspaper. Corroven's impressions during the investigation led to her involvement in the relief of Budapest's refugees and their children. To raise funds, she kicked off a large relief endeavor, notably a shipment to the children of "4 large trunks of garments and 100 Swiss francs." Swiss professors Ryser and Vis took part in another investigation, after which they concluded that "the misery they saw here is not to be seen elsewhere."[90] Liber expressed his appreciation of these investigations, because their result was "the blessed help of foreign missions." If the missions' benevolent activity were to cease, "this misery" among the children and families of the middle class would further escalate, since several who had been arrested belonged to the middle class.[91]

The class dimensions of the refugee situation were clear to many observers; though quick to critique the degradation of lower-class refugees, they treated the displaced middle class more gently. Liber reasoned that middle-class refugees could not be held responsible for their poor circumstances, because their specialized training did not prepare them to be able to secure their daily bread through conventional labor. He appealed for solidarity with the intellectuals, who "now more than ever" needed external and "beneficent help." He explained that the inhabitants' life circumstances had been mostly influenced by the "exceedingly bad" dwelling situation of the "nearly 60,000 fugitives" of which "755 families, live actually in wagons." Liber wished to remind visitors to Budapest who saw the "full show-windows, the radiantly illuminated coffee-houses and filled localities of theatres" to keep in mind that there existed a sad "reverse of this shining surface." Indeed, the brilliant shops, theaters, and entertainment venues, he argued, might still have customers, but they were no longer the old middle-class customers who, in the coming years, would not have the resources to follow the "call for cultural development."[92]

In a book titled *It Might Have Happened to You*, Dawson similarly challenged educated foreign readers' temptation to reassure themselves that Hungary's horrors were distant problems. "You," he told his middle- and upper-class readers, "are probably exactly the sort of person who, had you been born in Central Europe, would have gone to the bottom first." He anticipated and contested their belief that their intelligence, specialization, and social background would have spared them from social decline. Precisely because they gained their living with their brains, not their hands, they would have been unable to endure in such dire circumstances. He used direct confrontation to make his readers comprehend that those suffering and impoverished were doctors, professors, engineers, artists, musicians, businessmen, and lawyers and that the intellectual wealth of the nations was about to perish.[93]

Foreign reporting emanating from transnational humanitarianism revealed the international perception of postwar poverty. Already in the late nineteenth and early twentieth centuries, slumming and social photography had been sparked by an interest in spectating misery. American social photographers Lewis Hine and Jacob Riis showed in 1890 how "the other half" of American society lived to reveal the plight of workers, the poor, immigrants, and children. Using children to advocate for social reform, the American anti–child labor movement was becoming fused with Progressivism.[94] Slumming in American workshops and cramped apartments differed from slumming in Budapest's impoverished and refugee dwellings in one important aspect: while people such as Hine and Riis wanted to cross social boundaries, the humanitarian encounter in Budapest's postwar refugee camps and lowly tenements often enabled moments of social identification. Here international relief workers entered the private space of destitute refugee families. Inside the railway cars they encountered many people who were highly educated, had belonged to the middle or upper class, and arrived in Hungary as part of a displaced intellectual and economic elite. Since the relief workers were often from a similar social and educational background, they identified strongly with the refugees and felt compassion for their sharp social decline. Thus, their focus lay on those who were newly impoverished and displaced.

The recollections of children were considered especially worthwhile to report. Knowing the value of children's testimonies, Julia Vajkai asked fifty children from her workrooms (discussed in a later chapter) to write "little autobiographies."[95] Vajkai reported in a meeting of the foreign missions that these autobiographies represented valuable propaganda material and would be at the disposal to any relief organization interested.[96] After their translation into English, these individual children's stories were publicized in an article in *The Record* by SCF's Eglantyne Jebb titled "Life Stories of Hungarian Children." Instead of simply printing the stories, Jebb embedded these "typical biographies," as she called them, into her own narrative and interpretation. They provided an alternative to "any number of dry, statistical, adult-written reports" and were intended as a means to explain "the need for bringing succor to the starving children of the slums." In the same way that "'atmospheres' and 'experiences' came to constitute one of the central and longest-lasting features of international cooperation" at the time, so did the search for and representation of children's "authentic" and subjective experiences and their feelings shape humanitarian reporting.[97] Jebb selected a number of condensed narratives of children's experiences. Their stories reflected on the departure, disappearance, and death of fathers; on the lack of income, proper food, housing, heating, and clothing; on hunger and everyday struggles to obtain food or other goods; on illnesses and the death of mothers, infants, and siblings; on displacement, permanent migration, and lost homes. In capturing these reflections on the war's intrusions into children's everyday lives, Jebb gave a voice to the child "victims of war, starvation, disease and penury." One of the children, Ellen, wondered whether "perhaps I am much too young to write my life's story. It is true that I have lived only a few years, but my life has had variety enough."[98] The dense life stories reveal how grown-up the children had to become.

Some of the recollections center on children's experiences with displacement and migration. Ellen had fled twice from Transylvania to Budapest, first after its occupation in 1916 and again in 1919. Many of her recollections of her early childhood in Transylvania were happy memories. "I possessed everything my heart could desire," Ellen wrote. But of her departure from her former home and her arrival to Budapest in August 1919, she explained that "here we suffer very much," and "here I have not even got a warm room." Another story from a Transylvanian girl explained that "the end of the war took a bad turn for us," because her family was "banished" from their home and hometown. She remembered that they had "lost and suffered much," first living in a railway car and then dwelling in "one little room." A boy from Transylvania dated the outbreak of the war to 1916, not 1914, because it was "not the outbreak of the Great War but the invasion of his "beautiful native village'" that mattered to him.[99] Personal accounts like these allowed Jebb to elicit compassion and raise funds among British audiences. The article ended with a note that grants by the Save the Children Fund for work in Hungary so far totaled £91,648.[100]

Solutions to meet the special needs of the displaced families and their children were hard to come by. An American Relief Administration (ARA) cablegram to London in 1921 about the situation in Budapest acknowledged that, while general relief work was done to some extent, there occurred "many cases where worthy members [of the] intellectual classes are in great misery." Mrs. E. F. Hansen reported in December 1921 about the distribution of relief by the American Commonwealth Fund (ACF). Food packages worth $10 were distributed to "educators, teachers, professors" in Budapest and its suburban neighborhoods, who were in special need of relief. Leftover packages were distributed among "active and pensioned officials, judges, lawyers, physicians, artists, writers, actors, army officers." The ACF considered the situation of these professionals—both locals whose income no longer guaranteed their

Fig. 1.2. Idyll in the coach street. Caricature by Károly Mühlbeck, *Új Idők* 26, no. 6 (February 22, 1920): 115.

everyday survival and those who had been displaced—"particularly serious." Yet due to the intellectuals' abrupt financial decline, some were "too reserved to ask for help." In response, the ACF circumvented the customary system of investigation and simply sent packages out to the deserving intellectuals.[101]

High-profile publicity for the refugees' plight came on May 30, 1920, when American journalist William L. Chenery published a lengthy article on the railway-car dwellers in the *New York Times*. The article relied on a series of eyewitness reports, many of which had been made for the ARA, SCF, and the ICRC. Quoting Ronald Campbell Macfie, a Scottish physician and a representative of the English Quakers investigating in Budapest, Chenery echoed many of the class-based sympathies in other reports. Macfie described finding the train cars "a very pathetic sight." In one of them he had found a family of ten who all looked "miserably ill and wasted." Chenery wished to remind American readers that many of the refugees were "people of position and refinement." A personal encounter with one poor woman who, during their talk, broke down and wept when she described her happy home back in Transylvania especially aroused Macfie's, and Chenery's, feelings of compassion.[102]

Some criticized how the postwar condition forced the middle-class refugees to adapt their everyday routines to the inappropriate circumstances. A caricature titled "Idyll in the Coach Street," shown in figure 1.2, sarcastically presents railcar dwellers' everyday life. The apparently unmitigated adaptation of the most ordinary daily activities to the train is captured by people going to the barber, taking care of an infant, and cleaning dishes.

Ridiculing the need of refugees to pretend to live a normal daily life, just now in a train compartment, the caricaturist denounced the effect of the

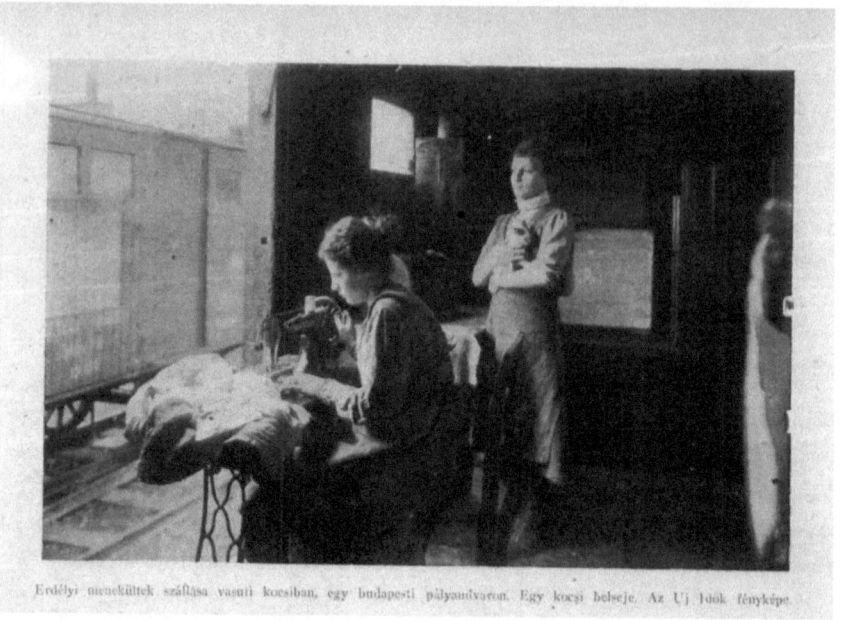

Fig. 1.3. Transylvanian refugees in a railway coach in Budapest. Unknown photographer, *Új Idők* 26, no. 3 (January 24, 1920): 56.

peace treaty for its disruption of people's lives. The railcar dweller becomes here the hero of the postwar. While many reports decried or satirized the refugees' social decline and filthy living conditions, others heroized middle-class refugees' resilience to create a semblance of normal life under the inhuman housing and living conditions. As figure 1.3 suggests, many refugees continued to perform respectable work, as represented by the woman at the sewing machine.

Major international humanitarian organizations like the ICRC, SCF, and SCIU used the most innovative media of the time to share their findings with potentially sympathetic audiences. Alongside articles, books, and reports, photographs and documentary movies visually captured the refugee, housing, and food crises. Of four movies the ICRC commissioned in 1921, one titled *Organisation of Help in Favor of the Hungarian Children in Budapest* recorded various forms of inappropriate housing in Budapest, including barracks, communal homes, and railway cars.[103] The film probes the lives of both children and professionals who came as refugees to Budapest, selecting a teacher, a lawyer, and a judge living in the destitute railway cars. The focus on a few individuals—with their names and titles—removed the anonymity of the refugee mass. Portrayals of the suffering of these homeless individuals, it was hoped, would evoke compassion among middle- and upper-class viewers and donors in the West.

Visuals and reports alike presented individual cases to exemplify widespread suffering. One ARA report from 1921 profiled four stories. Fifty-eight-year-old Sam Gross, a "graduate scholar of various European Universities," was reported to be living under the "most deplorable circumstances." Due to the exorbitant cost of living, his inadequate monthly pension brought him to the verge of starvation, caused his shabby appearance, and forced him to live in a stable. Vince Reichmann, an industrial high school faculty member with a family of four, had fled from Fiume, where he had been robbed before departing to Budapest. Once in Budapest, the Reichmanns found shelter in an empty railcar. His wife and two children developed severe cases of bronchitis. The narrative description of this "utterly destitute" family represented the story of the entire "deplorable situation of the Hungarian intellectual classes." The ARA's E. F. Hansen denounced the inconceivability of these "deserving, educated and well-born families" having to "exist" in abject conditions.[104] Relating here to the intellectual's class belonging and social entitlement, Hansen contributed to inscribing Hungary into a victim narrative.

These individuals were identified not as former soldiers but as the new deserving poor, who had to unfairly suffer from hardships and privations beyond description. Hansen closed her report with the story of a married couple of the intellectual class who now owned only a single pair of shoes between them, which compelled either the wife or the husband to stay at home while the other was out looking for bread. This couple, like many displaced families, was forced to sell all of their personal belongings, even "their last suit of clothing," to survive. Hansen observed that gifts of charity or charitable donations "from kind people" and foreign missions were the sole means of relief.[105]

Children in Refugee Housing

Families residing in both the railcars and the city's refugee barracks and colonies endured substandard living conditions. They often had no heat, toilet, or cooking facilities. Social photographer and police reporter Kornél Tábori tried to capture this existence on camera. He regularly joined the police on their razzias to the dwellings and documented the human misery found there.[106] Some of his documentary photographs, such as figure 1.4, were reprinted in American newspapers or in humanitarian publications such as the Save the Children Fund's *The Record* and aimed to capture scenes of everyday life.

Fig. 1.4. The inside of a railway car. Photo by Kornél Tábori, in Tábori, *Egy halálraítélt ország borzalmaiból, no page number.*

This type of documentary photography aimed to "present their human subjects as ordinary people who were temporarily down on their luck, hoping that viewers would make the imaginative leap to apply the message to themselves."[107] Pictures of the interiors of the railcars accompanied reports exposing the refugees' dire living conditions. Preparing food and keeping the wagons clean were everyday challenges, but changing weather conditions presented a serious risk to families' survival. The dense concentrations of people in confined areas facilitated the spread of contagious illnesses, and images documented the unacceptable conditions for the sick in this temporary "railway city."[108]

In addition to attempts to appeal to donors' sense of class empathy, class empathy, the fate of children and the innocence of youth were common themes in efforts to gain international supporters. "The figure of the child" played a central role in contemporary media "representations of poverty," attracting the rapt attention of national and international readerships and donors.[109] As Iain Wilkinson has argued, "'the visual' is a vital component of social experience and serves as a motive force of social action."[110] In postwar Budapest, images of children living in the railway cars became a powerful symbol of Hungary's traumatic experience and elicited strong feelings of sympathy and compassion. Reporters relied on close, detailed descriptions of the impoverished children and their living conditions to arouse readers' concern. The humanitarian reporters in Budapest of the 1920s shared many of the internationalist "concerns about what people felt [which] came to drive virtually every aspect of international life, from politics to leisure, from education to health."[111] Publicizing humanitarian images and reports and eliciting specific emotions among the local and international audience were central features of the humanitarian endeavor at the time.

The dynamics of childhood and family life in the railcars, observers reported, exhibited the consequences of displacement. Julia Vajkai reported in 1920 seeing "a little baby, one week old. It had been born there on Christmas Eve and was wrapped up in an old petticoat and blue with cold." "The wind [was] blowing through the cracks and gaps." In such extremely difficult living conditions, she wondered, "How many of their children have died during the winter, victims of pneumonia?" Due to the severe weather that winter, many of the railcar dwellers had to "remain in their beds—such beds as they had—all day long," because they had no clothes and no shoes to warm their bodies and feet. Most of the families had lost all their furniture because they had had to sell it bit by bit to raise money for food, which meant that the railcars were often very bare and ill-equipped. Nevertheless, in most of the wagons, all members of a family "gather[ed] round a little stove, for the most part fireless, to mingle their misery together." The children were trapped in "these dark and loathsome dens for whole days," while the parents were either working or looking for work. Vajkai continued with stark warnings. "Seeing the dreadful sufferings of their children" and being unable to change their daily lives, "many a father and many a mother have gone mad." She was convinced that a "horrible mental and physical decay" would befall these families.[112] The lack of heat inside the railcars contributed to the spread of diseases and a high infant mortality. Such ills plagued the railway wagons and Budapest's impoverished neighborhoods alike.

Because space inside the railway wagons was cramped, many older children would leave and spend the day roaming outside in the railway station area, as shown in figure 1.5. In addition to leaving the railway cars as a means to escape the tight living spaces, refugee children also went out to forage for firewood, food, and other critical supplies, as shown in figure 1.6. As a result, children often became partial providers for their families, and their work contributed significantly to their comfort and survival, especially when their parents had not yet obtained employment from the Hungarian state. There were reports of children being overburdened with responsibilities. Reports from

Fig. 1.5. The street of the railway-car dwellers. Unknown photographer, January 1920, Signature 321-1948, Hungarian National Museum, Budapest.

Fig. 1.6. Children delivering firewood from the forest. Unknown photographer, January 1921, CH AEG AP 92.105.78 (2).

1920 expressed the fear that some children would turn into thieves. When they "see food somewhere which is for the moment unguarded, . . . the dull pain in their empty little insides suddenly becomes a gnawing spasm" and they are tempted to simply "take the food and eat it." The children's hunger was seen as the prime cause of antisocial and criminal behavior, which was mounting alarmingly. If the children began by stealing bread, they would later "steal money or anything in order to buy food." Child relief workers were convinced that, once the children started "sliding down the slope, there [was] . . . no stopping!"[113]

Some organizations tried to deal with this problem before it grew out of hand. William Chenery observed that the Hungarian National Child Protection League had successfully been "searching in the quarters of the poor," and thus prevented their "turning to wrongdoing." Nevertheless, Budapest had radically changed and now had "a child criminality almost as great as that of England's seven largest cities put together, London included." Responsibility for the city's "social decline" was placed squarely on the postwar redrawing of Hungary's national borders and the state's inability to deal with all the problems that had been unleashed.[114]

Since many parents could not provide sufficient care, bands of vagrant children frequented the railway areas and surrounding neighborhoods. The "more than 50,000 young vagrants on the streets of Budapest"—the number by 1921—constituted a massive social problem.[115] Some of these child vagrants were war orphans, whereas others had traveled to the city from the lost territories.[116] Much public debate circulated about the "hundreds of thousands of fatherless and motherless children, illegitimate children, orphans, vagrants." How were they to be "saved for respectable society"?[117]

Inspectors of life in the barracks in 1920 concluded that illness and unemployment were, of course, devastating, but the lack of a father amplified the woe to the remaining family: "Hunger, rags, dirt, the depravity of children emerge from the father's grave."[118] Even if refugee children still had accommodation at the railway stations, they faced severe problems in their everyday lives. Ongoing reorganization of the temporary housing even caused refugee children to get lost. An account of "Hungary in the Third Peace Winter" by Captain Prentiss N. Terry, who was reporting on the American feeding scheme, noted that sometimes, "when a child returns from the bread line, with a loaf of bread or empty-handed," it would often "not know where to find his 'home,' for it has been shunted over to another track or railroad yard."[119]

In the winters, the railcar families' situation worsened. Because of their poverty and inability to find appropriate accommodation or properly paid

Fig. 1.7. Half of the children have no shoes. Unknown photographer, 1920, CH AEG AP 92.105.77.

work, former "government officials, even of the higher class, . . . filed affidavits that their children could not attend school because they [had] neither clothes nor boots."[120] Various reports mention that, during the winter, siblings shared one pair of shoes and took turns going to school. Photographs, such as figure 1.7, captured children without boots, especially among the dwellings of poor and refugee families. This lack of adequate footwear became a serious health concern.

During the winter months, a report from 1921 mentions, a number of children "with chilblains of the second or third degree on their feet were nursed by the ambulant surgical clinics."[121] This lack of proper clothing made it impossible for many refugee children to attend school or go outside—thus affecting their education and social standing and making their integration into Budapest society even more difficult. The children's state of education had already been a problem before their departure from the outlying lands. As Julia Vajkai explained, "When the Hungarian schools in the parts of the country occupied by Rumania were closed, 160,000 children in those territories were left without schooling."[122] In collaboration with the British Save the Children Fund and with its financial support, Vajkai established schools and vocational training for children ages twelve to fourteen, where they could learn a practical handicraft to help support their families.[123] This initiative is examined in the final chapter of this book.

Politics of Displacement

The story of Budapest's refugees and railcar dwellers and the handling of displaced people in the wake of World War I reveals how refugees were used for propaganda purposes in the dispute over borders and populations. Doomed to live for months, even years, at railway stations in the city, the standstill demonstrates the Hungarian postwar state's ambivalent stance toward the refugees. Could they not return home? Was Budapest really their final destination? Would they really have to be integrated into the new Hungarian state? The fact that the refugees remained in such a precarious situation for so long reinforced Hungary's hope that the refugees might return to where they came from. The political implications of Budapest's refugee situation were widespread. Many Hungarian press sources, especially during the war and its immediate aftermath, envisioned the return of refugees to their real "homelands" in Transylvania and other lost territories. In August 1920, only a few months after the signing of the Treaty of Trianon, a reporter for the daily *Nyírvidék* expressed a collective wish for the "urgently expected and ardently desired opportunity" to "expel the hyenas"—Romanians—from Transylvania and to "lead our railway dwelling refugees who are eating bread, salted through the tears of statelessness, back to their neglected homes." It was, this reporter said, "our hidden and instinctive conviction that the current state cannot be eternal."[124] But regardless of the desire for their return, the misery in Budapest required relief, which had further political implications both domestically and internationally. Because the refugees represented a rather elite class and were regarded as "ethnically valuable," their integration was seen as an important step in the ongoing nation-building process in Hungary.

The grim situation at the city's train stations was a locus of contestation with political and social implications. Captain Terry observed during his visit to the freight wagons in 1921 that "loyal Hungarians" were now forced to live wretchedly with a family of four to ten in a railcar just "because they would not swear allegiance to their victorious enemies, the Jugo-Slavs, the Roumanians, and the Czecho-Slovaks."[125] His observations directly linked Hungary's domestic refugees to issues of international policy. Both local and international relief workers feared the social consequences of the mass displacement. Endre Liber, the Hungarian commissioner to the United States, believed that "all good-will" would be "in vain" if "our poor compatriots, expelled from their homes, are not enabled to return."[126] A 1920 report from the ICRC on its mission to Budapest explicitly addressed the refugees' agony: "True to their oath, true to their country, they suffer the fate of the martyrs. Driven from their homes without clothes, without money, without hope, they suffer and perish, crowded into barracks or railroad cars like beasts."[127]

Although the June 1920 peace treaty had codified the territorial loss, the American Relief Administration's Hansen referred in 1921 to Hungary's lost territories as "occupied" territories, thereby fundamentally questioning the status of Hungary's new borders in humanitarian circles.[128] Fearing political chaos and Bolshevism, both local and international relief workers helped institutionalize the rhetoric of Hungary's victimhood in various ways. Close documentation of the social and physical decline enabled the Hungarian state, along with its relief organizations, to present the whole nation as victim of an unjust treaty, threatening grave social consequences. The refugee discourse was ammunition for the politicians publicly questioning the fairness and social sustainability of the postwar European order. One publication, prepared to be circulated at the Paris Peace Conference in 1919, made a eugenic argument against territorial loss, observing that those areas would lose the "cream of the socially selected." At the same time, the intellectuals' migration to Hungary would constitute an even greater social danger, because they would share the misery of a "fallen proletariat." If they were not able to make a decent living, their families would not thrive, and the class would soon become extinct. Intellectual mothers would not be willing to raise large families and give birth to Hungary's future generations in this difficult situation. And this would be the end of the Hungarian nation.[129]

Ideas of mass suffering were ideal ammunition for a political elite eager to gain supporters demanding a revision of the Treaty of Trianon.[130] The highly publicized "great national energy" surrounding the Hungarian refugees could also be used to strengthen Hungarian national identity beyond borders and help "restore" the postwar Hungarian state.[131] Yet the success of this national project largely depended on the international postwar community. The Trianon treaty was, after all, an international agreement. For this reason, revisionists invested tremendous effort in bringing international attention to the refugee issue, which was used to press the need for political and geopolitical reassessment of the peace agreement. The results were mixed. While the campaign succeeded in arousing much sympathy at home and abroad, it failed to change the minds of the treaty's international signatories. Propagating the cause of Hungary's minorities and its stateless or homeless refugees was yet instrumental in enabling this former enemy country to participate in international discourse in the interwar period.

On September 18, 1922, Hungary gained a seat in the League of Nations, from which the country's representatives consistently lobbied for revisionism and "protests against its neighbors' treatment of their Magyar populations."[132] As the League "theoretically served as the protector of Hungarian minority rights in Transylvania" and elsewhere, the country used this platform to gain international visibility for the conflicts with its neighboring countries and to push for a more "coherent policy of minority protection."[133] However, this policy never came into being.[134] While the effort to use the refugees' plight to delegitimize Trianon and the new postwar order was in the end unsuccessful, it did manage to anchor an "ethnic-exclusive" understanding of national belonging among Hungarians (irrespective of which side of the country's borders their homes were).[135] The story of the Hungarian railcar dwellers is thus more than a story of wrecked lives; it is also one of territorial and international power struggles.

Conclusion

Massive migration and displacement took the capital's destitution to a new dimension and initiated a victim discourse centered on the city's "deserving" middle-class refugees. The public discourse about the forced displacement of hundreds of thousands of Hungarians reveals the government's unwillingness to accept its new geopolitical status. The destiny of one special group of refugees in Budapest at the time—the railcar dwellers and their children, whose homes were railcars in the sidings of rail stations—was instrumental in drawing attention to the capital's suffering. The plight of these impoverished refugees served the Hungarian state and its popular media outlets in their open denunciation of the "traumatically felt" peace terms, entailing major loss of territory and relinquishing a valuable section of Hungary's population.[136] The stories of these homeless Hungarians who came to epitomize the politics of removal bring to light the intertwined relationship between the discourses of displacement and advocacy for political revisionism. While migration impaired the everyday lives of Budapest's civilian population and its children in this social melting pot and was instrumental in laying the basis for territorial revisionism, the destitution of these migrants was further aggravated by a severe food crisis in the early postwar years, as the next chapter will explore.

Notes

1. American Relief Administration European Children's Fund, *Final Report*, June 1, 1920, 1.
2. Lévai, "Az elhanyagolt gyermekegészség," 153.
3. Conklin, *Statelessness*, 104–6.
4. Proctor, *Civilians in a World at War*, 110.
5. On ethnicity in relation to migration, see Puskás and Ålund, "Ethnicity," 13.
6. McCagg, *A History of Habsburg Jews*, 204.
7. Gatrell, *A Whole Empire Walking*, 197.
8. Szűts, "Optálási jegyzőkönyvek"; Ablonczy, "Menni vagy maradni?"
9. Zimmer, "Nationalism in Europe," 424.
10. Thomas and Babac, *Armies in the Balkans*, 8.
11. Malkki, "Refugees and Exile," 496.
12. Mócsy, *The Effects of World War I*.
13. Udvarhelyi, "'You People Would Keep on Dwelling': Twentieth-Century State Responses to Homelessness in Hungary from Above and Below," 695; Bender and Schorske, *Budapest and New York*, 164.
14. Recent academic publications, and even a documentary film, have attempted to reconstruct the everyday life of the railcar dwellers through oral and written recollections. See Dékány, "Csonka Vágányon." See also "Dér Zoltán diákkori emlékei a háborús évekből." On the intertwined history of the Hungarian state railway organization and the railcar dwellers, see Szűts, "Vasutas vagonlakók és a MÁV menekültpolitikája." See also Csóti, "Vagonlakók, barakklakók, menekültek."
15. "A menekültek szállásán," *Világ* 10, no. 143 (November 25, 1919), 8.
16. Kádár and Sarbó, *A nagy vihar hajótöröttei*, 33.
17. Liber, "Budapest a Menekültügy Szolgálatában," 33, 66.
18. "Egy székely város anyagi támogatást kér," *Budapesti Hírlap*, July 21, 1918, 9.
19. Minka, "A hontalan," 307.
20. "Menekülők: Rudnay Gyula képéhez," *Új Idők* 24, no. 39 (September 29, 1918): 256.
21. Dragoman, "Linguistic Pluralism," 289.
22. "Menekülők: Rudnay Gyula képéhez," 256.
23. Arendt, *The Origins of Totalitarianism*, 276–78.
24. Barth, *On Cultural Rights*, 61.
25. American Society of International Law, "Treaty between the Principal Allied and Associated Powers and Roumania," 324–32.
26. Motta, *Less Than Nations*, 373.
27. Case, *Between States*, 28.
28. "Miért olyan sok a vagonlakó Csonkamagyarországon?" *Melléklet az Erdélyi Hírek* 1, no. 41 (November 14, 1920).
29. Egry, *Etnicitás, identitás, politika*.
30. Brubaker et al., *Nationalist Politics*, 68.

31. "Treaty of Peace between the Allied and Associated Powers and Hungary and Protocol and Declaration," Signed at Trianon, June 4, 1920 (hereafter Treaty of Trianon), https://wwi.lib.byu.edu/index.php/Treaty_of_Trianon.
32. Rürüp, "Lives in Limbo," 114.
33. Sömjén, "Az állampolgarsági opció," 3.
34. Treaty of Trianon, Article 63.
35. For the interconnection between the end of empires and migration, see Brubaker, "Aftermaths of Empire."
36. Treaty of Trianon, Article 63.
37. Sömjén, "Az állampolgarsági opció," 4.
38. Mócsy, *The Effects of World War I*, 180.
39. Gatrell, *The Making of the Modern Refugee*, 53; Brubaker, "Nationalizing States," 415–16; Graupner, "Statelessness as a Consequence," 36.
40. Thorpe, "Displacing Empire," 102.
41. Petrichevich-Horváth, *Jelentés az Országos Menekültügyi Hivatal*, 37.
42. Pearson, "Hungary: A State Partitioned," 99.
43. Kürti, *The Remote Borderland*.
44. Ripka, "Emlékezés," 102.
45. Szűts, "Vasutas vagonlakók és a MÁV menekültpolitikája," 101, 94.
46. Chenery, "Starving Budapest," 2.
47. Petrichevich-Horváth, *Jelentés az Országos Menekültügyi Hivatal*, 37.
48. "Menekültek javára," *Pesti Hírlap* 42, no. 135 (June 1920): 4.
49. Petrichevich-Horváth, *Jelentés az Országos Menekültügyi Hivatal*, 12.
50. "Ahol a Menekültek Városa Épül," *Virradat*, March 22, 1922.
51. "A barakok világából," *Népszava* 48, no. 218 (September 15, 2020): 3.
52. Petrichevich-Horváth, *Jelentés az Országos Menekültügyi Hivatal*, 12.
53. "The American Red Cross in Hungary," 1921, Sheet 3, Records of the American National Red Cross 1917–34, WWI, 953.08 Hungary, Budapest Unit, Reports, Statistics, Surveys and Studies, NARA.
54. Chenery, "Starving Budapest," 2.
55. The stations included Keleti, Nyugati, Józsefvárosi, Dunaparti, and Dunakeszialagút.
56. Chenery, "Starving Budapest," 2.
57. "Sohase felejtsetek!" *Erdélyi Hírek* 1, no. 20 (June 19, 1920): 1.
58. "Miért olyan sok a vagonlakók Csonkamagyarországon."
59. Brubaker, "Aftermaths of Empire," 160.
60. "Patkányok," *Budapesti Hírlap* 42, no. 170 (July 28, 1922): 6.
61. Mócsy, *The Effects of World War I*, 176.
62. "A miniszterelnök beszéde a jóvátételi bizottság előtt," 1.
63. "Napihírek: Temesvárról kiutasított magyar családok," 1.
64. "1920. Június 14 én Budapest különböző pályaudvarain marhakocsikban tengetik életük," *A Melléklet az Erdélyi Hírek*, June 19, 1920.
65. "A vagonlakók és menekültek lakásügye," 2.
66. "Miért olyan sok a vagonlakók Csonkamagyarországon," and "Névsora azon keletmagyarországi vaggonlakó hazátlanoknak," *Melléklet az Erdélyi Hírek*, 1, no. 20 (June 19, 1920). Hungarian refugees played an active role in the radicalization of politics toward the right in 1919 and the subsequent White Terror. See Mócsy, *The Effects of World War I*, 176.
67. In the most complete Hungarian database of contemporary newspapers and journals, Arcanum Digitális Tudománytár, the keyword *Csonka magyarország* [truncated Hungary]

yields almost three thousand results, indicating the frequent use and widespread acceptance of this self-ascription. https://adtplus.arcanum.hu/en/.

68. Haynes, "Hungarian National Identity," 95.
69. Roszkowski and Kofman, *Biographical Dictionary of Central and Eastern Europe*, 1023.
70. Zeidler, *A magyar irredenta kultusz*; Zeidler, *Ideas on Territorial Revision in Hungary*.
71. Brubaker et al., *Nationalist Politics*, 95.
72. Kürti, *The Remote Borderland*, 96.
73. Dawes, *That the World May Know*, 1–2.
74. Barnett, *Empire of Humanity*, 34.
75. Givoni, *The Care of the Witness*, 4.
76. Klose and Thulin, *Humanity*, 11.
77. Dawson, *It Might Have Happened to You*, 41.
78. "Entretien avec M. MacKenzie, représentant de L'Union Internationale de Secours aux Enfants," 1–3, 1, AP 92.21.3, Secours á la Hongrie, Correspondance, rapport du CICR (1920–22), Assemblées des mission étrangères et des organisations nationales, Procès verbaux (1920–21), CH AEG.
79. Tábori, *Háborús Album*, 84.
80. Chenery, "Starving Budapest," 2.
81. Romsics, *Hungary in the Twentieth Century*, 95.
82. Julia Vajkai, "The Car-Dwellers," Budapest, January 1920, CH AEG AP 92.21.2 (1).
83. Vajkai, "The Car-Dwellers."
84. Ibid.
85. Dawson, *It Might Have Happened to You*, 39–40.
86. "L'activité du comité international de la croix rouge á Budapest," Comité International de la Croix-Rouge, Budapest 27 January 1922, Mission en Hongrie, ACICR B MIS 4.5/1108 à 1219, Archive of the International Committee of the Red Cross, Geneva (hereafter ICRC, Geneva).
87. Julia Vajkai, "Supplementary Report on the Conditions of Children in Hungary," January 20, 1920, 1–6, 1. CH AEG AP 92.21.2 (1).
88. Report of R. Vajkai . . . concerning her visit in the suburb of Budapest called "Angyalföld," Budapest, January 2, 1920, CH AEG AP 92.21.2.
89. Rozsi Vajkai, "In the Slums of Budapest," 131.
90. Andrew/Endre Liber, "Account on Circumstances of Subsistence in Budapest," Budapest, October 21, 1921, 1–35, Hungary, Folder 2 (1920–21), International Commissioners' Reports and Correspondence, EJ 155 21/18, Eglantyne Jebb Papers (SCF/A409/EJ), Save the Children Fund Archive (hereafter SCF Archive), Cadbury Research Library, Special Collections, University of Birmingham, Birmingham.
91. Liber, "Account on Circumstances," 1, 31.
92. Ibid., 2–4.
93. Dawson, *It Might Have Happened to You*, 2–3.
94. Riis, *How the Other Half Lives*; Freedman, *Kids at Work*; Yochelson and Czitrom, *Rediscovering Jacob Riis*; Duerden and Hine, *Photographer and American Progressive*, 78.
95. Jebb, "Life Stories of Hungarian Children," 27.
96. "Protocol of the Meeting of the Foreign Missions and Home Institutions," March 22, 1921, 1–2. CH AEG Archives privées 92.21.2.
97. Scaglia, *The Emotions of Internationalism*, 196.
98. Jebb, "Life Stories of Hungarian Children," 27, 31.
99. Ibid., 28–32.
100. "Protocol of the Meeting of the Foreign Missions," 2.

101. Hansen, "Third Distribution of Food Packages," 39–41.
102. Chenery, "Starving Budapest," 2.
103. "Actions de secours en faveur des enfants hongrois à Budapest," ICRC/Save the Children 1921, ICRC Digital Archives.
104. Hansen, "Third Distribution."
105. Ibid. See also "A vagonlakók," *Népszava*, July 9, 1920, 3–4.
106. Tomsics, "Tábori Kornél."
107. Marien, *Photography: A Cultural History*, 279.
108. Petrichevich-Horváth, *Jelentés az Országos Menekültügyi Hivatal*.
109. Wells, "The Melodrama of Being a Child," 277.
110. Wilkinson, "The Provocation of the Humanitarian Social Imaginary," 262.
111. Scaglia, *The Emotions of Internationalism*, 3.
112. Chenery, "Starving Budapest," 2.
113. Ibid.
114. Ibid.
115. Bowden, "Economic Conditions and Relief," 12.
116. Praise of the governmental relief of war orphans can be found in "Százhatvanhárom hadiárva," *Népszava* 46, no. 180 (August 4, 1918): 7.
117. "A senki fia," *Budapesti Hírlap* 42, no. 184 (August 1922): 6.
118. "A barakok világából," 3.
119. Terry, "Hungary in the Third Peace Winter," 41.
120. Chenery, "Starving Budapest," 2.
121. "The Starving Children of Hungary: Babies Dying by Hundreds."
122. Chenery, "Starving Budapest," 2.
123. Julia Vajkai, *Child Saving and Child Training*, 5.
124. "Mozgósításról," *Nyírvidék (Nyíregyháza)* 41, no. 183 (August 12, 1920): 1.
125. Terry, "Hungary in the Third Peace Winter," 41.
126. Endre Liber, "Government Commissioner of Refugees," Budapest, March 13, 1920, RG 59 Department of State, Decimal File, 864.42/9–864.511/2, Sheet 3, NARA.
127. "Rapport de la mission de la CICR à Budapest, 1920," ACICR B MIS 4.5/533 à 4.5/434, 1001–1130. 1–3, 1. Archive of the ICRC, Geneva.
128. Hansen, "Third Distribution."
129. Hungarian Territorial Integrity League, *The Consequences of the Division of Hungary*.
130. On the radicalization of refugees, see Egry, *Etnicitás, Identitás, Politika*, 110.
131. Petrichevich-Horváth, *Jelentés az Országos Menekültügyi Hivatal*, 35.
132. Rothschild, *East Central Europe*, 164.
133. Cameron Watson, "Ethnic Conflict," 173.
134. Francis Deák, "The Rumanian-Hungarian Dispute."
135. Gammerl, *Untertanen, Staatsbürger, und Andere*, 333.
136. Kuzmics and Haring, *Emotion, Habitus und Erster Weltkrieg*, 34.

2

HUNGER

Starving in the Capital City

WHILE (FORCED) MIGRATION FROM THE CEDED TERRITORIES IMPAIRED the everyday life of Budapest's civilian population in this social melting pot, people's destitution was exacerbated by a major food crisis in the early postwar years. World War I and its aftermath created one of the most severe food shortages in twentieth-century Europe. Migration and food scarcity were also closely intertwined. "Tidal flows of population inevitably strained the food supply of each city" in Europe after the war, as Thierry Bonzon and Belinda Davis note.[1] But Budapest was special. The lack of food in Hungary and especially in the capital was the result of various economic, political, and social factors that mutually impacted one another. Along with the large-scale displacement of Hungarians, which brought thousands more mouths to feed, the war's legacy of territorial losses and disrupted imperial infrastructures severely hampered the production and delivery of food supplies.

This chapter explores how Hungary's capital became a hungry city whose civilians, and especially its children, struggled to survive. The chapter scrutinizes the multiple causes of the city's postwar food crisis, going beyond a narrow focus on the impact of the economic blockade on Europe's civilian populations and children. As the war and dissolution of the Austro-Hungarian Empire disrupted both the production and transport of food, this chapter explores how the loss of territories and political turmoil altered and prevented the cultivation, harvesting, delivery, and consumption of food.

Food and Warfare

Economic warfare during and after World War I was seen as the main cause of children's hunger and overall deprivation in the defeated nations. In postwar Hungary, the economic blockade, imposed by the Allied powers from 1914 to the summer of 1919 (extending beyond the Armistice), played a significant role in reducing the availability of certain commodities. It also affected the import and export of important industrial goods, with serious repercussions on trade and on the overall economy.[2] Food scarcity can alter historical settings and relations in a very profound way. In *Home Fires Burning*, Belinda Davis sheds light on the central role food plays in history, explaining that food is "a fundamental human need" that involves "pleasure or danger in choosing well or poorly" and has the power of "mediating human relations."[3] In postwar Hungary, the hunger crisis created a nutritional, material, economic, and emotional vacuum. Karen Hunt has stated that the "disinterring of everyday life on the diverse home fronts of the First World War" provides a "new way of understanding the war itself," especially when attention is turned to the "most basic necessity of daily life—food." During the war, "almost everything else in everyday life could be allowed to suffer, such as the cleaning of the home, person, or clothing," but the "requirement for daily food" could never be neglected; a family's very survival was at stake.[4]

The aftermath of World War I saw an immense need for public feeding in the countries affected by the war and its aftermath. While veterans' bodies had to be healed and reconstructed, the collective body of the largely malnourished postwar populations had to be nursed back to health. For that purpose, it was not only that food had to be properly distributed; a new public awareness for this kind of bodily suffering also had to be raised. An inherent problem was that while "bloody death"—death during wartime fighting—"excites you, prints indelible images on the mind," as Lizzie Collingham argues in *The Taste of War*, "death by famine lacks drama." In contrast to the mourning over physically injured bodies, she observes, it was "the quiet and unobtrusive nature of death by starvation" and the "vast slow dispirited noiseless apathy" of those "who died of hunger" that explains why these victims are "largely forgotten today."[5] Yet famine in postwar Austria and Hungary was no longer silent and unobtrusive. It was gaining attention and came to be publicly acknowledged as a humanitarian crisis. In the postwar years, Austria, like Hungary, "would successfully export its national [food] crisis to the world and become a rallying point for postwar internationalism."[6] Like many other humanitarian crises, it came to be staged as a visual "melodrama."[7]

Before World War I, the bulk of Hungary's grain grew in Bácska and the Banat, but the milling center was Budapest, and most of the milled flour was earmarked for export. War fundamentally disrupted systems for the production and distribution of grain across the European continent. Two years into the war, in 1916, Romanian grain exports to Hungary—which had accounted for 30 percent of the needs of the Austro-Hungarian Empire—were cut off.[8]

Due to a poor harvest in 1916 and 1917 caused by unfavorable weather during harvesttime, along with difficulties gathering crops in Austria-Hungary because of the reduced labor force, wheat supplies dropped severely, creating a dearth of bread.[9] By 1917, the harvest in Austria had been reduced to 40 percent of its peacetime production, and the country became dependent on imports, which had until then mostly come from the Hungarian part of the empire.[10] But Hungary was no longer in a position, or no longer willing, to export to Austria as much food as was needed there.[11] Hungarian exports of grain and flour went down by "2.4 per cent of their pre-war average," creating a severe imbalance among different parts of the empire.[12] Declining food production in Hungary in turn resulted in fewer food exports to Austria, where the food situation was becoming "truly critical." The Viennese media accused Hungarian peasants of setting up a "Hungarian blockade" against Austria. Historian Peter Pastor argues that these food quarrels contributed "to the drifting apart of the two halves of the [dual] Monarchy."[13]

Yet, in the first years of the war, up to the occupation of its territories, the Hungarian part of the empire was in a better situation than the Austrian part or the German Empire. A *Washington Post* report of September 5, 1916, on the "exodus from Hungary" claimed that "food is still plentiful." The correspondent himself "had eggs, ham and butter, the latter unlimited, all for breakfast," at a time when these things were "unobtainable in Berlin." But eventually Budapest, too, had no white bread; it was the last city in the Central powers to replace it with war bread.[14] By 1917–18, "fat, flour, poultry and pork" were able to command "astronomical prices" on the black market, with the "profits ending up in the pockets of producers and middlemen."[15]

To many observers, the food problem was the major issue of the war for the Central powers. Wolf von Schierbrand, an American journalist who was in Austria-Hungary for several years, had inquired, among other topics, into the empire's food situation. In 1917 he published a report, later a book, titled *Austria-Hungary: The Polyglot Empire*. "This food danger and food urgency," he wrote, "hammers and knocks at every door three times a day." It calls for "instant attention, instant solution," he continued, because it was "not only a stomach question, but one of the soul," and it would determine the countries' futures.[16] Von Schierbrand drew attention to the emergence of famine, the scarcity of food, and the high price of foodstuffs, and he was concerned about their impact on the people's general health. From his own observations and drawing on official data, he concluded that the "feeble and sickly, the babies, women, children and the aged" were the ones who were injured the most. Due to lack of milk, he observed a level of infant mortality that was, by 1917, three times higher than it had been in 1914.[17] He could have argued that food conditions were "vastly better in Hungary than in Austria," because Hungary was less industrialized, more agricultural, and less dependent on imports. But Budapest had long relied on food deliveries from the countryside, and the war created shortages virtually everywhere.

During the war, imports of many basic food products stopped, including the import of milk for feeding infants and children.[18] In December 1915, when milk for children was already scarce, critics noted that Budapest's "coffee houses and the confectioners still receive[d] milk."[19] Such harsh criticism drew attention to the inequality of access to certain food products. Whereas the better-off classes in the capital city could still afford to go to coffeehouses and bakeries, others, especially destitute children, were unable to access basic, essential items. Anne, a Hungarian girl, recalled in 1922 that "milk, I only know by hearsay.[20] Milk deliveries to Budapest decreased dramatically between 1916 and 1919.[21] Thus, it was becoming "impossible to deliver milk against [ration] cards for the sick, old people and babies," while some "people have secured milk who were not entitled to it." The food office decided in 1918 to "centralize the handling and distribution of milk in order to facilitate the control."[22]

Some sources argue that people were troubled less about the drastic price increases for certain food products than about the complete unavailability of various essentials. In the summer of 1918, flour supplies were so limited that "there were families that were for three to four days entirely without any bread, because they could not redeem their flour vouchers."[23] High prices, one eyewitness maintained, "do not matter so much, if only the food could be obtained" at all. Budapest's inhabitants might soon need to "follow the example of the Parisians in 1870 and eat rats and mice."[24] Desperately, on February 9, 1918, Austria-Hungary signed the so-called Bread Peace Treaty, which created a "Ruthenian Crownland out of eastern Galicia and the Bukovina," recognizing the existence of Ukraine "in exchange for the delivery of at least a million metric tons of grain." Though this "bread peace" prevented the spread of revolution in the spring of 1918, some scholars have argued that it was decisive in bringing about Austria-Hungary's dissolution.[25]

World War I "reduced life once more to its prime essential: a sufficiency of nourishment," reviving "primordial instincts" of hunger, as in the "age of the cave man," von Schierbrand observed.[26] Food represented the foundation of every wartime economy.[9] Nutritional deprivation during the conflict was the result of a decrease in both quantity and quality of foodstuffs. The war triggered a kind of "minor revolution" in attitudes toward food, which was now thought of as "a tool" for maintaining and improving the soldiers' physical condition and fighting capacity.[27] "Wars cannot be fought without food,"[28] Ina Zweininger-Bargielowska has argued, because "physical activity increased significantly," making a high intake of calories necessary. "The war helped redefine nutrition as an issue of national security" and accelerated the scientific approach toward food.[29]

A new scientific language had emerged in the second half of the nineteenth century for describing the human body. As Rudolf Kučera has observed, the body was no longer a "mechanical machine" but rather a "modern motor," "driven by various fuels." The idea of rationalizing food gained prominence, as did the notion of calories. Calories were fuel that had to be transformed into energy to guarantee the proper and effective functioning of the body. By the end of the nineteenth century, "physiologists, biologists, biomechanics," and like-minded scientists were regarding the human body as a type of industrial motor and a key (if not *the* key) element in industrial production.[30] "Such numerical quantifications," expressed in the calculation of calories and the composition of certain foodstuffs, "replaced subjective individual expressions of satiety with a scientific determination of what nutrition an individual required in order to be in a state of health."[31] Nutritious food became not just a means of survival and a source of individual enjoyment but also guaranteed the maximum labor efficiency from workers. During World War I, all the combatant countries invested much effort into harnessing "the new science of nutrition." They tried to "maximize the efficiency of food distribution" and hoped "to squeeze as much physical labor as possible from soldiers and civilians." This conceptual revolution also significantly altered the ways food was conceived, prepared, processed, packed, and transported. During war, which placed an "immense strain on the food system," soldiers and the army—mostly men—were the focus of food provisioning.[32] Civilians and children came second.

Apart from prioritizing soldiers over the civilian population, a major cause of the decline in the processing and production of food during the war was the absence of male labor. In the Austro-Hungarian Empire, the recruitment of "increasingly wider age-groups of men for military service" caused severe shortages in the local and national workforce; as a result, jobs were filled by women and prisoners of war.[33] When at the front and in prison camps, Hungarian men were missing from running farms, working the fields, and harvesting. An American report of 1917 claimed that "3,000,000 men, mostly of the agrarian class" had been "removed from their vocation." Their places in the fields and in agriculture were then filled "by old and infirm men and women and children."[34] Mobilization also affected the empire's industrial productivity, as industrial production became "subordinated to the war effort" and productivity declined due to the labor shortage. Because agriculture was still the bedrock of Hungary's economy, men's absence was heavily felt.[35]

Many men who served in the army did not return when the war was over. Some spent years in prison camps and could not return home.[36] The absence of men who had been held as prisoners of war (POWs) in Russia even three years after the end of hostilities continued to affect Hungary's agriculture and food production. Of the 1.6 million to 2.1 million POWs of the Austro-Hungarian army in Russia, an estimated 500,000–600,000 were Hungarians. POWs of the Central powers were sent to comparatively "more inhospitable areas of the Russian Empire," including "the Urals, the White Sea Area, Siberia, or to Russian Central Asia"; of the 300,000 Austro-Hungarian soldiers who died, many were Hungarians.[37] An emotionally loaded 1921 appeal from the Hungarian National Assembly's War Prisoner Release Committee to the House of Commons Russian Relief Committee addresses "the human sentiments of the wives and mothers of our former enemies and appeals to all civilized nations of the world." The document stressed that hundreds of thousands of Hungarian prisoners of war had "fallen victim to the ravages of disease," were "starving and perishing," and were suffering from "physical and mental anguish." The text emphasizes the link between the absent POWs and the Hungarian civil population back home, explaining that "only the Hungarian mothers, only the Hungarian wives and children are left lamenting, kept pining—endlessly—for the home-coming of their beloved." Sixty thousand Hungarian families reported they found themselves in "pitiable anxiety."[38] The appeal called on the League of Nations to hasten the repatriation of the Hungarian POWs to secure the survival of their left-behind families, the agricultural sector, and the grieving society as a whole.

While Hungarian soldiers were missing from the picture in Budapest, thousands of (mostly Russian) prisoners of war (POWs) were held in the capital city. Before their repatriation through the International Committee of the Red Cross, the POWs needed to be fed, putting another burden on the Austrian and Hungarian governments. The state tried to avert the problem by having prisoners essentially feed themselves. A 1917 American newspaper article reported that half a million prisoners were "set to work in Austria and in Hungary for the planting and harvesting seasons."[39] When inspecting POW camps in Austria-Hungary, von Schierbrand listened to prisoners' grievances, which revolved mostly around "insufficient food, unaccustomed food, food not cooked to their liking; about alleged spoiled or tainted food, about unfair distribution of it; about favouritism shown, about thefts of food." He found that, "in all prison camps, the stomach is indeed found the most important organ of the body." Von Schierbrand judged Russian soldiers' appetites as generally unappeasable; if they could, they would all "devour three big loaves of bread a day." The natural appetite of an average Russian was "twice as big as that of an Austrian soldier," von Schierbrand continued. But now they were imprisoned in "semi-starving nations." Whenever the Russians complained about the food situation of its POWs in Austria-Hungary, the governments replied that England and France, who were Russia's allies, were responsible for the economic blockade being used against the Central powers as a measure of war.[40] It would be unfair to their own populations, officials argued, if the prisoners were to receive more food than local citizens.

The war disrupted nearly all aspects of the food systems supplying Budapest, from grain deliveries to workers to harvest to additional mouths to feed. The food shortages reached all levels of society and affected children and adults alike.

Discontinued Infrastructures: From Blockade to the Empire's Dissolution

The wartime disruption of international trade likewise had a damaging effect on food supplies, exacerbating the internal supply issues in Austria-Hungary and Central Europe. Before World War I, Britain had been an important trading partner with Hungary. Germany and the other Central powers had been dependent on the continuous "flow of international trade" as well.[41] An Eastern Blockade Committee had been established in Britain to coordinate and control the naval blockade on the Central powers, and it blockaded not only Germany's seaports but also imports to Austria-Hungary from 1914 to 1919. On May 26, 1915, the Italian government, in alliance with Britain, also declared a blockade along the "Austro-Hungarian coast from the Italian frontier on the north to the Montenegrin frontier on the south, including all islands, ports, bays." Although all ships attempting to trade with the Allies' enemies were to be blocked, friendly and neutral ships were to be allowed free entry and departure from the blockaded zone.[42]

Food thus "functioned as a weapon" under the blockade, resulting in "severe undernutrition and mass starvation."[43] Disrupting a world economy in which food had regularly been transported across the world's oceans to the urban populations of Europe, the blockade put "pressure on civilian food supplies" to crush the morale of civilian populations.[44] Herein, to Herbert Hoover, lay a core problem of the food blockade. He denounced the fact that "soldiers, government officials, munitions workers and farmers in enemy countries would always be fed" and that the real impact of the blockade fell "upon the weak and the women and the children."[45] A study of data and statistical analyses of children's nutrition and weight decrease in Germany during the blockade has led Mary Elisabeth Cox to judge the naval blockade as a kind of "hunger game" that had a clear negative impact on children's well-being.[46] Economic warfare had indeed been one of the successful instruments in crushing the Central powers, which ended up unable to feed their own civil populations.

The Hungarian economy suffered extensively from the impact of the Allied forces' naval blockade. The importation of foodstuffs continued to be barred until the summer of 1919. Several ordinary household items were unobtainable. In the villages, salt, tobacco, and matches were the least available; in the towns, wood and coal were scarce. In the capital, the "consumption of gas and electricity was restricted, with businesses being forced to close after noon, restaurants and coffee-houses at ten o'clock in the evening."[47] Although Britain officially supported the continuation of the naval blockade beyond the end of the war, by May 1919, articles were appearing in newspapers such as *The Observer* questioning its legacy: "Nearly six months after the Armistice, the blockade is still inflicting some of the most frightful miseries of war on all Central Europe, especially on the women and children amongst a population of over a hundred million souls." The suffering of children and fear of the famine's long-lasting impact on Europe's future generations were used to call for the end of economic warfare. Adults were seen as guilty of starting the war, but children were presented as innocent and undeserving victims. Acknowledging that he should not refer to men as victims, the author of *The Observer* article pressed the case of women and children: "Mothers cannot suckle their babes" and "cannot give strength to the infants they have borne," so the children of the poor or impoverished "pine or die." "Lacking milk and eggs and other elements of normal nourishment," great numbers of the surviving children, whom the author judged "as innocent of all guilt as our own children," were "doomed for life to be rickety, scrofulous, tubercular, feeble-minded, defective, the premature prey of maladies." He appealed to the humanity of "people of British breed," who were not, and should not, be "accustomed to make war like this, not only on a whole civil population [but] on its women and children" well after the actual "war and its necessities are at an end."[48] In Britain, the United States, and other victorious or neutral countries

Fig. 2.1. "Les enfants s'amusent." Unknown caricaturist, *L'humanité*, January 15, 1920.

throughout Europe, the call for ending hostilities became stronger as the appeal for humanitarian relief of the victims' suffering grew. Finally, on July 12, 1919, the naval blockade was lifted so that food could again reach Hungary and the defeated nations.

Even as the blockade was lifted, postwar peace treaties continued to create challenges for a return to normalcy in food networks. On November 7, 1919, an article judged the blockade "the most horrible and most effective weapon of war," whose resulting hunger crisis strangled Hungary. Linking the blockade with detailed descriptions of the physical state of Hungary's children was a widespread strategy. Hungary's "innocent little ones, whose skinny arms were thin to the bone and their sunken faces were covered in paleness" were the most wounded of this political battle.[49] A caricature in the French communist journal *L'humanité* from January 15, 1920 (fig. 2.1), titled "Les enfants s'amusent" (The children have fun), illustrates with bitter irony the implications of the postwar peace negotiations on Hungary's children.

In the image, four Hungarian children are playing famine. The oldest child suggests: "We are going to play Hungary: you will starve of hunger while I am Clemenceau and laugh." Published just days before the Paris Peace Conference's closure, this caricature reads like a last rebellion against the harsh prospective peace conditions. The children's game about hunger serves here to criticize the victorious nations, and especially France, for playing with the children of the defeated nations, such as Hungary, a game with real hunger.

The occupation and then loss of Hungarian territories—major geopolitical consequences of the war—played a central role in escalating postwar food shortages. The reconfigurations of postwar Central and Eastern Europe contributed to the scarcity of certain agricultural and industrial goods, bringing the production and domestic processing of some foodstuffs to an almost complete halt. Maureen Healy explains that it was not the blockade that had the most "drastic consequences" on the availability of food in Austria-Hungary; the nation had been, for "the most part, self-sufficient in food production before the war."[50] It was the country's radically diminished agricultural production and the violent disruption to old intra-imperial systems of transport of foodstuffs that contributed most substantially to the hunger crisis.[51] Writing in 1923, Oszkar Jászi, a Hungarian social scientist, judged the dissolution of Austria-Hungary to be an economic Armageddon: "Large economic units" that were "many centuries old" and had been "linked together by ties of ... free trade, were broken to pieces." Jászi denounced new customs barriers, because they "stopped the natural blood-circulation of many ancient economic organisms," as if "their veins had been gripped in an iron vice."[52] The delivery of food was impaired in the process of the territorial losses and the implementation of the imperial dissolution. Whereas Poland had been "drained of her foodstuffs ... by her military occupants," the main problem in Hungary was that the nation had lost access to many productive agricultural territories.[53] By February 1919, meat, milk, and fat were scarce, although Hungary had been a "land of milk and honey." Contemporary media described the occupying forces as "invading aliens" who subverted Hungary's ability to meet its own nutritional needs. Hence, the Hungarian population was called on to "enlighten the world, Europe, and America" about the fact that "the Banat had given us our grain and fat and the Uplands our milk."[54]

With the loss of two-thirds of its territory, Hungary lost access to important industrial and agricultural areas, especially coal mines in Vojvodina and rich agrarian lands in Transylvania. Hungary's extensive animal husbandry, including pig breeding and cattle rearing (mostly in the Transylvanian mountains), had been cornerstones of the country's agricultural sector before World War I. With the loss of "traditional livestock-rearing regions" during and after the war, Hungary's ability to produce and export meat products decreased greatly. Agricultural production dropped to half (or less) of what it had been in the prewar period, and Budapest's processing facilities became heavily dependent on the import of raw materials.⁵⁵ The capital's postwar civilian population had trouble accepting privations and was apt to search for culprits.⁵⁶ Because "the very existence of hungry bodies implies an external source of responsibility and therefore of blame," Hungary's postwar authorities and civilian population blamed the victorious nations for Budapest's and Hungary's postwar hunger.⁵⁷

Various multilingual publications sought to prove the disastrous impact of the peace regulations on Hungary's economy. A small academic book was published in 1920 by the Hungarian minister of commerce Gyula Rubinek. *Magyarország Gazdasági Térképekben* (*The Economy of Hungary in Maps*) was printed in Hungarian, French, and English, hoping to reach international audiences. The book presented a series of maps that illustrated statistical data on Hungary's agricultural productivity before and after the treaty. It was a scientific attempt to quantify Hungary's economic losses and utilize data for territorial revision.⁵⁸ Relying on official statistics, the maps represented the impact of territorial losses on the stock of cattle, pigs, mines, wheat, cereals, coal, and gas. The book's message was that the nation's economy had heavily depended on the fertility and productivity of the recently ceded territories, especially the Bácska region spanning Vojvodina and Transylvania. Once Hungary lost access to these fertile regions, as early as 1918, the capital began suffering. Rubinek used economic data to critique terrorital loss.

Destruction of infrastructure, "including ports, railways, and communication lines," in former Austria-Hungary and elsewhere further disrupted food supply processes.⁵⁹ In Hungarian territory, infrastructure was permanently undermined with the occupation and loss of territory to Romania, Czechoslovakia, and the Kingdom of Croats, Serbs, and Slovenes (later Yugoslavia). The former Hungarian harbor of Fiume, for instance, was occupied by the Yugoslav state, and railway stock was detained so imports could not get through.⁶⁰ Even when some regions of the former empire, such as Bohemia, had supplies or even a surplus in certain foodstuffs, they were often unwilling to export any of it without good "compensation in manufactured articles or other goods."⁶¹ This reluctance caused a drastic decline in circulation.⁶² The Hungarian authorities were no better. In February 1919, authorities worked to prevent the delivery of large stocks from the south of Hungary and Croatia to be sent across Hungary to German Austria, because, they claimed, "these goods really belong to Hungary and not the Serbs who have occupied the territory."⁶³

The lack of coal was particularly significant because it hindered rail traffic. Oszkár Charmant, Hungarian consul in Austria, wrote to Charles Daniel

Bourcart, Swiss ambassador to Vienna, on January 3, 1919, warning that, due to coal shortages, traffic had been so reduced that it had become impossible to transport the milk needed for Budapest's diseased children. Charmant blamed the occupation of Hungary's mines by the Romanians and Serbians, while imports from Austria or Prussia were being hindered by the Czecho-Slovaks. The "terrible lack of coal," he warned, would result in a "terrible catastrophe and even to anarchy." Out of such fears, Hungary called on the Swiss to guarantee the safe import of coal from occupied territories.[64] This letter was forwarded to Herbert Hoover and the American Commission to Negotiate Peace, in the hope that Hoover would negotiate in Hungary's favor during the peace talks. However, US relief to Hungary was provided only once the "Bolshevik danger" had passed.

The lack of coal also had serious repercussions on industry. To Hoover, coal "was just as essential as food." The division of the former Central European empires into fourteen states was disastrous for the delivery of coal in the region, he lamented.[65] Coningsby Dawson observed in 1921 that there were over a thousand industrial factories in Budapest, but only a hundred were in operation, some only partially, because of lack of coal. Furthermore, there was almost no wood in Hungary, because it was "a land of tillage" rather than woodland. Most of the mines were now in other countries, nearly eliminating domestic coal supply and impacting the industrial productivity of the entire country.[66] Before the war, 18 percent of the population had been employed in mining and manufacturing, activities that contributed up to 25 percent of national income; now the key mining regions were annexed to Romania, and Czechoslovakia received Hungary's salt mines, more coal mines, and small gold and silver mines.[67] Budapest's suburban industrial area, Újpest, "the Newark of Hungary," which had "teemed with the sounds of a thousand industrial activities" before the war, was now "asleep" and "as quiet as a churchyard." Újpest had become "a forest of smokeless factory chimneys and deserted streets," unable to offer employment to the former workers or to refugees.[68] A large majority of industrial workers were now unemployed.[69]

Austria-Hungary had been a functioning economic entity before the war, but the dissolution of the empire also meant the collapse of economic solidarity people had known. In the old empire, rural areas, such as the Hungarian plains, had traded their food for manufactured goods and raw materials from urban areas in Austria, Bohemia, and Silesia. This general rural-urban trade pattern did not disappear within new nation-states, but it changed fundamentally with new international borders between those regions. As the intra-imperial infrastructure broke down, urban populations—especially in

Vienna, Prague, and Budapest—experienced economic disintegration firsthand. This accounted, among other factors, for the food scarcity in the cities. The discontinuation of imperial trade patterns compounded the transportation restrictions of new international boundaries.[70]

Beyond the trade and infrastructure challenges, the sheer poverty of the new Hungarian state meant that the material and technical infrastructure of the dissolved monarchy "soon fell into disrepair."[71] As technological infrastructures formed the "physical basis for transnational flows of people, goods and services," their disruption prevented the delivery and distribution of commodities and foods. International trading partners relied on infrastructures to "expand," "renegotiate," and "transform ... relations with each other," but the damage and disruption to these relationships was dire.[72] Throughout the nineteenth and early twentieth centuries, the rapid circulation of labor, capital, and commodities had resulted in "new connections and dependencies spanning the world." Now, the restructuring of the geopolitical territories of Central and Eastern Europe broke many of the transnational ties that had been established.[73] The new borders interrupted railway connections and created new taxes and ideological animosities between neighboring states.

Hungary's rail network, which had been founded in 1846 had crossed the country's new borders, was now reduced from twenty-two thousand to eight thousand kilometers. The state railway, Magyar Állami Vasutak (MÁV), also lost countless freight trucks and locomotives.[74] To make matters worse, Hungarian railcars were regularly confiscated when outside the borders. Austro-Hungarian successor states still thought of rolling stock as "common property."[75] An International Committee of the Red Cross report by a Dr. Munroe, dated November 3, 1918, recounts an incident in Borossebes, a Hungarian town in western Transylvania occupied by Romanian forces, where the villagers were forced to hand over railway wagons. End to end, these wagons spanned fifteen kilometers.[76] The transportation system suffered, too, because new, uneconomical highways and railroad lines had to be constructed.[77] Under the direction of the Supreme War Council in Paris, an Allied Railway Mission was established in Trieste, charged with rehabilitating and reintegrating the Central European railway system.[78] American civil engineer Lt. Col. William Bowdoin Causey served as the mission's president in Austria-Hungary. In a 1919 telegram, Causey recommended to the Allied powers "that traffic be immediately resumed on all the railroad lines entering the city of Budapest, at least that the transportation of food supplies from the adjacent territory be allowed to move freely to the city." The interruption of railroad transportation had caused additional hardship, he explained, because it not only stopped carloads of foodstuffs but also prevented Budapest's citizens from traveling to neighboring countries to purchase supplies.[79] Disruptions to previously domestic, now international, transportation and food distribution networks contributed to the hungry circumstances in Budapest and would continue to do so.

Urban Food Scarcity and Useless Money

How did food scarcity directly affect the city's inhabitants and their children? The fate of children in Budapest was especially severe, and they suffered more from food scarcity than children in rural regions. Children's access to food was particularly affected, because they were mostly passive recipients of food. While industrialization and urbanization had already created problems of child neglect and abandonment, children now faced severe malnutrition.[80] Food scarcity in Hungary involved price increases, inflation, urban shortages, long lines, rationing, rural hoarding, and riots. The war limited the food supply, causing a host of economic consequences, including a drastic increase in food prices in Hungary. The price of milk and meat products—butter, veal, pork, beef, and fat—rose considerably, as did the price of flour. One report claimed that, in 1920, certain foodstuffs cost "over a hundred and thirty times pre-war prices," while wages had "only doubled, trebled or quadrupled" with inflation. In other words, the cost of living increased 13,000 percent, while wages increased just 200 percent to 400 percent. For instance, the price of white bread in 1914 was 0.4 krone per kilo; in 1920, the price was 35 kronen. The price of meat increased from 1.2 to 90 kronen, pork from 1 krone to 110 kronen.[81] The most remarkable price increase was on clothing. "Textiles were particularly hard hit," and the massive "shortage of cotton and wool" affected not only civilians but the troops, "who were reduced to wearing shoddy and makeshift clothing."[82] The price of shoes increased from 16 kronen per pair to 2,500 kronen, and an overcoat obtainable for 70 kronen came to cost 10,000 kronen.[83]

The unavailability of food also influenced the value of the Hungarian currency, and thus the everyday life of Hungary's civilian population. The *Hungarian Statistical Yearbook* of 1919–22 included a table on the "weekly expenses of a worker's family for foodstuffs containing 82,800 calories" between 1914 and 1922. While a family spent 20 kronen on its weekly allowance in June 1914, by June 1919, that spending had risen to 170 kronen. Then it began to soar. In June 1920, the family outlay was 780 kronen; in June 1921, 631 kronen, and in 1922 (after another jump), it was 1,740 kronen. Hungarians in the postwar period experienced far more dramatic price increases than they had in the war years.[84] The year 1920 brought escalating inflation to Hungary (sometimes referred to as hyperinflation), which lasted until the mid-1920s. Though workers received more money, the money had substantially lost its purchasing power. The inflation was partly caused by the budget deficits the government ran up between 1919 and 1924 and an "increasing volume of loans and discounts . . . at a very low interest rate."[85] The price increases around 1920 were closely linked to the immense inflation the country was experiencing. The combination of rising prices, food shortages, higher weekly food expenses, and escalating inflation drove down living standards. The living standard of an average day laborer decreased around 70 percent compared with the prewar standard. For an industrial worker, the decrease was 61–74 percent, and for army officers and civil servants, the standard of living dipped 82–87 percent.[86]

A 1921 MÁV publication with the overtly revisionist title *Megcsonkított Allamvasutak* (The Mutilated State Railway) set income against weekly expenses for a variety of workers' families between July 1919 and April 1921. The weekly expenses of a worker's family with four children rose immensely after 1919. The document contrasted the increase of weekly expenses to the incomes of various worker families, arguing that (a) the weekly expenses of a typical worker's family increased significantly and did not correspond to income; (b) the expenses of a family whose father was employed at MÁV increased far less and corresponded to the family's increased earnings; and (c) the expenses of families employed at MÁV and receiving food supplies at a reduced price remained stable and were well below the family's earnings. In this way, railway employees were arguably less affected by inflation and therefore safer from hunger.[87] The source reveals that unequal access to foodstuffs was not only dependent on rural/urban division and class but also on one's profession and the related (dis)advantages.

Another impediment to the functioning of Austria-Hungary's agricultural markets came from officially fixed maximum food prices. Famous Austrian businessman and coffee maker Julius Meinl decried the "price-ceilings" on agrarian products. Meinl's memorandum of March 6, 1919, was signed by several prestigious Austrian businessmen and presented to the Paris Peace Conference in 1919. The imposition of maximum food prices meant that the Austrian food authorities, including the food controller Dr. Löwenfeld-Russ, would not allow Meinl to sell imported potatoes in Vienna above the fixed prices, even when potatoes had been unobtainable for quite a while. Nor could "German Austria . . . for any length of time, get its grain from abroad, especially from America" because of high freight rates and the cleavage between food prices in Austria-Hungary and actual world market prices. The memorandum argued that if farmers "were paid the real world-market prices they would be encouraged to produce [so much more]" that production would "exceed the peace production" and the country would "be able to feed itself." There might be some truth to this; farmers were sometimes unwilling to sell their foodstuffs for fixed prices, because they could earn far more on the black markets. As things stood, the harvest of 1919 was still untouched, and Hungarian farmers refused to sell their products at the official maximum prices. The report concludes that economic decline was not a "natural result of the war" but an unfortunate result of governmental *Zwangsbewirtschaftung* (coersive state management) together with the profit making of "privileged monopolised companies." Due to this governmental maladministration, large quantities of food—especially perishable products—had been left to spoil. Almost half of the potato crop, which was left out in the winter, went to rot. Even cattle were left to perish. The report charges that, even during the war, there should have been enough vegetables, fruit, grain, and potatoes in Austria to feed everyone.[88]

To address food shortages and pricing problems, rationing systems were introduced in cities and towns, in both Austria and Hungary. The combatant countries sought to regulate national food consumption by means of individual household rationing.[89] Austria began rationing in 1915, the second year of the war, and the number of rationed products increased with each passing year.[90] Imperial authorities were forced to begin bread rationing as early as 1915.[91] In Hungary, ration cards were introduced in January 1916.[92] A cablegram of October 16, 1916, regarding the food situation in Budapest notes the introduction of one ticket "for general victualing, a general kind of a ticket without which single tickets for bread, maize, potatoes are useless," and another for every "inhabitant to buy half a pound of beans per month." These two rationing coupons were the latest additions to eighteen others that were already regulating consumption in Budapest at the time.[93]

Because most fathers were fighting at the front, it was women and children who "stood for many weary hours in queues (often from midnight until late the next morning) in order to receive provisions."[94] A girl named Cornelia remembered that she had to take her mother's place in the food queue at five o'clock each morning shivering with cold. "This was hard," she explained, "but I felt I must take on myself a part of the sorrows of my home." Many other children did the same. "I was always standing in the queues for bread," another girl remembered. "I caught [a] cold [and] was ill for a year. I was in

Fig. 2.2. From Budapest's streets. The people queuing warm themselves. Unknown photographer, *Új Idők* 26, no. 4 (February 1, 1920): 95.

hospital." Once the mother fell ill, too, and because the father was away at war, the daughter had to take over all the household chores on top of working to earn the family's living.[95]

The end of the war and the establishment of more widespread relief agencies did not end the ubiquity of bread lines. In November 1919, contemporaries observed that the American food relief action produced as many food lines as there existed schools in Budapest. Even in the wealthier districts of the city, children lined up early in the morning in front of their schools for food. On the poorer outskirts of the city—on Thököly, Grassalkovics, and Csikagó Streets, for example—hungry parents led long lines of hungry children to the bread lines.[96] The *Continental Times* reported on "women with their babies on their breasts under the same shawl," standing and waiting in front of "the bakers' the butchers', coal stores, and potato shacks of Budapest." They were in line at two o'clock in the morning to be first when the shops finally opened at eight. The queues had their own social dynamic; "women nursing babies had the right to step in line before the others," which is why "mothers often lend their babies to friends, or to the mothers" who had older children. They had to secure food "by stealth or force." Sadly, many babies spent whole winter nights on the streets—and died as a result. Older children often stood for entire nights in front of the shops. In the public media, photographs such as figure 2.2 captured children's attempt to keep warm while queuing at night. When school opened in the morning, mothers arrived and took their children's place in the line.[97] Even after many hours of standing in line, they often returned empty-handed, because there simply was not enough food for everyone.[98] Consequently, "war widows, orphans and disabled ex-servicemen" found themselves in "poverty-stricken circumstances."[99]

Though rationing systems were originally introduced to prevent hoarding and to guarantee the "entitlement to food of all sections of the population," processes of "exclusion and denial" soon emerged and significantly affected the fair and "equal distribution of food."[100] Because the rationing system did not successfully secure access to food, thieving and hoarding were common in the capital. Hoover recalled that "everyone who could, grabbed for food and hoarded it," that "there was at the beginning some rioting and pillaging of the countryside," and that "towns and cities were for a time much worse off than they had been before the Armistice when there were rigid controls."[101] While the displaced middle-class refugees had lost their homes and thus also their access to homemade canned foods, the well-to-do and farmers were reported to hoard masses of foodstuffs. Wolf von Schierbrand observed that they "have hidden away immense stores of eatables not easily perishable, such as smoked meats, bacon, ham, sausage, also flour, macaroni, rice, peas, beans, lentils, sugar, coffee, tea, [and] cocoa." He was convinced that "many millions of pounds of these various comestibles have been hoarded, while the poor in only too many instances are in dire need of food of any kind," which had "completely disappeared from the open market."[102]

Governmental control mechanisms could not prevent illicit and black-market (*Schleichhandel*) trade from flourishing, since two-thirds of the population depended on it.[103] It was "impossible [to] imprison all culprits," so the government imposed a penalty of whipping and other punishment.[104] Even when some hungry city dwellers managed to obtain and smuggle in foodstuffs, they faced seizure of black-market goods. In 1920 in one of Budapest's barracks, a woman was found sobbing desperately. Her husband had been in the hospital for three months, so she went to the countryside for some flour, of which she wanted to sell half and use the other half for her two children, ages six and nine. She finally managed to obtain an unbelievable thirty kilos of flour, but the flour was taken away from her at the station, leaving her even more desperate than when she had set out.[105]

The lack of food "exacerbated deep inequalities and a new 'food hierarchy.'"[106] Wealthier individuals initially could still barter their belongings for food, but once they had nothing left, they had trouble earning their daily bread. Workers, on the other hand, had little to barter other than their labor, which nevertheless remained valuable during and after the war. Still, industrial workers who had been employed in Budapest's larger factories had almost no means left to secure food for their families if and when those industries shut down. During wartime, "food had become the most prized commodity," and this, as Alexander Watson points out in *Ring of Steel*, "upturned the social order." The middle classes experienced this social disruption especially traumatically, because "an education, cultivation or profession brought few rewards in wartime." For a person of middling rank, a previously prestigious desk job turned into a "burden when competing for food against social inferiors in armament factories."[107]

Like class, the rural/urban division also played a crucial role in access to food. Hungary witnessed huge disparities between its capital and its less urban areas, as farmers naturally had more direct access to foodstuffs. Already before the war, the Hungarian part of the Austro-Hungarian Empire had suffered from a "deleterious imbalance in the distribution of farmland" and an "overdominance of big estates," so that a "disproportionately large area of land was in the hands of disproportionately few." Ignác Romsics finds this a "specifically Hungarian feature." It blocked equal access to Hungary's land and property. In the early twentieth century, Hungary's economic focus on agriculture had resulted in the dominance of industrial food processing, mostly based on cereal production and flour milling.[108] But once the delivery of these items from the countryside to the capital was interrupted, owing also to the lack of other commodities such as coal, the capital city could no longer process foodstuffs and supply was largely cut off.

In contrast, farmers in the countryside continued to grow and harvest wheat, vegetables, and fruit. They could slaughter their own pigs if meat was no longer available in the shops. Thus, a new stereotype of the "greedy farmer" began to circulate: the notion of the farmer or landowner who would hoard his food and not deliver the surplus to urban areas, thus creating extreme inequalities between country and city. To prevent the unequal distribution of food between rural and urban spaces—and its impact on civilians and children—authorities attempted to control farmers. As early as 1916, a "systematic search in every town, village and farm" was instituted in Austria and Hungary to confiscate "all hidden stock."[109] Hoarding continued after the war. An American Relief Administration report from July 1919, two weeks before Béla Kun's Hungarian Soviet Republic was overthrown, estimated that there was probably enough food in the country overall, but the peasants were unwilling to deliver it to Budapest, "both because of their opposition to the system of government and because the Bolshevist money with which they are paid is virtually worthless." With no goods the peasants wished to spend their money on, the government extorted a large part of Budapest's food supply from the peasants "by sheer violence." Even for those who favored the Bolshevist government, everyday life in Budapest was becoming "one of very great hardship," because "everyone gets a fair quantity of poor bread."[110]

While the notion of well-being had a subjective dimension during the war and in the postwar period, most people shared a common desire to maintain some of their old standard of living and had trouble abandoning certain foods and eating habits.[111] In most wars of the twentieth century, it was "lack of fat, combined with [a] very limited quantity of animal protein in the form of meat, eggs or cheese" that especially caused "a nagging sensation of hunger, even if the food contained sufficient calories."[112] In their neighborhoods and communities (those "social and geographical entities around which ordinary people construct their daily lives," in Jay Winter's words), and independent of provisions from the state, people sought different ways of obtaining the commodities they considered necessary for their physical and moral survival.[113]

Public expressions of despair over food scarcity resulted in violence and even riots.[114] By 1917, social discontent in the Austro-Hungarian Empire resulted in many occurrences of "looting of food stockpiles."[115] Transylvanian refugees were reported to be raiding shops after waiting for hours in unserved queues.[116] Added to the problems was the long registration time before the refugees could receive any support. On one occasion in Vienna, a large procession of "haggard, desperate and famished" women and children walked through the city, attempting to "make a public and striking demonstration" of what hunger looked like to pressure the mayor to "provide and equally distribute sufficient food for the needy."[117] There was similar action in Újpest, a suburb of Budapest, where women "stormed the town hall" after waiting for hours in vain outside shops to "get a pound or two of potatoes." A large number of rioters, mostly women, were arrested, but they defended themselves, arguing that they could not buy any food if they got their money only "after eleven in the morning, by which time the shops would have sold out their scanty stocks."[118] Another riot broke out between vendors and purchasers in

Budapest's main market hall at the end of 1916. Even the tramway traffic was stopped, and "shouting and yelling filled the air." The object of the fight was "some chicken and ducks," but the police were powerless to restore order. The story even reached the *New York Times*, which emphasized that the rioters were "not hungry working women" but women of the better class, who were trying to secure precious birds for New Year's Eve. The author denounced the contrast between the "pomp of the coronation" of Emperor Charles I/IV on December 30, 1916, and the everyday misery in Budapest's main marketplace, and hoped to draw attention to social and economic inequalities.[119]

The pattern of food production and consumption during the war continued to affect people's cooking and eating behaviors after the war. Just as "changes in food consumption in the French countryside after the war" can be "directly attributed to how rural soldiers had eaten in the army," the need to feed large-scale armies with products that were rich in nutrition but easy to prepare and consume also left an imprint on the production and consumption of food elsewhere. In postwar Budapest, due to lack of wood and fuel, many households were unable to prepare cooked food at all. An American Relief Administration cablegram estimated that under 10 percent of Budapest's population was supplied with fuel, so the large majority of the population had no fuel for cooking their scarce rations, presumably left to be eaten cold.

Refugees living in railcars at the train stations were doomed to prepare and consume their food either outdoors or in the cattle cars. Social photographers captured images of food preparation in cattle cars. One image in *Az Érdekes Újság* (the Interesting Journal) from December 1919 (fig. 2.3) depicts a refugee mother preparing a simple dish for her son on a stove in the railway coach. Although the scene captures a moment of food preparation, the caption stressed the inappropriate living conditions, noting that "this is how a refugee family from Transylvania furnished its railcar flat."[120]

Similarly, *Erdélyi Hírek* (Transylvanian News) documented "Mrs. G.O. wife of a judge of the county court is seen cooking dinner."[121] In stressing the inappropriateness of a wife of a county court judge having to cook dinner at a railway station, such reports and images pointed to the social decline of this displaced middle class. The utterly improvisational character of making and eating meals in railway coaches at the train station nourished feelings of social degradation among the affected middle class. Portrayals of refugees' everyday life, including their daily food preparation and consumption, were instrumental in drawing attention to the social decline of Hungary's "valuable" class if no relief was provided.

Így rendezkedett be vaggonban levő lakásán egy erdélyi menekült család
(Szőnyi Lajos fölvétele.)

Fig. 2.3. This is how a refugee family from Transylvania furnished its railcar flat. Photo by Szőnyi, *Az Érdekes Újság* 7, no. 48 (December 25, 1919): 48.

Anti-Bolshevism and Food Relief

Beyond the postimperial difficulties, the struggle over food and food relief also had ideological dimensions. Americans witnessed the postwar turmoil from afar, recoiling at the spread of communism in Central and Eastern Europe following the Russian Revolution of 1917. The continuation of the food blockade beyond the Armistice was "supposed to help suppress a communist revolution" and pressure the countries of Central Europe to "settle for peace on the most unfavorable terms."[122] As we have seen, drastic price increases during the war were accompanied by an uneven distribution of food among different classes. The unfairness and desperation this caused may have helped Béla Kun and his supporters achieve a Bolshevik takeover in Hungary on March 21, 1919.[123] Unfortunately for Budapest's starving children, the revolution delayed US food aid until the communist government was removed.

Kun had become one the most famous "POW champions of the Bolshevik cause," and, after his return from Russia, fought to bring the revolution to postwar Hungary.[124] Bolsheviks in Russia had demanded more humane treatment of prisoners, and many of the POWs returned to their Central and East European home countries attracted to Bolshevist ideologies and new ideas to implement them. An article of January 5, 1919, warned the Allies that Kun was "making the most out of the lack of coal, the closing of factories, the growth of the food shortage and the steadily-soaring prices of the necessities of life." He seemed most successful at carrying his "appeal to the war-stricken, unemployed elements of the proletariat and is fast acquiring a large following."[125] Kun was feared among the victorious nations, who were willing to go to great lengths to stop the further spread of Bolshevism.

Yet when Kun was finally in power, he was unable to solve the food and supply crises. Budapest was still "starving and the peasants [were] determined to resist the confiscation of their crops ordered by Béla Kun."[126] Although originally in favor of communism, the Hungarian Jewish writer Arthur Koestler, "a poor fourteen-year-old" in 1919 Budapest, changed his mind after his family "found it hard to buy most food with the Béla Kun regime's ration cards and worthless paper money." The sole food available to Koestler that summer, he claimed, was "vanilla ice cream, presumably because it was not price controlled."[127] In the spring and summer of 1919, the Hungarian Red Army initiated a postwar armed conflict against Romania to regain former Hungarian territory and "secure great quantities of foodstuffs which it possesses."[128] However, the Romanian units defeated the Hungarians and occupied Budapest, staying there from August 4 until November 14, 1919. In the meantime, Kun's Soviet-type government was overturned on August 1, 1919. The *Manchester Guardian* stated that, just ten days after the communist government had failed, the "general food situation" in Hungary was "becoming increasingly difficult every day."[129] Budapest's "rational citizens" were warning that, unless the Allies acted speedily and were willing to "dispatch adequate armed forces, every coalless and foodless day" would "bring the Bolshevik elements of Hungary just that much nearer to controlling the entire country."[130]

Months before, on June 26, 1919, the Council of the Principal Allied and Associated Powers received a proposal from a Mr. McCormick to President Wilson, petitioning that the blockade on Hungary should be lifted once the Kun government had withdrawn "its military forces within the lines fixed by the Allied and Associated Powers" and stopped any "military operations against surrounding States."[131] But it still took months before the blockade was finally lifted. On August 4, 1919, Herbert Hoover proposed a relaxation of the blockade, "opening of the Danube and the supply of foodstuffs to Hungary from the Banat." He suggested to the council that the "new Government, though very radical" could be used as a means to "upset Bolshevism." Hoover's proposal was adopted, and the Inter-Allied Trade Commission at Vienna was instructed to end the blockade. A surplus of food in the Banat region was considered "the only source from which Budapest could be fed." However, the Serbian government jeopardized these export attempts. The lifting of the economic blockade was closely related to the Allies' estimation of Hungary's ability to fulfill all the political and economic conditions of the Armistice, including demobilization and the delivery of reparations.[132] Hoover recalled in his memoirs that the Romanian army occupied Budapest "in defiance of direct orders of the 'Big Four'" and stressed the illegality of this military invasion. He found it equally horrible to the Bolshevist invasion. The Romanian army "looted the city in good old medieval style," even taking the supplies he had provided for the children's hospitals; as a result, children died.[133]

Apart from "looting art galleries, private houses, banks, railway rolling stock, machinery, farm animals—in fact, everything movable which Béla Kun had collected," Hoover recalled, the Romanians issued an ultimatum dependent on the delivery of "20,000 carloads of food." To Hoover, this was the last straw. He intervened, sending a "vigorous protest" to the Big Four members (Great Britain, France, Italy, and the United States) on August 6, stating that "there was not such an amount of food" to be had.[134] In response, the four nations appointed four generals on behalf of the Inter-Allied Military Mission to examine and report on the situation and to oversee the withdrawal of the Romanian occupying forces: Colonel Harry Bandholtz for the United States, General Gorton for Britain, General Mombelli for Italy, and Colonel Loree for France.

Bandholtz, a US army officer and the American representative, helped address these troubling international circumstances. He arrived in Budapest on August 11, 1919, and stayed until February 9, 1920. A week after his arrival, he noted in his *Undiplomatic Diary* that the Romanians had begun "to loot Hungary," taking automobiles, locomotives, railcars, "all the arms, munitions, and war material" and shipping them to Romania. They were also "clean[ing] the country" of "farm implements, cattle, horses, clothing, sugar, coal, salt, and in fact everything of value."[135] The vanishing of the railway wagons and locomotives was witnessed by others as well.[136] Some reports described the "robbery" of Hungary's "seed grains," and proposed this as one cause of the "present breadstuff shortage."[137] Meanwhile, Hoover reported, "1,000,000 people in Budapest were desperate for food," and the capital's children were dying. Nevertheless, the Romanians continued to seize food arriving at Budapest from the Hungarian countryside. While Hoover kept on providing food for twenty-five thousand children, the Romanian soldiers kept seizing "train-loads of food and machinery, hundreds of locomotives, thousands of cars" and again "plundered the children's hospitals."[138]

Hungary, as a defeated nation, was originally obliged to pay reparations to the Allied nations, but its postwar turmoil challenged this requirement. The Reparation Commission reminded its members that it should not be forgotten that Hungary had declared at the Paris Peace Conference that, due to the ravages committed by the Romanian army during the country's occupation, its economic conditions were catastrophic.[139] As Hungary could hardly cope with its postwar condition, Hoover sought in the meantime for options to feed the country's destitute children. Having developed his own concept of "rational nutrition" in prewar Germany,[140] Max Rubner criticized the Allied powers for starving out the former enemy by means of the "hunger blockade" in the immediate postwar period.[141] In contrast to the logic of the economic blockade that prevented the delivery of food for political purposes, Hoover soon realized that his mission to stop the spread of communism could be accomplished in the opposite manner—via the delivery of food. The United States had entered the war at a late stage, and for Americans it had "a quite different meaning"; they saw it as "essentially a European conflict." But they seized the opportunity to intervene both economically as well as militarily, pursuing the ultimate aim of rescuing and reforming Europe politically.[142] Only once Kun was out would Hungary no longer be treated as a defeated enemy country. Before that, Hoover's prime mission had been to "organize and determine the need of foodstuffs" only among the "liberated populations in Southern Europe," by which he meant "the Czecho-Slovaks, the Jugo-Slavs, the Serbians, Roumanians, and other."[143] Now that the Bolshevist threat was neutralized, Hoover would also deliver food to Hungary.

Photographers accompanied the first feedings in Budapest (see fig. 2.4) and captured the moment for both the Hungarian and American public. An image of a group of the first children who had been selected for admission to the American feeding station was accompanied by a note observing that "American flags were conspicuous" at the opening ceremony of the American relief station in Budapest, and both famous Hungarian generals as well as the poorest soldiers "brought their children for the great necessity: food." The caption declared that "without American aid starvation awaits rich and poor alike."

Hoover comprehended the immense nutritional needs of the children in Central and Eastern Europe and fully realized the political, economic, and

Fig. 2.4. Opening of child feeding in Budapest. Unknown photographer, August 1919, American Relief Administration European Operational Records, Box 859, Folder 2, HILA.

social potential of providing food relief. He defined the severe food shortage as "both a core vulnerability in the international order and an instrument of US influence."[144] The body of the child could serve as a site of transatlantic health intervention by means of public feeding. It was not only the "advent of the state" but also the emergence of transnational health and relief organizations that placed "nutrition at a crossroads where citizenship, culture, economy and health played a meaningful role."[145] The hunger crisis in postwar Budapest and other Central European cities persuaded Hoover of the need for a "practical economic organization" of Europe, which he envisioned as starting with an extensive food relief program for Europe's starving children under the umbrella of the American Relief Administration.[146]

Conclusion

In December 1919, Hoover claimed that "the real, the deciding battle of the war" was still to be fought—not on the front, but on the farms of the Central powers. He was convinced that the enemy had collapsed not primarily from military and naval defeat but from total economic exhaustion. This exhaustion, caused by the countries' crumbling economic condition and lasting through the early 1920s, manifested itself particularly in the city's postwar food scarcity and the resulting malnutrition and hunger. The Great War, the economic blockade, and the dissolution of the Austro-Hungarian Empire dislocated and discontinued both the production and transport of food. The loss of territories and political turmoil altered and prevented the cultivation, harvesting, delivery, and consumption of food. This scarcity of essential foodstuffs in Budapest was one of the key factors for children's destitution and suffering. While the countryside was far better off in terms of access to food, Budapest was cut off from the production sites and was unable to provide for children the items that were necessary for their proper nutrition and growth. The city's refugees and their children were especially prone to suffering from the city's food scarcity, but systematic relief was on the way.

Notes

1. Bonzon and Davis, "Feeding the Cities," 307.
2. Paul, *The Politics of Hunger*.
3. Davis, *Home Fires Burning*, 21.
4. Hunt, "Gender and Everyday Life," 150.
5. Collingham, *The Taste of War*, 1.
6. Burrin, "Clemens Pirquet," 45.
7. Wells, "The Melodrama of Being a Child."
8. Pastor, "Hungary in World War I," 173.
9. Von Schierbrand, "The Food Situation in Austria-Hungary," 49.
10. Wargelin, "A High Price for Bread," 762.
11. Von Schierbrand, "The Food Situation in Austria-Hungary," 50.
12. According to Wargelin, this happened because "the railroads were running out of coal" due to "a sharp drop in German deliveries from Silesia." Wargelin, "A High Price for Bread," 773.
13. Siklós, *A Habsburg birodalom felbomlása 1918*, 81. Pastor, "Hungary in World War I," 173.
14. Von Wiegand, "Exodus from Hungary," 1.
15. Romsics, *Hungary in the Twentieth Century*, 85.
16. Von Schierbrand, *Austria-Hungary: The Polyglot Empire*, 206.
17. Von Schierbrand, "The Food Situation in Austria-Hungary," 48.
18. Ibid., 50.
19. "Országos kenyérjegy-rendszer," 11.
20. Jebb, "Life Stories of Hungarian Children," 27.
21. Étienne Clouzot, "Secours aux enfants en Hongrie," extract from *Revue internationale de la Croix-Rouge* 3, no. 26 (February 15, 1921): 137–43.
22. "Milk," in *Food Situation Hungary*, reprinted from *Neues Politisches Volksblatt*, November 30, 1918, 3, United States Food Administration Records, Alphabetical File, Austria Hungary, Food Ministry, Box 95, Folder 14, Regulations, Hoover Institution Library & Archives (hereafter HILA), Stanford.
23. "A 'kincses' város ínségben," 3.
24. "Famine in Hungary While Women Riot," 2.

25. Wargelin, "A High Price for Bread," 784, 788.
26. Von Schierbrand, *Austria-Hungary: The Polyglot Empire*, 206.
27. Collingham, *The Taste of War*, 10.
28. Burrin, "Clemens Pirquet," 42.
29. Collingham, *The Taste of War*, 8.
30. Kučera, *Rationed Life*, 16.
31. Burrin, "Clemens Pirquet," 44.
32. Collingham, *The Taste of War*, 9–10.
33. Romsics, *Hungary in the Twentieth Century*, 85.
34. "Inured to War, Vienna Crowds Theaters, Cafes," 7.
35. Romsics, *Hungary in the Twentieth Century*, 85, 23.
36. For a recent study on prisoners of war, see Pathé and Théofilakis, *Wartime Captivity in the 20th Century*.
37. Pastor, "Hungary in World War I," 174–75. On Jewish life, see István Deák, "Strangers at Home"; Hanák, *Zsidókérdés, Asszimiláció, Antiszemitizmus*.
38. Stephen de Rakovszky and Aladár Kontra, "From the Hungarian National Assembly's War Prisoner Release Committee," to the House of Commons Russian Relief Committee, Budapest, August 11, 1921, F.O.371, Political Central Hungary, Files 8–99, TO P.P.8663, 1921, 6100, National Archives, Kew.
39. "Inured to War, Vienna Crowds Theaters, Cafes."
40. Von Schierbrand, *Austria-Hungary: The Polyglot Empire*, 278–83.
41. Janicki, "The British Blockade during World War I."
42. "Italian Blockade of Austro-Hungarian and Albanian Coast," reprint from *London Gazette*, June 4, 1915.
43. Zweininger-Bargielowska, "Introduction," 2.
44. Hunt, "Gender and Everyday Life," 151; Davis, *Home Fires Burning*, 21.
45. Hoover, *Memoirs of Herbert Hoover*, 257.
46. Cox, "Hunger Games," 629.
47. Romsics, *Hungary in the Twentieth Century*, 95.
48. "First Steps to the Real Settlement: Raise the Blockade," 10.
49. "American Relief Administration European Children's Fund," 5.
50. Healy, *Vienna and the Fall of the Habsburg Empire*, 37.
51. Herwig, *The First World War*, 271.
52. Jászi, "Dismembered Hungary and Peace in Central Europe," 276.
53. American Relief Administration, *American Relief Administration European Children's Fund Mission to Poland: 1919–1922*, 7.
54. "Hús, tej, zsír," cover.
55. Romsics, *Hungary in the Twentieth Century*, 23, 130.
56. Bonzon and Davis, "Feeding the Cities," 312.
57. Weinreb, "Embodying German Suffering," 485
58. The French title is *La Hongrie Economique En Carte*. Rubinek, *Magyarország Gazdasági Térképekben*.
59. Cox, "Hunger Games," 622–23.
60. Mayor of the City of Budapest to the American Committee, Budapest, February 5, 1919, American Relief Administration European Operational Records, Paris Office Countries File, Hungary Correspondence, January–June 1919, Box 364, Folder 4, Reel 427, HILA.
61. Julius Meinl, "Memorandum," in *Food in German Austria & Neighbouring States*, March 6, 1919, 1–5, 2, F.O. 608, Peace Conference: British Delegation, Correspondence and Papers, Files 829/1/2 to 869/2/2, 1919 (221), National Archives, Kew.

62. Anastasiadou, *Constructing Iron Europe*, 110.
63. "Introductory Letter to Julius Meinl, 'Memorandum,'" in *Food in German Austria & Neighbouring States*, March 6, 1919, 1–3, 1, F.O. 608, Peace Conference: British Delegation, Correspondence and Papers, Files 829/1/2 to 869/2/2, 1919 (221), National Archives, Kew.
64. Oszkar Charmant to Mr. Charles Daniel Bourcart, American Relief Administration European Operational Records, Box 36, Folder 4, 3, HILA.
65. Hoover, *Memoirs of Herbert Hoover*, 317.
66. Dawson, *It Might Have Happened to You*, chap. 5.
67. Romsics, *Hungary in the Twentieth Century*, 23, 130.
68. American Relief Administration European Children's Fund, *Final Report*, 10.
69. Bowden, "Economic Conditions and Relief in Hungary," 10–11.
70. American Relief Administration, *A Sketch of the Child-Feeding Operations*, 3.
71. István Deák, "The Habsburg Empire," 134.
72. Badenoch and Fickers, *Materializing Europe*, 2.
73. Arsan, Lewis, and Richard, "Editorial," 158.
74. Detailed railway and canal map of the Austro-Hungarian Empire in 1910, https://www.geni.com/projects/Austro-Hungarian-Empire/25791.
75. Anastasiadou, *Constructing Iron Europe*, 110.
76. Dr. Munroe, "Rapport de la mission du C.I.C.R. à Budapest," November 3, 1918, 1–4, 3, Rapports de la mission du C.I.C.R. à Budapest, ACICR B Mis. 4.5/349 à 4.5/432 Archive of the ICRC, Geneva.
77. István Deák, "The Habsburg Empire," 134.
78. Adlgasser, *American Individualism Abroad*, 303.
79. "Notes of a Meeting of the Heads of Delegations of the Five Great Powers Held in M. Pichon's Room at the Quai d'Orsay, Paris, on Monday, 11 August, 1919, at 3:30 p.m.," in Papers Relating to the Foreign Relations of the United States, The Paris Peace Conference, 1919, vol. 7, Office of the Historian, Foreign Service Institute, United States Department of State, https://history.state.gov/historicaldocuments/frus1919Parisv07/d33.
80. Hegedűs, "Kleinkinderpflege- und Kinderschutzbewegung während der k.u.k. Monarchie," 185.
81. American Relief Administration European Children's Fund, *Final Report*, 5.
82. Straka, "Peace and Reform," 3.
83. American Relief Administration European Children's Fund, *Final Report*, 5.
84. Országos Magyar Kir. Statisztikai Hivatal, *Magyar Statisztikai Évkönyv, 1919–1922*, 100–103.
85. Sargent, "The Ends of Four Big Inflations," 57, 61.
86. Romsics, *Hungary in the Twentieth Century*, 137.
87. Kelety, *A megcsonkított államvasutakról*.
88. Meinl, "Memorandum," in *Food in German Austria and Neighbouring States*, March 6, 1919, 1–5, 2. F.O. 608, Peace Conference: British Delegation, Correspondence and Papers, Files 829/1/2 to 869/2/2, 1919 (221), National Archives, Kew. Meinl was involved in an Austrian peace initiative after 1915. See "Individual Peace Initiatives—Julius Meinl and Heinrich Lammasch," in *Peace Movements and Efforts in the First World War*, http://ww1.habsburger.net/en/chapters/individual-peace-initiatives-julius-meinl-and-heinrich-lammasch.
89. Allen, "Food and the German Home Front," 174.
90. Straka, "Peace and Reform," 3.
91. Romsics, *Hungary in the Twentieth Century*, 85.
92. Pastor, "Hungary in World War I," 171.
93. "Famine in Hungary While Women Riot," 2.

94. American Relief Administration European Children's Fund, *Final Report*, 12.
95. Jebb, "Life Stories of Hungarian Children," 32, 29.
96. "American Relief Administration European Children's Fund," 5.
97. "The Starving Children of Hungary, Babies Dying by Hundreds."
98. American Relief Administration European Children's Fund, *Final Report*, 12.
99. Romsics, *Hungary in the Twentieth Century*, 85.
100. Collingham, *The Taste of War*, 11.
101. Hoover, *Memoirs of Herbert Hoover*, 301.
102. Von Schierbrand, "The Food Situation in Austria-Hungary," 50–51.
103. Meinl, "Memorandum," 2.
104. "To Mr. Murphy," cablegram, Budapest, December 11, 1920, American Relief Administration European Operational Records, Box 36, Folder 2, Reel 57, HILA.
105. "A barakok világából," 3.
106. Teuteberg, "Food Provisioning on the German Home Front," 68.
107. Alexander Watson, *Ring of Steel*, 359.
108. Romsics, *Hungary in the Twentieth Century*, 22–23.
109. "Search Homes for Foods," *Washington Post*, February 25, 1916.
110. Pottle and Durand, "Conditions in Hungary," 30.
111. Winter, "Paris, London, Berlin," 11.
112. Collingham, *The Taste of War*, 13.
113. Winter, "Paris, London, Berlin," 4.
114. Von Schierbrand, "The Food Situation in Austria-Hungary," 48–49.
115. Romsics, *Hungary in the Twentieth Century*, 86.
116. "Famine in Hungary While Women Riot," 2.
117. Von Schierbrand, "The Food Situation in Austria-Hungary," 48–49.
118. "Famine in Hungary While Women Riot," 2.
119. "Hungary in Straits for Food Supply," *New York Times*, January 8, 1917, 1.
120. "Igy redezkedett be vaggonban levő lakásán egy erdélyi menekült család," 48.
121. *Erdélyi Hírek Melléklete* 4 (November 7, 1921).
122. Collingham, *The Taste of War*, 25; Breen, "Saving Enemy Children," 224.
123. On Kun's Bolshevik Republic, see Hajdú, *Az 1918-as Magyarországi Polgári Demokratikus Forradalom* and Borsányi, *Kun Béla.*
124. Pastor, "Hungary in World War I," 175.
125. "Famine, Freezing and Bolshevism Menace Existence," I1.
126. "Revolt in Budapest," 2.
127. Macrae, *John Von Neumann*, 82.
128. "Famine in Hungary While Women Riot," 2.
129. "Serious Food Situation in Hungary," 8.
130. "Famine, Freezing and Bolshevism Menace Existence," 11.
131. Sir Maurice Hankey to the Secretary-General, Paris, June 26, 1919, F.o.608, Peace Conference (British Delegation) Files 812/1/1–829/1/1, 2, National Archives, Kew.
132. S. P. Waterlow to Earl Curzon of Kedleston, Foreign Office, August 5, 1919, 1–2, H.S.B.217, ADM. 2739, National Archives, Kew.
133. Hoover, *Memoirs of Herbert Hoover*, 400.
134. Ibid., 401.
135. Bandholtz and Krüger, *An Undiplomatic Diary.*
136. MacMillan, *Paris 1919*, 268.
137. Von Wiegand, "Exodus from Hungary," 1.

138. Hoover, *Memoirs of Herbert Hoover*, 401–2.

139. Reparation Commission, "Annex 1148: Delivery of Livestock, Paragraph 6. Annex IV of the Treaty of Trianon," 5, F.O. 371 Political, Central, Hungary, Files 21471–24102, 1921, 6144, National Archives, Kew.

140. Treitel, "Max Rubner and the Biopolitics of Rational Nutrition," 11.

141. Weindling, "From Sentiment to Science," 204.

142. Nolan, *The Transatlantic Century*, 52.

143. "Mr. Hoover Going to Europe at the President's Request to Organize Food Relief," *The Official U.S. Bulletin*, November 11, 1918, 7. Reprinted in Bane and Lutz, *Organization of American Relief in Europe*, 37.

144. Cullather, "The Foreign Policy of the Calorie," 349.

145. Barona Vilar, "International Organisations," 130.

146. "Central Powers' Greatest Battle," 3.

3

DEGENERATION

Embodying Postwar Suffering

At the beginning of World War I, the mobilization of children at the home front was the central element of visual propaganda related to Hungary's youth, but during the war's final years, the degeneration of children's health became the key theme. Hunger, severe malnutrition, epidemic disease, and physical neglect shaped children's everyday lives and physical condition. As their most basic needs had often not been met during the war and were not fulfilled in its aftermath, children's bodies started to deviate from the norms of natural growth. The health and well-being of a generation were being threatened, and there were outbreaks of infectious disease. Examining how epidemics, poor health care, lack of food, and inadequate housing affected children sheds light on children's particular vulnerability. Children's harmed corporality played a central role in the contemporary media and in lobbying and fundraising campaigns at both local and international levels. This chapter explores the emotive utilization of the child's damaged body in visual representations, which made it the "embodied experience of war" and a symbol of the continuing havoc.[1]

The Political Meaning of the Child's Body

In a 1920 article in the *New York Times*, Julia Vajkai, head of the Hungarian National Child Protection League, recalled how she had entered the room of a poor family in which the mother "showed [her] . . . a bundle, which [she] . . . had not noticed before, as it was hidden in the bed. It was a baby. No: it was a sort of horrible little living corpse: its greenish skin hanging in folds round the bones of its wizened little face."[2] The material body had been transformed into a starving, sick, fragile, rickety, impaired thing that embodied and made horribly visible the war's brutal effects on children's bodies and health. In this way the "reality of war" was not "just politics" but rather "politics incarnate, politics written on and experienced through the thinking, feeling bodies of men and women"—and children.[3] War became an "indisputable turning point in the body's politicization."[4] The child's particular vulnerability during and after the war was caused by combinations of geographic displacement, orphanhood, neglect, malnutrition, lack of appropriate housing, and limited access to health care, welfare, and education. The frail physical state of children throughout Europe was a constant reminder of both the insanity of this destructive war and its aftermath. The destitute child's body, indeed, prompted the humanitarian demand to ensure the relief of children, which turned into a new "battlefield"[5] of politics, both symbolic and real. In this battle, we can identify what Keith Watenpaugh calls the shift from "a narrow focus on the relief of human suffering to a broader effort to address the very root causes of that suffering." New knowledge was to be sought and applied to alter children's bodily constitutions, meet their nutritional needs, and avert the multiple causes of their suffering. Unwittingly, children's destitute bodies instigated an international "formation of humanitarian knowledge."[6]

When parents' bodies were severely affected, they could not provide for their children adequately. The mother of the greenish-skinned child described by Vajkai above was unable to get out of bed and had sent the baby's young brother out to fetch milk, which he was only able to obtain after searching for four days. Vajkai's description of the child's body was meant to evoke emotions of pain and the threat of inevitable death unless well-wishers acted immediately to relieve the child's physical suffering. Descriptions and depictions of children's suffering bodies were closely linked to appeals for humanitarian relief. In contrast to the invalid soldiers, damaged children represented wholly innocent victims of the war who had done nothing to deserve their plight. Before the child's body gained widespread public attention, the "invalid's dismembered material body" constituted an "unpleasant reminder" of wartime defeat for the losers.[7] This made the recovery and regeneration of physical harm caused by the war a pressing concern. The unprecedented corporal destructiveness of the Great War, ruthlessly inflicted by new technological weaponry, found its classical expression in the severely injured, disabled male body, the wounded soldier, and the invalided war veteran. Photography had become a means to document diseases with the professionalization of medicine.[8] Casualties became icons bearing witness to the war's uncompromising and destructive effect on those involved in fighting. War invalids' disabled bodies, as "living relicts" and "ambiguous symbols" of the war, shaped the ways that postwar societies dealt with the conflict's social consequences. Because the wounded men had actively participated in conflicts, they represented not just the war's victims but also its perpetrators.[9] Nevertheless, what remained after the fighting was over was the disabled male body, a haunting image that evoked simultaneous calls both for individual compensation and for a peaceful world order.

The damaged body of the war veteran was not the only potent symbol of the times; the damaged bodies of children, too, came to symbolize the negative repercussions of the war and its aftermath on the physical integrity of whole populations. While soldiers were wounded or killed during direct engagement in battle, children were affected in a more indirect way. Since they were large dependent on their parents or on their countries' welfare systems, children faced almost total deprivation if their caretakers were unable to supply food and care. The consequences to children themselves could spurn calls to action. In July 1918, children's doctor Ödön Lévai drew people's attention to the fact that "children are taking their share in suffering the miseries of the war." He appealed to the people and the government "not to allow the war to destroy the child and in that way, also, the regeneration of the nation."[10]

In Lévai's view, the health of children represented the health of Hungary's entire postwar population. While Hungary's unfolding territorial losses were considered, by the Hungarian Territorial Integrity League, a "dissection of Hungary," so were children's damaged, starving, and dying bodies seen as a symbol of the nation's rapid decline.[11] The conclusion to this line of thinking was that the future of the nation be could assured only if the children could be saved. The recovery of injured soldiers and the suffering of adults were important, but "it would be the greatest short-sightedness if the state and society failed to recognize the need to build, develop and enlarge child protection and children's health care." Lévai acknowledged that "due to the current budget," it was indeed very difficult to provide "useful governmental child and successful health care." Yet, especially because of the "ghastly losses to the nation," Hungary needed to secure "the renewal of human manpower and building of the future generation." To reach this goal, he argued, required investment in a professional system of "most intensive and most careful child protection."[12]

Children's starving bodies were turned into icons of postwar suffering for lobbying in international political and humanitarian campaigns in victorious and neutral nations. As Alice Weinreb explains, hunger creates "a universalized, absolute, and apolitical bodily identity," and "personality and individuality are erased, subsumed by the experience of hunger"; also, the masses of starving children in Budapest lost much of their individuality in the contemporaneous propaganda.[13] Interpretation rested not on children's complaints about the scarcity of food and their feelings of hunger but on their physical appearance. The public estimation of the "severity of an individual's level of hunger" did not rely on self-reported symptoms; a "starving body must look starving to actually be starving."[14] This is why few documents can be found that speak of children's estimations of their own food provision and hunger. Instead, detailed descriptions and visuals of the destitute bodies of children were featured in the pages of journals and newspapers, mobilizing domestic and international compassion for these young victims of war. While war propaganda and its imagery had focused on technological weaponry and combat on the battlefield, the postwar period rediscovered human vulnerability, especially of the noncombatants, as a "'new visibility'... [was] brought to the experience of human suffering."[15] It was no longer the heroism of war that stood in the foreground but war's destructiveness and its effect on the everyday lives of those it touched.

Children and the Spread of Epidemics

During and after the war, diseases spread throughout Europe and beyond due to the advance of soldiers, the displacement of people, and the lack of food and proper hygienic conditions. It became clear that "epidemics could cause higher causalities than military actions."[16] In the aftermath of war, diseases were carried across borders as soldiers were imprisoned, crowded together in railway stations, or returned home, and as refugees and displaced people moved about. With every traveling person, infectious diseases could easily spread, and the overcrowded European capital cities were laid open to the outbreak of epidemics. Allied nations were concerned about the situation, aware that diseases could spread to Western Europe and even be carried across the Atlantic. Even if Western Europe had "no direct interest" in the matter, it was to its own benefit to fight the further spread of disease. Not "even an island like Great Britain [could] count itself wholly safe" if typhus were to spread from Russia or Poland.[17] In the United States, discourses about tuberculosis intersected with "new fears about ethnicity, gender and dependency." Seen as a threat to the United States, tuberculosis was associated with war-torn Europe and was used to "scapegoat... the European immigrants who sought refuge in American cities" and who were linked to the importation of various diseases.[18]

Indeed, in Europe, various epidemics were spreading dangerously, and Budapest's children were prominent among the suffering victims. The challenges of feeding children were closely related to the risk of contagion. Because many fathers were away, families became increasingly impoverished, and amid the growing numbers of children in the capital's state asylums and poor neighborhoods like the Mária Valéria barrack, it became difficult to secure children's proper feeding and hygiene. In 1922, for example, the lack of adequate kitchen spaces in the barracks necessitated that the food for the barracks' destitute children had to be prepared in the kitchen of the state asylum. Then the food had to be delivered by car to the barracks' babies and small children. En route, the food cooled down, later went bad, and quickly caused cases of "dysentery and gastritis" among the children. It was not only the city's "little ones" wasting away; even the healthy ones got sick.[19]

In July 1918, Lévai observed that the "number of child diseases and epidemics rose significantly" and that malnutrition resulted in "the weakening of [children's] resilience against many diseases, and especially against tuberculosis."[20] Famine and disease were closely linked, because undernourished or malnourished bodies were more likely to contract the diseases and epidemics that were spreading in Hungary at the time. The weakened immune system of a starving child's body was highly receptive to contagious diseases. In an interview in 2013, István, a Hungarian who had been a child in the early 1920s, recalled what it was like for the city's impoverished children: "They died, [because] life circumstances at the time were so bad, the nutrition so poor [and because] nutrition played a central role when it came to tuberculosis. . . . There did not exist any penicillin [and] there weren't any doctors."[21]

The Hungarian statistical yearbook of 1914–23 reveals that tuberculosis and influenza were widespread causes of death. Tuberculosis accounted for 15 percent of recorded deaths in 1916,[22] about the same in 1917, and 13 percent in 1918. The so-called Spanish flu appears for the first time in the statistical yearbook of 1916–18.[23] In 1916, it affected only 0.09 percent of the population,[24] whereas in 1918 it was responsible for the deaths of 53,201 people—or 11.24 percent of Hungary's entire population.[25] Influenza broke out in Hungary in the summer of 1918. Its first peak was reached in mid-July, while a second larger wave happened in mid-September. A source from July 3, 1918, notes the arrival of the Spanish flu to Budapest on June 10, when sixty Russian prisoners brought the disease to Budapest's Zita Hospital. In 1919, influenza was still taking its toll—2,757 people (717 under age seven and 2,040 above). In 1920, the casualties were 5,683 (1,224 under age seven and 4,459 above). In the following years, the impact of influenza decreased, but tuberculosis kept raging. In 1919, tuberculosis killed 38,764 people and in 1920, 41,033.[26]

Mothers' diagnoses of influenza, in particular, disrupted children's everyday lives. Infants and toddlers were often forced to be (temporarily or permanently) raised by distant family members, foster families, or state institutions. Older children were also impacted by their mothers' absence. One Hungarian girl recalled that when she was twelve, "dear mother left us and died. Latterly, she was so weak that she readily caught influenza, which was followed by inflammation of the lungs and so she died in 1919 after six months suffering in the hospital." Since her father had gone to war, her mother had taken "great pains" to keep the four children "in order and tidy" and send them to school.[27] The departure of fathers obliged mothers to earn income while taking care of the children at the same time. This double burden and the precarious food and housing situation provided an ideal breeding ground for the spread of diseases. Once mothers became ill, family responsibilities fell on the shoulders of the remaining family members—typically the children. Ottilia described her family's situation and the burden it placed on her: Once the "war struck [her] . . . little home like a thunderbolt" and her father was killed in the battlefield, her mother "fell ill owing to overwork and . . . had to be taken to hospital." From that point on, she stated, "all the cares of the household were now on my shoulders." At night, "I was so tired that I fell asleep at once."[28]

Contemporaries debated how to protect the children from the contagion of the Spanish flu. Crowded housing blocks and state institutions were judged to be risky to children's health. Hungarian authorities repeatedly questioned whether to close schools and for how long. While pediatricians reported at the time that the flu was at least as prevalent in young children as in adults, they also acknowledged that it had a much milder, less lethal outcome among children. In the initial stage of the pandemic, masses of young children, infants, and toddlers became ill, but the number of infected schoolchildren increased as the epidemic progressed.[29] On September 21, 1918, four hundred children contracted the disease in the city of Szekszárd.[30] By October 9, 1918, the flu already had a "devastating" impact in Hungary, an article claimed. In response, some "semi-rules" were implemented to protect children from the disease. Schools in the capital closed, although daycare institutions were allowed to remain open. Later, the daycare in Maria Theresia Square had to close because several children got ill. When schools were scheduled to reopen, parents wrote letters to the city arguing that the virus was still spreading, and that if the situation did not change, their children should not go back to school.[31]

Contemporary sources listed the daily number of the infected and narrated individual tales of woe of infected children. In one report from September 27, police were called to Pozsonyi Street, where two children were reported to be dead. Once the police car arrived to the flat, they found not only the two reported girls but also eight-year-old István Fröhlich and three-year-old Ferenc Fröhlich dead from the disease.[32] In another news story from October 1918, sixteen-year-old maid Ilona Molnár fell ill with influenza in the house of her employers. Because they feared becoming infected themselves, they sent Ilona away to the hospital. On the way, Ilona collapsed on the capital's main boulevard. A nearby police officer called an ambulance, which refused to take her. While waiting for three hours for the special car of the *Fertőtlenítő Intézet* (Disinfectant Institute)—which had been opened in Budapest in 1913 for the sole purpose of treating highly infectious diseases such as tuberculosis—Ilona died. Now they needed a hearse.[33]

Other contemporary Hungarian media captured horror stories of children's suffering from influenza. One of these stories, "The Tragedy of Kálmán Zsolnai," explains how a father lost his wife to influenza and how his son also got sick. One Tuesday morning in September 1918, Zsolnai returned home to his wife and two small children. The older child, Kálmán, was two and a half years old. The father was "more than surprised" to find his wife dead while his older son slept next to her cold body. On Wednesday, Kálmán developed a high fever. Because the father had to prepare his wife's funeral, Zsolnai's sister-in-law "carried the little sick child on her neck" to the city to bring him to a hospital.[34] Although the boy was sick, the Stefánia Hospital refused to admit him because he was contagious. They sent him to the White Cross Hospital, where he was again denied after a doctor diagnosed him with the Spanish flu and diphtheria. Kálmán was then sent to the Szent László Hospital, where he was also rejected. Only in the fourth hospital, the Szent István Hospital, did a Dr. Rosenberg write him a referral for admittance back at Szent László. They waited for hours with the referral in hand, but still Kálmán was never admitted and finally returned home. He was lucky and survived the disease. The story ends with an explanation of why Rosenberg did not admit the contagious child at Szent István: it would have put the other children in danger. This story conveys the experiences of masses of influenza victims with a single narrative. It furthermore criticizes the unprofessional and inappropriate handling of the little sick boy by the hospital.[35]

Especially in the postwar years, eyewitnesses visited the hospitals to survey the conditions. American Captain Prentiss M. Terry went to visit epidemic victims and described the hospital as "shameful and disgusting." In one room, which was "dirty, stale and nauseating," Terry encountered thirty newborn babies wrapped in paper instead of linen, all screaming. Some of them had mothers; others did not. Only two nurses were there to take care of the infants. He wondered whether some of the babies were breathing at all. In another room, "with no fresh air," he found forty older children, ages six to twelve, who were weak and emaciated. The children had neither stockings nor shoes; the rooms had neither enough mattresses, nor sheets, nor pillows. Comparing his experiences at the front with his impressions at this hospital, Terry concluded: "I have seen hell on a battlefield, but this sight was worse than that."[36]

A booklet by the Save the Children Fund titled *What Have We Done?* addressed the problem of infant death through a story from a hospital in Vienna, not unlike hospitals in Budapest. Mothers who had just given birth there, though pale and exhausted, had joy in their eyes as they brought "new life into the world." But their "great sacrifice will have been in vain," the witness observed, unless more fuel could be brought to the hospital. The writer recounts a previous incident wherein two babies, born healthy, died of "cold, of pneumonia" and "slipped away quietly, without a cry." A week later the same thing happened. But this time, it sparked a revolt among the mothers, who were so "mad with despair they jumped from their beds and their bitter cries filled the hospital. 'We will not bring forth children for death,' they wailed."[37] This story touched on one of the core issues of why children were such powerful symbols of suffering. "My little brother died at the age of twenty-two months," another girl recalled. "This event caused great sorrow to my parents as he was the only son."[38] With the rising number of infants wasting away, anger over individual infants' preventable deaths developed into a collective fear of the nation's decline. The increased infant mortality rate, alongside the physical suffering of surviving children, drew out powerful negative feelings among concerned adults.[39]

In the territories of postimperial Hungary, a vigorous struggle raged over national survival in which the discourse and politics surrounding child relief focused on children's wasting away. In *Pricing the Priceless Child*, Viviana Zelizer argues that the twentieth century, which witnessed the widespread implementation and professionalization of child welfare services, experienced a "magnification of child mourning." The situation, Zelizer asserts, signified a deep "transformation in the cultural meaning of childhood—a move toward an "exaltation of children's sentimental worth." If a "child life was sacred," the prospect of a child's death, especially through preventable causes such as hunger or the lack of heat, would provoke "not only parental sorrow but social bereavement as well." Thus, the call for emergency relief to prevent the further wasting away of innocent children developed into a concern of "national priority."[40]

Heated debates raged in the contemporary media. "The Funeral of Little Ferenc Csaba," a Hungarian article from March 1917, contrasts the perspective of a father and steelworker, József Csaba, with that of the head of the Budapest state orphanage, Sándor Szana. The widower father claimed that when he temporarily placed two of his children in the state orphanage, they were both healthy. When he returned, his four-month-old son, Ferenc, had died of meningitis. In contrast to the father's accusation, Szana publicly responded that, on his admission, Ferenc already "suffered from severe rickets and visible anemia." The head of the clinic was astonished that the father could blame tuberculosis at the institution, "when it was obvious that the mother that had died from that very same disease had infected the rickety and anemic child."[41] The city of Budapest was heavily involved in providing professional care to those children who could no longer rely on family. Stories such as the Csaba family's, even if dramatized, touched two sensitive points: they questioned the quality of the public child protection system and emphasized the danger of spreading epidemics like tuberculosis and hunger-related diseases like rickets in the postwar period.

Depicting Children's Misery

The story of Budapest's children, their destitution, and their relief is a visual story. Accounts of the children's plight and the humanitarian intervention to relieve it throughout the twentieth century could not be written without taking into account their massive visual output. World War I had introduced a new perspective on the mutilated, starved, and suffering human body. Unleashing a "culture of violence," this first "total war" left populations "unable to see how deeply and irreversibly affected they were by its brutalization"—until it was shown to them in the bluntest of images.[42] "The practice of representing atrocious suffering as something to be deplored, and, if possible, stopped, enters the history of images with a specific subject: the sufferings endured by a civilian population at the hands of a victorious army on the rampage."[43] Early on, British philanthropists such as Emily Hobhouse and Thomas Barnardo had used photographs of poor children (not always in a truthful way) to create publicity and drum up donations for relief.[44] Jack Thompson has pointed out, in the context of missionaries' depictions of Africans, "in an age before television," loaded visuals had "a powerful effect" not only "on how the western public... perceived people from other cultures" but also on how they behaved toward these people after seeing the images."⁴⁵

Eyewitness reports and visual materials documenting the suffering of civilian populations brought the public's attention to the problematic treatment of the former Central European enemy by the victorious nations. A 1920 eyewitness report in the *New York Times* employed the bodily description of a "bleeding wound" to describe the suffering of the civilian populations in Central Europe. Hungary, he judged, was the region's most destitute country; "millions of human beings" were "literally naked and cold, hungry and diseased, impoverished and hopeless."⁴⁶ While photojournalism during World War I had "maintained the traditional conception of the enemy as dehumanized other," the postwar imagery tried to advocate for the suffering "other's" relief.⁴⁷ In the postwar period, different images were employed, depending on whether they were meant to stoke or to calm certain fears. The ubiquity of the images reflects public uneasiness about what the war had done to the state's vulnerable subjects. The "powerlessness of the suffering subject" tugged and people's hearts; they felt for "the subject's lack of structural power and capacity that signifie[d] the impossibility of being culpable for his or her own suffering."⁴⁸ Humanitarian visual and verbal rhetoric countered the old politically propagated stereotype of the undeserving enemy—the villain to whom no sympathy could be extended.⁴⁹

The emerging public and international awareness of war victims' suffering resulted in increased references to the children's plight in public discourse, and many visual images were publicized. Visual depictions of the needy and their suffering gained momentum once it became clear that the war had affected the physical integrity of whole societies and populations. The figure of the child took a central role in representations of postwar destitution, serving to attract the undivided attention of national and international readerships and donors.⁵⁰ As Michael Barnett has argued, "it was not the child known or recognized but rather the child as an abstraction, as a symbol of what the world might become"⁵¹ that appealed to the adult population. Now imagery of suffering children exerted a moral force on viewers, engaging their sympathies and their instinct to offer assistance. Contemporary media outlets played an important role in stirring the philanthropic effort. In postwar Europe, the "conjunction of philanthropy, politics and cultural diplomacy was critical to... [humanitarian] communication practices," enabling them to formulate a "publicly palatable message about the [humanitarian] cause."⁵²

Because child victims were so powerless, the distant spectator was to be mobilized to relieve their suffering. Key humanitarian figures expressed their deep concern for "the physical and moral restoration of the peoples of Eastern Europe, in giving them a chance for life and happiness, in changing their attitude of despair to one of hope."[53] A commentator on the situation in Budapest recalled that "poverty wherever [I met] it, ha[d] the same distressing effect upon me. The deterioration of the human soul and body touche[d] me ... as a pathetic canvas, irrespective of nationality, race, or environment."[54]

The image of the destitute child can be thought of as a "visual act," which, as Annette Vowinkel explains in *Agenten der Bilder*, "prompt[s] us to act" in the same way as a speech act does. As visual acts, images of children's suffering force the observer to do something to relieve the children's pain. In the postwar period, pictures, especially documentary photographs, were employed "as an argument in the public sphere with the aim to influence public debates and political decision-making processes."[55] Photojournalists and humanitarians who used such images sought to change public opinion, both about the war and about Hungary, a former enemy country. With the increasing production and dissemination of photographs, "images became a preferred means to capture and immortalize emotional expressions and to prove what people actually felt."[56] The image of the starving child figured in the printed media as a common postwar visual trope. Finding donors for the relief activities required extensive lobbying and fundraising. Humanitarian visuals exploited the power of identification, so that "the spectator [was] invited to viscerally identify with other people's experience, particularly their suffering and the incontrovertible unfairness of their situation."[57] This could be a highly successful way to reach the hearts (and wallets) of target public sympathizers.

Bodily representations of children's hunger and poverty in Central Europe were presented in countless American and British newspapers of the time. Images and detailed descriptions of the suffering body were used as visible and unambiguous evidence of the war's unprecedented brutality. Particularly after the war had ended, the everyday life of children was closely documented in national and international press outlets. American Red Cross reports mentioned how crucial it was from a propaganda point of view to keep "in constant touch" with the press, including the weekly and monthly papers, magazines, and even international journals.[58] Professional photographic footage, drawings, posters, paintings, postcards, and other visual material accompanied almost all the contemporary written accounts. Photography, in particular, quickly proved to be a potent means of conveying the suffering that had to be relieved, and then of documenting the "rescue" benefactors had effected. These images documented the children's suffering before the relief activities; showed relief being given; and bore witness to the children's transformation that relief had made possible.

Save the Children Fund Founder Eglantyne Jebb affirmed that photographic images had initiated her own activism, in addition to creating publicity for her cause.[59] During the early Balkan wars (1912–13), Jebb traveled to the conflict zone to deliver money to the Macedonian Relief Fund. The plight of the Muslim Albanian refugee children made a deep impression on her.[60] Shortly afterward, World War I started, and the neglect, starvation, and illness that children faced in the Eastern parts of Europe radically intensified. Jebb remembered her sister coming back from Central Europe with some of the first images of the suffering children. This led Jebb to start publicizing the children's misery on the streets of London by simply showing the photographs to passersby. At first, the idea of supporting the enemy's children generated opposition and even outright hostility. The power of these photographs, however, was undeniable. Images of the innocent, vulnerable, and destitute child body aroused protective instincts in viewers and readers. The images were exhibited abroad in an attempt to transport the experience of suffering across borders—a "means of bridging [physical and geographic] distance."[61] Irrespective of who actually published the calls for support, all the public appeals had a number of common elements. The child relief program was explained in simple, emotional language aimed directly at prospective donors, and the images were chosen for their effectiveness in eliciting emotions (because it is emotion, not reason, that usually dominates visual perception). Karen Wells has explained this as a "visceral sensation." "We feel the injustice, our desire for the injury to be repaired is intuitive rather than rational."[62] The physical fragility of children and the call for immediate help evoke compassion.

As early as 1917, the American Relief Committee for Hungarian Sufferers in New York published a poster challenging the American public with a question: "What is a child worth to you?" Readers were explicitly asked how many children they would support "if five cents would feed a hungry child for a day, if a dollar and a half would feed a child for a month, if ten dollars and a half would feed a child through the winter."[63] The question was posed with the overt intention of eliciting moral guilt. "The cry of hollow-eyed women and shivering children in Prague or Buda-Pest, in Lodz or Vienna or Petrograd" come "from our fellow-creatures" for whose distress "we ourselves are in great part responsible."[64] The United States, the public was reminded, had participated in the war, and therefore had moral responsibility for what was happening in its wake. Awareness of this simple fact lay at the root of all philanthropic activism in America.

Humanitarian Advertising as Propaganda

Postwar humanitarian materials were propagandistic. They sought to evoke "the emotional satisfaction that the western psyche obtains from images of child-saving in emergencies."[65] It did not much matter who the children depicted in relief appeals and materials were; as visual objects, they simply had to fulfill certain criteria—to be underfed, pale, poorly clothed, dirty, or obviously orphaned. Divorced from context, images of the strained, suffering body of the child became a "moralizing metaphor of a collectively made experience of war."[66] It became one of Europe's main "embodied memories" of what the conflict had brought about.[67] "Photo-centered appeals forged communities of emotion and action" that extended beyond national borders.[68] The documentation of humanitarian child relief was a fairly new invention, but it was extremely effective.

In general, humanitarian imagery was and still is far from subtle. It bypasses "political and social complexities" in favor of "apparent simplicity and directness of emotional address." Successful focusing of the "viewer['s] attention on suffering" is achieved through the complete elimination of distracting individuality or detail.[69] In *Regarding the Pain of Others*, Susan Sontag comments on the immense fascination humans have with the iconography of suffering. Sontag muses on why images of severely harmed human bodies—mutilated, slaughtered, tortured, or killed—have become an essential component of reporting. This "disaster imagery," in which the media latch on to catastrophe, plays heavily on feelings of empathy, compassion, and pity with the aim of generating immediate activism.[70] The imagery relies on the power of "spectatorial sympathy" and our strange "fascination with pain" for its appeal.[71] It works at a distance, and its effects are subtle.[72] In the postwar era, the foundation for future fundraising projects was successfully laid.

Both American and British child relief organizations relied heavily on advertisements and imagery in their fundraising to support the cause of children in Central Europe. Eglantyne Jebb and her sister Dorothy Buxton campaigned against the Allies' starvation policy and, in early 1919, distributed leaflets in Trafalgar Square, London. The leaflet showed a baby close to death and was titled *A Starving Baby—And Our Blockade Has Caused This*.[73] On November 15, 1921, Jebb published a warning against "cheap publicity," explaining that the "task of looking after hundreds of thousands of children was so great that it would be impossible to do the work without the support of the British public." The Save the Children Fund decided to take the "bold step of advertising on a large scale, proclaiming to the world what it was doing and why it was asking for help." "Advertising [was]," Jebb confessed, "a scientific but dangerous business."[74] However, it had been shown to pay off and without such an appeal to the public, raising sufficient money would be impossible.

A 1920 documentary titled *Starvation, the Camera Drama of a Hungry World*, which recounted Herbert Hoover's child relief activities, featured "pictures of the worst cases of children, with protruding bones, swollen abdomens, and tight eyelids." Shown to those who had made donations to the relief mission, the film aroused "sympathy and tears and relief at the thought that America was doing something to alleviate their sufferings."[75] As Sontag put it, photography had become one of the "principal devices for experiencing something, for giving an appearance of participation."[76] The imagery of suffering put out by humanitarian organizations was often supplemented with depictions of the immediate alleviation these organizations brought. It was a dichotomist visual language: children suffering before relief, and then their transformation, which the provided relief had made possible. Textual propaganda followed the same route, stressing the dependent relationship between the lucky recipient and the beneficent humanitarian. As Paul Betts explains, Europe's "Eastern fringes . . . emerged as a new theatre of humanitarian imagination" and intervention, which helped to justify British and American "moral and global leadership."[77]

Accounts and pictures could either wipe away the familial, national, local, ethnic, and political particularities of children's suffering to broaden their appeal, or, as they often did in the Budapest case, they could emphasize a specific nationality. Aid imagery often relied on a "dynamic of abstracting children from their historical, cultural and political location, as already inscribed within dominant ideologies and cultural representations of childhood."[78] But in *From the Horrors of a Country Condemned to Death / Egy halálraítélt ország borzalmaiból*, Cornelius / Kornél Tábori aimed to draw attention to Hungary's suffering, addressing both a local and an international readership in the hope of raising funds from both spheres. The booklet's cover (fig. 3.1) shows an, emaciated mother, surrounded by a crown of thorns, holding her starving child aloft. The drawing illustrates the hopelessness Hungarian mothers felt on seeing no way of escape "from the horrors of a country condemned to death" other than to give a starving baby away.[79]

Fig. 3.1. Cover drawing by Lajos Szántó. Tábori, *Egy halálraítélt ország borzalmaiból*.

The depicted drama of suffering and child abandonment evokes compassion, empathy, and pity. The image conveys the overall purpose of Tábori's booklet in two ways: on the one hand, it depicts the horrors of the aftermath of war; on the other, it depicts a mother trying to protect her child from war-induced starvation by giving it away. The appeal is directed at the international humanitarian community, pricking consciences so that donors will "help and save the children." In this particular picture, the child and mother are visually reduced to a one-dimensional expression of a single experience: the physical experience of hunger. The child's survival appears impossible, and an international savior must come to the rescue. Tábori acknowledged, "We need the help of those who are better off than we are, who have not suffered so greatly," because their "money has not lost its purchasing power as ours has."[80]

Authorities and reporters made many unwelcome inspection tours of Budapest's impoverished dwellings to take photographs and gather details for reports. Poor industrial neighborhoods—especially the Sixth, Seventh, and Eighth Districts—were rife with evictions, homelessness, and overcrowded flats. The Budapest police chief's 1913 report stated that especially families of the "inferior classes" flocked together in overcrowded apartments in the Eighth District.[81] A 1922 letter from the American Red Cross in Hungary to Col. Ernest P. Bicknell, the ARC commissioner for Europe in Paris, judged the Sixth District "the poorest and most wretched." "People were living in what are called Pavilions, each pavilion containing forty rooms nine feet square." The writer described the local population as consisting of "refugees of all classes; of the families of men who were in jail for Bolshevism."[82] In the overcrowded districts, entire families who had been evicted for nonpayment of rent had to leave their apartments; some squatted with all their furniture for weeks in front of their former homes.[83] István, an interviewee, recalled that one could often see evicted "families sitting with their furniture in front of their houses ... simply because they could not pay their rent." His family escaped eviction, but just barely.[84]

To fight the spread of cholera and other epidemics in the late nineteenth century, Budapest officials had established emergency housing—cheap and relatively healthy shelter for families who had become temporarily homeless in the capital. But contrary to their original purpose, these emergency shelters turned permanent.[85] Growing social conflicts and tensions over housing in the early twentieth century led to increased public awareness for the necessity of improved municipal housing.[86] In March 1909, István Bárczy, Budapest's mayor, launched a large-scale housing program.[87] But despite a number of prewar attempts to alleviate the city's housing shortage, the postwar situation with its massive influx of refugees escalated the housing problem and made it a common subject of visual public attention.

Increased municipal attention to housing coincided with increased police presence, and authorities initially possessed great confidence in images as evidence. Budapest police had begun "to exercise increasing surveillance over urban spaces" in the late nineteenth century, showing less and less tolerance toward diverse "manifestations of private life" in public spaces.[88] The police officers who controlled the poor districts to prevent neglect, vagabondage, and delinquent behavior took many photographs. Some razzias in postwar dwellings took place at night, thus taking on the tone of an even more invasive practice of social surveillance and control. Figure 3.2 is an example of the visual output of such a tour, when a Hungarian documentary photographer captured three sleeping children, dirty, half naked, and without blankets.

The picture's caption, originally in French, identified the neighborhood as Budapest's Grassalkovits [sic] Street. A 1920 report on children's life in Budapest assumes that photographs of these tours must "tell the truth." It stated that members of the Entente missions "inspected the dwellings of poverty shown in ... photographs and ... convinced themselves of the truthfulness of the particulars stated." Based on this experience, they felt committed to "limit ... [them]selves to reporting true facts that could be verified by means of names and addresses or other adequate evidence."[89]

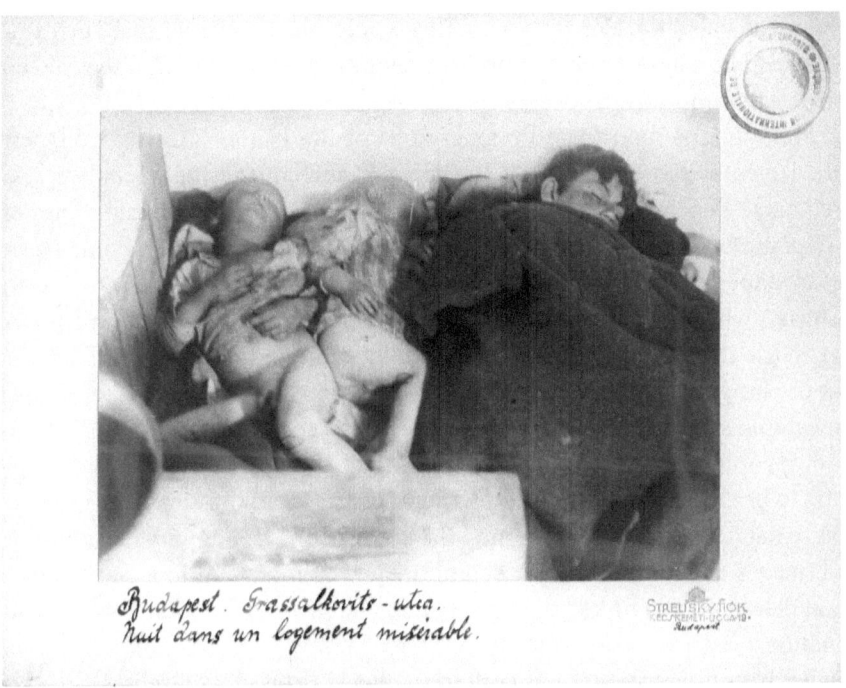

Fig. 3.2. Budapest, Grassalkovits Street, night in a miserable lodging. Photo by Sándor Strelisky 1920–21, CH AEG AP 92.105.76 (1).

In a report for Save the Children titled *How Is Life in the Capital?* Endre Liber, a contemporary Hungarian observer, painted a very dark picture, seeing the children's plight as a main cause for the city's growing criminalization. Liber recalled that a raid organized by the police revealed "the fearful misery of the children of our capital," and he described the many "miserable children" who were lying "in their empty beds without any clothes." He also observed an "increase in the number of those demoralized or needy and abandoned children" who came before the police tribunal. He noted that there were several among the arrested children who "belong[ed] to families of the middle class," fueling fears of degeneration.[90]

Amid this international sympathy there was believed to be a close link between children's physical condition and their moral development. Reporting on his trips to Budapest and Austria in 1923, Andrew Cherna, honorary commissioner of the American Red Cross, stressed the connection between physical and psychological development. He argued that "physical poverty means moral degeneration," which would lead to "rheumatism of the soul." Due to poverty, children would become "symptomatic" and exhibit demoralized and delinquent behavior. For that reason, it would be "inevitable that such immense and horrible physical disabilities should cause the children to grow up imbecile and morally degenerate."[91]

Many of the reports and photographs of life in the slums of Budapest were driven by sensationalism. "The conventional journey of journalists and foreigners, who were interested in the famous and infamous misfortunes of Budapest always took them to the barracks and to their dwellers," one Hungarian paper reported.[92] Reporters seized on the prevalence of suicide in Hungary, which was (and still is) higher than in other European countries. A 1921 article in *The Record*, the Save the Children's Fund's journal, told readers that in Hungary suicide was "increasingly general as a means of escape from unbearable starvation and misery, the victims ranging from children of ten to old people of eighty-eight most of them of the middle class. Sunday appears to be the favorite day. A recent Sunday produced the appalling number of seventeen suicides."[93] Combining the account of suicides with descriptions and images of the "unheated, wet and dreary" living conditions of the poor, the article explicitly linked the two phenomena in a call for compassion—and donations.

Because international humanitarian agents wanted to reach as wide an audience as possible with their humanitarian propaganda, they adapted and modified images from their inspection tours and the accompanying captions. Humanitarian reporting and propaganda often distorted the context of an image to convey the most effective message. For example, the caption of a picture from 1920, shown in figure 3.3a, reads: "Starvation has made them sell their mattress. A young girl after having been forced by Roumanian soldiers threw herself into the Danube."[94] In the Hungarian context, the phrase "having been forced" implies that the girl was raped, the reason for her suicide. The same image (fig. 3.3b) was reproduced in the *New York Times*, carrying the caption, "Here amid rags on the floor were found three children.... The husband's body was recovered from the Danube."[95] In the US newspaper, the caption shifts the focus to the suicide of the breadwinner, throwing the three children into absolute neglect and poverty; the mother was assumed to be away. In Hungary, the caption and image suggested, suicide had become the only escape and children's lives were put in peril. Irrespective of what actually happened, this was a useful approach in embittered Hungary, because it stressed the undeserved fate of the family.

The propagandistic uses of humanitarian images and texts created opportunities for distortion. A problem with using visuals for fundraising purposes

Fig. 3.3a. Starvation has made them sell their mattress. Photo by Kornél Tábori, in Tábori, *Egy halálraítélt ország borzalmaiból*, 114.

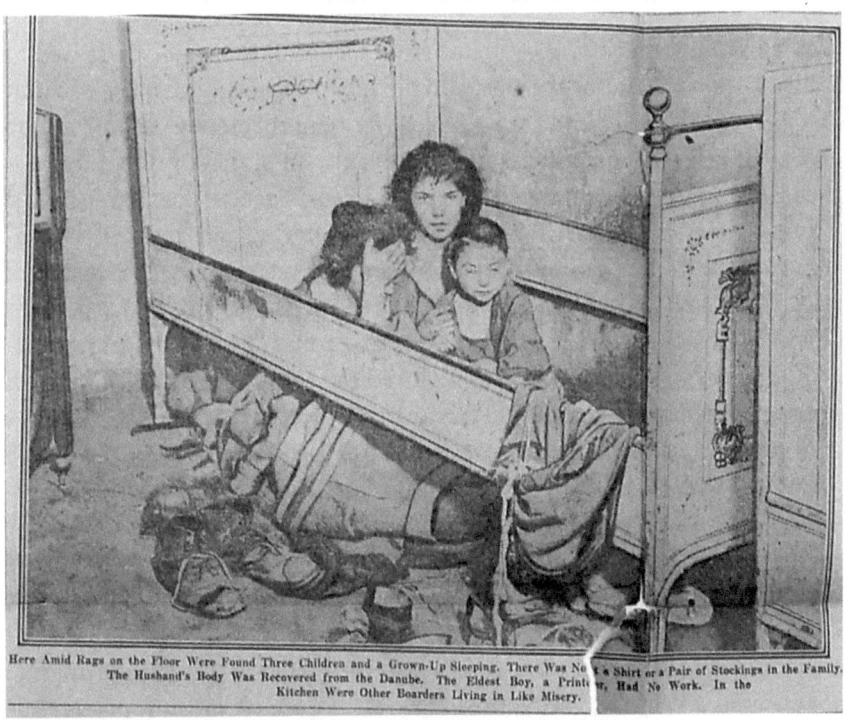

Fig. 3.3b. Here amid rags on the floor were found three children and a grown-up sleeping. Photo by Kornél Tábori, in Chenery, "Starving Budapest," 2.

was that they were easy to modify. Thus, an image's truthfulness and its possible manipulation would be questioned. British child philanthropist Thomas Barnardo had manipulated images of destitute children in the late nineteenth century. Barnardo gained a reputation for "artistic fiction," when he staged children for photographs and exploited the images as marketing tools for philanthropic purposes.[96] But even when intentions of humanitarian visual imagery were good, there were problems with the representation. The images might be too abstract or, conversely, too graphic for comfort. In 1919, the *Manchester Guardian* wrote that there were "photographs of Central European children which are too awful to bear reproduction" in the editor's office and "authenticated stories which scar one's mind with their horror."[97] So the paper assigned artists to produce drawings that were thought more appropriate for fundraising purposes. With drawings, fundraisers could not only convey their message but adapt it to the visual sensibilities of specific audiences. The visual representations reflected children's "real needs" and exploited how the images "function[ed] within the psychic, cultural, and financial economies of aid."[98]

Childhood Innocence and Social Fears

In contemporary sources, the capital city's frail children were presented as victims of the war and of the postwar turmoil—especially the loss of Hungary's former territories and the massive migration that followed. Appeals on their behalf reflected a new and outspoken criticism of the impact of the violent conflict and postwar turmoil on vulnerable subjects in affected societies. In Hungary, it was not solely the war but also its afterlife that "marked the moment when children became an object of international relations."[99] The fate of innocent children had a particular appeal at the time. As Michael Barnett has argued, "While children are always in need of constant care and protection, the children of the postwar period required another–very physical– type of support and protection that would secure their very survival."[100] Descriptions and depictions of suffering European children played on both sympathetic emotions toward innocence and warnings based in fear, representing both optimists like Herbert Hoover and humanitarians of a more pessimistic or cautionary bent. Children's innocence animated Hoover's and others' efforts to treat them as blameless victims, not enemies. Fears, on the other hand, were based on foundational questions: What kind of adults will these children grow up to be if they are deprived of nutrition, a proper upbringing, and education? What might be the longer-term outlook for Europe and European society if these children were to become its future leaders? Famine and poverty were seen as the catalysts for children's irreversible degeneration. Throughout Europe, the move toward "helping children was synonymous with reconstructing damaged nations and ensuring a successful biological and political future."[101] Positive emotional appeals focused on rescuing the children; negative emotional appeals focused on sparing the children from degenerating into the next generation of European social danger.

The *Manchester Guardian* in 1919 identified "the complete moral and physical wreckage of thousands of children" that was due to come as the result of this starvation.[102] A subsequent article from March 1920 urged the public to give wholehearted support to the Save the Children Fund to save Europe's future citizens, who, if unaided, would turn into cripples. Eglantyne Jebb pointed to the unresolved risk of "children now suffering the consequences of war in starvation, cold, and diseases, which, if they do not kill, threaten to reduce the population of Europe to multitudes of cripples, cretins, and rickety idiots . . . numbered by millions."[103] Hoover went even further and stressed the threat to American children: "Some time in the future, unless these children are preserved and cared for, our children will be infected by them." He was employing the image of a viral epidemic that might spread through the multitude of Central European children unless they were saved from starvation. He was not worried about the former combatants but rather the next generation: "This mass of undernourished, underfed, mentally, morally and physically destitute children" were, to him, "the real wastage of the war." In twenty years' time, these children would "form the basis of civilization of Eastern Europe."[104] If nothing was done, Hoover foresaw these same children as a generation begging on Europe's streets or "fill[ing] the jails of Europe and the United States."[105] Associations to similar situations at home were evoked to help viewers imagine what the European children's situation might be like. To get an idea of abandoned children "left to a life of idleness without supervision or discipline," the would-be donors were asked to "imagine a crowd of 5,000 New York street Arabs let loose" in a place "where they knew cocoa, milk and rice were to be distributed free of charge."[106]

Visual representations of the physical impact of the war and its aftermath on children's bodies served especially to produce a "revolution in seeing and hearing."[107] They mobilized compassion—even from afar—for direct relief from the victorious nations. As Karen Wells has noted, "The transparent emotional demand made by the figure of the child and the simplicity of the solutions offered to their problems contribute[d] to the moral legibility" of humanitarian relief actions.[108] Iain Wilkinson has argued that "humanitarian culture and experiences of humanitarian impulse" can be identified "as integral features of the dominant social imaginaries of our time."[109] The image of children's destitution had enormous propagandist potential, from which the relief organizations benefited. Children were seen as "bodies to be fed and cured, as emotional beings to be loved, as politically neutral citizens, and as future citizens."[110]

Many newspaper articles emphasized the sharp contrast between the abysmal living standards of poor children in distant cities and the luxury enjoyed by British donors. Successive appeals piled on emotional pressure to provoke instinctive, urgent reactions from targeted prospective donors. Although they might be sitting in their homes enjoying a cup of tea and the daily paper, readers were accosted by child relief appeals giving the impression that if they did not act immediately, they would be responsible for the deaths of innocent children. For example, one read as follows: "Another helpless child is dead—another, and another while you read and hesitate."[111] Playing with feelings of guilt and moral obligation, the visuals also took advantage of British society's self-image. Nonsectarian and nonpolitical, relief campaigns implied that the British were, at heart, a magnanimous people. "Ironically, rhetorical strategies and appeals . . . celebrated the natural generosity of the British and Britain's position as a world leader" while at the same time condemning callousness.[112] Only by being forced to "experience 'moral-emotional dissonance,'" Wilkinson explains, could people be "provoked into critical thinking and action."[113]

Thus, in Britain in particular, strong feelings of responsibility emerged toward the innocent victims in Central and Eastern Europe. A "new imperative to save Europe (and particularly its children) altered the geography of British humanitarianism, shifting its focus beyond the British Empire into a new 'international' area."[114] It highlighted the obligation people felt to the war's victims: "Let us do all we can before it is too late, so that none can say that WE have lived and that OTHERS died in vain."[115] Appeals for the relief of the former enemy's children aroused moral solidarity and compassion for the suffering distant other.[116] Based on these feelings, a new social sensibility emerged among the victorious powers, altering policies and channeling concern for children toward social change. As Didier Fassin defines them, "moral sentiments" are those "emotions that direct our attention to the suffering of others and make us want to remedy them."[117] Yet the usefulness of such triggered emotions is questionable. As Jane Lydon has argued, compassion contributes to "the notion of the human that is partial, limited and exclusive."[118] Nevertheless, in a massive effort to stir emotions, visual images played a key role because they could "evoke emotions and visions about how the world might or should be."[119] Images of starving and destitute children in war-stricken Europe also helped the donors and their nations and organizations feel that they were making the world a better place.

Visuals and closely narrated eyewitness reports brought about a new awareness of children's special vulnerability in times of economic and political turmoil. A British article from 1920 wished to remind its readers that "one may like one race better than another, but in this vision of common suffering, distinctions disappear, and where children are concerned, only the irresistible appeal of childhood is heard."[120] As Emily Baughan observes, in humanitarian relief just as in anti–child labor campaigns, "children were imagined as objects of affection, which placed them 'above' economic calculations of their worth."[121] As embodiments of innocence, children represented an optimistic vision of the postwar future. Lord Weardale, chairman of the Save the Children Fund, called Europe's destitute children "the tomorrow of society," the "raw material of the League of Nations." The Save the Children Fund was invested in caring for "the little shivering mite, oft-times homeless and an orphan," because each one was "a potential father of the race, a citizen of the future."[122] Erica Burman observes that, in the context of aid to Third World countries, images of children often served as a prototypical political projection screen. Hugo Slim summarizes Burman's main research conclusions, stating that "Western fantasies about an ideal childhood state have consistently been projected into humanitarian endeavor." Such projections were based on the infantilization of the recipients in distant countries, encouraging such "obsessive child-saving policies, which act to separate children from their communities."[123]

Political figures such as Herbert Hoover and other leaders sensed that childhood was a politically neutral topic on which most nations and people cooperate. Hoover used children to convey his own convictions about the legacy of the war, proclaiming that children were "the real optimists of the world, those who have known sorrow and suffering, yet who still hope."[124] He saw children as better than adults, capable of forgetting and forgiving and of creating a different future. Hoover drummed up solidarity among Americans by equating the starving children of the former enemies with children in the United States. "These children are no more my children than they are your children," he argued, but "the obligation of every man and every woman in the United States after he has cared for his own children or his neighbors' children."[125] Regardless of the children's origins, he urged, they should be rescued. In a similar vein, Eglantyne Jebb pursued her vision of internationalism, which was for her "a project of feeling."[126] She was driven by her conviction that by means of children's relief, future "peace would be built upon the friendships forged between people from across Europe," while international humanitarians would be "guiding the general public toward greater sympathy for people of different nationalities."[127] Dr. Armstrong Smith, the European relief director of the Save the Children Fund, expressed hope that Hungarian children could turn into cultural mediators. After the children had stayed for a whole year in Britain, he trusted that they could serve as a means of "drawing closer together the peoples of Britain and Hungary," between whom there had always existed close cultural ties. Smith also hoped that children's relief would result in an after-care scheme, so that Hungarian children could continue enjoying English games, dance, literature, and drama. Children and their relief would reestablish peaceful international relations.[128]

In postwar Central Europe, children's physical and mental suffering from the war's side effects confronted the victorious nations with the question of what peace had done to Europe. Citing the eyewitness observations of Coningsby Dawson, Hoover acknowledged that most of the victimized children were "not born when the war was started." They had been born into a world where "many of them have never known what it is to be warm and not to be hungry," in which "'joy' is a word utterly meaningless." Hoover confronted Americans with the fact that "two years after our madness has ended," Europe's children were "still paying the price of the adult world's folly." Hoover emphasized his belief in the power of child relief as one key "way of wiping out animosities."[129] The "culture of sensibility steadily broadened the arena within which humanitarian feeling was encouraged to operate, extending compassion to . . . previously despised types of persons," such as the children of the enemy.[130] Seeing children's bodies suffer from hunger and malnutrition, Hoover felt obliged to protect the "biological immaturity of children," because, as "growing creatures, they suffered more lastingly from malnutrition" than adults.[131]

A statement titled "Intervention on Behalf of the Children in Countries Affected by the War," addressed to the Assembly of the League of Nations in December 1920, reveals the fears related to children's suffering and starvation. Giuseppe M. Motta, Swiss delegate to the league, reminded delegates that "all rivalries, all racial or religious antagonisms have vanished in face of the agony of the children who are the sacred heritage of the human race." The conflict had inflicted the "most disastrous consequences on the health and the growth of children," Motta emphasized. He observed that "the whole world has been moved to pity by the fate of these innocent victims, destined to disease and death through insufficient food, through privations of all kinds, and through lack of heating and clothes."[132] A public letter in the *New York Times* of

September 30, 1919, argued that funds for Hungarian children—passive victims of the war—should be prioritized to save them from starvation. The author pleaded that one hundred thousand starving children in Budapest should be fed by outside help, because "the children of Hungary have no politics and they have been the victims of terrible circumstances" and during the time of "revolution, invasion, and lawlessness they have played no part, save to go hungry."[133]

In the United States, the close ties between Central Europe and American communities formed by European migration were often referenced as a key argument in securing funds: "Our population is made up of people who migrated from all parts of Europe and nearly every family over there has a friend or relative in the United States. Their faith in America . . . is unbounded."[134] One organization argued that "there is no other source of revenue than the friends of Hungary in America. Without this continuous support, the desperately needed relief must cease."[135] Thus, Hungarian Americans in particular, and representative organizations such as the American Relief Committee for Hungarian Sufferers, were urged to act on these ties and raise funds to keep the relief work going. They collected money and donated it to the Hungarian government and its child welfare committee.[136] Using an approach similar to the images that were used to elicit emotions and bring in donations, Julia Vajkai, of the Hungarian National Child Protection League, wrote and spoke about the sorry condition of Budapest's children, inspiring individuals abroad to send donations. In 1919, letters with personal donations from all over the world reached Budapest: "An English woman sent a golden chain watch, a poor launderer sent her one-day income, someone sent a headkerchief, and another one a wedding ring"—all wishing that Hungarian children should never again experience need.[137]

Appeals for children's relief abroad were sometimes directed to other children. In 1921, the advertisement shown in figure 3.4 was published in the *ARA Bulletin* (see fig. 3.4) with the title "Bring a Gift and Watch the Child Grow."[138] It asked American schoolchildren to help their undernourished peers in Central Europe. A picture of a child's head was outlined in dots, seemingly fading away. With every dollar donated, two adjacent dots could be connected. When all the dots were joined, the child's head would appear complete, symbolizing the saving of ten real children. The emotive utilization of the child's damaged body in visual representations turned the hungry child into the embodiment of the postwar and into a symbol of the continuing havoc. Having established the high stakes and misery among Budapest's children suffering after the war and the potential amelioration from relief, the international

Fig. 3.4. "Bring a gift and watch the child grow!" Unknown artist, *American Relief Administration Bulletin* 2, no. 11 (April 1921): 35.

community successfully employed children's suffering bodies to inspire relief from abroad. Domestic and international humanitarians were alarmed at the disheartening consequences of the war, making children's bodies the cornerstone of their relief efforts in the postwar years.

Conclusion

Extending the discussion of the causes of destitution in Hungary's capital, this chapter analyzed the ways in which the war affected children's bodies and their health, engaging with concerns at the time about children's physical and moral "degeneration." Children's (distant) suffering and their use as "moral iconographies"[139] help us better understand how Budapest's dire conditions were exhibited to the outside world to appeal for humanitarian aid. While the invalid soldier had symbolized the war and combat, the starving child became the quintessential icon of the turmoil that followed. Through numerous circulated sketches and photographs, the wasted bodies of famished children became icons of postwar austerity, drawing the attention of humanitarians outside and within Hungary's borders. Philanthropists in the victorious and neutral nations used the impaired body of the child as a projection screen for public appeals to end and relieve the suffering of the crushed nations. Children served very well as innocent victims. Furthermore, they helped raise awareness about the urgent need for national welfare and humanitarian relief, some of it motivated by concern about Europe's next generation.

Notes

1. Canning, "Feminist History after the Linguistic Turn," 394.
2. Chenery, "Starving Budapest," 2.
3. McSorley, *War and the Body*, 1.
4. Canning, "Feminist History after the Linguistic Turn," 394.
5. Kallio, "The Body as a Battlefield."
6. Watenpaugh, *Bread from Stones*, 93–94, 62.
7. Sabine Kienitz, cited in Ahlbäck, *Manhood and the Making of the Military*, 93.
8. See Lammers, *Fotografie und Medizin*.
9. Kienitz, *Beschädigte Helden*, 12–14.
10. Lévai, "Az elhanyagolt gyermekegészség," 153.
11. Apponyi, *The American Peace and Hungary*, 11.
12. Lévai, "Az elhanyagolt gyermekegészség," 153.
13. Weinreb, "Embodying German Suffering," 466.
14. Ibid., 467.
15. Wilkinson, "The Provocation of the Humanitarian Social Imaginary," 262.
16. Wróbel, "Foreshadowing the Holocaust," 191.
17. "The Typhus Epidemic in Central Europe," 117–19.
18. Feldberg, *Disease and Class*, 105.
19. "Tüdövész és egyéb nyavalyák pusztitják," 6.
20. Lévai, "Az elhanyagolt gyermekegészség," 153.
21. István, narrative interview with the author, Budapest, November 30, 2012, collection of the author.
22. Of those who died, 6,316 were younger than age seven, and 53,317 were over age seven.
23. A Magyar Kir. Központi Statisztikai Hivatal, *Magyar Statisztikai Évkönyv: 1916, 1917, 1918*, 60.
24. Flu sufferers included 120 children younger than age seven and 222 people over age seven.
25. Of those who died, 11,752 were younger than age seven, and 41,449 were over age seven.
26. *Magyar Statisztikai Évkönyv: 1916, 1917, 1918*, 60.
27. Jebb, "Life Stories of Hungarian Children," 29.
28. Ibid.
29. Géra, *A spanyolnáthu Budapesten*, 224.
30. "Terjed a spanyol influenza," 7.
31. "A spanyol járvány," 6.
32. "Pusztít a spanyol járvány," 5.
33. "A spanyol járvány," 6.
34. "Zsolnai Kálmán tragédia," 5.
35. Ibid.
36. Terry, "Hungary in the Third Peace Winter," 42.
37. "What Have We Done?" EJ 166: Hungary: Loose papers on SCF work, Eglantyne Jebb Papers (SCF/A409/EJ), SCF Archive, Birmingham.

38. Jebb, "Life Stories of Hungarian Children," 29.
39. Zelizer, *Pricing the Priceless Child*, 23.
40. Ibid.
41. "A Kis Csaba Ferenc temetése," 8.
42. Audouin-Rouzeau, Becker, and Smith, *France and the Great War*, 227.
43. Sontag, "Looking at War," 42–43.
44. Koven, *Slumming*, chap. 2; Godby, "Confronting Horror."
45. Thompson, *Light on Darkness?*, 1–2.
46. Chenery, "Starving Budapest," 2.
47. Chouliaraki, "The Humanity of War," 328.
48. Wells, "The Melodrama of Being a Child," 281.
49. Mahood and Satzewich, "The Save the Children Fund," 57.
50. Wells, "The Melodrama of Being a Child," 277.
51. Barnett, *Empire of Humanity*, 86.
52. Colpus, *Female Philanthropy in the Interwar World*, 177; Mahood, *Feminism and Voluntary Action*, 211.
53. "Our Help Is Needed and Must Be Given," *New York Times*, May 18, 1920, 10.
54. Andrew Cherna, "Report to the American Red Cross on Investigation in Austria and Hungary," September 1923, 5, Records of the American National Red Cross 1917–34, 953.08, NARA.
55. Vowinkel, *Agenten der Bilder*, 8, 18.
56. Scaglia, *The Emotions of Internationalism*, 196.
57. Wells, "The Melodrama of Being a Child," 281.
58. Paul Zentai, "Education, Propaganda and the American Red Cross," 953.62/08 Commission to Hungary, WW1 Reports, 24, NARA.
59. See Mahood, *Feminism and Voluntary Action*, chaps. 9–10.
60. Rappaport, "Eglantyne Jebb," 1:333.
61. Kennedy, "Selling the Distant Other," 1–2.
62. Wells, "The Melodrama of Being a Child," 281.
63. "What Is a Child Worth to You?" poster, 1917, Ball State University Library, Archives and Special Collections, http://libx.bsu.edu/cdm/singleitem/collection/WWIPosters/id/294/rec/1.
64. Buxton and Buxton, *The World after the War*, 59.
65. Slim, "Editorial: Disasters," 190.
66. Kienitz, *Beschädigte Helden*, 15.
67. Canning, "The Body as Method?" 506.
68. Fehrenbach and Rodogno, "Introduction: The Morality of Sight," 4.
69. Ibid.
70. Sontag, *Regarding the Pain of Others*; Burman, "Innocents Abroad," 238.
71. Halttunen, "Humanitarianism and the Pornography of Pain," 307, 318.
72. Sontag, "Looking at War," 86.
73. Zahra, *The Lost Children*, 38.
74. Jebb, "Cheap Publicity," 68.
75. "Starvation Seen in Film," 0.
76. Sontag, "On Photography," 177.
77. Betts, "Universalism and Its Discontents," 57.
78. Burman, "Innocents Abroad," 239.
79. Tábori, *Egy halálraitélt ország*, 1.
80. Ibid., last cover page.

81. Bálint, "Nyomor az utcán-"; Perényi, "Urban Places, Criminal Spaces," 144.
82. American Red Cross in Hungary to Col. Ernest P. Bicknell, American Red Cross Commissioner for Europe, Paris, June 27, 1922, Records of the American National Red Cross 1917–34. World War I. 953.08, NARA.
83. Angelika, "Nyomor az utcán-.".
84. István, narrative interview with the author, Budapest, November 30, 2012.
85. Umbrai, "A hatósági kislakás-építés története Budapesten," 8.
86. Gal, "Borrowing Ideas."
87. Umbrai, "A hatósági kislakás-építés története Budapesten," 58–59.
88. Perényi, "Urban Places, Criminal Spaces," 135.
89. Tábori, *Egy halálraítélt ország*, 1.
90. Endre Liber, *Account of Circumstances of Subsistence in Budapest: How Is Life in Budapest?* Budapest, October 21, 1921, 34 pages, 29–30, Eglantyne Jebb Papers Hungary, A 0407, EJ 155 Hungary, Folder 2, 1920–21, SCF Archive.
91. Cherna, "Report to the American Red Cross," 14; "The Meaning of Starvation: An Appeal for the Babies of Central Europe," *Manchester Guardian*, October 15, 1919, 14.
92. "A barakok világából," 3.
93. "Unheated, Wet and Dreary," 121.
94. Tábori, *Egy halálraítélt ország*.
95. Chenery, "Starving Budapest," 2.
96. Koven, *Slumming*, 113.
97. "The Meaning of Starvation," 14.
98. Burman, "Innocents Abroad," 239.
99. Granick, *International Jewish Humanitarianism*, 198.
100. Barnett, *Empire of Humanity*, 85.
101. Granick, *International Jewish Humanitarianism*, 198.
102. "The Meaning of Starvation," 14.
103. Nevinson, "The Black Outlook in Europe."
104. Hoover, "The Children Must Be Saved," 2.
105. Hoover, "Central European Relief."
106. "Misery Tales from Europe," 1.
107. Last, "Putting Children First," 195.
108. Wells, "The Melodrama of Being a Child," 279.
109. Wilkinson, "The Provocation of the Humanitarian Social Imaginary," 264.
110. Marshall, "Children's Rights and Children's Action," 352.
111. "Agonising Deaths of Children at Easter-Tide," 7.
112. Mahood, *Feminism and Voluntary Action*, 178.
113. Wilkinson, "The Provocation of the Humanitarian Social Imaginary," 270.
114. Baughan, *Saving the Children*, 19.
115. "Ghastly Tragedy of Europe's Children," 3.
116. Wilkinson, "The Provocation of the Humanitarian Social Imaginary," 269.
117. Fassin, *Humanitarian Reason*, 1.
118. Lydon, *Photography, Humanitarianism, Empire*, 5.
119. Chouliaraki and Blaagaard, "The Ethics of Images," 254.
120. Nevinson, "The Black Outlook in Europe."
121. Baughan, *Saving the Children*, 31.
122. Weardale, "The To-Morrow of Society," 33.
123. Slim, "Editorial: Disasters," 190.

124. "1,000,000 Children Saved by America," *New York Times*, November 16, 1919, 20.
125. Hoover, "The Children Must Be Saved," 2.
126. Baughan, *Saving the Children*, 80.
127. Ibid.
128. Armstrong Smith, "Budapest Revisited," 264.
129. Hoover, "What Peace Has Done to Europe," 29.
130. Halttunen, "Humanitarianism and the Pornography of Pain," 303.
131. Marshall, "Children's Rights and Children's Actions," 355.
132. "Motion Proposed by the Swiss Delegation to the Assembly of the League of Nations, Explanatory Statement, Intervention on Behalf of the Children in Countries Affected by the War," Geneva, December 2, 1920. Motta to Monsieur Paul Hymans, 5. F.O. 371. 4717. Political. Central. General. Files 9861–15096, National Archives, Kew.
133. "Plan Found to Save Starving Children," 16.
134. Hortense McDonald, "Generation in Peril."
135. "Hoover Wants 1,000,000," N1.
136. "Cablegram by Richardsen to Mr. Bland, Budapest, March 19, 1919," American Relief Administration European Operational Records, Box 35, Folder 4, Reel 56, HILA.
137. "Külföldi Magyar gyermekekért," *Új Nemzedék* 1, no. 66 (December 16, 1919): 4.
138. "Bring a Gift and Watch the Child Grow," *ARA Bulletin* 2, no. 12 (May 1, 1921): 35.
139. On moral iconographies, see "Moral Iconographies" (blog), *Hypotheses*, https://moralicons.hypotheses.org; Knoch and Möckel, "Moral im 20"; and Glover, *Humanity*.

4

INSTITUTIONS

The Genesis of Child Protection

THIS CHAPTER EXPLORES THE PARADOXICAL ROLE OF THE war and its aftermath in causing not just children's suffering but also eliciting widespread attempts to alleviate children's everyday destitution. It tests the provocative conclusion of Deborah Dwork that "war is good for babies and other young children" by showing how the urgent mission to save, in this case, Budapest's children translated into diverse child protection services.[1] Children's displacement, uprootedness, neglect, malnutrition, and frail health required the expansion of the public child protection system during and after the war. In such a crisis situation, Hungarian postwar child protective initiatives built on preexisting institutions and models, even if they had to be rethought and reinvented or supplemented.

In 1920, the child welfare system in Hungary, especially in the capital, was by no means as backward as some incoming American relief workers had imagined. This chapter investigates the National Child Protection League, founded in 1907, and the National Stefánia Association for the Protection of Mothers and Infants, founded in 1915. I explore the role of the global and local conflict in altering, expanding, and modernizing the vernacular child protection system without which international relief could not have reached Budapest's children. I also examine the leading role of women in the making of the Hungarian child welfare system, highlighting the work of a few key women child relief workers who lay the foundation for the future cooperation between Hungarian and international child relief organizations.

The Child Protection League

"There was nothing new about a children's charity in 1920," Linda Mahood notes in her biography of Eglantyne Jebb, founder of the British Save the Children Fund. Child protection was well established in postwar Europe;[2] indeed, huge advances had been made throughout the continent and in Hungary specifically. The late nineteenth century and the first decades of the twentieth century "marked a transition" from "traditional social medicine" to the "modern medical management of childbirth and childrearing."[3] As Jan Behrends and Martin Kohlrausch stated, the fin de siècle can be understood as the "start of a dramatic era that has been called classical or high modernity, an era of unprecedented upheaval." In this period of rapid transformation, professionalization, and change, cities such as Budapest turned into a "stage on which new states had to prove their legitimacy." This notion included the "construction of representative government buildings, national libraries, and theaters" alongside the professional handling of long-term "social problems."[4]

In that era, children gained rights to appeal for protection from the "most extreme consequences [of] poverty, ignorance, vice and cruelty."[5] It would therefore be misleading to depict developments in the years after World War I as "markers of an entirely new world order." Rather, the new initiatives of the time "breathed fresh life into older forms."[6] What was lacking, however, was the centralization and coordination of local efforts to better alleviate the suffering of the destitute, the marginalized, the elderly, and the young. Children's protection especially developed into a social arena that required close cooperation. Children's care was negotiated between the fields of pedagogy, medicine, nutrition sciences, and psychology. Its everyday implementation involved close collaboration between families, nurses, educational and health care facilities, doctors, philanthropists, faith-based organizations, and state representatives.

In Hungary, concern for child protection was a key feature of prewar society. Though the war severely impaired the efficiency of the Hungarian child protection system, professional organizations caring exclusively for children had been active since the late nineteenth century and especially the first decade of the twentieth century.[7] Hungary, according to József Szénásy, "preceded the great European states" in its care system, unifying mother and infant protection "as an organic whole" as early as 1915—before Germany, France, Italy, and England.[8] Budapest took the lead, with a massive expansion of initiatives and organizations geared to take care of the country's orphaned, disabled, and neglected children. Rapid modernization, industrialization, and urbanization had revealed children's defenselessness. Certain districts were infamous for substandard living conditions for children. Poverty grew constantly due to ongoing industrialization and social division. Many unregistered poor did not even figure in the districts' lists. Throughout Europe at this time, religious and philanthropic organizations were responding to the

Fig. 4.1. The headquarters of the Hungarian National Child Protection League. Unknown photographer, in Rottenbiller, *Az Országos Gyermekvédő Liga*, 23.

increasing exploitation and mortality they saw among children in the industrialized labor market. In 1903, Budapest's charities were reported as trying "to bandage the wounds of society" and "alleviate the misery of society."[9]

By the end of 1905 (or 1906 in some accounts), one of the two most important child welfare institutions, the Hungarian National Child Protection League (*Országos Gyermekvédő Liga*, hereafter, the League), had been founded. The League would go on to become the official child protection organ of the Ministry of the Interior.[10] Its main office, located at 6 Wesselényi Street, coordinated the administration of the humanitarian child relief work, including the reception, management, and controlled distribution of the arriving relief goods (see fig. 4.1).[11] From its inception, the League distributed foodstuffs, clothing, utensils, and money to children in need; it ran dispensaries and recreational centers for sick children; it offered a free legal service to children and minors; and it provided information to child protection institutions and individuals.[12] In 1907, Count Edelsheim-Gyulai explained how all this had become necessary because of the growing social problems and the increasing "poverty" that accompanied the rapid "growth of [Hungary's] major cities." Although several child welfare initiatives had been launched previously, institutionalized "child protection" (*gyermekvédelem*) lacked both "cooperation between the various humanitarian initiatives" and a central, professional organ that could take over coordination of the various activities assumed. The League therefore aimed to serve as the "central office" for the entire emergent child protection movement, the hub of a "system of practical preventive child protection."[13] Its goal was to provide public child protection to "Hungarian children and minors, regardless of class and religion."[14]

The League established recreational institutions for sickly children, relief kitchens for mothers and their offspring, orphanages for orphans and war orphans, boarding schools (especially for orphaned students), and teaching facilities. It also offered free legal assistance to minors.[15] It supervised sixty-four institutes with around six thousand children. Placing "properly selected children" with "good foster parents," it allocated other children to hospitals and to various institutes specializing in serving the "deaf and dumb," the blind, and the "poor" as well as those training domestic servants (*cselédképző intézet*). It had industrial schools, grammar schools, and even a music academy. The League equipped disabled children with "medication, bandages, artificial legs, [and] glass eyes." It helped out parents by providing clothing.[16] By 1926, the National Child Protection League was running two infant-and-mother homes, four homes for war orphans, one daycare home, two nurseries, three medical practices, four boarding schools, two holiday venues, and two homes for learning an industrial craft.[17]

The League's founding leadership notwithstanding, it was especially women from the middle and upper classes who engaged with the cause of child welfare.[18] According to Linda Mahood, the British Save the Children Fund was "not just the playground of wealthy and well-known women."[19] However, in postwar Budapest, I would argue, local child relief was still heavily reliant on the wives of important politicians, wealthy aristocratic widows, and middle-class women. "I have always felt that unemployed royals might find useful scope in this direction!" Eglantyne Jebb once exclaimed when Archduke Albrecht and his mother, Archduchess Isabella, welcomed her enthusiastically to a child protection congress in Budapest in 1924.[20] Years prior to this event, in 1911, Countess Adelma Vay and Countess Márta Zichy gave a talk before the Federation of Hungarian Women's Associations (*Magyarországi Nőegyesületek Szövetsége*). Founded in 1904, this was the umbrella organization of Hungary's women's movement.[21] The countesses argued that women had to step together on the "road of morality," overcoming any "egoistic attitude" and working "for the future and the benefit of the people."[22]

These statements contained a veiled criticism of the unearned privileges of upper-class women. It was "not us, the privileged of life," but rather the "wretched, battered, wounded, defenseless" who needed support. The speakers tried to rouse women's compassion for destitute children, appealing to their maternal instincts: "According to the laws of nature," the being closest to the woman was the child—if not her own, then another's. This intrinsic feeling of compassion for the child should be put into action. There was no more real and serious type of women's politics than the saving, protection, and education of children, because they would later "drive and constitute the nation"; in that role, they would either "strengthen and raise" the homeland or let it become "stunted and wither away."[23]

Child protection reached beyond the elite and turned into a widely shared middle-class trend. It rendered women visible and united them with other women.[24] As was the case elsewhere, a great number of charity and child relief organizations were run by middle-class women. Philanthropy enabled women of the upper and middle classes to "play a public role" even without the vote."[25] When it came to the class composition of relief staff, Herbert Hoover was invested in using child relief to "neutralize class hatred" and create a "social melt" by "bringing the upper classes into the range of labor." Hoover recalled in 1921 that he "recruited from every class, ranging from princes, counts and barons, to street sweepers and scrubwomen." His aim was to diminish the "strong and even bitter class distinction," especially in postimperial Central Europe. He was convinced that "a princess stirring broth in a soup kitchen is the best argument for democracy that could possibly be found."[26]

Another prominent group who rallied to the child welfare cause in Hungary was religious women. Women were considered to have "a natural aptitude for compassion" and a "stronger religious sensibility" than men, leading them to take an interest in the poor.[27] As voluntary workers, nurses, or midwives, women were at the heart of the creation and professionalization of child welfare in Hungary.[28] In Europe and beyond, the war had promoted the profession of nursing—and the woman (child) relief worker—as "the feminine counterpoint to battle-scarred masculinity."[29] The countesses promoting the work of the League linked their Christian faith to their appeal for social rapprochement and the leveling of huge social class inequalities. They hoped to put an end to the "great isolation" that separated the better classes from the poor and less privileged. The innocence of children was a concept that was easy to meld with religious ideas. The countesses said that the initial question a child should be asked was whether he or she believed in God. Guided by

Christian morality, they argued that the League's work was respectable for women in providing relief to illegitimate or abandoned children. Any child living in misery or who is abandoned or debauched should be asked, "Are you hungry? Are you cold?" Count Edelsheim-Gyulai agreed with this approach. In 1909, he explained that initially there should be no fuss about finding out the child's name, age, address, and beliefs; the League should simply help the child. Only later should more information be sought. The League's workers, Count Edelsheim-Gyulai explained, had been explicitly instructed to examine and question the children they had taken in about their parents' social standing, native language, religion, and their talents and flaws in terms of a child's future upbringing.[30] The question about religious denomination was intended to facilitate placement of children with institutions or in families of their own belief—"the Catholic children into Catholic families, the Reformed children to Reformed foster parents and the Israelite children into families of the same faith."[31]

In general, the League's mission was to provide child and juvenile protection, offering support both on the practical and theoretical level.[32] During the first general assembly of the National Child Protection League on November 28, 1907, politician Kálmán Széll argued that child protection should not be just a "philanthropic, humanitarian, charitable" concern but a "national" one.[33] The League was particularly concerned with combating the causes of children's neglect and deprivation. Edelsheim-Gyulai drew attention to the curses of alcoholism, tuberculosis, and venereal diseases, which he believed not only blighted the lives of many deprived families but could also ruin a child's life from the moment of its birth. He also identified bad nutrition, bad housing, and the "sinful, immoral and criminal environment" of the slums as major causes of the "degeneration of a whole generation."[34]

The League served as a hub of child protection services and worked to strengthen the connection between private charities and the state.[35] During a speech to the League on March 28, 1909, Edelsheim-Gyulai made it clear that the organization aspired to serve as the central headquarters, coordinating the amazing "machinery" of child protection, which "the state and society had to maintain" together.[36] The League was an intermediary between the state and childcare institutions. It also took on state responsibilities, such as "the care of foreign children and the education of children who were endangered by moral ruin."[37] The "pulse of society's heart" would be felt in the League's vital mission. Hungarians needed to understand that if they saved waifs, they were not simply practicing clemency, they were fulfilling an essential "social duty."[38]

The League's structure mimicked that of both state bureaucracy and families. According to its basic rules, the League's membership included "an honorary president and honorary members as well as other founders, patrons, and full and external members (*kültagjai*)." Only people of Hungarian nationality were eligible to be members.[39] The various institutions were to be headed by professional pedagogues. The children were to be divided into "families" with a woman head or "matron" (*családanya*), who would guarantee cleanliness and neatness. A woman "who handled the children with love" was needed for the children's spiritual upbringing, and she should also bring some joviality and homeyness to their lives.[40] The League was financed through bonds and capital, membership fees, governmental support, and donations. A large portion of the money raised was invested in propaganda for the organization's cause. In 1905, a monthly *Child Protection Journal* (*A Gyermekvédelem Lapja*), published by Edelsheim-Gyulai, was created, which served as an academic outlet for research in the field of child protection. It became the official mouthpiece of the League.

An important occasion sponsored by the League was the annual Children's Day (*gyermeknap*)—a nationwide event to raise money to fund the League's programs and activities (see fig. 4.2).[41] The tradition began with the first Children's Day on May 26, 1906.[42] In the first year, Children's Day was celebrated in 46 communities and cities.[43] The next year, 612 communities and cities participated, and in 1908, this number rose to 2,262. Edelsheim-Gyulai saw in this swelling support proof of increasing public awareness of the importance of child protection.[44] By 1914, Children's Day was a major event. A small publication about the Annual Assembly of the League and its Children's Day for that year listed every fundraising station in the city of Budapest and every female volunteer collecting money for the ongoing work. A hundred stations were announced, in prime locations: in front of the Auguszt Confectionary; the New York, Keleti, and Angol coffeehouses; at all the bridgeheads and main squares; by important churches such as the Franciscan and the Deák Square churches; near the casino on Nádor Street; at the main train stations; on Andrássy Boulevard; at the Oktogon; by the main city rings of Károly Körút and Múzeum Körút; next to the savings bank; by the Parisian fashion house; and in the main food market.[45]

All these sites in the city were places where people would already be spending money—for bridge tolls, food, entertainment, pleasure, fashion, long-distance travel, and church alms. Placing the fundraising stations in these spots was a strategic attempt to encourage people to donate their coins to philanthropy. Some stations were staffed by a single woman; others might

Fig. 4.2. Fund-raising activity for the Hungarian National Child Protection League. Unknown photographer, May 2–3, 1931, Signature 74.21, Hungarian National Museum, Budapest.

have more than thirty women staffing the location at various times. Because the volunteers were often the wives of important public and political figures, one motive for placing such large groups in one place must have been to create publicity and so boost the raising of funds. Children's Day featured organized entertainment that required an entrance ticket, which added a considerable amount of money to the cause.

With funding in hand, the League's overriding concern was to reach Budapest's "debauched children" (*züllött gyermekek*), for whom nobody cared. At a tender age, these children had been "thrown onto the street" to suffer hunger and cold. Deprived of any proper upbringing, they were considered capable of any type of offense or crime. One eleven-year-old boy had run away from his sixth foster family and was stealing, mugging, and setting fires. The boy ended up in an institution where he was "bound to the foot of the bed" to restrain him. Though he should have been placed in a corrective institution, relief agent Sándor Karsai recalled, there were not enough places. Indeed, most at-risk children could not be accommodated in an appropriate setting, because it was feared that they would affect other "children in a house, a village, a street."

Moreover, they would likely end up in prison. In Karsai's view, "the rescue of these children" should be the main child protection mission of the state and society alike. The social derailment of some children was considered so severe that only placement in an institution could save them.[46]

These institutions bore in mind the children's futures and sent many on to receive an education and learn a profession—in agriculture, trade, or industry. This vocational slant was intended for the child's good, not exploitation. Karsai was convinced that if children showed signs of social or moral "degeneration," it was the result of the "social milieu" they came from and their "neglected education." Even after a short time in the ameliorating atmosphere of the National Child Protection League's institutions, he believed, a child could be "healed" and transferred to a family to ensure continued flourishing. If a child was not "saved" after a year in an institution, the only option was transfer to a "corrective institution." Always, the main focus should be on education, so that children "could be of use to the nation and the economy."[47] Through these and various other impulses initiated by the League, the organization became highly influential in laying the basis for the slow genesis of a state system of a Hungarian child welfare. The National Child Protection League helped to create the infrastructure for the care of those children who fell through the cracks in the system of family care well before the Great War broke out.

Neither Money nor Things: Securing Postwar Child Protection

During World War I, countless male breadwinners were killed in battle or returned home physically or mentally impaired. Hence, the traditional system of family responsibilities was often broken, threatening children's everyday care, feeding, and education.[48] The destruction wrought by the war and the dissolution of the empire also brought material poverty and strain on child protection facilities. Yet the expansion, centralization, and professionalization of children's welfare in many parts of Europe went, as Tara Zahra points out, hand in hand "with the new responsibilities assumed by wartime governments." These included not only "the health and morale of citizens on the home front" but also "the physical, education[al], and moral welfare of children."[49] The war signaled "the beginning of the end of private charity's monopoly on relief."[50] The evident war and postwar distress of the child population in Budapest triggered a "renewed sense of the importance of child life" and an expansion of the welfare services offered.[51]

The war and its aftermath severely strained Hungary's child protection system, but by no means destroyed it. A local infrastructure was still in place. But while Hungary's "board of charities" was "virtually intact," it was "without supplies to distribute," lacked materials and medical equipment, and activities had almost come to a complete stop.[52] On May 15, 1920, Julia Vajkai wrote to Eglantyne Jebb, explaining that the condition of the League, which she considered the "most splendid organization to work on a quite neutral basis," weighed "most heavily" on her heart. The League's many children's asylums and homes had been doing excellent work for many years, but if the Save the Children Fund could not offer financial support, facilities would have to close, sending three thousand children out onto the streets.[53] In this new postwar era, the League's and Hungary's domestic child relief institutions needed additional support to address monumentally greater needs.

Child protection in postwar Budapest was a reversal of Hungary's previously robust system. Rose Vajkai, delegate of the Save the Children International Union (SCIU) in Hungary, later recalled that, because of the "hitherto unimaginable misery," the Hungarian welfare organizations found themselves "in the strange position of being compelled to [seek] emergency relief," though they operated in a country "where such work had long been . . . of a high standard." Budapest was well known for its "excellent child welfare work" and, "naturally," in better times, had provided children with an appropriate education.[54] Vajkai relied on her deep personal connection with Jebb, who had set up a European network of child relief workers, embracing every "nationality, religion or political attitude." Between 1918 and 1928, Vajkai was apparently Jebb's closest colleague, implementing in Budapest many of the children's rescue and protection ideas that Jebb had envisioned for Europe's children.[55] The SCIU recognized that "hardly any help from National Relief organizations [could] be counted upon," as "they themselves depend[ed] largely on gifts from foreign missions."[56]

Only eight child asylums survived into the postwar period. These were located in Budapest, Debrecen, Gyula, Kecskemét, Pécs, Szeged, Szombathely, and Veszprém. Additionally, perhaps around seventy-one orphanages, homes, and special institutes remained part of the domestic Hungarian childcare system. Children in orphanages located in territories that had been ceded from Hungary, such as those in Kassa (Košice) and Rimaszombat (Rimavská Sobota), were either distributed to the other orphanages or integrated into the welfare system of the new states.[57] Institutions of the League that lay outside the redrawn borders of the Hungarian state were cut off from the main administration in Budapest. Among them were "homes for agricultural apprenticeship" in Nagyvárad (Oradea), Temesvár (Timişoara), Kolozsvár (Cluj), and Pozsony (Bratislava), and the Szilányi children's home in Szalonca (Slavnica). These were now administered by Romania or Czechoslovakia.[58]

Identifying the nationality of contested children to be saved could be politically fraught. In October 1920, 111 "impoverished and neglected" Slavic-language-speaking children, who, prior to the war, had been institutionalized in state orphanages in the southern Hungarian city of Pécs, were meant to be "repatriated" to childcare institutions in the formerly Hungarian and now Serbian city of Subotica (Szabadka). The "origin of 99 children was doubtful," and according to the available documents, some considered them perhaps of Hungarian origin while only their family names were Slavic. But because most of these children were considered to have been originally Slavic prior to some kind of "Magyarization," they were to be transferred to a Serbian orphanage in Subotica rather than remain in the Hungarian orphanages in Pécs. The Yugoslavian ministerial secretary Milan Damjanovits proposed in a letter to the Hungarian state authorities that Slavic children who had been placed in Hungarian foster families in Hungarian villages near Pécs should also be "repatriated" to state asylums or foster families in Subotica. In case their birth parents would "wish to take their own children back in their own care," the Serbian authorities would allow this without any difficulties. The main aim of this repatriation action was to help the state asylum in Pécs, "which found itself in a severe crisis." The proposal was intended to enable the orphanage "to better care and feed the children of Hungarian origin" and to place the Hungarian children in Hungarian foster families in the nearby villages.[59] This discussion over children's repatriation reveals the difficult and often unclear national belonging of the children of former Austria-Hungary. Hungary's territorial losses and the wish to draw clear boundaries between the new nation-states caused the forced transfer of children, even if their citizenship was far from unambiguous.

The war and its aftermath alone did not account for the ensuing children's neglect, poverty, and hunger. As a Hungarian schoolteacher observed in 1918, "there were already serious problems and deficits in the pre-war period"; one "can't make the war accountable for everything." The war brought to the surface "old problems and urged us again and again to solve" them.[60] The existing system of child protection, then, had its shortcomings and weaknesses. In *Empire of Humanity*, Michael Barnett observes that the demands of the war situation and food shortage "highlighted the limitations of improvised charity and the necessity of an institutionalized philanthropic and aid sector."[61]

The war thus triggered the professionalization of children's welfare. Several international aid workers reached the same conclusion on Hungary's dire need for international assistance to bolster domestic child relief efforts. When British doctor and journalist Haden Guest traveled to Budapest to report for the *Manchester Guardian* on child welfare immediately after the war's end, he was shocked by what he saw. In October 1919, he wrote that "the present government cannot keep order, and apparently does not want to." He went on to emphasize that "a strong international force to guarantee free elections and to prevent the people from tearing themselves to pieces" would be required.[62] International humanitarian aid in the form of money and relief agents would be needed to make up for local deficiencies and to revive and equip Hungary's child protection system. Captain James G. Pedlow, director of the American Red Cross in Budapest, also assessed the situation of existing relief as seriously challenging. On July 27, 1921, he reported to superiors in Washington that he feared the Hungarian government would "not be able to take proper care of these people" and that "outside assistance will be needed for some time to come"; many new arrivals would have to "live in freight cars," and he described the housing conditions as "so utterly bad that it would seem impossible to take any additional population.[63]

That was why child relief workers appealed to international aid organizations for help. Foreign money was absolutely necessary if the system of child relief was to be revived and made fit for task. The Hungarian national child relief organizations therefore sought help from abroad, as a retrospective report by the League states. Fülöp Rottenbiller, undersecretary of the League, recalled the shift from national to international support in the child-saving movement of the 1920s. While Hungary's better-off population had supported Hungarian philanthropy "with great love for decades," it was now "so occupied with its thoughts about its everyday survival, that it had become unimaginable to practice charity." For that reason, he argued, it was necessary to reach out to the foreign countries that were willing to help and acquaint them with the League's projects and institutions.[64] Hungarian child protection officials like Aladár Pettkó-Szandtner confirmed that the Hungarian system of child protection was tottering. "The war, the revolutions, and the so-called peace" had impoverished the middle classes, "who were always ready for altruistic cooperation" in good times but whose "unselfish and beneficent work" was paralyzed in the "extremely hard conditions of life" that now beset them.[65]

Postwar scarcity made postwar relief work considerably more expensive, further inhibiting domestic efforts. A report for the Red Cross by Count

Széchényi, head of the League, blamed the excessive prices on food, clothing, and other children's goods for the trouble charitable organizations had in functioning. Costs were ten times higher in 1920 than they had been in 1918. The League could only survive "from day to day" and had tremendous difficulty in obtaining necessary materials. Because Hungarian society was suffering as a whole, people were far less willing to "make sacrifices" than before. He appealed to nations in better economic circumstances to send material relief in the form of food, clothes, and money so that the League could carry out its "greatest social undertaking"—protecting Hungary's children in these desperate times. He called for solidarity among the international community to aid stricken Hungary, warning that if Hungary's "cry for help [should remain] without an echo," thousands of innocent children would be exposed to "physical and moral ruin."[66] In the same year (1920) as the League of Nations was founded, with its program of transnational cooperation to secure world peace, Széchényi was strident in his lobbying of international organizations like the International Committee of the Red Cross, beseeching them to intervene and bolster Hungary's strapped domestic organizations on behalf of its children.

War, Nurses, and Children's Relief

The war played a crucial role in elevating women's active contributions to public and philanthropic life. Women were active in the League's efforts well before the war's outbreak, but the conflict brought them a much greater role. A 1917 article in the *Chicago Daily Tribune* acknowledged that Central and Eastern European "women of gentle birth were no laggards when war came," as they "immediately entered the hospitals or went to the front as nurses." The author observed that there was "scarcely an aristocrat or feminine member of the great imperial family who [had] not dedicated herself to her country's cause." When the "history is written of Austria-Hungary's part in the world war," the writer noted, the "chapter treating the work of women should be one redounding to the credit of womankind for all time."[67]

Women experienced "a period of economic and emotional vulnerability" at the home front, but nevertheless succeeded in becoming "more self-reliant" in the service they offered. They took over a leading social role as "heads of household, breadwinners, and protectors of their children and property"— roles that they were not readily willing to give up once men returned from the battlefield.[68] Women nurses, in particular, were active at the front, in prisoner of war camps, and in hospitals in the heartland. They were indispensable

Fig. 4.3. Mrs. Julia Vajkai. Unknown photographer, *Új Idők* 2, no. 34 (September 28, 1946): 565.

in providing relief to the wounded, disabled, captured, and orphaned.[69] The untrained Red Cross volunteer nurse performed the "most noble service."[70] The war also helped professional nurses and social workers achieve social recognition.

Mostly working as newly trained nurses, women started to shape child protection institutions. They had the opportunity to prove their value. Particularly after the war, they were needed in children's work. The war had caused a diversification of the nursing profession, and the new trained, professional nurses pushed for modern, scientific child-rearing practice.[71] Before World War I, most nurses, many of them nuns, had had little formal training, but the war changed that. Red Cross nurses completed a one-year course with placement in a Red Cross hospital. Infant nurses usually went through an intensive six-month course and gained a diploma or, if they were among the most promising fifteen trainees in their cohort, received a year of training (practical and theoretical) at Budapest's White Cross Hospital. Due to their professional training, the postwar infant nurses were considered to be of "very superior quality." The National Stefánia Association for the Protection of Mothers and Infants offered a six-month course to fifty visiting nurses who provided home care to children and young mothers. Finally, the Central Tuberculosis Dispensary in Budapest trained its own nurses to help at hospitals and make home visits.[72]

In the postwar crisis, with its explosion of children's needs and corresponding expansion of child welfare services, infant nurses were in high demand from the governmental welfare stations, which always had a staff of three. The evident need for nurses resulted in a "definite feeling" within the Ministry of Public Welfare that a national public health nursing service should be developed.[73] This view was shared by the press, and several Hungarian women rose to prominence in these efforts. Giant steps had been taken toward women's equality and social empowerment. In the Hungarian weekly *Új Idők*, Julia Vajkai reflected on women's contribution to Hungary's "peaceful revolution." Vajkai herself, shown in figure 4.3, was a living example.

Born in 1879 into a Catholic family of manufacturers (her father was Armin Weisz, and her mother Emilia Illencfalvi Linzer), Vajkai dedicated her life to the protection and education of impoverished children. She was one of the key figures to create links between local Hungarian child protection institutions and international organizations. Through her actions, letters, and travels, she established and maintained cooperation between Britain, Geneva, and Budapest. She headed the Hungarian National Child Protection League in Budapest, served as delegate of the Hungarian Red Cross, and was a local relief worker for the SCF. In a letter to the SCIU in Geneva, she identified herself as the "delegate of a foreign organization" whose role should be "absolutely restricted to serving as an intermediary . . . to draw attention to the needs of my country and to identify possible means to help it."[74] Her self-defined role was to raise international awareness of the plight of postwar Hungary's poor. When she was invited to visit Britain, she "gave many vivid accounts of the distress among children and expectant mothers."[75]

Julia's sister, Rose Vajkai, was heavily involved in local child protection work, too. She served as the Hungarian delegate of the SCIU and as the secretary of the International Committee of the Red Cross in Budapest and Vienna. Rose and Julia perfectly embodied the "sisterhood" that Linda Mahood finds to be a typical feature of late-Victorian philanthropic and voluntary organizations. Their sisterhood was both figurative and literal—sisters by birth sharing a common mission.[76] Vilmos Neugebauer of the National

Child Protection League gave Rose an office in Budapest, and she received a salary for her work.[77] Julia believed that the war had liberated women enough for them to show some of their true mettle. "In the war, we showed" not only "that we are as capable as men" but that "every area . . . has a side that women understand better than men."[78] She was referring to the "family court, orphans' court, [and] children's court," for which one "absolutely needs a law degree," but also human understanding. She was convinced that "Europe made the greatest improvement in the field of worker's welfare when they nominated women as industrial inspectors."[79]

Women's increased role in public life, especially as nurses and volunteers, continued beyond wartime. Women were actively involved in the rehabilitation of wounded soldiers as well as in caring for destitute children. Their new visibility coincided with many women's expectations of greater equality. In an American Relief Administration report on the "Mother's and Babies' Breakfast Action in Hungary," Hedwig Singer described how nurses from the National Stefánia Association for the Protection of Mothers and Children were selected to assist in every child dispensary as child specialists. Because these nurses were "notified of every birth taking place in Budapest" and were thus in "constant contact with the mothers of new-born infants," the incoming foreign relief workers felt "greatly assisted" by their presence. In addition to these sisters, the American Relief Administration welcomed help from women involved in the "various ladies' associations," who helped make up "a fine group of young women."[80]

Yet women's wartime and postwar activism did not necessarily result in women's long-term liberation. Some of the accomplishments toward women's emancipation could not be upheld throughout the interwar period, as Ingrid Sharp and Matthew Stibbe make clear. Once men returned from battle, societies aimed at "reintegrating the men into civil society so that 'the natural order of things' would be restored." Some women would then step back into "domesticity and maternity."[81] While women's activity in the field of child relief in postwar Hungary was still encouraged, it was expected that the work would be performed according to clearly demarcated gender roles that were considered instrumental in the regeneration of the nation. The profession of nurse fit the conservative pattern of divided gender roles, which recognized women's "inherently feminine capacity for comfort and healing."[82] Women's position was thus somewhat equivocal. Eve Colpus describes female activism, captured in the idea of the "active cheery worker," as mirroring "a specifically gendered conceit of the interwar period," which facilitated "the positive expression of selfhood."[83] Clearly, women's postwar activism in the child protection arena laid the foundation for innovative notions and practices of women's activism for decades to come.

Relieving the Capital's Destitute Children and Mothers

The Budapest Central Aid Committee (Budapesti Központi Segítő Bizottság) was established in 1914. It had its own social welfare departments, including one for the protection of children and one for mothers. Under the leadership of József Madzsar, a department for the protection of mothers was set up because financial help to mothers from the state was found to be insufficient, as "women struggled with the difficulties of the last stages of pregnancy and during childbed." Furthermore, in times of war, "one needs to take twice as much care of infants," since "infant mortality rises as a result of the worsening economic conditions." The department's roles were to protect mothers "during the last weeks of pregnancy"; to ensure "hygienic handling during [their] children's birth"; to extend special "care for mothers to recover during the first days after birth"; and to help "mothers succeed with breastfeeding their children themselves." The department for children's protection put its energies into the establishment and running of children's daycare centers and schools; providing food and clothing; and offering entertainment, education, and children's placement in orphanages and night care.[84]

Building on the work of the Budapest Central Aid Committee since 1914 and making use of the infrastructure it had set up, Budapest's first Welfare Center (Budapest Főváros Népjóléti Központja) was launched in June 1916.[85] It took over the task of protecting mothers and children in Budapest. Hugó Csergő, the center's first director, stated that two years in, the staff were still only "at the very beginning" of implementing a governmental system of child and mother protection.[86] But the center could rely on the work done by its predecessor, the Budapest Central Aid Committee. The Welfare Center was under the guidance of Budapest's then mayor, István Bárczy. Its aims were to overcome "the weaknesses of the old incomplete system" and to address "new miseries, needs, illnesses and other currently burning concerns that are calling for help."[87] The 1919 *Red Book of Budapest's Misery (A Budapesti Nyomor Vöröskönyve)*, published by the center, refers to the city as the "capital of the poor," noting that industrial growth had not gone hand in hand with the "economic growth of its inhabitants" and their social empowerment.[88]

Because child and infant mortality were seen as a consequence of poor living conditions and a lack of modern care for mothers and children, the Welfare Center offered a range of provisions to pregnant, delivering, and nursing mothers. However, the center was pulled between opposing demands for the centralization and professionalization of mother and child protection and a wish to maintain and support local welfare initiatives. In the *Red Book of Budapest's Misery*, the center maintained that "proper mother's protection" required some form of "decent decentralization" to preserve the various welfare organizations' agency and autonomy. At the same time, trained personnel should be employed in every welfare station to improve the quality of the overall work, and a central office should coordinate and control the welfare system of the entire country.[89] Against this background, the Welfare Center was meant, at last, to provide systematic governmental backing to what until then had been a mostly "humanitarian" endeavor, finally "minimizing the need for poverty relief."[90] The center was tasked with exercising "guidance, supervision and control" over the capital's various existing welfare activities. It also had the task of establishing "links between social and governmental organizations" active in the field of social welfare, so that government and society initiatives were able to "smoothly complement each other."[91]

Sándor Szana, the director of the state asylum, stressed in 1917 the importance of close cooperation between doctors and medical facilities and welfare and child protection institutions. His experience in the state asylum had taught him that it was not enough to tell mothers "to give their children better food, and warmer clothes, and to send them in the summer to a village," if they were perfectly aware that "the mother could not do this." Instead, he suggested that a care worker should "stand next to the unlucky mother" and organize all these important items for her. Such a person could come from one of Budapest's many philanthropic organizations. A worker with the necessary knowledge of available social welfare services could obtain "dresses, shoes, lunch, milk, bread, summer vacations, swimming at Lake Balaton, all for free."[92]

The Budapest Welfare Center was organized into twelve departments. Departments 6, 7, and 8 dealt, respectively, with the "protection of mothers and infants" (*anya- és csecsemővédő szakosztály*), the "protection of children" (*gyermekvédő szakosztály*), and the "provision of children's clothing" (*gyermekfelruházó szakosztály*). Other departments looked after public health, feeding, financial support, and legal protection among other things. The Department for Mothers and Infants, under the leadership of József Szterényi, was charged with establishing a link "between public authorities, associations, bodies and institutions" in the capital, in the field of welfare. It aspired to function as a "think tank" (*véleményező*) and preparatory body, offering guidelines for maternal and infant protection, which it would help implement. It was to professionally guide, support, develop, and give advice to daycare centers and institutions that helped with children's feeding, placements overnight or in orphanages, allocation to summer colonies during the holidays, and anything else related to the protection of children. The Department for Children's Clothing saw to material relief.[93]

When they were due to give birth, mothers were free to decide where their baby would be delivered—at home or in a maternity hospital. If the birth was to be at home, women were offered "midwife vouchers" so they could be attended by a midwife during labor. In 1917, 1,401 midwife vouchers were issued, and in 1918, the number was 1,219. These are large numbers for a new initiative, but they represent a small fraction of the overall of births. An expectant mother's more usual route was to utilize one of the maternity homes (*szülőotthon*). The Welfare Center might take care of the mother's other children, who would either be placed with extended family or join the mother in the "Márta [birth] ward," so that they would not "remain without care."[94]

In the first four to five months after a child's birth, breastfeeding mothers were entitled to financial help of "10 crowns monthly" from the Budapest Welfare Center. Breastfeeding mothers were also prioritized in access to milk and foodstuffs. To help with aftercare, the center equipped very poor mothers with an "infant box," which contained "diapers, baby dresses, small shirts, underwear, pajamas, elastic pacifiers, and Nestlé milk powder." In 1917, the center could buy a large stock of necessary supplies for the infant boxes from the Budapest Central Aid Committee, though purchasing cotton turned out to be difficult. Instead of cotton, the center bought "linen flour sacks" (*vászon liszteszsákocska*), from which diapers and small dresses could be made.

By 1918, four years into the war, however, the economic situation had worsened. The center had difficulties filling infant boxes and obtaining items such as pacifiers. By the winter of 1918, children were reported to be "dressed in uncomfortable paper." Due to a "painful lack" of money, the center had to postpone opening a "transitional children's home," needed mainly for war orphans, and could barely implement its far-reaching welfare plans. To assist working parents and to prevent the exposure of unsupervised minors to "debauchery," the Welfare Center invested in the extension and institutionalization of daycare (*napközi*) for schoolchildren. The initiative was not new; it relied on already existing schemes. Many of Budapest's schools already had daycare facilities, supported by the Children's Friends Association (Gyermekbarát Egyesület), which was established in 1887 and provided cooked school dinners. When the number of children in need increased dramatically during the war, the schools turned to the National Relief Committee for Veterans

(Országos Hadsegélyző Bizottság) to back the Children's Friends Association financially.[95]

Midwives for Mothers: The Stefánia Association

Though the Budapest Welfare Center was in charge of the capital's child and mother protection initiatives, a National Stefánia Association for the Protection of Mothers and Infants (Országos Stefánia Szövetség az Anyák és Csecsemők Védelmére) was established for those who lived outside the city.[96] Founded in June 1915, the association took over the task of "the country-wide organization of mother and child protection."[97] This organization was essential for the expansion of women's activism and their training in the field of institutional child protection. The association was named after Crown Princess Stéphanie (Hungarian: Stefánia) from Belgium, who had become crown princess of Austria through her marriage to the Austrian crown prince Rudolf.[98] The Stefánia Association was headed by Count Albert Apponyi and a board composed largely of female aristocrats.[99] Its establishment represented the next step in the implementation of a state system of child protection in Hungary. The country was suffering an alarming decrease in birth rate and a rise in infant mortality as well as the "terrible waste of humans on the battlefield." The Stefánia Association aimed to provide emergency care to infants and mothers to remedy the first problem and to "strengthen" and "repair" the nation's "human material" as a response to the second.[100] There was a nationalist element in this: the Stefánia Association prioritized the care of pregnant mothers and infants in the belief that these two groups were essential to the rescue and rebuilding of the Hungarian nation.

The "existing state child protection and social movement" had been unequal to this "absolutely necessary" task, Lajos Keller explained in a report on the first ten years of the association's work. It was vital for "the future of the nation" that Hungary's high infant mortality rate of around 21 percent be lowered, and this required the systematic training of professionals and the continuous education of mothers. Before the Stefánia Association's founding, some of this work had been carried out by the Feminist Association for the Protection of Mothers and Children (Feministák Egyesülete Anya- és Gyermekvédelmi Bizottság), which had paid for visits to hospitals' maternity wards,[101] but a wider approach was necessary.

A main office for the Stefánia Association was set up at 10 Vas Street in the center of Budapest. In addition to a social welfare department, there were medical, publicity, and legal departments and, of course, a general department for administration. Establishing the various departments and local dispensaries was a difficult undertaking in itself, but the greatest challenge the Stefánia Association faced at the time was "lack of material means." Without funds and materials, the association could not really start its work. It succeeded nevertheless in opening "milk-kitchens, nurseries, daily nurseries, homes for pregnant [women] and mothers, convalescent homes, hospitals for children and infants."[102]

The association's key objective was to provide welfare to all mothers in need; it promised that it would not discriminate. "Racial, linguistic or religious differences" did not bar access, and it matter not whether a child was born "in or out of wedlock."[103] Marius Turda has explained other objectives as well: to "stimulate the activity of the state in management of child welfare services" and "to increase public awareness of the eugenic role of motherhood."[104] The Stefánia Association did not see itself as a classical charity organization but as a prime mover in building a physically healthy population. Its policy toward the mothers of Hungary was fourfold. First, it aimed to prevent them from falling into hopeless economic circumstances because of their pregnancy and child-rearing. Second, it discouraged them from delivering their babies at home, as was customary. Third, it urged mothers to breastfeed personally and not give their babies over to a wet nurse. Finally, it offered mothers professional advice about the best way to care for their newborns.[105] Instead of aftercare, the Stefánia Association believed in the power of preventive care.[106] It sought to educate by means of a publicity campaign that included "pictures, pamphlets and lectures." This campaign tried to impress on the population how important it was for mothers to raise their infants healthily. Where there was ignorance, poverty, or bad habits, it sought to "correct public opinion from a moral, religious and patriotic point of view."[107] The emphasis was on educating "healthy mothers" instead of simply solving health problems for them.[108] Already during the war, training courses for home health visitors had started in Budapest, Kassa, Kolozsvár, Nagyvárad, Pécs, Arad, Temesvár, Szeged, and Szombathely. While all these cities were becoming equipped with maternity homes, milk kitchens, and children's homes, with the Treaty of Trianon, the Stefánia Association lost access to the now cut-off cities where it had established many of its activities and thus had to discontinue its services there.[109]

One of the Stefánia Association primary undertakings was to collect and publicize knowledge about the proper upbringing of children. To disseminate knowledge on infant nursing and care, it produced a publication titled *Anyák kiskátéja* (Mother's little catechism), issued to provide guidance for mothers to use in their everyday lives.[110] In its push to propagate

Fig. 4.4. A mother school. Unknown photographer, *Melléklet a Magyarság*, February 26, 1925, 11.

its educational work, the association also relied heavily on word of mouth. "Mothers' schools" (*anyák iskolája*), as shown in figure 4.4, in every town and village had a Stefánia dispensary where popular lectures were held. Mother schools were also increasingly set up in the districts of Budapest. Doctors gave partly scientific, partly educational talks while the midwives of the Stefánia Association took care of any children who had been brought along, giving them afternoon tea and reading them stories. It was believed that Hungary's high infant mortality rate was "caused by the ignorance and superstition of the people," who had been further "corrupted" by the war and its aftermath.[111] So the mother's schools were heavily publicized and attempted to draw in as many mothers as possible.

The Stefánia Association invested most of its energy in the systematic training of midwives. The first training for midwives took place in November 1915, and this quickly became one of the association's core programs. It spearheaded the comprehensive and systematic professionalization of child protection based on "skilled and professional work." A central midwives' office (*védőnői iroda*) was set up in Budapest, and in 1917, thirty-two midwives were already employed there. The midwives not only provided mothers with "health-related and social guidance" but represented them in dealings with the authorities and associations. They were equally involved in helping the

Child Protection Department of the County Guardianship Authority (*árvaszék*), which took care of children who had been born out of wedlock and had been abandoned.[112]

Lajos Keller, director of the Stefánia Association, maintained that the "social and preventive worker" in Hungary had to "overcome quite different difficulties" in modernizing birthing and child-rearing from the social workers in "Western Europe." Essentially, he argued, "protection of mothers and infants" was the most difficult of all the kinds of social work because of the "cultural state of people" and their unwillingness to follow the midwives' advice. He gave examples from the "small communities and farms" where nurses had not even been allowed to enter the house and dogs had been set on them. Even in easier cases, it took time to gain women's trust. The nurses had to battle against local "superstition," "popular customs," the "antipathy of relatives," and "charlatans" who gave contrary advice. There could be no comparison with conditions in the Western European nations. These had "financial means" and the "cultural level" was "more developed." Hence, Keller asked that the Hungarian people be "satisfied" with the work and results being accomplished by the Stéfania Association's nurses.[113]

Addressing infant mortality became a central piece of the Stéfania Association's effort. Some years before Keller made his plea, József Madzsar, head of the Department for the Protection of Mothers, had compared Hungary's birth and mortality rates for 1901–5 with the corresponding statistical tables for Western and other Central and East European countries. He concluded that the main problem for Hungary was not its birth rate but its high mortality rate, which was 21 percent for children below the age of twelve months.[114] "Scientific determination" of the causes of child mortality was needed.[115] Madzsar was able to identify two major causes of child mortality: "poverty and [the] mothers' ignorance." The Stéfania Association should counter these, first, by developing "means to economically protect mothers" and, second, by making great efforts to "enlighten, educate and control infant care."[116] Keller even went so far as to calculate the economic value for the Hungarian state of "the saving of one human life." On average, the sum was five hundred pengős. According to contemporary sociologists, "human life" had enormous value. Keller therefore concluded that investment in mother and infant protection did "not represent an investment without profit" and that the Hungarian state could have no "more economical, more useful, more necessary, and more important work" than to cut mortality rates. In the "dismembered state" of Hungary, investment in infants and children, so that they grew "in number and in strength," was the sole way to construct a better national future.[117] Any mother whom the Stefánia Association could successfully help to bear, nurse, and rear a child was judged to contribute more to the "wealth of the nation" than if she were employed.[118]

The Stefánia Association realized that it could lower mortality rates if infants were better fed. Under the leadership of Madzsar, the association sent out "trained, good spirited and reliable noble women" to achieve this. The organization then fought a fierce battle against the "artificial" and inappropriate feeding that was judged to have caused infants to "waste away." It invested eighteen crowns per person per month to incentivize mothers to nurse and raise their infants themselves and not use wet nurses.[119] It went so far as to implement regulations prescribing which mothers were entitled to receive milk products and which were not. According to Madzsar, "mother milk" alone was "at least as important as all other measures put together" for an infant's well-being. He advocated a huge publicity campaign.[120] As Susan Zimmermann argues, meeting the needs of children in poverty made an ideal cause for social legislation. At times, mother and child protection developed into an instrument that controlled mothers and worked against vagrant and "asocial" children.[121] The Stefánia Association used various control measures to ensure that "every mother breastfed her own child" and that only mothers whom a doctor had certified unfit to do so could receive artificial "infant food from the milk kitchen."[122] The issue had become an instrument of social control over the mother's body, and the Stefánia Association an important engine in the practices of mothering and the nationalization of welfare.

Institutionalizing Children's Welfare

To achieve its aims across the country, the Stefánia Association worked closely with local communities, authorities, and the state.[123] The year 1917 was decisive in the institutionalization of social welfare and child protection in Hungary. After the human losses in the first two years of the war, the government realized the necessity of seeing to the country's regeneration. Emperor Charles IV, King of Hungary (Károly Király), was crowned in Budapest on December 30, 1916. He and his wife, Zita of Bourbon-Parma, encouraged the establishment of a system of governmental welfare. The *Pesti Hírlap* in June 1917 expressed admiration for the young king's support and the publicity it generated for the government's plans. It was something completely new for the royal family to be concerned with "guaranteeing political rights to the people," and even more novel for it to want to further "welfare" measures. The trials of the war had made this necessary, for only in "a secure, comfortable and calm house could [people] forget and recuperate from the sufferings [they had] experienced." King Charles "really want[ed] to help and solve the problems," and, under his leadership, the new government was committed to realize "point by point" what the "social workers" (*szellemi munkások*) had been "fighting for" for years.[124]

In June 1917, at the same time as a similar development in Austria, a Hungarian Ministry of Labor and Social Welfare (Népjóléti és Munkaügyi Minisztérium) was founded.[125] Questions of labor, insurance, housing, child welfare, health care and social welfare, and care for war invalids and orphans came within its remit.[126] The masses of orphaned, displaced, neglected, and impoverished children in Budapest and beyond were so large that the Hungarian state considered bringing child protection under government control. Child protection started to evolve into child welfare. The government placed the Stefánia Association in control of the management and implementation of the Hungarian system of protection for mothers and infants.[127] The decree to this effect was issued by Gábor Ugron from the Ministry of the Interior.[128] The Stefánia Association was to "direct and to develop the organization for the protection of mothers and infants in Hungary."[129] On the basis of this decree, a Hungarian national system of mother and child protection slowly took shape.[130] Much energy was invested in health education, public lectures, publicity, and practical publications. Officially this all came under the authority of the Ministry of the Interior.[131] The Stefánia Association made mother and child welfare a serious, central, and national undertaking.[132]

The Stefánia Association's new Institute for the Protection of Mothers and Infants had three departments: one for the protection of mothers, one for infants, and a social department. The department for the protection of mothers supervised "homes for pregnant, birthing, puerperal and nursing mothers" as well as a free gynecological clinic and a counseling center. It also addressed mothers' hygiene and education.[133] The infant department oversaw an infants' hospital, an infants' home, a milk kitchen, an institute for infant care, and a model day nursery.[134] There was also a laboratory, a clinic for toddlers, and a consultancy for nursing mothers. The social department maintained a library, a permanent exhibition hall, traveling exhibitions, journals on mother and infant protection, an office for publicity, and a counseling room. It ran courses and residential schools for professionals, doctors, midwives, and social workers as well as an agency to register and employ midwives and infant nurses.[135] By 1920, the Stefánia Association had established fifty-eight dispensaries, twenty health centers, and a range of maternity rooms, mothers' homes, and infant hospitals both in cities and rural areas.[136]

Circulating Material Items

Material objects started to be circulated among families in need and expectant mothers. "Poor pregnant women" were given "mobile birthing boxes" (*szülészeti vándorládák*), and needy parents could obtain "mobile infant beds" (*vándor kosarak*).[137] Many local child welfare activities were supported by international relief organizations that wanted a visual testimony of donated gifts. Figure 4.5 shows one of the mobile infant beds donated by the Stefánia Association but financed by the Save the Children International Union (hence the large SCIU emblem) and made from materials contributed by Pope Benedict XV.[138] Demonstrating the bed's usefulness is a real infant—mirroring the SCIU emblem and visually bringing the organization's philosophy to life. The beds were typical material objects lent to mothers who could not afford to buy them. Such items helped ensure their baby's survival in the first weeks after birth. As the mobile beds circulated among families in need, this initiative enabled the relief organizations to target large groups of mothers and children. A "wandering baby outfit system" was also distributed through the various institutes of the Stefánia Association. Since clothing and linen were scarce in the capital, the association relied, to a great extent, on material gifts from the American Red Cross.[139]

The infant beds also came to symbolize the professionalization of child protection and the emerging child welfare system.[140] These institutions, and then the state, were becoming increasingly accountable for the protection of children and mothers. Objects such as a birthing box helped make the birth safe; infant beds helped infants survive their first weeks. As these physical objects circulated between expecting mothers and the relief organizations, they created close linkages between those in need and the providers. These objects furthermore "helped to create a sense of belonging" and were essential in forging "social ties" and "shared identities" among those in need.[141] The mothers who could not afford an infant bed or linens shared this destiny with one another, and this sharing was expressed in the circulation of the objects.

Donated and borrowed clothing performed a similar role. Because "textiles often function in intimate contact with the human body," donated clothes for the infants functioned as a material bridge between the donor and the recipient. The Stefánia Association's maternity equipment became ubiquitous, part of the everyday lives of mothers and families. Beyond their

Fig. 4.5. Mobile infant beds. Unknown photographer, CH AEG AP 92.105.75 (4).

economic, monetary, and cultural value, the items also carried social and medical value.[142] They exemplified an emerging culture of child and mother protection and education while equally representing a culture of shortages, where maximal utilization mattered. The beds were only to be borrowed, then passed on. Practices of frugality and reuse enabled the relief organizations to help more needy families. The beds also testified to a new "culture of control." Before, during, and after the birth of her baby, a mother was expected to follow the established guidelines. Insofar as materials serve as "important means for groups to distinguish themselves from others," the Stefánia Association distinguished itself from previous philanthropic organizations by providing professional welfare and medical objects that implied new practices of motherhood. The association gained a new social "power over things and via things."[143] We know little about how the donated gifts, beds, clothes, and boxes were received. Nevertheless, these objects showcase how ideas of child protection became translated into practical, everyday life. They helped families provide for their children during the challenging postwar years.

Conclusion

The destruction of war and the dissolution of the empire not only brought material poverty and strain on child protection facilities; the social and economic crisis simultaneously forced change and triggered the expansion and professionalization of child protection. A variety of old and new local initiatives were brought to bear on the problems of infant mortality and child starvation. Techniques from the new nutrition sciences, educational displays, restorative summer camps, midwife training, orphanages, and material objects all played their part.

The postwar child rescue initiatives relied on several decades of preparatory work that informed the infrastructure of philanthropic, medical, and child protection endeavors. Prior to the ravages of war, Hungary was far from backward in this field. The system of care in the country was, as this chapter has demonstrated, a forerunner of the welfare systems that were to emerge in Europe as a whole. Especially in the capital city, many child protection organizations and facilities were active. During the first decade of the twentieth century, social welfare organizations had been professionalized and institutionalized. Volunteer organizations and local women relief workers dominated the missions to the destitute children and to expectant mothers and families in need. In the aftermath of the war, however, the city's organizations were destitute and ran with few resources; thus, international help and intervention was an essential partner and supplement to domestic endeavors.

Notes

1. Dwork, *War Is Good for Babies*, 211.
2. Mahood, *Feminism and Voluntary Action*, 167.
3. Ladd-Taylor, *Mother-work: Women, Child Welfare, and the State*, 33.
4. Behrends and Kohlrausch, *Races to Modernity*, 3, 8.
5. Mahood, *Feminism and Voluntary Action*, 168.
6. Arsan, Lewis, and Richard, "Editorial," 164.
7. Under the government of Sándor Wekerle (1906–10), new social reforms sought to counter the harmful social consequences of industrialization, especially the exploitation and neglect of children.

8. Szénásy, "Országos Stefánia Szövetség (1915-1941)," 415-17.
9. "Szegénység és jótékonyság," 11.
10. Zimmermann and Melinz, *Gyermeksorsok és gyermekvédelem*, 44.
11. [Valentin Clouzot?], "Abrégé du compte rendu de l'activité de la Ligue pour la protection des enfants en Hongrie," in XII. Rapports de Budapest. ACICR B Mis 4.5./640 a 4.5./693, 1254, ICRC Archive.
12. Ibid.
13. Talk given by Sándor Karsai at the yearly assembly, November 28, 1907. See Sándor Karsai, *Jelentés az Országos Gyermekvédő Liga 1906-7 évi működéséről* (Budapest: Thalia Nyomda, 1907), [1, 3].
14. "Abrégé du compte rendu."
15. Ibid.
16. Karsai, *Jelentés az Országos Gyermekvédő Liga*, [13].
17. "Az Országos Gyermekvédő Liga intézményei," *A Gyermekvédelem Lapja* 15, no. 1 (March 1926): 39.
18. On interwar philanthropy, see Colpus, *Female Philanthropy in the Interwar World*.
19. Mahood, *Feminism and Voluntary Action*, 211.
20. Mulley, *The Woman Who Saved the Children*, 112.
21. Schwartz, *Shifting Voices*, 14.
22. Vay and Zichy, *Az Országos Gyermekvédő Liga ismertetése*, 3.
23. Ibid., 14, 3, 9.
24. Zimmermann and Melinz, *Gyermeksorsok és gyermekvédelem*, 39; Wingfield and Bucur, *Gender and War*, 4; Sharp and Stibbe, *Aftermaths of War*, 6.
25. Cabanes, *The Great War*, 257.
26. Hoover, "Children's Relief and Democracy," 1.
27. Cabanes, *The Great War*, 257.
28. On nurses, see Irwin, "Nurses without Borders."
29. Gill, *Calculating Compassion*, 188.
30. Vay and Zichy, *Az Országos Gyermekvédő Liga ismertetése*, 7-8; Karsai, *Jelentés az Országos Gyermekvédő Liga*, 3.
31. Talk given by Sándor Karsai, [8].
32. Neugebauer, *Az Országos Gyermekvédő Liga Alapszabályai*, 1.
33. Talk given by Kálmán Széll at the yearly assembly, November 28, 1907. See Karsai, *Jelentés az Országos Gyermekvédő Liga*, [6].
34. Karsai, *Jelentés az Országos Gyermekvédő Liga*, [3].
35. Zimmermann and Melinz, *Gyermeksorsok és gyermekvédelem*, 38.
36. Karsai, *Jelentés az Országos Gyermekvédő Liga*, [3].
Jelentés az Országos Gyermekvédő Liga 1907-8 évi működéséről, 3.
37. "Abrégé du compte rendu," 1254.
38. Karsai, *Jelentés az Országos Gyermekvédő Liga*, [12].
39. Neugebauer, *Az Országos Gyermekvédő Liga alapszabályui*, 4-5.
40. Karsai, *Jelentés az Országos Gyermekvédő Liga*, 14, 3.
41. Zimmermann and Melinz, *Gyermeksorsok és gyermekvédelem*, 38.
42. Neugebauer, *Az Országos Gyermekvédő Liga alapszabálya*, 1.
43. Karsai, *Jelentés az Országos Gyermekvédő Liga*, [13].
44. "Közgyűlés," in *Jelentés az Országos Gyermekvédő Liga*, [3].
45. Prohászka, *Az Országos Gyermekvédő Liga*, 24.
46. Karsai, *Jelentés az Országos Gyermekvédő Liga*, [14].

47. Ibid., [3, 14].
48. On women's bodies and war, see Canning, "Feminist History after the Linguistic Turn."
49. Zahra, "Each Nation Only Cares for Its Own," 1383.
50. Barnett, *Empire of Humanity*, 87.
51. Dwork, *War Is Good for Babies*, 212.
52. "Relief Problems in Hungary: First Reports on Work Being Done by Red Cross in Cooperation with Other American Agencies," *Red Cross Bulletin* 4 (February 8, 1920): 7.
53. Julia Vajkai to Eglantyne Jebb, May 15, 1920, Western Aid and the Global Economy, Series 1: SCF Archives, London, Reels 15–35. EJ 151. Hungary I/3: League for the Protection with Children and Holiday Homes: Correspondence, 1920, microfilm, Columbia University.
54. Rozsi Vajkai, "In the Slums of Budapest," 131.
55. "Heroische Frauen," *Pester Lloyd* 83, no. 170 (July 26, 1936): 4–6, 6.
56. "Union Internationale de Secours aux enfants: Extract from Report of Bunier. Delegate of C.I.C.R.," 1920/10, 1–2, 2, Eglantyne Jebb Papers Hungary, A 0407, EJ 155 Hungary, Folder 2, 1920–21, International Commissioners Reports and Correspondence, SCF Archive, Birmingham.
57. Pettkó-Szandtner, *Child Protection by the Royal Hungarian State*, 5–6, 16–25. The figures are from 1926.
58. Prohászka, *Az Országos Gyermekvédő Liga*, 24.
59. Asyle d'Enfants de l'Etat á Pécs, Concerne: Repatriment des enfants d'origin Slave a Szabadka, Rapports de Budapest. Mis. 4.5./694 á 4.5/790, 1352–1502. Archive of the ICRC.
60. Lévai, "Az elhanyagolt gyermekegészség," 153.
61. Barnett, *Empire of Humanity*, 86.
62. Guest, "Starvation and Misery in Hungary," 6.
63. James Pedlow to A. Ross Hill, Budapest, July 27, 1921, Sheet 5, Records of the American National Red Cross 1917–34, Record Group 953.62/08, Commission to Hungary, WWI Reports, NARA.
64. Rottenbiller, *Az Országos Gyermekvédő Liga Harminc Évi Működése*, 23.
65. Pettkó-Szandtner, *Child Protection by the Royal Hungarian State*, 11.
66. "Abrégé du compte rendu."
67. "Inured to War, Vienna Crowds Theaters, Cafes," 7.
68. Wingfield and Bucur, *Gender and War*, 6.
69. See Rachamimov, "'Female Generals' and 'Siberial Angels'"; Healy, "Civilizing the Soldier."
70. Schultheiss, *Bodies and Souls*, 161, 168.
71. Ladd-Taylor, *Mother-work*, 33.
72. Selskar Gunn, "Public Health in Hungary," December 13, 1924, Collection RF, Record Group 1.1., Series 750J, Box 4, Folders 37–38, 102–24, 121, Rockefeller Archive Center.
73. Ibid.
74. Mrs. Julia Vajkai to the Secretary General of the International Save the Children Union, Mission de la Croix Rouge Hongroise en Suisse, March 29, 1920, CH AEG AP 92.21.2 (1). Julia Vajkai died on October 13, 1956.
75. "General Conditions Hungary," 1919, 1–2, 2, Hungary-Causes of Distress in Central Europe, 507, Eglantyne Jebb Papers, Baltic States Finland EJ 77–96. A413. EJ 240. Continent and the East. Various. SCF Archive.
76. Mahood, *Feminism and Voluntary Action*, 143.
77. Mr. W. A. MacKenzie to Julia Vajkai, January 31, 1922, CH AEG AP 92.21.2.
78. "Békés forradalom," 565.

79. "Julia Vajkai," mentioned in "Békés forradalom," 565.
80. Singer, "Mothers' and Babies' Breakfast Action," 35.
81. Sharp and Stibbe, *Aftermaths of War*, 7, 13.
82. Schultheiss, *Bodies and Souls*, 6.
83. Colpus, *Female Philanthropy in the Interwar World*, 3.
84. Bárczy, "A főváros segítő munkája," 2, 8, 7.
85. Some sources cite 1917 as a founding date. However, many from 1916 already mention the Welfare Center; for example, "A hatóság és a társadalom együttműködéséről." See also Bihari, *1914: A nagy háború száz éve*.
86. Csergő, *A Budapesti nyomor vöröskönyve*, 95.
87. "'Népjóléti Központba szervezik Budapest jótékonysági akcióját," 4.
88. Csergő, *A Budapesti nyomor vöröskönyve*, 13.
89. Ibid., 108.
90. "'Népjóléti Központba szervezik Budapest jótékonysági akcióját," 4.
91. "A hatóság és a társadalom együttműködéséről és a Népjóléti Központról," 69.
92. Szana, "A gyermekkor közegészségügyének bajai," 206–8.
93. "A hatóság és a társadalom," 70, 73.
94. "A magyar gyermekvédelem kettős jubileuma," 95–96.
95. Csergő, *A Budapesti nyomor vöröskönyve*, 95, 98, 116, 118–19.
96. Even today, the association's headquarters is used for child welfare activities.
97. Országos Stefánia Szövetség, *Jelentés a Stefánia-Szövetség működéséről*, 53.
98. Stefánia was originally crown princess of Belgium, but after marrying Crown Prince Rudolf of Austria, she became a member of the Habsburg dynasty.
99. These aristocrats were the wives of György Bánffy, Count István Czebrián, Count Sándor Teleki, István Bárczy, and Count Rafael Zichy.
100. Keller, *Országos Stefánia Szövetség*, 8.
101. Ibid., 8–9.
102. Ibid., 7–9. Vilmos Tauffer and János Bókay, two well-known professors, headed the medical department (*orvosi osztály*) of the Stefánia Association. The propaganda department was run by Count Rafael Zichy and Pál Ruffy, the legal department by state secretary Béla Kozmai Kun, and the administrative department (*közigazgatási szakosztály*) by Sándor Kőszegi.
103. "A Stefánia-Liga az anyák és csecsemők védelmére," *Fővárosi Közlöny* 25, no. 71 (October 30, 1914): 1.
104. Turda, *The History of East-Central European Eugenics*, 216.
105. "A Stefánia-Liga az anyák és csecsemők védelmére," 1.
106. Keller, "A magyar anyavédelem," 3.
107. Keller, *Report on the Activities of the National Association for 1928*, 8.
108. "A Stefánia-Liga az anyák és csecsemők védelmére," 1.
109. Lajos Keller, History of the Stefánia Society: Its Activities and the American Red Cross, NARA 953.62-08, Commission to Hungary, WWI Reports, 5.
110. Keller, *Országos Stefánia Szövetség*, 9.
111. Keller, *Annual Report on the Activities of the Stephania National Association*, 5–6.
112. Keller, *Országos Stefánia Szövetség*, 9–11.
113. Keller, *Report on the Activities of the National Association for 1928*, 3.
114. Madzsar, *Az anya- és csecsemővédelem országos szervezése*.
115. Madzsar, *Mit akar a Stefánia-Szövetség?*, 5.
116. *Königin Zita Anstalt*, 4–5.
117. Keller, *Report on the Activities of the National Association for 1928*, 6–7.

118. Lajos Keller, History of the Stefánia Society, 4.
119. "Mari és a gyermeke," *Az Est* 7, no. 55 (February 24, 1916): 5.
120. Madzsar, *Mit akar a Stefánia-Szövetség?*, 11.
121. Zimmermann and Melinz, *Gyermeksorsok és gyermekvédelem*, 8.
122. "Tájékoztató a magyar anya- és csecsemővédelem," 33–34.
123. Országos Stefánia Szövetség, *Jelentés a Stefánia-Szövetség működéséről*, 54.
124. "Népjólét," 1.
125. "Népjóléti minisztérium," 218.
126. Turda, *Eugenics and Nation*, 15.
127. Hungary's prime ministers were fast changing: István Tisza was prime minister until June 15, 1917; Móric Esterházy then took over until August 20, 1917; Sándor Wekerle, August 20, 1917, to October 31, 1918; and then Mihály Károlyi.
128. Keller, *Annual Report on the Activities of the Stephania National Association*, 5.
129. Keller, *Report on the Activities of the National Stephania Association for 1928*, 7.
130. Keller, *Országos Stefánia Szövetség*, 11.
131. Kiss, "Egészség és politika," 111.
132. Stefánia Szövetség, *Jelentés a Stefánia-Szövetség működéséről*, 60.
133. Stefánia Szövetség, *Országos Magyar Anya*, 2; Keller, *Országos Stefánia Szövetség*, 13.
134. Keller, *Országos Stefánia Szövetség* 13.
135. Stefánia Szövetség, *Országos Magyar Anya*, 2.
136. Keller, *Országos Stefánia Szövetség*, 13.
137. Pettkó-Szandtner, "Anya- és csecsemővédelem," 1.
138. Delegate of the ICRC in Budapest to SCIU, Budapest, October 18, 1921, Eglantyne Jebb Papers Hungary, A 0407, EJ 166 Hungary, Folder 2, 1920–21, International Commissioners Reports and Correspondence, SCF Archives, Birmingham.
139. Stefánia Association to Ernest J. Swift at the ARC, Budapest, January 12, 1925, 953.42, Hungary, Budapest Uni, W.W. I. Clothing (infant layettes), Records of the American National Red Cross, NARA.
140. For a valuable introduction to the history of things, see Gerritsen and Riello, *Writing Material Culture History*; and Derix et al., "Der Wert der Dinge."
141. Charpy, "How Things Shape Us," 212.
142. Kelley, "Time, Wear and Maintenance"; O'Connor, "Anthropology, Archaeology, History," 79.
143. Charpy, "How Things Shape Us," 205, 209, 214.

5

INFRASTRUCTURES

Materializing "Glocal" Relief

Throughout Europe and beyond, hunger and hunger relief, especially for children, became key postwar issues. Having explored the domestic child welfare institutions in the previous chapter, this chapter shifts the perspective to the new international solidarity for starving civil populations that manifested itself in children's relief in Budapest. The chapter scrutinizes the creation of an international humanitarian relief infrastructure in Hungary's capital city by tracing the humanitarian connections between Budapest, Geneva, the United States, and Great Britain. Children's destitution and hunger made the temporary migration of relief organizations and relief workers to Budapest necessary. The discussion here explores how relief efforts were established and coordinated, detailing the cooperation between the American Relief Administration, the Save the Children Fund and its international union (the Save the Children International Union), the American Red Cross, the International Committee of the Red Cross (ICRC), and local Hungarian institutions. These were the so-called foreign missions who sat, literally, at a common table, where children's relief was debated and planned. Examining the infrastructure that was necessary for the delivery of food aid and other relief endeavors enables us to understand the "glocal" dimension of food politics—the interaction between the local and the global, between the humanitarian donor, local relief workers, and the child recipients. Exploring the humanitarian feeding stations for schoolchildren and milk kitchens for mothers and infants, the chapter details how the foreign missions and local relief workers cooperated in providing for Budapest's hungry children.

Assessing Local Needs

International aid to Europe began in 1914 when Herbert Hoover organized a Commission for Relief in Belgium to aid the civil population in the

German-occupied country, which had been plunged into a serious food crisis.[1] He had gained some experience working on food relief in France and knew that he could help stricken Europe and its children by providing food.[2] Once the United States entered World War I in 1917, the US Food Administration was created, charged with shipping food supplies to the nation's European allies and to neutral parties suffering from lack of food.[3] Hoover was in charge. Initially, he restricted relief efforts to "the relief of such populations in Europe and countries contiguous thereto, outside of Germany, German Austria, Hungary, Bulgaria, and Turkey."[4] As the American nutritionists Ralph Kellogg and Alonzo Taylor made clear, even this was an "immediate and very great, but not impossible, task" America had undertaken to ensure a "sufficient and regular supply of food" not only to the "armies of our fighting Allies" but also to the "no less great armies of working men and women in the war industries, and finally, of their women and children at home." Maintenance of food supplies was "an absolute necessity ... for the successful prosecution of the war."[5]

In February 1919, the American Relief Administration (ARA) was formed. President Woodrow Wilson appointed Hoover its director general and gave him full authority to oversee the distribution of food and clothing.[6] The ARA had a budget of $100 million, and the intention was to spread American ideals of democracy and humanitarianism along with these donations. American action was energetic. In 1921, Hoover claimed that US charitable associations had provided relief "through food, clothing, shelter and medical service" to "upwards of fifteen million" children in Central Europe since the beginning of the war.[7] Between November 1918 and September 1919, he arranged for the delivery of more than four million tons of food and other supplies. The United States had much spare food to ship to Europe.[8] By the summer of 1918, Hoover recalled, an "abundant crop" and "enormous savings" had secured the United States an immense advantage in this war on food.[9] Using food to provide aid to starving Central and Eastern Europe was not only a way of "divesting the United States of surplus food supplies" but also a way to "hold its agricultural competitors in European neutral states at bay."[10]

Before international relief reached Europe, the humanitarian organizations involved in distribution sent delegates on missions to the target countries to collect information. They went by ship or train, usually to the capital cities, and met with local politicians or welfare workers. Hoover himself went to London and Paris on July 11, 1918, accompanied by nutritional adviser Alonzo Taylor. Hoover wanted to discuss the nutritional needs of the Allied powers before setting up the Inter-Allied Food Council in the summer of 1918.¹¹ "Impressed by the simplicity of [Clemens von] Pirquet's mechanical method of determining the needs of children,"¹² Hoover brought the Austrian nutritionist to the United States shortly after the war, where Pirquet quickly became a key figure in the study of nutritional deficits and the physiological impact of starvation. Pirquet was particularly involved in the fight against rickets and tuberculosis, because they both seemed to be closely related to nutritional deficiencies. He had found that rickets resulted from the "combined effect of deficiency in the diet of a specific food constituent (vitamin) and lack of direct sunlight."¹³ In 1920, together with Harriette Chick, Pirquet developed the Pirquet System of Nutrition, a program designed to eliminate rickets among the children of Vienna. He conducted experiments with rickety children in an "American children's charity clinic in Meidling" with financial support from the ICRC.¹⁴ He promoted the scientifically based "rule of fighting rickets by '*Licht, Luft, Leberthrahn*'—air, light, cod-liver oil." Pirquet propagated his belief in children's proper, regular feeding as "the best means of preventive medicine." Most importantly, he recommended that artificial infant nutrition have "a much higher energy value" to quickly restore the infants' harmed health and constitution. ¹⁵

This new understanding of food and feeding spread through Europe and beyond. Yet this nutritional knowledge, as Amy L. Sayward observes, had already emerged in the late nineteenth and early twentieth centuries, when "scientists, doctors, scholars, and government bureaucrats gathered at the nexus between agriculture, nutrition, and public health" and agreed that nutrition science could "greatly benefit humankind—if it could be widely disseminated, understood and written into policy, not just nationally but internationally."¹⁶ It was in the postwar years that "these transnational nutritionists increasingly defined both national and international nutrition policy agendas," as in these times of nutritional crisis, they had been vested with increasing power to put their nutritional knowledge into practice.¹⁷ As child populations were suffering across Europe, standardized knowledge of the nutritional state had to be produced. Pirquet was aware that to obtain credible "statistical results," he would need to apply his "proper feeding principles" not just to individual children or small groups but to the masses. The "science of nutrition" needed to become a fundamental part of education so that "every individual" could profit from it. Pirquet revolutionized the understanding of hunger. Previously thought of as simply not having enough food, hunger was now seen as something more complex: the lack of certain nutritional elements in the diet.¹⁸ New knowledge about the ideal everyday diet triggered a new appreciation of "the calorie," which "allowed Americans to see food as an instrument of power."[19] Pirquet was fully aware that in "normal times" there should be "no general condition of hunger, and we daily satisfy our desire for food"; "deprivation of food and rest" were "exceptional conditions of life."[20]

Pirquet's method seemed ideal for the relief of hunger because it found the individual "judgment of doctors on the nutritional needs of individual children unnecessary" and created statistical knowledge for "administering relief during a famine period."[21] The "emergence of experimental knowledge and its transfer into social practice"[22] was the foundation on which the identification of nutritionally disadvantaged children was now based, and it determined the levels of supplementary feeding. Yet Pirquet was later criticized for his obsession with weight and calories and his unwillingness to consider unique bodies. By the 1940s, relief work discussed questions about how to determine need. It was by then widely acknowledged that "need varies . . . from case to case." Every social worker knew that "any attempt at sweeping mechanical methods of determining need result in grave inequities and serious hardship in individual cases."[23]

During the summer of 1918, the US Food Administration sent exploratory missions to Austria-Hungary and other Central and East European countries to determine levels of hunger, malnutrition, and food shortages in the region. Inspectors employed scientific methods to assess the children's physical condition and determine the availability of certain foodstuffs. Many reports highlighted the situation in Budapest, though many of these relied on local newspaper accounts. A report of August 10, 1918, originally published in the *Neues Pester Journal*, noted the high market prices of commodities such as eggs and fat and described how "women and children were standing at dawn waiting at the fat depots with their cards."[24] A telegram a month later reported that crops had been ruined by "snowstorms in June." The wheat had been so badly damaged that "the crop [would] probably be 30 per cent smaller than usual"; fruit crops and corn were still in good condition.[25] A special report on the crop situation in Hungary, dated July 13, 1918, complained that in the whole general area, the "potato, turnip and cabbage crops have been badly damaged by the late frosts."[26]

Whereas in previous years Hungary had exported much of its grain to Austria and other European countries, in 1918 this had to be discontinued because of a drastic shortage.[27] A "scientific" review of the availability of food products in Hungary helped the ARA determine which products needed to be imported. The ARA asked local authorities, charities, and welfare organizations to "contribute such native food supplies as were available."[28] American intervention would provide imports of "such necessary foodstuffs as were not locally available, such as milk, fats, and an inspection service for the purpose of maintaining the efficiency of the system."[107] Prices were assessed, because it was more economical to receive imports of "sugar and cocoa" from the United States at rates "considerably cheaper than local."[29]

The Rockefeller Foundation became similarly involved, sending delegates to determine the public health conditions. Between June and October 1920, Edwin R. Embree, secretary of the Rockefeller Foundation, visited Austria, Hungary, Poland, Yugoslavia, Germany, France, and Switzerland. In Budapest, he met local health workers and representatives of international relief organizations. He visited health care and relief facilities, making specific recommendations on how to relieve people's physical suffering and improve care in hospitals. In "general conversation" with Walter Lyman Brown of the American Red Cross, Embree tried to ascertain the character and mentality of Hungarians. In a subsequent report, he described them as being "entirely different creatures" from Americans, with emotions, reactions, and thoughts that were almost "Asiatic." It would be impossible "for Americans really, thoroughly to understand them." Character judgment was thought important in determining the ways to best meet local needs.[30] Two years later, in March 1922, the Rockefeller Foundation sent Selskar M. Gunn, a public health expert, to Budapest to submit a report. He observed that child welfare in Hungary had, up to then, been based on public assistance and did not take "matters of hygiene" into account.[31]

Several relief organizations tried to map nutritional needs. On September 1, 1921, the ARA published a "Hunger Map of Europe" in its bulletin, shown in figure 5.1. The map differentiated between "areas from which the ARA has withdrawn" (including Romania and Armenia) and "areas in which the ARA is now operating." The "Russian Famine Area," Hungary, Austria, Czechoslovakia, Poland, Estonia, Latvia, and Lithuania were still benefiting from ARA support. The Russian famine area faced the most urgent need; text below the map stated that, there, "distribution to children and invalids will not wait the result of the surveys."[32] A year earlier, in October 1920, Save the Children had published a similar map of "Europe's Need" in its monthly journal, *The Record*. Poland, Crimea, and Armenia had been identified as the areas with the "greatest distress," but, as a city, Budapest was also singled out in that category. Parts of Austria, Czechoslovakia, Estonia, Latvia, and Lithuania were also identified as regions where children were in danger. Maps such as these were used to show the target areas for relief, both to the organizations' working members and to current and potential donors. When scientific reports and nutritional maps indicated that relief measures were urgent, the international

Fig. 5.1. "Hunger Map of Europe." Unknown artist, *American Relief Administration Bulletin* 2, no. 16 (September 1921): 1.

humanitarian organizations acted quickly to ease the situations. Having calculated the possible food trade America would make with postwar Europe—the Americans wished to "earn a profit on this business"—and extolling the enormous efforts of his own nation, Hoover started exporting surplus food to Europe.[33]

Food Relief and Immediate Postwar Politics

Food relief to Central and Eastern Europe in the postwar era was embedded in the politics of the time. With the US relief program, Hoover and the ARA were pursuing political and ideological aims as well as economic and humanitarian ones.[34] The United States aimed to both scientifically relieve the greatest needs on the continent and help establish favorable circumstances in Europe for American foreign policy and business interests. A key aim was to prevent the westward spread of communist influence from the new Soviet state.

In Hungary, it looked as though this spread was indeed taking place. Between March 21 and August 1, 1919, a Soviet-style government came to power. Hoover did not allow delivery or distribution of food in this "red" zone. He kept strictly to his plan and, when he started bringing relief to Central European countries, excluded Bolshevist Hungary from donations altogether. Reporting on conditions in Hungary, an article in the *New York Times* of December 17, 1919, blamed the Bolshevists for the extensive pauperization of the children there. Its author argued that "the privations due to the war were enormously increased by the misrule of the Bolshevist Government," which Hungarian leaders had apparently "invited in" with hope "of winning a better boundary from the Peace Conference." The writer condemned this behavior, which brought "terrible harm" as no "territorial gains could have been worth the suffering which Hungary endured under the rule of Béla Kun."[35]

Hoover saw in Bolshevism a great threat, not just to "American social, political, economic and ethical values" but "to freedom and hope for Europe."[36] Instead of using the "obvious method" of employing "force to catch Béla Kun and his growing Red Army" and then crush them, Hoover decided on the alternative plan of "No Food for Bolshevists."[37] Already on March 26, 1919, five days after Hungary had proclaimed itself a Soviet republic, a letter from the ARA to the American Commission to Negotiate Peace highlighted the politically problematic role of food shipments to postwar Hungary. A consignment of twenty-five wagonloads of pork, which Hoover had sold to the Hungarian government, was on its way to Budapest from Trieste when it was stopped by the Yugoslav authorities in Zagreb. They did not want it to reach its destination and fall into the hands of the Bolshevists.[38] By July 5, 1919, Hoover was publicly reflecting on the danger of Bolshevist influence in Hungary. He feared that communist ideas were "impregnating the working classes throughout the area" and stated his conviction that "unless some means could be devised of abating the infection, the economic regeneration of Central and South-Eastern Europe would be difficult."[39]

On August 1, 1919, Kun's Bolshevist republic came to an end, just 133 days after its inception, and two weeks later, on August 12, 1919, the ARA started feeding twenty thousand children in Budapest. The ARA hoped to use food to discourage any further Bolshevik infiltration of the Hungarian state.[40] As Jacklyn Granick argues, "Food relief was America's answer, both humanitarian and political, to social chaos and revolution."[41] The Americans were particularly concerned about the situation in the capital city, which had been regarded as "the most American city in Europe" before the war.[42] The plight of the children in Budapest drew considerable attention. Departing from his original plan of supporting only former allies and neutral countries, Hoover started providing child relief to former enemy territories, shipping large amounts of food, cotton, clothing, coal, and medical equipment to Hungary. The food shipments were an especially telling gesture, because Kun had not been able to secure a stable food supply.[43] Hoover could plug the gap by providing massive food relief and believed this was the most effective way to fight Bolshevism.

"Mr. Hoover," the *Washington Post* declared, knew from experience that "people do fall into bolshevism when their condition becomes desperate," when "bolshevism means bread and anti-bolshevism means starvation," but they "defy bolshevism" when they have enough to live on.[44] In an ARA report of July 25, 1919, on the condition of Hungary, Emery Pottle (Interallied Food Commission) and Dana Durand (US Food Administration) observed that "[food] conditions ... will become far worse during the winter and everyone looks forward to a period of frightful destitution." For that reason, they concluded, "this foresight of the situation to come is one of the chief reasons why the people want to change the government."[45] It was in response to such observations that Hoover installed a food distribution system in Hungary, with American officers in control. He wanted to convince both Hungarians and Austrians that it was best to "be on the side of freedom and order rather than on the side of bolshevism."[46] Retrospectively, and in a reference to the Russian Revolution of 1917, Hoover's massive relief program was believed to have "prevented this period of crisis from becoming Europe's 'October.'"[47]

The ARA initially received substantial congressional funding and was, in consequence, very flexible. In July 1919, Hoover established a separate ARA European Children's Fund to continue child relief work in Europe beyond Congress's initial allotment on a more private basis. Speaking about Czechoslovakia, Hoover told Americans, "The children's food program will remain an urgent need for at least another year. . . . This has enormous importance for the future of the new republic, and I urge you to give it your special support."[48] Thus, the ongoing work of children's relief was privatized and transformed into a new undertaking, though very much under Hoover's leadership. Although several other organizations ran parallel relief efforts during the immediate postwar period, the European Children's Fund was the only one to make its work permanent.

Throughout the fall of 1919, Hoover established a canteen system in Hungary for starving children. He opened soup kitchens and milk stations, which served a meal a day to thousands of recipients. His American "child welfare

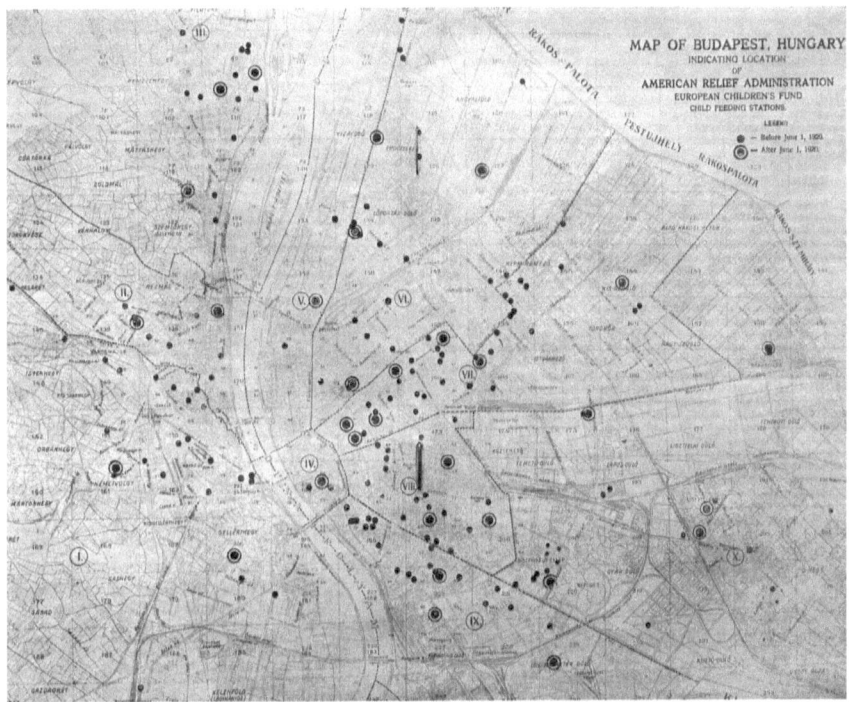

Fig. 5.2. "Map of the American Feeding Stations in Budapest." Unknown author, in *Final Report of the Work in Hungary*, 14–15.

mission to Hungary" was associated with "a warm bite, a nutritious dish, a warm tasty lunch" to the many "emaciated, dehydrated, underdeveloped, badly fed Hungarian children." Although Europe was judged for still debating how to handle the food crisis, America, "where the woman is holy and the child is holy," was praised for "already offering a helping hand."[49] Food was provided in "15 hospitals" and "27 public institutions," including orphanages, kindergartens, schools, and other distribution places, centers to combat malnutrition and hunger. Most of the relief premises were located in Budapest but also in the industrial suburbs and in the mining districts of Miskolc and Diósgyőr as well, bringing the total to about "60 kitchens."[50]

The relief kitchens served early midday meals to children ages three to fourteen, every day except Sundays and holidays.[51] Some children also received breakfast, consisting of white bread, cocoa, condensed milk, and sugar.[52] To apply nutritional science methods to the starving children of Budapest, the ARA set up relief stations scattered throughout the city, targeting the most poverty-stricken districts. The incoming relief workers of the ARA could rely on preexisting local child welfare and health care institutions along with schools, which were used to deliver the relief goods. An ARA food relief map, shown in figure 5.2, illustrates the distribution of the relief kitchens as they were located in Budapest on June 1, 1920.

Because Pest was the more urban, industrialized, and densely populated part of the capital, it had far more relief kitchens than Buda. The international food relief facilities represented what could be called "food islands," where an accumulation of foodstuffs drew starving and malnourished children. Not only did they form a particular food infrastructure in Budapest, they altered the physical bodies of the children of certain neighborhoods. Each day, in Budapest's ten districts, the ARA fed 38,402 children attending schools and kindergartens; in the suburbs, its kitchens fed another 41,455 children; local child protection institutions fed a further 9,353; and the hospitals fed 1,592 more. This amounts to 106,328 children fed daily in the capital, a figure that far exceeds the 15,526 children who were fed in other parts of Hungary. The most feedings in schools happened in three districts in Pest: District Six (7,688 children), District Seven (7,646 children), and District Eight (4,452 children), compared with, for instance, 420 children in District Four.[53] These three districts had the highest populations in the city and a significant number of people experiencing homelessness. The suburbs were also in need of American feedings. The children of the suburbs—Kispest, Csepel, and other industrial neighborhoods—received even more than the children of Budapest proper.

Under the financial and organizational aegis of the ARA, Pirquet supervised the child-feeding programs. He started his work in Austria on May 5, 1919, and went on to oversee the program in Hungary starting on October 13.[54] Pirquet had developed methods of selecting and feeding the children most in need while at Vienna University Children's Hospital. He devised an ideal nutritional diet, known as the NEM system (Nutrition Equivalent Milk),[55] which was adopted by all the ARA missions in Eastern Europe.[56] Pirquet later recounted how, when the American feeding mission first started in Austria, fourteen-year-olds "were several centimeters below the normal in height." Observing this, he decided to make "a special [nutritional] study of several thousand apprentices who received American food." He found that "with these additional meals, they began to grow again, twice as fast as the normal rate of growth for that age," and concluded that, if their feeding could be continued, they should "reach normal size."[57]

On the basis of this type of nutritional science, a few selected American "humanitarians" coordinated the US child relief program in Budapest.

Fig. 5.3. James Pedlow. Unknown photographer, *Az Érdekes Újság* 9, no. 7 (February 17, 1921): cover.

Two individuals figure especially prominently in the sources. The first was George Richardson, the ARA's chief in Budapest and assistant to its Central Executive Commission for Children in Hungary. The second, pictured in figure 5.3, was the popular James "Uncle" Pedlow, the American Red Cross (ARC) commissioner who even made the cover pages of local Hungarian journals.

In February 1919, Hoover had written to Henry Davison, the American Red Cross's chairman, asking whether the organization would be willing to undertake relief work systematically throughout Central Europe, because the work was to be "so largely purely charity." Hoover stressed that the ARA wanted to "cooperate whole-heartedly" with the American Red Cross (ARC) and support it with "real assistance."[58] Founded as far back as 1881, the American Red Cross had provided noncombatant relief in Europe

The Ultimate Consumers.
The foodstuffs after traveling over 6000 miles from America to Hungary by ocean steamer, canal barge, freight train, auto truck and wagon, finally reach the ultimate consumers.

Fig. 5.4. "The Ultimate Consumers." Unknown photographer, in *Final Report of the Work in Hungary*, 27.

throughout the hostilities and provided massive amounts of relief afterward to the countries in need. In Hungary, the ARC inaugurated a Child Health Action program.

Throughout the relief countries, the ARA saw to the logistics of delivering its abundant supplies of foodstuffs to the starving regions by establishing a reliable transport infrastructure. In November 1919, large shipments of cocoa, condensed milk, rice, coffee, and fat had already arrived at Budapest.[59] By the early twentieth century, it had become "technologically possible to stretch the distance between food producer and consumer," and neither national borders nor oceans were insurmountable hindrances.[60] With the transport systems in place, the entire undertaking expanded. In 1919, along with ninety-eight tons of white flour, the ARA shipped ninety-five tons of milk to Hungary. By May 1920, the milk quota had risen to 224 tons, having more than doubled in half a year.[61] The success was all due to a strong and stable infrastructure. An image in the ARA's Final Report on the Work in Hungary (fig. 5.4) explicitly linked this professional infrastructure to the child recipient.

Emphasizing the role of the United States in technological progress, the photograph caption underlined that transport logistics that made such a massive delivery of foodstuffs possible: "The foodstuffs after traveling over 6000 miles from America to Hungary by ocean steamer, canal barge, freight train, auto truck and wagon, finally reach the ultimate consumers." So long as Hungary was unable to provide for its children, humanitarian relief would come to these "ultimate consumers."[62] Moreover, the transport of relief supplies would help establish economic ties that could later be used for other forms of transatlantic trade and economic investment.

Though humanitarian in its conception, the giving of material assistance followed clear economic and capitalist goals. The moral ambivalence of the whole mission lay in the fact that "humanitarian reform not only took courage and brought commendable changes" but also "served the interest of the reformers."[63] Through material shipments of aid, recipient countries could easily be made economically dependent on the donor country. Commodities are products "intended principally for exchange" and emerge, in Arjun Appadurai's words, "in the institutional, psychological, and economic conditions of capitalism."[64] Humanitarian material gifts, whether in the form of food commodities or clothing, ensured future capitalist economic ties between the donor and recipient countries.

To accommodate private giving through commercial channels, in November 1920, Hoover established a few "strategic centers" for private gifts of food, sent to the stricken lands by "three or four million families" in the United States who had relatives or old friends in Central and Eastern Europe.[65] The food to Hungarians was to be distributed by means of a network of warehouses, such as that depicted in figure 5.5, which were to be run by the American Relief Warehouse Corporation. American Relief warehouses were set up in European cities in need, including Warsaw, Hamburg, Budapest, Vienna, and Prague. The intention behind them was to prevent the "utter loss and waste" of foodstuffs people had tried to send individually.[66] Rather than shipping individual parcels, the warehouses stocked basic food supplies, such as flour, pork, milk, sometimes coffee, and canned beef for distribution to the "designated persons."[67] The delivery of foodstuffs and goods at these warehouses was carefully documented in photographs, as shown in figure 5.6.

The warehouse system was an attempt to overcome disappointment and muddle. When Americans had sent gifts of food or money to their overseas cousins, results were not always as they would have wished. Károly Huszár, Hungary's prime minister, advised that sending individual packages was impractical, because transportation facilities were "so disorganized"; sending

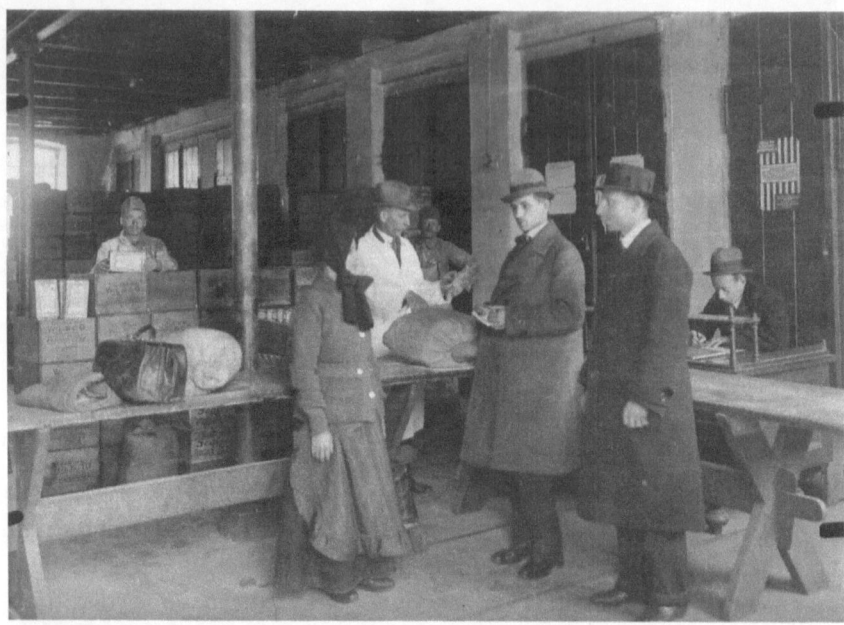

Fig. 5.5. American foodstuffs for Hungarians. Unknown photographer, American Relief Administration European Operational Records, Box 851, Folder J, HILA.

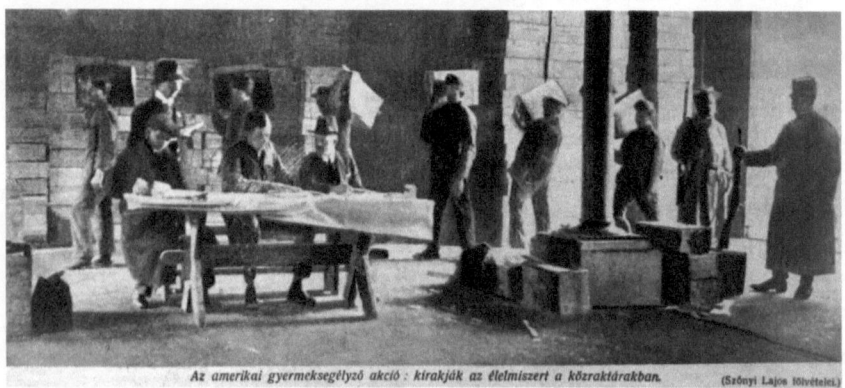

Fig. 5.6. The American child relief action: They stack the food in a public warehouse. Photo by Lajos Szőnyi, *Az Érdekes Újság* 8, no. 48 (December 25, 1919): 48.

cash remittances was not a viable solution either, because "essential foods cannot be purchased locally." It was particularly difficult to get foodstuffs delivered to Hungarians in the occupied (and later ceded) territories such as Transylvania. In 1920, Lee Krouse, a Texan of Hungarian origin, tried to get food and a letter delivered to his family in Arad. An ARA staffer tried to take the package to Arad by car, but the car broke down on the way, so he had to continue by train and cross the Romanian frontier. At last, he "located the family." Krouse's relatives "wept for joy," because this was the first news they had had from him in three years. Such deliveries, however appreciated, were prohibitively impractical on a large scale.[68]

To prevent such difficulties, Hungarians in America were advised to simply deposit money, which could then be transferred to the "designated persons" in Europe to obtain "food drafts" or supplies from the warehouses. Access to these relief goods was strictly controlled to avoid "abuse, inefficiency and delay." Any profit would go to the children's welfare program. Relatives could go to the warehouses for clothing as well. Because, for the most part, only raw materials such as leather and cotton could be delivered to Hungary, many of the garments had to be made locally. Relief recipients were entitled to order the tailoring of their individual garments. The warehouses had to compile lists of "name, address, and garments, and sizes" for each beneficiary.[69] Thus, while most international relief efforts addressed generalized needs across the population, some initiatives accommodated individualized aid donations—but in ways that still strengthened transatlantic economic ties.

Yet the prime focus of the relief agencies was children. As ton upon ton of wheat and corn was shipped overseas, American food became the essential "medium of exchange between the United States and many nations of Europe."[70] As the years went by, and the demand for relief food failed to decrease at the rate expected, Hoover came to the conclusion that the task of saving the entire adult population of Europe was not feasible after all. The undertaking would go on forever, and the goal would never be fully attained. "It is pitiful to feed only the children, to ignore the adult populations," he acknowledged, "but this latter is a problem far beyond the possibilities of private charity."[71] Despite this stricture, the provision of aid to the children continued. Children were dear to Hoover's heart, and philanthropists and political leaders were anxious to prevent the "degeneration" of Europe's future population, which they saw as a real peril. All profits gained from the sale of the foodstuffs on the dollar basis and the shipments of food and clothes to adults were "used for extending the present child relief activities of the administration in the countries" to which the packages had been shipped.[72]

Foreign Missions in the Capital

Between 1918 and 1920, the ARA is reported to have provided "6 million children" in Central and Eastern Europe and the Near East with "a substantial meal" each day, saving them from starvation. But by the summer of 1920, the

ARA's resources were "threatened with exhaustion."[44] It was clear that the US government could no longer cover all the expenses, so there remained "no other means for the continued support of these children except the public charity of the American people."[73] The ARA needed successors that were funded through public donations rather than federal dollars, paving the way for the coordinated efforts of American charities under the European Relief Council, and roles for the ICRC, the SCF, the SCIU, and other relief organizations, internationalizing aid efforts beyond the early US efforts in Hungary. Hoover expected in 1919 that "the governments and private charity in [the aided] countries should pay . . . the entire cost of maintaining the distribution system" themselves. He had also expected that American humanitarian intervention was only to take the "form of the initial organization, instruction as to method, and the continuous import of such necessary foodstuffs as were not locally available, such as milk [and] fat." Hoover acknowledged that "an inspection service for the purpose of maintaining the efficiency of the system" should be provided by the ARA.[74] But he hoped that the drain of providing actual supplies would, in short order, be shifted away from the US government. Now he realized that the target countries and populations were unlikely to succeed independently.

Accordingly, on April 25, 1919, Hoover formulated an "Appeal to European Nationals in the United States for the Support of Child Feeding." In the document, he stressed how essential it was to "amalgamate former bodies, or create out of important nations, committees for each of the [relief] countries" to "solicit from their own nationals, and possibly from a sympathetic public, support for their child feeding." National committees could then "continue their charitable assistance to these European committees" after the US withdrawal.[75] Hoover called for humanitarian cooperation in relief efforts between the ARA, ARC, Jewish Joint Distribution Committee, American Friends Service Committee, Young Women's Christian Association (YWCA), Young Men's Christian Association (YMCA), and various church organizations. He appealed to them for "joint and co-operative action in the effective organization of American charity to meet the piteous call of these helpless children."[76]

On September 23, 1920, a conference was convened to develop a plan to arrange for this "American charity toward 2,500,000 destitute children in Europe, [this] coming winter."[77] Finally, on September 27, 1920, the European Relief Council was established as a partner in US child relief efforts.[78] Now it was even more important to gain the support of the American people for relief efforts. Campaigners used both textual and visual representations of destitute children to wring financial backing from the general public. "Without America's help they are condemned to death," ran a 1920 European Relief Council appeal for donations to help Europe's "ragged kiddies."[79] It combined pictures of starving children fed by employees of the European Relief Council with emotionally laden statements about the devastating situation the children were in.

Other bodies pressed for transnational cooperation in the field of child relief, notably the League of Nations and the ICRC. "The rescue of the children" should not lie only with the ARA; it should be "one of the most noble tasks of the League . . . to make sure that none of the countries who have suffered from the war see their children forgotten and their sufferings ignored."[80] Though the ICRC is best known for its work in the field of public health, in Budapest the feeding program was the absolute priority.[81] Any other type of relief work came second.

Redistribution of responsibilities was not always frictionless. When, in the fall of 1920, discussions took place about the shift of responsibilities from the ARA to the ICRC in Hungary, Walter Lyman Brown, director of the ARA in Europe, received a cablegram from his superiors stating that the ARA "disappove[d]" of the ICRC's desire "to distribute its supplies through local authorities" and insisting that "kitchens supported by us should be absolutely under our management and control." The ICRC should "turn over whatever money they have" and let the ARA "manage [the] entire affair," thereby "eliminating [the] ICRC," because it had "no personnel" and "no ideas about child feeding." Yet, in the end, the rivalry was overcome. "Our kitchens" (in the ARA's words) were used by the "same committee" of relief workers, and the "menu" and "arrangements" remained "exactly [the] same as ours." It was only the delivered foodstuffs that had new institutional backing, though there was some rearranging of personnel, and the American flag was replaced by the flag of the ICRC.[82] The transfer of management from the ARA to other international and local relief organizations happened throughout the European countries, where these newcomers "found themselves cooperating and competing to feed continental Europe."[83]

Despite the initial feuding, the ICRC offered to provide funds to feed "25,000 other children" in the ARA's kitchens.[46] In cooperation with various Save the Children chapters, the program worked effectively. Mr. Burnier, the delegate of the ICRC at the time, took the opportunity of the first meeting of the Foreign Missions held on November 2, 1920, to announce that the Save the Children International Union, supported by the Save the Children Fund and the Rädda Barnen, the Swedish section of Save the Children, was able to continue the children's feeding program.[84] Posters bearing the announcement and the SCIU emblem appeared outside the schools where the meals were provided.[85]

International relief organizations expected the city of Budapest, with the support of the Hungarian government, to cover the administrative costs of the relief work, which included the provision of kitchens, kitchen staff, basic utilities, and transportation. The Hungarian government nominated Count Széchnyi, head of the National Child Protection League, to handle the administration of foreign relief organizations in Hungary. In a letter of November 19, 1920, Count Rodolphe Reding-Biberegg of Switzerland, in his function as ICRC delegate in Budapest, wrote to the SCIU in Geneva pleading for support to finance the feeding of fifty thousand Hungarian children. He pointed to the "disastrous distress of the children of this country who die from cold and famine." Of course, the Hungarian government was ready and willing "to do anything to maintain the kitchens, the heating and the necessary personnel."[86] Reding-Biberegg committed to "the strictest neutrality" and abstinence from any form of political manifestation.[87] He was instructed to gather as much information as possible on the local situation, including details of the ongoing organization of relief and its flaws, with suggestions for improvement. The ICRC expressed the hope that he would enable its cooperation with the American mission and, if possible, arrange to take it over eventually.[88] It was expected that "millions of children saved from rickets and death" will "remember, when grown up, the debt they owe to the League of Nations," and will "labor to cement the structure of universal brotherhood of which the first stones were laid by the Assembly."[89] Immensely important to the ICRC mission in Budapest was ongoing documentation of the work done. Reding-Biberegg was required to submit a fortnightly report, which was to include detail on the physical transformation of the children bodies and the improvement in their nutrition.[90]

Cooperation among organizations was extensive. Besides collaboration between the American Relief Administration, American Red Cross, International Committee of the Red Cross, Save the Children, and Save the Children International Union, a host of other international organizations surfaced in Budapest, and these had to be pulled together somehow. The ICRC established a close working relationship with the National League of Child Protection, charging Vilmos Neugebauer with the task of serving as liaison officer.[91] The SCIU and ICRC took the lead.[92] The joint endeavor became known as the Foreign Missions (sometimes known as the Budapest Mission). The ARA, at 31 Váci Street, was charged with feeding the children; the ARC, located in Hotel Dunapalota, distributed hospital supplies, drugs, linen, and some of the food; Swiss agents distributed linen, clothing, food, drugs, and bandages; the Action Lodge Famine Relief Fund, located in Hotel Hungaria, distributed milk for children's centers, maternity hospitals, and dispensaries as well as drugs, linen, and clothing, and it furnished the hospitalization scheme for children; the Dutch Mission, run by C. Fledderus (at 4 Kossuth Lajos Street) ran children's hospitals and provided other hospitals with linen, drugs, bandages, food, and shoes. Norwegian Action, run by A. Gregereen at 3 Lónyay Street, distributed food, clothing, layettes, drugs, and bandages. The Swedish Red Cross and the Rädda Barnen maintained a public kitchen, helped children's hospitals, and distributed clothing, food, drugs, and bandages. The Danish distributed clothing and bed linen. The ICRC served as a "central clearing house of relief information," negotiating with all foreign agencies concerning relief work in Hungary.[93] This amalgamation played a major role as the "connecting link between all the missions," among whom a feeling of community developed.[94] Just like the internationalists surrounding the League of Nations, internationalists in the field of transnational child relief built and relied on a "transnational 'emotional community'" that was composed of "people and institutions that valued international contacts" and that shared a set of "emotions of internationalism" whom many believed "to be the only way out of war."[95]

To coordinate the work of the Foreign Missions, the various representatives of international relief met twice a month, sitting together at one table, discussing the everyday cooperation of American, Dutch, Swedish, Norwegian, and British relief organizations and of local child protection, health care, and religious institutions. Strength came from the cooperative character of the enterprise. The head of the SCF believed that, wherever and whenever possible, "aid should be delivered in partnership with local child welfare organizations" to strengthen existing provision and avoid "creating dependency."[96] Julia Vajkai believed that the warm "personal connections with the different relief missions" were largely due to her own and her sister's activism. To Vajkai, the friendly collaboration between the ARC and the SCIU was the "result of the sympathy that its leader," James Pedlow, had "for the work of my sister," Rose Vajkai.[97] The first of these joint meetings took place on November 2, 1920.[98] Reding-Biberegg had taken up the chairmanship of the Foreign Missions only the day before. Among the attendees at this meeting, and those that followed, were representatives of the ARA, the ARC, the ICRC, the Action Lodge Famine Relief Fund, the SCF, the SCIU, the Society of Friends, the Relief Committee for Foreigners, and various embassies, churches, and other organizations.⁹⁹ Local relief organizations also joined in these international talks. Among those that sent representatives were the Prime Minister's Relief Action, People's Welfare Ministry, Mission for Prisoners and Youthful Offenders, Hungarian Red Cross, and the city.

While the new nation-states of Central Europe were haggling and trying to get themselves onto solid footing after the war, international humanitarians around the table in Budapest were working on behalf of Budapest's children and trying to find solutions for the social distress that was still prevalent. In these talks, we can see the internationalization of relief and the close entanglement of internationalism and nationalism. As the international organizations had to report back to Geneva on a regular basis, their representatives, often with other international visitors, would go out to visit the poorer districts of Budapest and the smaller towns, documenting their observations in accounts that might be thirty pages long. For nearly a year, they undertook coordinated relief work in the city, feeding children by the thousands. In October 1921, when dissolution of the Foreign Missions was proposed, Pedlow suggested that the delegates should write to Geneva and declare their disagreement with the proposal: "The same telegramme is to unite the foreign delegates as well as the representatives of the country, in order to demonstrate the unity of all representatives in this question."¹⁰⁰

The Glocal Dimension of Relief

In Hungary and elsewhere, the international relief organizations were committed to the "most economical and practical form of administration." This meant that they seldom acted in isolation in the actual work of implementing relief. They chose to rely on the existing welfare infrastructures within their target countries. This was the most efficient way to reach the children in need. As the ARA made clear in the case of Poland, this meant entrusting work to local welfare organizations and workers, which they knew were in "competent . . . hands."¹⁰¹ Relief work, therefore, was an entirely transnational undertaking. A great deal of discussion, correspondence, and cooperation took place between Hungarian representatives and humanitarian relief workers. When the ARA, Save the Children, and American Red Cross came to Budapest, they made direct use of the available infrastructure of local child protection. Most nurses and relief workers belonged to the local Red Cross, the Stefánia Association, or the National Child Protection League. There was also heavy reliance on help from the religious orders. Roman Catholic bishop Ottokár Prohászka was vice president of the National Child Protection League

Children.¹⁰² Along with nurses and social workers, Catholic nuns contributed a great deal to the practical relief work.

The transnational and gendered composition of the relief committee, and of the whole initiative, is clear, not just in the written reports but in photographs. In many photos, the American James Pedlow is a central figure, shown surrounded by local nurses, Hungarian middle- and upper-class supporters, and various philanthropists. While it was mostly men (trained in the military) who ran the programs, women nurses and aides served the children, following the gender stereotype of women being best suited for child-related work. Sylwia Markowska-Kuźma observed a similarly concerning "gender dimension" in infant care in Habsburg Poland. "The relations between a mother and a physician were the relations of power" because of "the lack of professional equality or class disparities" as well as the male gender of most medical experts. While "motherhood and childcare were [considered] the most important female responsibilities,"¹⁰³ the fact that responsibility over women's bodies was given to men illustrates well the problematic gender dynamic in the emerging field of care for mothers, infants, and children.

The ARA kitchens were, for instance, largely run by women. A number of staged images show the kitchen employees, dressed in aprons, holding cooking utensils, and proffering certain items of food, such as the three loaves of bread depicted in figure 5.7—the most basic but most desired commodity. The work of these women was, of course, central to the entire relief operation. In other countries, glocal cooperation was just as tightly coordinated. A 1922 report on Polish relief stated that the ARA and the local Polish committee "were closely bound together" in their "interests and responsibilities," which required yet "closer coordination of their work."¹⁰⁴ In Czechoslovakia, the ARA collaborated with the new government and the national child welfare organization, the Czecho-Slovak Péče o dítě, which "fed a great proportion of the under-nourished children."¹⁰⁵ Everywhere there was a "wealth of local service," and it was possible to set up local committees of "leading citizens and especially women" in key cities and towns.¹⁰⁶ As the European Relief Council stated admiringly in 1921: "The local shelters for children are equipped and native service furnished by residents without charge on American charity."¹⁰⁷

In Hungary, the government agreed to furnish the kitchens, provide the personnel, obtain fuel, and pay the administrative expenses of relief work. For its part, the ARA imported the goods and brought in special workers to initiate and supervise activities.¹⁰⁸ The Hungarian Refugee Office (OMH) relied extensively on foreign relief. The ARA supplied the Hungarian organization

Fig. 5.7. Kitchen at Kispest. Unknown photographer, American Relief Administration European Operational Records, Box 851, Folder J, HILA.

with "sugar, cocoa, rice, condensed milk and fish conserves to the value of 300,0000 crowns."[109] Targeting children, large quantities of "milk, soap, medical supplies and special foods for infants were provided for these refugees."[110] At the same time, many local "restaurants and coffeehouse owners offered free or cheap lunch, dinner, breakfast and snacks to the refugees."[111] Profiting from the deliveries of free food packages from the ARA, the OMH also provided 361 families with groceries. And even before the ARA shipped food to Hungary, local initiatives had been set up that provided relief to the destitute refugees' and their children. Out of empathy with their "sad situation," Miklós Elemér organized a "table for Transylvanian refugees." Implemented not with the help of the city or the state but "with the enthusiastic support of the society," this initiative offered from September 1916 onward a free lunch "for those refugees that belonged to the middle class." The lunch was served in places of middle-class amusement, such as theaters, casinos, and ballrooms.[112]

The OMH served as a hub for distributing material donations from various international charities. Foreign charity missions in Switzerland, Sweden, and Scotland sent clothing, using the office of the International Red Cross as a delivery point. In May 1920, "a thousand cotton men's suits" arrived at the warehouse, which were duly distributed to refugee families. Large quantities of milk, soap, medical supplies, and baby food were provided.[113] Gifts that came via Pedlow of the ARC were of "such a great amount" that the organizers "succeeded in providing most of the refugees with much-needed clothing: rugs, flannel blankets, simple flannel, women's stockings, male cotton stockings, sweatshirts from cotton, hospital linen shirts, ready flannel dresses, flannel women's trousers, linen clothes for men."[114]

The OMH established a Mother and Child Protection Department, whose aim was "to place expectant mothers and infants in hospitals, institutions or private families." Five hundred homeless mothers were sent with their children (especially daughters) to these facilities. The OMH also embarked on a relief program encompassing three thousand families. Clothing went to 1,340 children between ages one and twelve; milk and cocoa went to 2,400 anemic mothers and children with medical prescriptions; and financial aid was offered to 1,642 mothers.[115] Temporary placements in state institutions were meant to improve children's' living conditions. Official government buildings, such as the municipal house of representatives, were used for this purpose.

Building on such local initiatives, the incoming relief organizations could develop and expand the relief infrastructure. For instance, the American Red Cross worked closely with local childcare institutions such as the National Child Protection League. In a July 1, 1922, letter to James Pedlow, ARC nurse Mary K. Taylor wrote of her vision for the close cooperation with the Stefánia Association. The aims of this association, she assured him, were "in close harmony with the aims of the [ARC's] Child Health Program," and the Stefánia Association was "heavily subsidized by the government," which made it "the natural agency for the carrying on of child health work under government auspices." A large number of health visitors "had received from 8 weeks to 10 months training under the Stefánia Society" and were already "visiting all the new-born children in certain cities."[116]

In general, to implement civilian relief, the ARC cooperated with the local board of charities. This was considered a good choice, because the board's "building, personnel, equipment and methods of work compared favorably with similar organizations in American cities," and during the war, its work had been of the "highest character."[117] The board of charities was placed under the direction of the ARC and was used to distribute incoming supplies "among the poor." While stressing the importance of relief donations to every single recipient, the ARC report was proud of the magnitude of the help extended: the ARC had assisted a total of 20,083 families and 88,081 individuals during 1920, its first year of intervention. The ARC was anxious to avoid any class discrimination and to distribute supplies "regardless of political affiliation." However, the board of charities had previously set up a hierarchical system of relief entitlement. Four classes were deemed "deserving" of relief: "state employees" were the "most worthy class"; second were "city employees"; third, the refugees living in freight wagons; and last, "ordinary cases."[118]

The ARC would not provide long-term relief in Hungary and the neighboring countries, which were expected to strengthen their own local relief agencies so that they could soon manage their own welfare system. It was the ARC's conviction that "relief and rehabilitation would work only if local populations would be ready to help themselves."[119] The ARC encouraged the "building up" of local "self-reliance."[120] Its ultimate vision was of humanitarian intervention as merely a means to establish and professionalize local welfare systems. The ARA, too, hoped "to develop from the native organization" a "permanent institution" that could, in the long run, function as a "country-wide child welfare organization."[121] Rather than "pauperizing Europe," its action should further a "fundamental policy . . . to build up self-help" and "stimulate the creation of institutions . . . directed to the permanent care of [the] waif, undernourished and orphan children" in the countries targeted.[122]

Local child relief organizations and charities were to "furnish transportation, warehouses, labor, clerical, help," and any material supplies that were available.[123] There was strong economic pressure behind this ideal; the less international relief agencies were able to cope with the financial drain of provision, the more local welfare organizations were required to fill the gap. While American and international aid organizations imported unobtainable items into the stricken countries, they were keen to use local raw materials and goods manufactured within the borders of Hungary, paid for by the Hungarian government.[124] They wanted to hand over administration and organization of the relief efforts as well to local management. The records document this shift. The breakfasts for pregnant nursing mothers were slowly but increasingly taken over by local welfare agencies and their employees. This meant that the children were examined by doctors from the National Child Protection League, and the mothers were selected from the lists of the Stefánia Association. The transition was done "for the benefit of mothers and children, in a satisfactory manner."[125] More and more, cooperation and mutual influence became important parts of humanitarian intervention.

Hoover put much effort into promoting the "creation of institutions" by the national communities in Europe. These could make use of the extensive "voluntary service," which "literally hundreds of thousands of women" provided, so that the "children of their race might be preserved." The faster the local communities could "recover in strength," the faster American relief organizations could withdraw their relief, though "without abandoning" Central Europe's children. However, in Hoover's view, European welfare workers could only become efficient with the backing of "American skill."[126] In conformity with this logic, ARC nurses were sent to Hungary not just to implement relief measures but, vitally, to recruit and train local nurses. Throughout Central, Eastern, and Southeastern Europe, the English-speaking ARC personnel faced a language barrier when dealing with mothers and children who spoke (what was to them) an unintelligible tongue. An ARC nurse recalled the difficulties faced during a mission to Serbia: "The language was difficult, but we managed to learn a vocabulary of useful words and everyday phrases.... Such words as *boli* (pain), *noga* (leg), *rooka* (arm)."[127] Obviously, this was not enough. Only trained local workers could deal with the relief recipients in their native languages and fully understand their needs. Besides, inviting local people to join the humanitarian intervention mobilized solidarity and empathy among the local population.

Highly motivated, the new Hungarian welfare workers were seen as being just as effective as their American counterparts: "The spontaneously arising need of the Hungarian woman to help, which was the need of her own aching soul . . . made up for the training and theoretical knowledge of the professional 'social worker.'" A 1923 ARC report explained how the grim aftermath of the Great War produced a new profession. "The theory of social work and the profession of the social worker was in Hungary until recently unknown." But the "physical and psychological suffering" brought about by the war aroused "among all noble spirited Hungarian woman that sincere desire, that moral value, that deals with the given situation ingeniously, selflessly and tirelessly, gently and rigorously and cannot rest until comfort and help are provided."[128] The report acknowledged the role of the ARC in encouraging a professionalization of social work and child welfare. Because "prenatal care of the mother and the baby" was considered a social undertaking, as it could save families from "trouble, pain and expense," the ARC was invested in generating the profession of 'social work.'"[129] At special events in almost every city hall throughout the country, local social and religious welfare institutions were informed about the work of the ARC. As the report concluded, the help of the ARC had "made life for many infants possible, who were our only hope for a Hungarian future."[130]

Emergency relief for those suffering most acutely dominated wartime and postwar child protection, yet the humanitarian mission to children was not limited to saving lives; there was the "desire to remove the causes of suffering" in the long term, too.¹³¹ The professionalization of hospitals and childcare facilities by means of modern equipment and thorough training of personnel transformed local health and welfare services. Mary Taylor, the ARC nurse quoted earlier, declared that the "enthusiasm and loyal support" of the local Hungarian staff brought "constant joy," and she especially appreciated their keenness to grasp "new ideas of work and organization." It made her feel that there was "hope of a real structure being built on the foundation" laid.¹³²

While the incoming relief agencies were eager to cooperate with local relief workers, Hungarians expressed a need for mediators on the international stage. In a meeting of the Foreign Missions in March 1921, Reding-Biberegg thanked everyone present for their excellent reports and photographs, which could "arouse great interest and make great publicity." He then went on to announce that he had been asked to "represent the cause of the poor of Hungary in Geneva." Julia Vajkai supported this strongly. She remembered how, in the previous year at Geneva, Vienna had been represented by Englishmen and Americans, while the delegates from Budapest had had to argue their own case and were "accused of not being able to be objective" and were ignored. Vajkai was convinced that "objectivity" and authoritative representation of Hungary could only be guaranteed through international humanitarians who were not of Hungarian nationality who could report "neutrally" on what they were witnessing. For instance, Mr. Boven, a foreign physician and a delegate of the ARC, was invited to "form for himself an opinion about the sanitary conditions of children of this country."¹³³ Vajkai admired what she saw as the unbiased objectivity of the English and American relief workers. In a farewell letter to Colonel Raymond Sheldon of the US Army, who had been involved in an ICRC mission to Budapest, she made a point of appreciating his predisposition, as a US citizen and soldier, to "judge things in a naturally unbiased way."¹³⁴ The combination of local and international expertise would be most effective in addressing Hungary's great needs on the ground in Budapest and advocating at the global level.

Conclusion

The creation of an international humanitarian relief infrastructure in Budapest started with exploratory missions by relief organizations, which assessed the city's level of starvation and identified children's nutritional needs. While the international relief organizations brought unprecedented resources and material to the relief endeavor, the local implementation of the American feeding stations and milk kitchens was dependent on the close cooperation between the Foreign Missions and Hungarian child protective institutions.

Examining the infrastructure of food aid in Budapest reveals the glocal interaction between the local and the global and between the humanitarian donors, local relief workers, and child recipients. Furthermore, the ongoing management of humanitarian food aid in the capital city showcases a shift from donated relief to self-help. Because international long-term relief was not an option, it became a crucial concern to strengthen and engage local relief agencies and agents so that the city and country could maintain child relief endeavors once the relief organizations departed.

Notes

1. Den Hertog, "The Commission for Relief."
2. Hoover, *Memoirs of Herbert Hoover*, 321.
3. Veit, *Modern Food, Moral Food*, 2.
4. "Hoover Made Head of American Relief," 18.
5. Kellogg and Taylor, *The Food Problem*, 4.
6. "Hoover Made Head of American Relief," 18.
7. Hoover, "Central European Relief," 107.
8. Hoover, *An American Epic*, xxi.
9. Hoover, *Memoirs of Herbert Hoover*, 250.
10. Clavin, "The Austrian Hunger Crisis," 271.
11. Hoover, *Memoirs of Herbert Hoover*, 259; "Food Control," *Monthly Labor Review* 8, no. 3 (March 1919): 128.
12. Abbott, *From Relief to Social Security*, 265.
13. Pirquet, *An Outline of the Pirquet System of Nutrition*, 45.
14. Gratze, *Terrors of the Table*.
15. Pirquet, *An Outline of the Pirquet System of Nutrition*, 45, 59.
16. Sayward, "Food and Nutrition," 110.
17. Ibid., 111.
18. Cabanes, *The Great War*, 225.
19. Cullather, "The Foreign Policy of the Calorie," 339.
20. Pirquet, *An Outline of the Pirquet System of Nutrition*, 18.
21. Abbott, *From Relief to Social Security*, 265.
22. Barona Vilar, "International Organisations," 130.
23. Abbott, *From Relief to Social Security*, 264.
24. "Market Prices," August 10, 1918, US Food Administration Records 1909–57, Austria-Hungary, Agriculture, Reel 118, Box 95.1–95.14, Folder 6, HILA.
25. "Special Report on Crop Situation," July 15, 1918, US Food Administration Records 1909–57, Office of Foreign Information, Austria-Hungary, Agriculture, Reel 118, Box 95.1–95.14, Folder 6, HILA.
26. "Crop Conditions-Hungary," September 14, 1918, US Food Administration Records 1909–57, Austria-Hungary, Agriculture, Reel 118, Box 95.1–95.14, Folder 6, HILA.
27. "Economic Situation, Austria-Hungary during the First Half of 1918," 1–21, 1, US Food Administration Records 1909–57, Austria-Hungary, Agriculture, Reel 118, Box 95.1–95.14, Folder 6, HILA.
28. Hoover, "Child Life in Central Europe," 1.

29. Mr. Mitchell to Childfund, cablegram, Budapest, March 2, 1921, American Relief Administration European Operational Records, Box 36, Folder 2, HILA.

30. Edwin R. Embree, "Log of Journey to Europe, Secretary Rockefeller Foundation, June 22–October 3, 1920," Rockefeller Archive Center. https://iiif.rockarch.org/pdfs/GWi7vznHmxjAjN2VMbqW9F.

31. Selskar M. Gunn, "Public Health Conditions in Hungary, March 20–March 23, 1922," 1–42, 19, Collection RF, Series 100, Box 57, Folder 567, Rockefeller Archive Center, Sleepy Hollow.

32. "Hunger Map," *American Relief Administration Bulletin* 2, no. 16 (September 1, 1920).

33. Walter Lyman Brown to Childfund Budapest, telegram, November 28, 1920, American Relief Administration European Operational Records, Box 36, Folder 3, R57, HILA.

34. See Surface and Bland, *American Food*. On Poland, see Kellogg, "Paderewski, Pilsudski, and Poland," 112.

35. "Where All Men Starve," *New York Times*, December 7, 1919, X1.

36. Curti, *American Philanthropy Abroad*, 271.

37. National "Hands Off Russia" Committee, *Russian Famine*.

38. Councellor, American Relief Administration to Joseph C. Grew, Executive Secretary of the American Commission to Negotiate Peace, Paris, March 26, 1919, American Relief Administration European Operational Records, Box 364, Folder 4, Reel 427, HILA.

39. Hoover during the Supreme Council meeting of July 5, 1919. See Hoover, *An American Epic*.

40. "Feeding Magyar Children," *New York Times*, August 13, 1919, 15.

41. Granick, *International Jewish Humanitarianism in the Age of the Great War*, 73.

42. Chenery, "Starving Budapest."

43. "Revolt in Budapest; Bela Kun Shot At," 2. Erdélyi was Hungary's food minister.

44. "Food and Bolshevism," 6.

45. Pottle and Durand, "Conditions in Hungary," 30.

46. "Food and Bolshevism," 6.

47. Patenaude, *The Big Show in Bololand*, 34.

48. "400,000 Czech Youths Fed," *New York Times*, August 28, 1919, 28.

49. "American Relief Administration European Children's Fund," 5.

50. Glant, "Herbert Hoover and Hungary," 99. Childfund to Mr. Quinn, cablegram, Budapest, January 6, 1921, American Relief Administration European Operational Records, Box 36, Folder 2, R57, HILA.

51. Bókay, "The Result of the Hungarian Mission," 10.

52. "Child Feeding in Hungary," *American Relief Administration Bulletin* 2, no. 5 (December 1, 1920): 31.

53. Gyuris, *Az Amerikai Gyermeksegélyző*.

54. Étienne Clouzot, "Secours aux enfants en Hongrie," Extract from the Revue Internationale de la Croix-Rouge 3, no 26 (February 15, 1921): 137–43, 137, CH AEG A.P. 92.21.1.

55. Pirquet, *An Outline of the Pirquet System of Nutrition*, 23.

56. Fischer, *The Famine in Soviet Russia*, 83.

57. Pirquet, *An Outline of the Pirquet System of Nutrition*, 63–64.

58. Robert Olds, ARC Commissioner to Europe, to Herbert Hoover, Paris, February 25, 1919, reprinted in Bane and Lutz, *Organization of American Relief*, 288–89.

59. American Relief Administration European Children's Fund, *Final Report*, 5.

60. Davis, *Home Fires Burning*, 21.

61. American Relief Administration European Children's Fund, *Final Report*, 5–6.

62. "The Ultimate Consumers," in American Relief Administration European Children's Fund, *Final Report*, 27.
63. On the capitalist roots of humanitarianism, see Haskell, "Capitalism and the Origins of the Humanitarian Sensibility."
64. Appadurai, *The Social Life of Things*, 5.
65. Brown to Childfund Budapest.
66. "Relief Problems in Hungary," 7.
67. Brown to Childfund Budapest.
68. Mr. Richardson to Mr. Brown, cablegram, Budapest, December 17, 1920, and Mr. Richardson to Mr. Smith, cablegram, Budapest, April 1, 1920, American Relief Administration European Operational Records, Box 35, Folder 4, R.56, HILA.
69. "Relief Problems in Hungary," 7; Childfund to Mr. Brown and Mr. Gay, cablegram, Budapest, May 12, 1921, American Relief Administration European Operational Records, Box 36, Folder 1, Reel 56, HILA.
70. Chenery, "Starving Budapest."
71. Hoover, "What Peace Has Done to Europe," BRM 1.
72. "Food for Europe by Personal Gifts," 12. See also "Distribution of Food to Poles, Czechs, Austrians and Germans Spurred," 8.
73. "Misery Tales from Europe," XX1.
74. Hoover, "Child Life in Central Europe."
75. Hoover to AMREFA, "An Appeal to European Nationals in the United States for the Support of Child Feeding, Paris, April 25, 1919," reprinted in Bane and Lutz, *Organization of American Relief*, 425.
76. Hoover, "Child Life in Central Europe," 3.
77. "To Aid 2,500,000 Children," 7.
78. The council comprised the ARC, ARA, JDC, the Federal Council of the Churches of Christ in America, National Catholic Welfare Council, YMCA, YWCA, and American Friends Service Committee. See Stöhr, *So half Amerika*, 160–64; Surface and Bland, *American Food*, 77–80.
79. "European Relief Council Feeds Starving Children of War Effected Countries in Europe" (video), Gaumont Graphic, 1920, *Critical Past*, http://www.criticalpast.com/video/65675030507_President-Herbert-Hoover_food-buckets_children-eating_European-Relief-Council.
80. "Motion Proposed by the Swiss Delegation to the Assembly of the League of Nations," Explanatory Statement, Intervention on Behalf of the Children in Countries Affected by the War," Geneva, December 2, 1920, 6. Motta to Monsieur Paul Hymans, 5. F.O. 371. 4717. Political. Central. General. Files 9861–15096, National Archives, Kew.
81. "Instructions," Berlin, January 11, 1921, 1–3, 1–2. Dossier Personnel de Reding, ACICR MIS 4.1 Correspondance concernant la Mission de Budapest. Archive of the ICRC, Geneva.
82. Childfund to Mr. Brown, cablegram, Budapest, November 30, 1920, and Childfund to Mr. Brown, cablegram, Budapest, February 18, 1921, American Relief Administration European Operational Records, Box 36, Folder 2, Reel 57, HILA.
83. Proctor, "An American Enterprise?," 30.
84. Delegate of the ICRC to the SCIU, Budapest, November 13, 1920, Rapports de Budapest, Année 1920–21, ACICR B Mis. 4–5/791 à Mis. 4–5/908, 1503 à 1707, Archive of the ICRC.
85. "In This School Lunch Is Served by the Save the Children International Union," CH AEG AP 92.21.1.
86. Delegate of the ICRC to the SCIU, Budapest, November 13, 1920.
87. "Convention between the ICRC and Rodolphe de Reding, October 18, 1920," ACICR MIS 4, Correspondance concernant la Mission de Budapest, Archive of the ICRC.

88. "Instructions," January 11, 1921, 1–3, 1–2. ACICR MIS 4, Correspondance concernant la Mission de Budapest, Archive of the ICRC.
89. "Motion Proposed by the Swiss Delegation to the Assembly of the League of Nations," 8.
90. "Instructions," 2.
91. "Certificat," February 28, 1920, ACICR MIS 4, Correspondance concernant la Mission de Budapest, Archive of the ICRC.
92. "Protocol of the Meeting of the Foreign Missions and Home Institutions, October 11, 1921," 1–6, 4, Hungary, Folder 2, 1920–1921, International Commissioners' Reports and Correspondence, From M. de Reding (& Others), EJ 155 21/18, SCF Archive.
93. Embree, "Log of Journey to Europe, Secretary Rockefeller Foundation, June 22–October 3, 1920."
94. Julia Vajkai to Eglantyne Jebb, Budapest, October 11, 1921, Hungary, Vajkai's Workrooms and Holiday Homes, January 1921–December 31, 1921, EJ 170 21/3, SCF Archive.
95. Scaglia, *The Emotions of Internationalism*, 17, 3, and 12.
96. Mulley, *The Woman Who Saved the Children*, 294.
97. Julia Vajkai to Eglantyne Jebb, Budapest, October 11, 1921.
98. Delegate of the ICRC to the SCIU, Budapest 133, November 1920, Rapports de Budapest, Année 1920–1921, ACICR B Mis. 4–5/791 à Mis. 4–5/908, 1503 à 1706, Archive of the ICRC.
99. Among the delegates were Armstrong-Smith, chief organizer of the Save the Children Fund; Julia Vajkai, British Save the Children Fund; Mrs. Singer, ARA; Asta Nilsen, Swedish Mission; Maud Cherry, World Students Christian Association; Mr. Müller, Dutch Relief Action; and Consul General Kienast, Countess Bethlen, and Mr. de Redersen of the Relief Action for Foreigners. The office of the ICRC was located in Hotel Dunapalota. Reding-Biberegg served as the ICRC delegate in Budapest. The office of the SCIU in Budapest was located at 8 Andrássy Street, where Rose Vajkai served as the secretary.
100. Protocol of the Meeting of the Foreign Missions and Home Institutions, October 11, 1921.
101. American Relief Administration European Children's Fund, *American Relief Administration European Children's Fund Mission to Poland: 1919–1922*, 9.
102. Julia Vajkai to Mrs. Mac Kenzie, May 31, 1921, CH AEG AP 92.21.2.
103. Markowska-Kuźma, "From 'Drop of Milk,'" 141–42.
104. American Relief Administration European Children's Fund, *American Relief Administration European Children's Fund Mission to Poland*, 13.
105. American Relief Administration, *A Sketch of the Child-Feeding Operations*, 7.
106. Hoover, *Memoirs of Herbert Hoover*, 322.
107. "The National Collection of the European Relief Council," 10.
108. Childfund to Mr. Brown, cablegram, Budapest, November 30, 1920.
109. Petrichevich-Horváth, *Jelentés az Országos Menekültügyi Hivatal*, 27.
110. "The American Red Cross in Hungary," 1921, Sheet 1–5, Sheet 3, Records of the American National Red Cross, 1917–1934, W.W.I., 953.08, Box 878, NARA.
111. Petrichevich-Horváth, *Jelentés az Országos Menekültügyi Hivatal*, 14.
112. "Menekültek asztala," 18.
113. "The American Red Cross in Hungary," Sheet 3.
114. Petrichevich-Horváth, *Jelentés az Országos Menekültügyi Hivatal*, 13
115. Ibid., 14.
116. "Letter by Mary K. Taylor," Society Service, American Red Cross in Hungary to Captain James G. Pedlow, Director of American Red Cross in Hungary, July 1, 1922," Sheets 1–4, Sheet 1. RG 200 Records of the American National Red Cross, 1917–1934, 953.08, Box 878, NARA.

117. Lt. Colonel S. A. Moffat, "Report of the American Red Cross Commission to Hungary for the Period Ending January 15, 1920," American Red Cross, Budapest, January 16, 1920, 2, XI Rapport de Budapest, ACICR B, Mis. 4.5/585–4.5/639, 1131–1250, ICRC Archive.

118. "Relief Problems in Hungary," 7; Lt. Colonel S. A. Moffat, "Report of the American Red Cross Commission to Hungary for the Period Ending January 15, 1920," American Red Cross. Budapest, January 16, 1920, 1–3, 2, XI Rapport de Budapest, ACICR B. Mis.4.5/585–4.5/639, 1131–250, Archive of the ICRC.

119. Rodogno, "The American Red Cross," 84.

120. Hoover, "Central European Relief," 108.

121. American Relief Administration European Children's Fund, *American Relief Administration European Children's Fund Mission to Poland*, 9.

122. Hoover, "Central European Relief," 107–10.

123. Hoover, "Relief for Europe," 111.

124. Cablegram from Budapest to London, April 10–11, 1921, ARA, European Unit, London Office Cable and Telegram File, Hungary "Yellow," Budapest to London, August 1920–February 1922, American Relief Administration European Operational Records, Box 36, Folder 2, Reel 57, HILA.

125. Singer, "Mothers' and Babies' Breakfast Action in Hungary," 38.

126. Hoover, "Central European Relief," 107–8.

127. Gardner, "American Red Cross Work," 37.

128. Lukács, "Az Amerkai Vöröskereszt," 41. She uses the English term *social worker*.

129. Charlotte Lukacs, "Social Work and the American Red Cross," NARA 953.62/08 Commission to Hungary WW1 Reports.

130. Lukács, "Az Amerkai Vöröskereszt," 41.

131. Barnett, *Empire of Humanity*, 21.

132. "Letter by Mary K. Taylor."

133. Protocol of the Meeting of the Foreign Missions, March 22, 1921, 1–2, CH AEG AP 92.21.3.

134. Julia Vajkai to Colonel Raymond Sheldon, US Army Budapest, Budapest, February 5, 1920, Rapport de la mission de la CICR à Budapest, 1920, ACICR B MIS 4.5/533 à 4.5/434, 1001–1130, 1–3, 1, Archive of the ICRC.

6

BODIES

Feeding Budapest's Hungry Children

IN POSTWAR BUDAPEST, THIS CHAPTER ARGUES, HUMANITARIAN INTERVENTION to provide food to the city's children can be considered a form of transnational biopolitical intervention. In his research on humanitarian relief, Didier Fassin interprets humanitarian intervention as one form of biopolitics, in that "it sets up and manages refugee camps, establishes protected corridors in order to gain access to war casualties, develops statistical tools to measure malnutrition, and makes use of communication media to bear witness to injustice."[1] Exploring the American feeding stations for schoolchildren and milk kitchens for mothers and infants, this chapter details how foreign missions and local Hungarian relief workers exercised power over the bodies of the hungry children.

The success of this international relief endeavor depended on efficient management of all incoming food and its distribution. Postwar hunger was caused largely by interrupted infrastructures, thwarted logistics, and discontinued flows of commodities within a framework largely developed in the imperial age. Paths for transport and local infrastructures had to be restored or reinvented to implement a new postwar humanitarian food economy reaching Budapest's swollen population, especially the children. Once the foodstuffs arrived in Budapest, the relief organizations applied knowledge and methods derived from the nutritional sciences to feed the city's starving children. Children had to be rated as clinically malnourished to be eligible for food relief. The power of food was even measurable, as children's modifiable bodies could be examined and evaluated after food intake. The everyday performance of food relief was contingent on the professional physical examination, treatment, control, and documentation of children's bodies in special examination rooms. This chapter discusses the problematic implications of certain acts of physiological controls of children's access to and consumption of food, uncovering how the modern management of children's bodies was instrumental in the postwar power struggle.[2]

Managing Destitute Bodies

Postwar relief was characterized by a scientific approach to bodies and nutrition. In May 1921, Carleton G. Bowden, who ran the American relief mission in Budapest, wrote a detailed report about the everyday routines of the American Relief Administration's feeding program. The monthly deliveries of foodstuffs to the kitchens were a combination of local available foodstuffs and imported goods. The amount of food received depended on the number of children to be fed by each kitchen and the number of rations per child per day. To make sure there was "no discrepancy" between the food delivered and the food consumed, the American Red Cross's "controllers examine[d] the books and the supplies of each kitchen at frequent intervals." Chemical analysis of the rations was made on a regular basis to ensure that the cooked food actually contained the "required quantities" of the nutrients prescribed. A standard menu for all kitchens, Bowden noted, made it "practically impossible for any misappropriation of our foodstuffs to be made." Nevertheless, a "few cases of petty thievery" had been reported, and the "offenders were severely punished." To control the fair distribution of American food relief among the children in need, a complex relief administration throughout Central Europe was set up. In Budapest it included a professional physical examination of the child's body by a medical doctor, who determined children's nutritional status, children's regular weight control, and the documentation of children's nutrition and bodily development. Only if the children were underweight and starved were they entitled to receive entry tickets to the feeding places. Bowden's report stressed the importance of weighing the children "at frequent intervals" to make sure that children whose weight was getting back to "the normal" were "excluded" to "make place for another undernourished one." In this way, the organizers made sure that only the neediest children received relief meals.[3] Bowden's report offers a representative snapshot of food aid in postwar Budapest, particularly with its strong emphasis on the "quantification" "of hunger and need."

It was made clear that food distribution should neither "be hurried" nor simply "given to local institutions" but "distributed under our supervision to individuals." This precaution was taken as the result of hard experience, and the ARA insisted that "greatest care must be exercised" to make sure it was not "being swindled."[4] Expenses had to be kept down anyway, because funding was limited and poverty was abundant. In other respects, the ARA pursued the principles of "impartiality, efficiency and science": admitting children for relief regardless of social, religious, or national background or belonging. Or so it claimed. However, Jewish children, in reality, faced greater obstacles than others.[5] "The urgency of [their] relief demanded a more limited goal of feeding and clothing as many suffering Jews as possible," a task that the Jewish Joint Distribution Committee aimed to fulfill in cooperation with the ARA and other American organizations.[6]

A general principle was that international food relief was primarily meant for children. Even if entire families were suffering from starvation, mothers and other indigent adults were mostly excluded from foreign help. Some child relief organizations strongly criticized this practice, pointing out that it endangered the unity of families, in which children were just one important element.[7] Even with the parents excluded, a child's need for additional relief feeding had to be backed with proof. A document from the pen of József Spritzer, a young schoolboy who answered a Save the Children International Union questionnaire in an elementary school in Budapest, offers a rare direct child's perspective on food aid after the war (see fig. 6.1). The questionnaire was designed to find out how often children were provided with a meal during a day. Out of the 540 children surveyed, 345 had had three meals, 185 had had two meals, and 10 had had only one meal or fewer. József was in this last group. Here is his questionnaire:

> *What did I eat for breakfast yesterday?*
> *I had nothing for breakfast.*
> *What did I eat for dinner yesterday?*
> *I had bread for dinner.*
> *What did I eat for supper yesterday?*
> *I had nothing for supper.*

To assess children's levels of neediness, doctors and nurses carried out physical examinations in special rooms in schools, gyms, or hospitals. The children's treatment was similar to the "medical supervision of diseases" at the time, employing "techniques of medical observation" and a "medically useful space."[8] Because starvation was a condition that could be thought of as a treatable disease, treatment required access to the children's bodies, "discipline," and a distinct "enclosure." Selected public premises were therefore turned into special medicalized spaces. While humanitarianism targeted children collectively, the act of assessment and selection singled out each individual. Alone in special spaces, staff appraised the children's "docile bodies." They were there to be registered, "subjected, used, transformed and improved."[9]

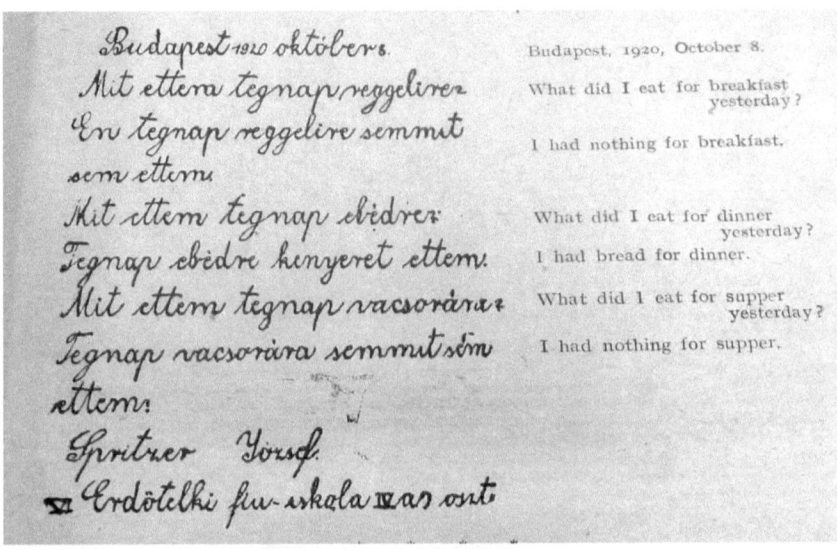

Fig. 6.1. Child questionnaire in "News from the Stricken Lands." Unknown author, *Record of the Save the Children Fund* 1, no. 2 (November 1920): 27.

The postwar child feeding programs employed strict medical supervision. A 1922 report claimed that "supplementary feeding was to be placed entirely on a medical basis"; yet social circumstances were also considered when destitute parents could not provide for their children.[10]

Owing to the American obsession with documenting the relief actions and amassing a photographic record to demonstrate the scientific methods used, we can see what these proceedings were like. Before the provision of food, "doctors, nurses, [and] school directors" in the "poorer districts" were asked to "select the poorest" and then "examine them" to find the "most undernourished." The children's bodies had to show deviation from the norm. Foucault has famously recounted how the classical age had "discovered the body as object and target of power," which can be "manipulated, shaped, trained." The children's examinations were in a way Foucauldian, separated by gender, often without the supervision of parents, undressed, and photographed to capture the children's malnutrition and resulting deformations.[11] The greater purpose of the examinations, however, was to aid children in need. Furthermore, the sites of humanitarian intervention were jointly populated by the incoming relief workers and local welfare personnel. The whole endeavor was based on and further developed the glocal cooperation. Examinations of children in Budapest were performed by local doctors. The medical staff of the University Children's Hospital examined children under the

Fig. 6.2. Girls on a scale. Unknown photographer, American Relief Administration European Operational Records, Box 859, Folder 7, HILA.

supervision of Dr. Andor Bosányi, a Hungarian pediatrician and director of the ARA's feeding stations.[12] Dr. Deutsch was responsible for the examination of the diseased children in the facilities of the Stefánia Association.[13] After a child's general neediness had been ascertained, his or her first step inside the relief premises led to the scales, as seen in figure 6.2.

Under a multistage control system, children ages three to fourteen with various weights below the target figure were considered in graduated order for free lunches at the schools and relief facilities. As scales and scientific tables determined children's entitlement to relief, children soon started to realize that a low weight was needed to qualify. "Do I weigh too much?" became a question that children asked fearfully while being measured.[14] For the weighing process itself, several doctors were employed to examine the children, with instructions that "the measurement of weight is to be carried out in robes, but without a heavy coat. . . . Those not satisfying the above conditions cannot be allowed food relief, and the doctor will destroy their recruiting card by tearing it across."[15] The doctors had to fill out a so-called recruitment ticket (*sorozó-jegy*) for every child (see fig. 6.3).

The card detailed the child's name, address, size of the family, the parents' occupations, and the size of certain garments. Although the original

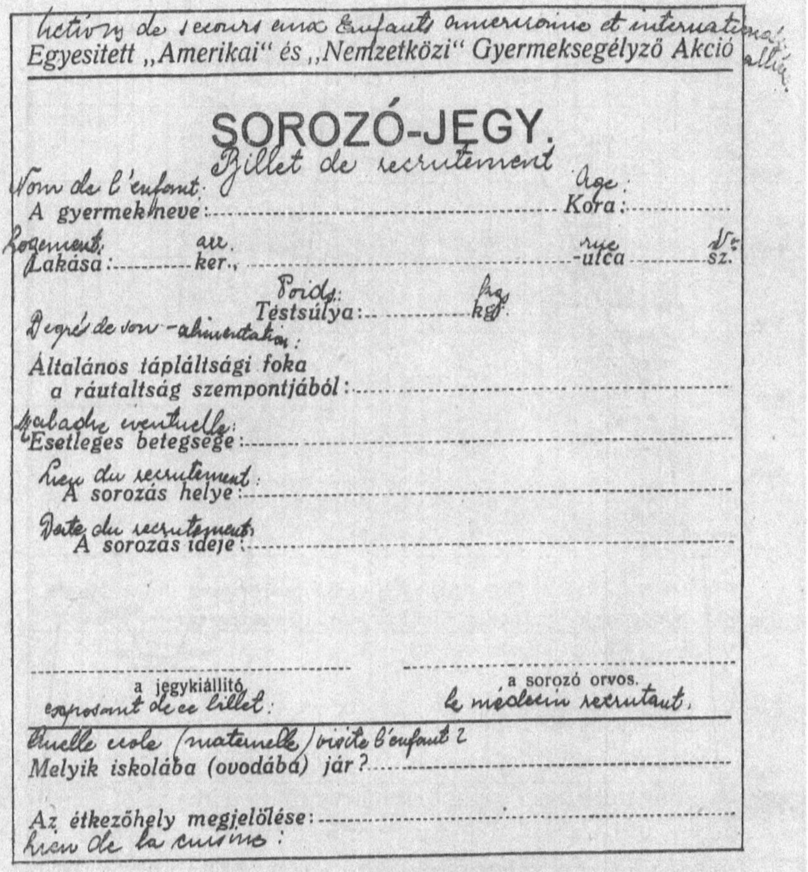

```
Action de secours aux Enfants américains et internationaux
Egyesített „Amerikai" és „Nemzetközi" Gyermeksegélyző Akció

              SOROZÓ-JEGY.
              Billet de recrutement
Nom de l'enfant:                              Age:
A gyermek neve:                               Kora:
Logement:       au                    rue              №
Lakása:         ker.,                 -utca            sz.
                      Poids:         kg
                      Testsúlya:     kg
Degré de son -alimentation:
Általános táplálísági foka
  a ráutaltság szempontjából:
Maladie éventuelle:
Esetleges betegsége:
Lieu du recrutement:
A sorozás helye:
Date du recrutement:
A sorozás ideje:



        a jegykiállító                  a sorozó orvos,
exposant de ce billet:              le médecin recrutant,
Quelle école (maternelle) visite l'enfant?
Melyik iskolába (ovodába) jár?
Az étkezőhely megjelölése:
lieu de la cuisine:
```

Actions américaine et internationale réunies (Fig. 4).
Feuille d'identité distribuée aux enfants des écoles de Budapest avant leur examen médical.
Le docteur remplit les blancs, et l'enfant suivant son degré de sous-nutrition
est admis ou non à bénéficier des repas scolaires.

Fig. 6.3. Recruitment ticket. Unknown author, in Étienne Clouzot, "Secours aux enfants en Hongrie," extract from *Revue Internationale de la Croix-Rouge* 3, no. 26 (February 15, 1921): 137–43, CH AEG AP 92.21.

forms were in Hungarian, the categories were often translated into French when the feeding was run by Geneva-based institutions such as the International Committee of the Red Cross or the Save the Children International Union, or into English if the ARA was responsible. This helped the international relief workers control and supervise the relief action. The tickets were a means of social sorting.

190 | Budapest's Children

Angolkóros gyermekek, akiket a sorozáson az étkezési akcióban részesedésre besoroztak. (Eiser fölvételei.)

Fig. 6.4. Rickety children to be recruited for participation in the feeding action. Photo by Mór Eiser, *Az Érdekes Újság* 9, no. 3 (January 20, 1921): 23.

Various reports at the time attempted to convey to the public the nature of the professional recruiting process. In depicting the selection process for the child-feeding initiative,[16] a photographer captured images of the children who had come to be weighed and categorized, and the report detailed the types of physical degeneration the children were suffering from. Children whose frail physical condition had been caused by hunger became prime targets of relief. The two children with rickets shown in figure 6.4 were part of the recruitment process. The photographers gave special attention to children with rickets, whose joints had become loose, their bones soft, and their legs bowed due to malnutrition. These images of severely underfed and "crippled" children were meant to drive home the urgent need for relief. Food and clothing were needed, as the images conveyed. These images were composed, adapted, and staged to create iconic figures of suffering. At the time, they were meant to evoke fears of the physiological impact of hunger, bad housing, and lack of hygiene on children's bodies and mental health. The mutilated body of the child was also a personification of what the collective body of the nation could become if the hunger was not relieved.

From the perspective of the humanitarian relief worker, hunger and malnutrition made the medicalization of the child's body a necessity. Children's

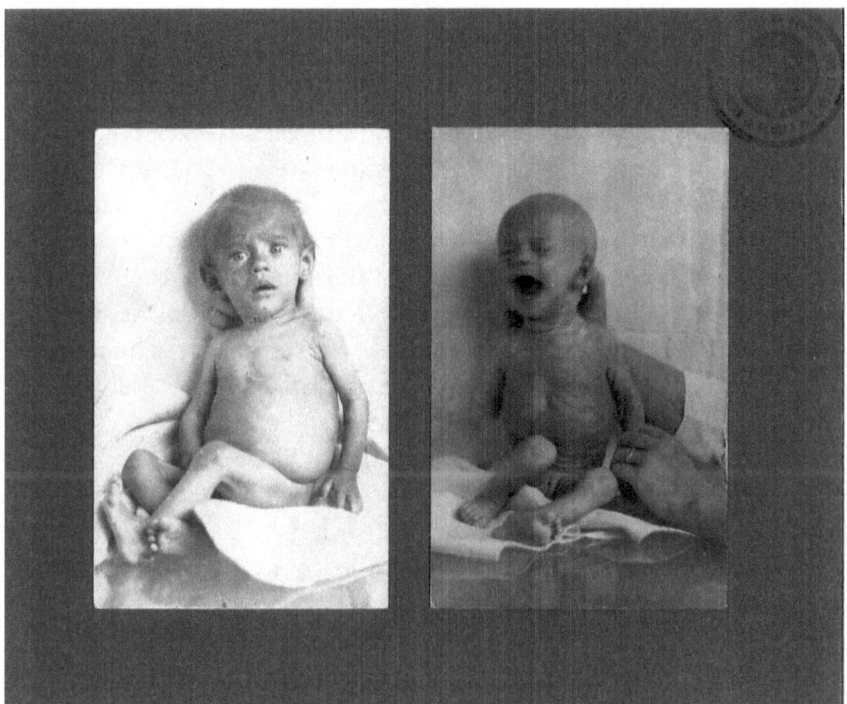

Fig. 6.5. Crippled children. Unknown photographer, 1920, CH AEG AP 92.105.76 (2).

bodies had become patients' bodies, bodies to be treated. The child's body, exposed to hunger and prolonged malnutrition, thus turned from an ideal child—a child who was well fed, active, and healthy—into a starved and sick body. Hunger thus expresses itself in a "universalized, absolute, and apolitical bodily identity," erasing the body's personality.[17] This is how the starving body of the child lost its individuality and gained a collective identity. The Save the Children International Union collected images of emaciated, crippled, or rickety infants encountered at Budapest's White Cross Hospital, such as those shown in figure 6.5, to document the children's obvious physical neediness.

Such neediness established an asymmetry between child and medical attendant. The necessity for rigorous medical control turned the child's body (in Foucauldian terms) into a "space of surveillance." In both images, the medical attendant keeps the child seated and directs the child toward the camera, as if in a puppet theater. Through the camera's lens, the intimate physical examination of the sick child becomes a public medical event. The publication or exhibition of such images abroad was intended to mobilize transnational solidarity; yet the images also played to sensationalism.

Apart from capturing children's starvation visually, statistical methods were widely used to scientifically evaluate children's malnutrition. For some decades already, governments had started "to regulate health indicators" within larger populations by collecting a "great deal of information."[18] Speaking to the Foreign Missions in March 1921, the physician Dr. Boven, delegate of the ARC in Budapest, stated that it would be "very helpful and desirable" to have the statistics of "the whole misery" of Hungary ready to hand, because the "quantity of the gifts" from the foreign relief organizations could be decided on the basis of those data.[19] Quantitative measures and standardizing tools were means to collect data on masses of humans and their bodies. And they were means of power. Through the use of statistics and other bureaucratic practices, governments and organizations could sort and organize social groups or entire populations. Biopolitical "mechanisms, techniques, and technologies of power" were now applied to the child population.[20] In the eighteenth century, the statistical table had become "both a technique of power and a procedure of knowledge" for "organizing the multiple" and mastering it through imposed "order."[21] Now, nutrition science and statistics, hand in hand with strict bookkeeping practices, enforced health "governmentality" over the targeted groups of infants and children. This was one of those moments when, according to Keith Watenpaugh, "the question of human rights and humanitarianism" developed into "a disciplining tool of Western institutions and colonialist agendas."[22] Though well-intentioned, humanitarians' statistics on starving children enabled relief organizations to seize power "in an individualizing mode" over the children's bodies and bring them "under surveillance."[23]

The process of assessment was mechanical and frightening to many children. Inside a poor suburban school on Aréna Street under the oversight of Adolf Juba, a Hungarian school doctor, for example, the children being examined were "all shaken when the tape measure reached them"; they seemed "afraid of the whole act like during some kind of medical surgery." After having their height and weight recorded, they were placed on a chair so the medical staff could ascertain the length of their upper body. The children's measurements were compared to British statistics, but it was only rarely that the Hungarian children exhibited similar weights and heights to children in Britain. To complete their medical history, children were asked the age of their fathers, but many could not answer because their fathers were lost to the war.[24] After they were examined, the children would be placed into social scientific categories of "well nourished," "medium nourished," or "undernourished" and appropriate relief feeding would be arranged, according to the recommendations at the place of examination—in a hospital,

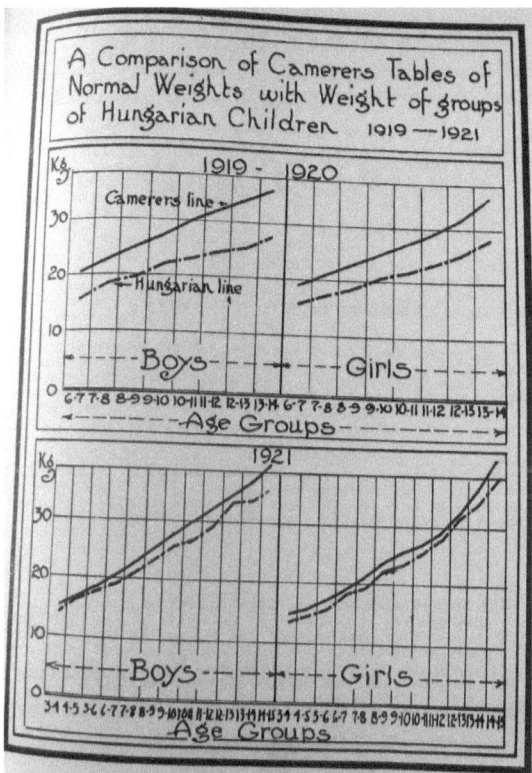

Fig. 6.6. "The Result of the 1921 Feeding from a Medical Standpoint." Unknown author, *American Relief Administration Bulletin* 2, no. 23 (April 1922): 46.

a state institution, or a district school.[25] The data collected by the ARA indicated, as shown in figure 6.6, a wide gap between the "normal weights" for children (as established by the German physician Wilhelm Camerer) and the weights of the Hungarian children assessed for relief. Hence, the immense nutritional deficit was scientifically proven and there could be a call for immediate improvement. This, in turn, paved the way for further measures of control, monitoring, and surveillance.

Children's Food Consumption

Once children had been assessed and an entitlement to receive a breakfast or lunch had been granted according to the strict criteria, the authorities issued them, or their mothers, an *étközőjegy* (food ticket), such as the one shown in figure 6.7, to relief premises.

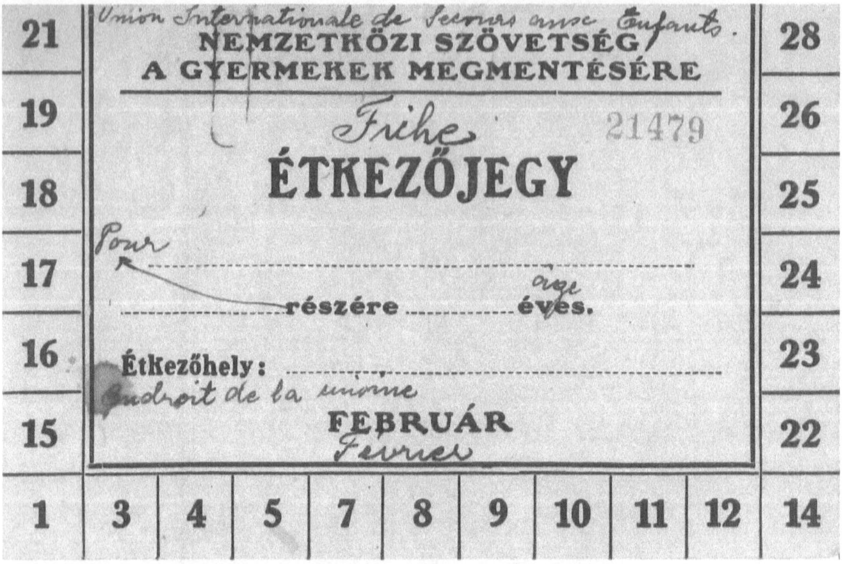
21 19 18 17 16 15
Union Internationale de Secours aux Enfants.
NEMZETKÖZI SZÖVETSÉG
A GYERMEKEK MEGMENTÉSÉRE
Friche 21479
ÉTKEZŐJEGY
Pour
részére .... éves.
âge
Étkezőhely:
Endroit de la ...
FEBRUÁR
Février
28 26 25 24 23 22
1 3 4 5 7 8 9 10 11 12 14

Fig. 6.7. Food ticket. Unknown author, 1920–21, CH AEG AP 92.21.3.

Relief organizations set standards for feeding operations and for charting children's progress, and evidence speaks to children's own reactions to the food relief they received in these contexts. The food available at the relief facilities mostly came from imports, which were now arriving on a vast scale. Tons of cocoa, sugar, milk, white flour, peas, beans, rice, and fats as well as soap were being shipped to Hungary. These items were first distributed in the schools and kindergartens of Budapest and its suburbs, then in other parts of Hungary, and in hospitals and institutions for the protection of children.[26]

The ARA's Herbert Hoover had decided that children should be fed at school to bring them "back to school life" and help "perpetuate the education idea in an environment of content."[27] Generally, relief meals were provided in primary schools, as compulsory schooling through age twelve made them a fairly reliable setting to reach children. That said, schools frequently had to close because there was no coal for heating, and on these occasions, the children missed their meals. Closures could be extended: an ARA cablegram of 1920 refers to a two-month period in the late fall of 1920, when, due to "lack of fuel for heating, all Budapest schools closed."[28] The housing shortage, which had "become a serious calamity" in Hungary, affected children's continuous schooling, too, as Julia Vajkai complained in 1926.[29] The ARA reported that not only the absence of fathers and brothers but years of being unable to live a normal life or attend school impaired the "moral[e] and physique" of Hungary's children "tremendously."[30] When school facilities could be heated, children ages three to fourteen were served early midday meals daily, except on Sundays and holidays.[31] From one relief shipment, "36,000 children in the hospitals, public institutions and schools were fed a breakfast."[32] Pediatrician Clemens von Pirquet's precise schedule for the "time and the amount of the feeding" could not always be followed to the letter,[33] and nutritional theory often "clashed with the reality of the situation in the field."[34] Humanitarian relief food came to be consumed not only in primary schools but in kindergartens, children's hospitals, and orphanages.

Once the children were entitled to relief, they had to eat on-site to prevent them from sharing their rations with their parents. To Hoover, the parents—especially soldier fathers—still carried the stigma of being the former war enemy. The children, in contrast, were "suffering through no fault of their own." The Quakers involved in humanitarian work disagreed with the idea of feeding only the children, believing that children were part of their families and should be fed within their natural environment.[35] Tara Zahra comments that "ARA policies were shaped by a profound mistrust of parents" and did nothing to support "family solidarity." Hoover's more cynical view was that "if food were distributed to parents," they would "simply eat it rather than share it with their children." For this reason, the ARA "mandated that children's plates must be cleaned on the spot in ARA cafeterias, under strict supervision."[36] In this way, child relief was a discriminatory process. It did not support impoverished families as an entity but offered help only to the children as innocent war victims.

What was the scene like in the relief kitchens? The children were seated at tables according to their category of "nutritional requirements." ARA workers were instructed to apply a "distinctive method of delivering calories to needy children" with efficiency. Great trouble was taken to distribute the food according to each child's nutritional needs: soup portions were exactly measured, and bread and cakes were sliced in advance in accordance with Pirquet's "hektonem" portions. The children ate everything they were served, and nothing was left over—it was seen as crucial that no food should be "turned into garbage." A central concern of the American feeding mission was that everything be done in the most economical way. Much of the tableware was old wartime issue. An eyewitness to an ARA kitchen in Vienna noticed that many of the children brought with them "military mess bowls," which their soldier fathers had brought home after demobilization. A report boasted, "The father and big brothers of these children" never "receive[d] in these mess bowls the same good and wholesome fare with which they [were] now filled at the American eating station."[37]

Despite their neglected appearance, the children were well behaved and appreciative. The way the children consumed the food they were given showed how famished they were. This was especially true of children coming for the first time, who reportedly wolfed down their portions with a "greedy gulping in a twinkling!" Due to hunger, they had lost much of their natural childlike behavior; there was little chatter and noise. Most of the time, they sat down "quietly and in orderly fashion." Everything was so well organized and "in readiness" that undue "waiting and tarrying of the children" was avoided. The subdued atmosphere changed somewhat during the session. Before their "thin hands" were allowed to "grasp the eating utensils," the children seemed uncomfortably silent. There was "no merry word, no play, no glad greeting of a comrade," because "hunger" had made them all "so tired, so silent, so sad!" But as soon as the smell of food came from the kitchen, it aroused the children's natural "impatience and joyful expectation."[38]

This discipline was not achieved without effort, and some reports suggest some unruliness. The ARA was worried that violent arguments and fights might break out between members of rival schools where food was distributed. Often, as many as a thousand children might eat in one dining hall, all at once, and sometimes "rowdy gangs" interrupted the proceedings. The local relief workers broke up troublemakers and relied on the help of "boy scouts" to prevent further violent behavior. Attitudes and expectations changed over time, and, once the children could rely on the daily provision of a warm lunch at their schools, the organizers found that "order has grown out of chaos."[39] Scenes with children in front of an ARA kitchen in Budapest were captured in images, such as figure 6.8. In the photograph, the children are being supervised by a few women relief workers, and military personnel are present to ensure good order.

In some cases, it was impossible "for sick and convalescent children, of which there [were] many," to leave home to come to the kitchens. The ARA remedied this by arranging for "warehouse profits" to be used to feed "sick and convalescent children in their homes." The organizers believed that, with "50,000 undernourished children" being fed in the kitchens and through the warehouse profit scheme for convalescents, the "situation in Hungary would be well cared for."[40] Thus, the feeding program was somewhat able to provide for the alimentary needs of children outside of their designated locations.

Fig. 6.8. "Hungary ARA. Feeding kitchens." Unknown photographer, American Relief Administration European Operational Records, Box 859, Folder 6, HILA.

How effective was the feeding program? After feeding starving children, the next step was to measure and statistically analyze the food's impact on their weight. This had to be meticulously documented, and, if necessary, adjustments were made to the children's diets. There was much discussion about the supply of fats because a weight gain could most easily be achieved by the intake of fatty foods. The "whole situation hinges on fats," one ARA cablegram proclaimed. Relief workers in Budapest echoed this view, asking for advice about "possibilities [of] assistance on [the] fat program."[41] An economic study on the humanitarian feeding of German children (in conditions similar to Hungarian children) claims that the efforts of humanitarian child relief organizations were "indeed successful in improving the well-being of . . . children most nutritionally damaged by the war."[42] Yet the children in Budapest received only 660 calories a day, which was just a third of what toddlers should consume and half of what children ages six to eight need for basic development. Hence, only modest weight increases were registered—for example, a gain of eight hundred grams after 161 meals in an orphanage.[43] But there is no record of infants or children *losing* weight, which would surely have happened if they had not received the free lunches amid postwar scarcity.[44] American relief, the sources suggest, not only won the war but also the subsequent war against hunger.

Saving Infants and Mothers: Milk Kitchens and an Assured Milk Supply

Whereas the American food mission initially targeted school-age children, from 1921 on, the operation expanded to address the needs of infants and expecting or breastfeeding mothers, whose health was taking center stage as a major concern. An ARA cablegram of February 1921 contains much discussion of the need to feed "children under 5, pregnant women and nursing mothers," noting that "nothing" was "being done [in] this country" to support them. Women and infants became newly entitled categories for relief.[45] Accordingly, the most indigent and undernourished "2,000 babies" and "200 pregnant women and nursing mothers" from the "poorer districts" were to be selected by local doctors, nurses, and school directors.[46] Milk, relief workers believed, was the solution to these types of problems.

The ARA established a breakfast initiative, using the facilities of the Stefánia Association. Hedwig Singer claimed in an October 1921 report titled "Mothers' and Babies' Breakfast Action in Hungary" that geopolitical instability had made food aid for mothers and infants essential. She wrote of the "pitiful sight of the little ones with heavy, large heads, bent legs, painfully awkward movements" who were seen all over the city. Rickets had badly affected "children conceived and born during the Red Rule and the Rumanian occupation," making their need greater than the older children. Singer was convinced that the children's disastrous physical state had resulted from the scant "bill of fare" available to mothers and babies during the Romanian occupation—"barley, marrow and potatoes ad infinitum, and even that in insufficient quantities."[47] Mothers and babies were fed "3 days weekly, cocoa, bread, and 3 days, milk and bread" in the relief premises.[48]

The breakfast initiative was heralded in local Hungarian journals such as *Az Érdekes Újság* (The interesting journal). A cover photo (fig. 6.9) from the publication showed the mothers and their young children who benefited. By February 1921, four "milk stations" for small children had been opened, too. The ARA distributed 650 tins of milk daily.[49] Because milk powder was easy to import, the ARA aimed to provide three thousand babies with milk throughout the summer months of 1921. It came in two-kilogram tins of Glaxo formula, because "Hungarian doctors know and approve of Glaxo" in contrast to "Hookers" Malted Milk Powder.[50] Especially when mothers could not breastfeed,

Fig. 6.9. "The little ones receive American breakfast."
Unknown photographer, *Az Érdekes Újság* 9, no. 14
(April 14, 1921): cover.

formula was considered an ideal means to prevent infant malnutrition and early death. Advertisements of Nestlé formula in the major Hungarian journals called on mothers to feed their children with Nestlé if they wanted to see them grow up healthy and beautiful and recover quickly from intestinal diseases.[51]

Because lack of milk was considered a major cause of children's starvation, relief workers put a lot of effort into importing and distributing milk in various forms. They saw it as the best way to improve infants' health. Relief workers were not alone in this thinking. For instance, in 1915 in the United States, the National Dairy Council conducted studies and began to promote milk as an "all-around healthy and nutritious food that was particularly good for growing children." A flood of publicity, including plays and films featuring milk, made sure that everyone got the message: the "consumption of milk was absolutely necessary for healthy childhood development." By the mid-1920s, consuming milk daily was considered "a basic requirement for healthy child growth and development."⁵² To lend scientific backing to the need for milk kitchens in Europe, research was conducted on the connection between infant mortality and the availability and consumption of milk. Statisticians had been accumulating data since the beginning of the nineteenth century in a general bureaucratic attempt to gauge the needs of societies and populations "before the aims of the state could be put into effect."⁵³ As Lorna Weir has suggested, mortality statistics serve as "a technique for rendering bare life as an object of governance," and statistics can be deployed "as collective representations of the nation."⁵⁴ Once "believable and spatially specific knowledge about the nation" was compiled in tables, it could be used to justify controls. Jason Hansen even claims that statistics transformed the ways in which "nationalism itself could be practiced, laying the groundwork for the practical application of nationalist ideology to everyday life."⁵⁵

In Hungary, statistical tables were published in the ARA's *Bulletin* showing correlations between mortality and birth rates and milk supply. A charted increase in the mortality rate was seen as the consequence of a decrease in milk availability. Thus, statistical practices were instrumental in proving Hungary's dramatic need for milk and in informing the needed capacity of the international relief organizations to remedy nutritional deficiencies. One statistical table from fall 1921 titled "Supply of Milk for the Children of Budapest" summarized how the need for milk in Budapest increased between 1918 and 1920 from 5,324 to 9,337 liters, and how the average age of children in need steadily declined over that same period; in 1918, the average age was two to three, in 1919, the average age was one to two, and in 1920, the average age was birth to one. The daily lack of milk amounted to 24,374 liters. The table draws attention to the increasing malnourishment of mothers and infants. Because infants were also the most dependent, providing relief to babies was the priority undertaking.

Many photographs from the time show mothers with their babies waiting for milk and food donations in front of some of the feeding stations in Budapest and its suburbs, as in figure 6.10. Lining up for food had become the a more general social response to scarcity. Normal shops and relief facilities alike saw bread and food lines, especially in the early mornings. Susanne Leikam argues that the masses of destitute people who daily waited in line for basic commodities were "prominently rendering poverty and hardship visible" and "challeng[ing] the functionality and competence of existing political and economic power structures."⁵⁶ Mothers and children queuing in postwar Budapest highlighted the inability of the Hungarian authorities to provide the food the population needed. In a society of shortage, they were turning to help from other nations, but in doing so they were developing new economic

Fig. 6.10. Recruiting babies and mothers in a suburb of Budapest. Unknown photographer, Administration European Operational Records, Box 859, Folder 4, HILA.

dependencies, particularly between the abundant United States and impoverished Central Europe. Hoover, who believed in treating relief like a business, was "cashing in on the deliveries to the defeated countries."[57] Many of the food deliveries, rather than being simply donated, were based on interstate loans.

To qualify for government-sponsored milk, mothers and infants had to undergo an examination and be issued "milk passes" (*Tejigazolváynok*). There were strict gradations: passes for one liter were given to pregnant or breastfeeding mothers and children under age two; passes for half a liter went to children between two and three. Sick and elderly people might also sometimes be entitled to milk supplies.[58] But the general rule was restrictive: the only adults who could get food relief were mothers bearing or raising the new generation. As in the other feeding facilities, the infants and toddlers taken into the ARA's relief scheme for access to milk kitchens had to undergo a scientific examination to assess their bodily constitution and weight; many were visually documented in the process. While the photographs of older children tend to focus on the large numbers of children attending, the visuals of the infants tend to narrow the perspective to the individual. A single malnourished child awaiting examination is shown in figure 6.11.

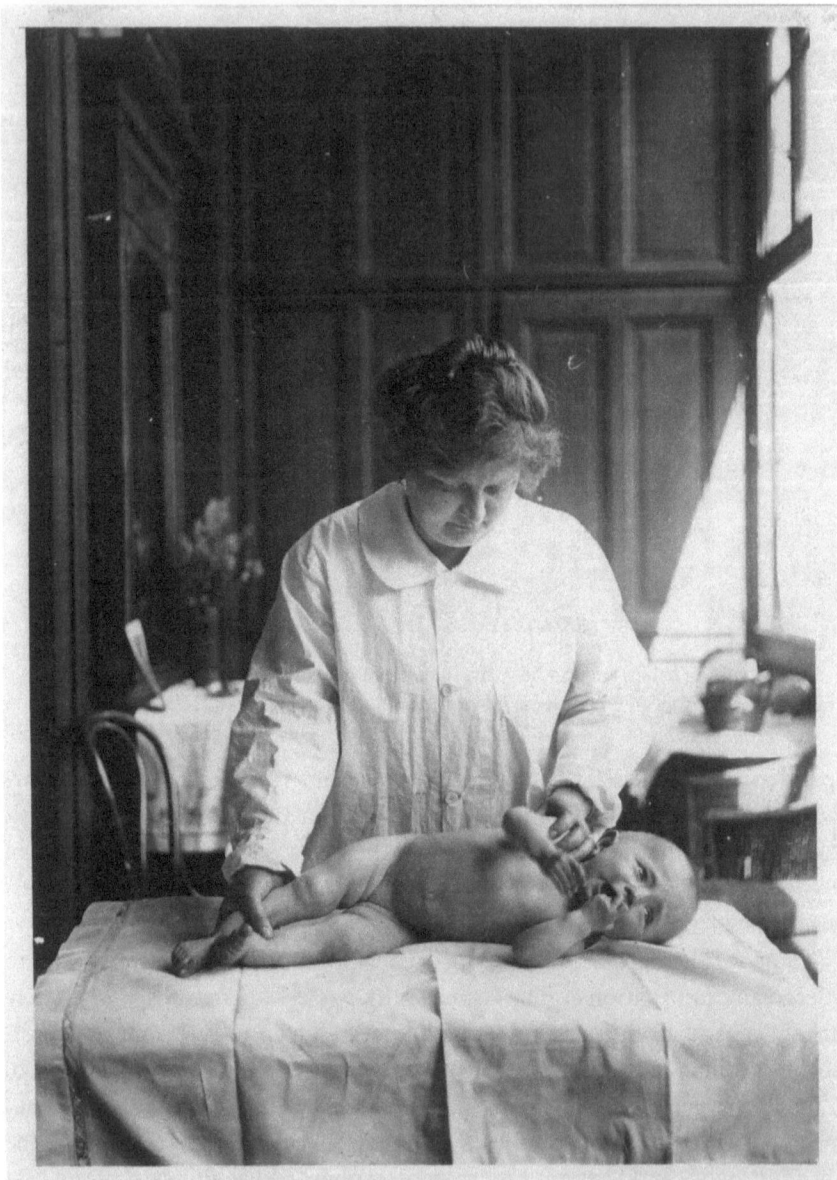

Fig. 6.11. Recruiting for ARA breakfast at the Association for the Protection of Mothers and Children. Unknown photographer, Budapest May 23, 1921, American Relief Administration European Operational Records, Box 851, Folder J, HILA.

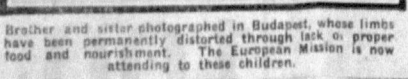

Fig. 6.12. "Budapest and London: Contrast in Child Life." Unknown photographer, *Birmingham Gazette and Express* November 23, 1920, CH AEG AP 92.21.1.

The examinations were conducted at the Stefánia Association premises by local nurses. It is uncomfortable to look at such images, as they intentionally expose bodily features indicating ill health and stunted physical development.[59] The specific social and local circumstances behind a child's suffering were often of only marginal interest.

Some photographs published in international journals, such as those shown in figure 6.12, contrasted the physical state of rickety children in Budapest with their well-fed peers in more prosperous Western cities such as London. The left-hand image is of two Budapest orphans, poorly dressed, with rickets, their bodies "distorted through lack of proper food and nourishment." How they contrast with London's "Little Miss Hazel Neilson Terry" on the right! Images of the shockingly divergent realities of the lives of children in these two European cities were used to drive home the urgent need to send food supplies to Hungary. They effectively combined a fundamental critique of the wealth of the better-off classes in Britain in a time of great need with a moral appeal to help Hungary's poor and physically disabled children.

"The British public's exposure to such suffering" would, it was hoped, raise money "to fight the famine," but, Rebecca Gill comments, it might "also bring British government and society to their moral senses."[60] Looking at images of the suffering of poor and bereft children from a safe distance forced people in the prosperous West to confront the realities in distant Central Europe. Yet this type of humanitarian imagery was also highly problematic from a political standpoint. As scholars Lilie Chouliaraki and Bolette Blaagaard have suggested, a "historical divide of viewing relations between Western societies of relative affluence and safety and developing countries of poverty and danger" often shapes humanitarian imagery.[61] Humanitarian relief for distant suffering and its visual representation never take place in a political vacuum but instead shape, and are shaped by, power relations.[62] This imagery mirrored and further enforced the political power relations between donor and recipient. Not only in war, but in peacetime, too, the victorious Western powers found it necessary to prove their economic supremacy by exposing the physical destitution of Budapest's children.

Stereotypes of women's and children's neediness, from which "humanitarian" photography never shrank, were deployed to evoke compassion and compel donations. Images taken for the SCIU in 1920 centered on mothers and their rickety, severely undernourished children hospitalized in Budapest's White Cross Hospital. Depictions of mothers and children like that shown in figure 6.13 draw on the religious pictorial iconography of the Madonna and Child and of the Pietà.

The visible suffering of the infants, just born and already destitute, combines with the desperate look on the mother's faces to make the viewer fear for the babies' lives. What lay in store for the mothers and babies? In her 1921 report, Singer observed that, "within a short time after receiving our breakfast[s]," mothers who had been "unable to breastfeed their infants in a sufficient manner" had "sufficient milk" so that extra milk rations to the infants were no longer necessary. In many cases, there was a difference of one kilogram in weight between infants of mothers who had attended the ARA's kitchen for a few weeks and other infants. In order not to shame the mothers and make them feel like beggars, the ARA "deemed it advisable, from the point of view of morale," to ask for a small weekly charge of two kronen for the breakfast rations. The money collected was set aside to "assist poor women" and "needy mothers ... in a worse plight than themselves."[63]

On September 1, 1921, the ARA handed over the "entire responsibility" for the breakfast initiative to the Stefánia Association and the National Child

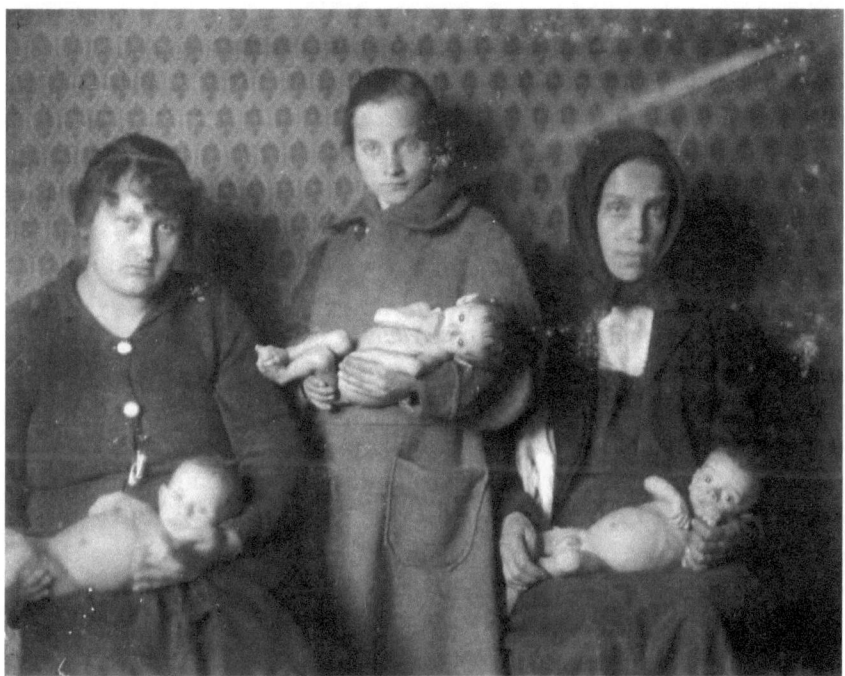

Fig. 6.13. Needy mothers with rickety infants in a clinic in Budapest. Unknown photographer, Budapest 1920, CH AEG AP 92.105.76 (2).

Protection League.[64] For the next nine months, up to June 1, 1922, another child feeding program would offer lunch to "15,000 undernourished school children" and breakfast to "approximately 3,000 nursing mothers and pregnant women," together with "2,000 babies."[65] The physical condition of infants and toddlers under age three was considered serious, because they were "born during communism."[66] In the course of the brief Soviet republic, it had been "impossible [to] obtain sufficient nourishment and attention."[67] In contrast, "older children" had had a better "start in life under more favorable conditions."[68] For the new relief action, the minister of public welfare Nándor Bernolák confirmed the Hungarian government would "pay the freight and transport expenses from the European port to Budapest of all commodities [the ARA] imported" for child welfare as well as "all expenses connected with the manipulation and warehousing of these commodities."[69] As in other cases, the ARA established an emergency measure, importing sorely needed milk powder, and then, having established a successful infrastructure, passed management to local relief organizations.

Shifting Responsibilities: From the Family to the State

Relief altered parental authority and expanded governmental authority in the feeding and care of children. Already in the late nineteenth century, modern states had begun to perceive food, and its related everyday practices, as a means to monitor and improve populations by altering their physical bodies.[70] Humanitarian intervention allowed certain authorities to gain access to, and power over, the destitute child and his or her body. Foucault identified children as part of the social "abnormal," by which he meant those social groups liable to be subjected and deprived of certain freedoms. Excessive "power is exercised over the mad, the ill, criminals, deviants, children and the poor," and this allows "mechanisms and effects of exclusion, disqualification, exile, rejection, deprivation, refusal, and incomprehension" to be forced on people in these social categories.[71] Especially in moments of economic, political, and social crisis, as in the aftermath of the Great War, parents were no longer in the sole position to secure their children's well-being, or even survival. Hence, parents passed part of their parental responsibility to the state.[72] In postwar Budapest, this shift from parental care to care through institutions played out in full. The child's undernourished body became a "site where regimes of discourse and power inscribe[d] themselves."[73]

After the scale of the destitution in Budapest had been ascertained, food relief "massified" and affected a whole generation. Access to the individual body was used to implement humanitarian relief, but relief became aimed at the capital's collective body of needy children. As Foucault formulated it during his famous lectures delivered in Paris, there existed a mechanism of collective surveillance and control. Such social control was also part and parcel of humanitarian relief. While Foucault speaks of a shift from the "first seizure of power over the body in an individualizing mode" to a "second seizure of power" that is "massifying," "directed not at man-as-body but at man-as-species,"[74] this humanitarian endeavor illustrates well how the individual child's body had to be measured and assessed so that the condition of the collective body of children could be altered. By employing various means of child relief, "British humanitarians" and those of other national backgrounds "worked to create physically healthy, mentally disciplined, and emotionally well-adjusted children across the globe."[75]

A combination of nutrition science and statistics with strict bookkeeping practices established health "governmentality" over Budapest's children and infants. The statistics needed masses of individual bodies, over whom power could be seized "in an individualizing mode" but "under surveillance."

Bringing these bureaucratic techniques to bear on the collective body of Budapest's destitute and starving children served to alter and govern the health and care of these child populations.[76] Beyond the body politics of individual disciplining and intervention in the intimacy of the child's body, the entire relief endeavor targeted and profoundly shaped Hungary's overall public health and child protection systems. Responsibility for the child lay no longer with the family alone but became increasingly a function of the state's competences. The state became a public paterfamilias.

Conclusion

In postwar Europe, destitution made it impossible for families to secure their children's survival. In such circumstances, children became dependent on food provided through transnational and transatlantic humanitarian intervention. Saving and healing the body of Budapest's children through food relief provided Western humanitarian organizations with an ultimate opportunity to alter the individual and collective body of distant children in need. Humanitarian child relief was only possible via invasion into children's most intimate lives, drastically altering the relationship between the family, the state, and the outsider. The agents of humanitarian food relief took up the responsibility for the survival of Budapest's starving, ill, abandoned, or destitute children, but in that process exercised power over the children's bodies. In that sense, postwar "history [was becoming] 'inscribed' or 'imprinted' onto [the] body," not solely through the destitution of the war's aftermath but also through the physical relief that was offered.[77]

Notes

1. Fassin, "Humanitarianism as a Politics of Life," 501.
2. See also Kind-Kovács, "The Great War."
3. Bowden, "Economic Conditions and Relief in Hungary," 13.
4. Childfund to Mr. Mitchell, cablegram, Budapest, March 7, 1921, American Relief Administration European Operational Records, Box 36, Folder 2, R57, HILA.
5. Adlgasser, *American Individualism Abroad*, 171–72.
6. Granick, *International Jewish Humanitarianism in the Age of the Great War*, 74.
7. Marshall, "Children's Rights and Children's Actions," 358.
8. Foucault, *Discipline and Punish*, 144.
9. Ibid., 141, 136–38.
10. Mary K. Taylor, Society Service, American Red Cross in Hungary, to Captain James G. Pedlow, Director of American Red Cross in Hungary, July 1, 1922, Sheets 1–4, Sheet 1, RG 200 Records of the American National Red Cross 1917–34, 953.08, Box 878, NARA.

11. Childfund to Mr. Brown and Mr. Mitchell, cablegram, Budapest, April 10–11, 1921, American Relief Administration European Operational Records, Box 36, Folder 2, R. 57, HILA. "Manipulated, shaped, trained" is from Foucault, *Discipline and Punish*, 136.
12. American Relief Administration European Children's Fund, *Final Report*, 24.
13. "Amerika a pesti gyermekekért," 6.
14. American Relief Administration European Children's Fund, *Final Report*, 24, 13.
15. "Daten zur Kinder-Recrutierung [sic], 1920/12/28," Eglantyne Jebb Papers Hungary, A 0407, EJ 155 Hungary, Folder 2, 1920–21, International Commissioners Reports and Correspondence, SCF Archive.
16. "Az amerikai vöröskeresztes misszió," 23.
17. Weinreb, "Embodying German Suffering," 466–67.
18. Youde, *Biopolitical Surveillance*, 18.
19. "Protocol of the Meeting of the Foreign Missions and Home Institutions: March 22, 1921," 3–4. CH AEG A.P. 92.21.3.
20. Foucault, *Society Must Be Defended*, 241.
21. Foucault, *Discipline and Punish*, 148.
22. Watenpaugh, "The League of Nations' Rescue," 1321.
23. Foucault, *Society Must Be Defended*, 242–43.
24. "American Relief Administration European Children's Fund," 5.
25. Bókay, "The Result of the 1921 Feeding," 44, 46.
26. Members of the American Child Welfare Mission in Hungary, "Child Feeding in Hungary," 32.
27. Hoover, "Children's Relief and Democracy," 1.
28. Cablegram to Mr. Murphy, Budapest, December 11, 1920, American Relief Administration European Operational Records, Box 36, Folder 2, R57, HILA.
29. Julia Vajkai, *Child Saving and Child Training*, 9.
30. American Relief Administration European Children's Fund, *Final Report*, 12.
31. Bókay, "The Result of the Hungarian Mission," 1.
32. "Child Feeding in Hungary," 31.
33. Pirquet, *An Outline of the Pirquet System of Nutrition*, 48.
34. Cabanes, *The Great War and the Origins of Humanitarianism*, 228.
35. Marshall, *Children's Rights and Children's Actions*, 356, 358.
36. Zahra, *The Lost Children*, 39.
37. Pirquet, *An Outline of the Pirquet System*, 52; "How Do the Children Eat?" 26–27, 26, American Relief Administration European Operational Records, Box 328, Folder 7, R379, HILA; Zahra, *The Lost Children*, 39.
38. "How Do the Children Eat?" 26.
39. American Relief Administration European Children's Fund, *Final Report*, 13.
40. Childfund to Mr. Brown and Mr. Mitchell, cablegram, Budapest, December 1, 1920, American Relief Administration European Operational Records, Box 36, Folder 2, R57, HILA.
41. Mr. Richardson to Mr. Brown, cablegram, April 15, 1920, American Relief Administration European Operational Records, Box 35, Folder 4, R56, HILA.
42. Cox, "Hunger Games," 629.
43. Étienne Clouzot, "Secours aux enfants en Hongrie," 2.
44. For a detailed analysis of children's weight increase, see Bókay, "The Result of the Hungarian Mission," 14.
45. Childfund to Mr. Quinn and Mr. Mitchell, cablegram, Budapest, February 28, 1921.
46. Childfund to Mr. Brown and Mr. Mitchell, cablegram, Budapest, April 10–11, 1921.

47. Singer, "Mothers' and Babies' Breakfast Action," 34.
48. Childfund to Mr. Quinn and Mr. Mitchell, cablegram, Budapest, February 28, 1921.
49. Childfund to Mr. Gay, cablegram, Budapest, February 2, 1921, American Relief Administration European Operational Records, Box 36, Folder 2, R57, HILA.
50. Childfund to Mr. Gay (Mr. Quinn), cablegram, Budapest, May 5, 1921, American Relief Administration European Operational Records, Box 36, Folder 1, Reel 56, HILA.
51. "Legnagyobb öröme," 22; "Nestlé Gyermekliszt," 14.
52. Meckel, *Urban Schools*, 185.
53. Porter, *The Rise of Statistical Thinking*, 17.
54. Weir, *Pregnancy, Risk and Biopolitics*, 37.
55. Hansen, *Mapping the Germans*, 10.
56. Leikam, "Visualizing Hunger," 584. See also Mann, "Queue Culture."
57. Glant, "Herbert Hoover and Hungary," 98.
58. Posters for milk passes, Tejakciója, Országos Hadsegélyző Bizottság, Collection of the Hungarian National Museum.
59. Thompson, *Light on Darkness?*, 2.
60. Gill, *Calculating Compassion*, 201.
61. Chouliaraki and Blaagaard, "The Ethics of Images," 253–54.
62. Orgad, "Visualizers of Solidarity," 296.
63. Singer, "Mothers' and Babies' Breakfast Action in Hungary," 36.
64. Ibid., 37.
65. Bernolák, "Agreement between the Royal Hungarian Government," 28.
66. Childfund, Cablegram to Mr. Quinn, Budapest, March 2, 1921, American Relief Administration European Operational Records, Box 36, Folder 2, HILA.
67. Ibid.
68. Ibid.
69. Bernolák, "Agreement between the Royal Hungarian Government," 28.
70. Weinreb, *Modern Hungers*, 3.
71. Foucault, *Abnormal*, 43–44.
72. Foucault, *Society Must Be Defended*, 256.
73. Butler, "Foucault and the Paradox," 601.
74. Foucault, *Society Must Be Defended*, 243.
75. Baughan, *Saving the Children*, 20.
76. Foucault, *Society Must Be Defended*, 242–43. See also Foucault, *The Birth of Biopolitics*.
77. Butler, "Foucault and the Paradox," 607.

7

(INTER)NATIONALISM

The Politics of Material Aid

THIS CHAPTER EXPLORES THE POLITICAL GOALS BEHIND THE feeding of Budapest's hungry children. In times of food scarcity, as Alice Weinreb reminds us, "food brings modern bodies in contact with political strategy." The chapter examines the methods international relief organizations adopted to boost their influence in distant Europe and gain future allies—children who would form the next generation. It identifies the crucial role of food and certain commodities in this transnational endeavor. In turn, the use of food in the postwar humanitarian relief efforts advances our understanding of the postwar "moral economy" and mirrored the professionalization of relief, which helped generate the rise of modern humanitarianism.[1] Humanitarian food relief furthermore reveals the social, political, and economic imbalances between the recipient and donor nations.

It is no surprise that complex power relations surrounded the food mission to Budapest's children. Food represents a field of power, as it generates "endless notions of good and bad: good and bad food, good and bad eating practices, and good and bad bodies," Jürgen Martschukat and Bryant Simon maintain.[2] Food is a basic: it "is essential to life and must enter our bodies daily in substantial amounts if we are to live."[3] But parents and children were unable to obtain it. Scarcity made people powerless to secure their own survival and created physical and cultural dependencies they had not known before. More widely, power imbalances manifested in the struggle over access to food, over the choice and processing of foodstuffs, and over spaces of food production and consumption. Paradoxically, in a period of internationalism, humanitarian relief for Budapest's destitute children often became an arena of postwar nation-building, territorial revisionism, and overt nationalism. This chapter argues that Hungarian nationalism and American patriotism represented fundamental driving forces behind the transatlantic relief efforts. And last, by examining how other material things gained a humanitarian meaning and contributed to the creation of personal and transnational relationships, this chapter contributes to the field of "material history."[4]

International Hierarchies and Supervising Local Efforts

The exercise of foreign power can be seen in a reshuffling of control over Hungarian relief organizations and local personnel. Many American Relief Administration reports, for example, stressed the need for this restructuring to better serve American priorities. ARA facilities employed many local Hungarian social workers, nurses, and auxiliaries, whereas American personnel tended to fill roles as managers, experts, and supervisors. In addition to imposing its own hierarchy, the ARA shook up European medical rankings as well. Whereas in Austria, "nurses [formerly] looked down on cooking as an art much inferior to nursing," ARA nutritional scientist Clemens von Pirquet selected his "best nurses for superintending the kitchen." To him, the kitchen was "more important than the pharmacy."[5] Reports telegraphed to London about the American-led relief work stressed its professionalism and efficiency. A 1921 report refers to "3 expert American lady assistants" who spoke Hungarian and served as "controllers" for the kitchens."[6] In *Bread from Stones*, Keith Watenpaugh notes that reports from the Middle East emphasized a parallel approach: a departure from the "sentimental missionary narrative" of the nineteenth century and a new reliance on scientific understanding and modern knowledge to ascertain conditions and the causes of suffering, and then to develop rationalized solutions. This type of reporting intersected with the "political and social expectations of the Western middle-class public sphere" and its "technocratic, disciplinary knowledge-driven—and sometimes rights-based—response to humanitarian need."[7]

Hungary had a longer tradition of child protection and welfare than the United States, but the American relief organizations wanted to manage the "whole show," using its "modern," rationalized systems. Much of the language in the US reports reveals the hierarchies its relief organizations had imposed on the everyday work at the stations. "We promise that our control will be efficient"—statements like this abound.[8] A 1922 report on the ARA's European Children's Fund Mission to Poland explains how American inspectors, "going from town to town and from kitchen to kitchen" to supervise local facilities, constantly demonstrated the "fundamental principles" of the relief initiative and exhibited the "point of view of the American donors." The American field inspectors clearly made it their task to "verify" that "the wishes of the American donors" were being fulfilled.[9]

Other factors set American relief workers socially apart as well. Local child welfare workers were often volunteers or, if paid, earned only a little, while American relief workers in Europe were far better off financially. To pursue their work efficiently, the Americans might be provided with "1 automobile, 1 secretary, 1 stenographer," and a "chauffeur as personnel."[10] Thomas Westerman has argued that American relief workers in Belgium in 1914 found themselves "in an amorphous space": they were "neither combatants, nor victims; neither occupied, nor occupiers," and they became at times "tourists, unofficial ambassadors of the USA, and agents of mercy to people threatened with starvation."[11] This was also true for postwar Budapest. The relief workers led their everyday lives there. They had their favorite restaurants. And they established relationships, made friends, and worked together with their Hungarian colleagues. Nevertheless, hierarchies can be identified in the written reports about the everyday relief work.

Former army personnel were prominent in relief organizations. Among the eighteen army officers in one branch, a report boasted, there were "6 Generals and none lower than Colonel."[12] Captain James Pedlow was the chief of the American Red Cross in Budapest; Captain George Richardson was the chief of the ARA in Hungary.[13] Their military training was directly put to use in the relief work of the ARA.[14] Another report proudly mentions an "organized system [of] kitchen control by pensioned Army officers." Indeed, it was to the military organization of routines that the "great success" of the kitchens was credited. Firm organization under army personnel was considered "much better than previous control by teachers, who had neither power nor ability [to] enforce rules."[15] The recruitment of officers and soldiers was considered "a masterstroke," because they were not only "physically fit [and] self-reliant" but "accustomed to . . . working with Europeans."[16] Infrastructures, responsibilities, and competences developed during the war were being applied in this postwar "campaign."[17] Herbert Hoover recruited many former employees from his staffs at the American Food Administration and the Commission for Relief in Belgium as well, having particular confidence in experts and engineers.[18] Yet some local relief workers considered them a "sheer waste [of] time and money," because work in Hungary was so concentrated that the control of feeding was easy.[19] They assured the ARA that they needed no assistance and wished to run the job alone.[20]

The European Children's Fund's Budapest office was required to report with continual updates about the state of the relief work. The London office, run by Walter Lyman Brown, maintained constant supervision. On November 13, 1920, Brown sent a telegram to Budapest, requesting that staff "report immediately" with precise details of the places where feeding took place, name lists of prominent local welfare workers, locations of greatest need, and local governmental donations. Budapest was to deliver "any letters or messages" reporting on relief work and supply photographs documenting the work.[21] American supervision via London was intended to convey thoroughness, efficiency, and oversight.

In Hungary, the foreign military and relief personnel were supported by the churches and synagogues and by local medical and child relief experts. János Bókay, professor at the Budapest University of Science and a "children's specialist of international renown," served as the president of the ARA's Children's Fund Executive Committee. On the advisory body were illustrious religious representatives, including Catholics, Lutherans, Calvinists, Neolog Jews, and Orthodox Jews. The Ladies' Committee, which reported on conditions in the relief kitchens, included the wife of the former minister of public health, Mrs. András Csilléry, the wife of the mayor of Budapest, Mrs. Tivadar Bódy, and the wife of the former prime minister, Mrs. István Friedrich. These women, listed explicitly by association with their elite husbands to lend authority, were aided by more than a hundred "ladies of all classes and interests in Hungary."[22] Social hierarchies and the politics of prestige in relief work were not only international but also domestic.

Political Lobbying and Restoring "Greater Hungary"

While relief work served American and Western political goals, it also intersected at times with Hungarian political goals. International relief organs were keen to assure their authorities that the Hungarian state appreciated their efforts and therefore arranged several joint "inspection tours" with the highest officials and public figures. Whenever such dignitaries came to inspect the kitchens, the press was drawn in to ensure full coverage. On February 2, 1921, Regent Miklós Horthy and the chief of the ARA in Hungary, Ulysses Grant-Smith, jointly "inspected [the] kitchens last Thursday and congratulated us [for the] efficiency [of our] operation."[23] Christian festivals were ideal times to propagate the close American-Hungarian friendship. Approaching the holidays in 1920, ARA Europe director Brown suggested that the relief workers get a "short Christmas message from, say, Horthy speaking for [the] children of Hungary to Hoover." A message of thanks could be transmitted to the "American people" and could be of great "assistance in [the] drive for funds."[24]

Fig. 7.1. From the American Relief Action. Photo by Mór Eiser, *Az Érdekes Újság* 9, no. 5 (February 3, 1921): 4.

Photographs displaying close cooperation between American relief workers and the Hungarian political elite were an essential and widespread propaganda tool. Many such images found their way to Geneva and beyond. Under the title "Pictures of the American Child Relief Action," a page in *Az Érdekes Újság* (The interesting journal) showed the visit by Horthy and Grant-Smith just mentioned. In the photo (see fig. 7.1), Horthy stands with a group of American relief workers, a medical adviser, and several women patrons approving a "kitchen, maintained through American relief, in which he sees poor children receiving free lunch."[25] After listening to the remarks of the worthy visitors, readers are told, the children were finally allowed to "taste the excellent food."

This image, along with many others, references Hungary's lost territories—places where postwar aid and revisionism became intertwined. Prominent on the wall of the relief facility is a map of Greater Hungary carrying the slogan "*Nem! Nem! Soha!*" (No! No! Never!), an example of the widespread propaganda against the territorial losses after the Treaty of Trianon. As international relief workers proudly posed with Horthy, they must have had the recent "red threat" very much in their minds. Affiliation with the right-wing revisionist government was distinctly preferable; restoration of the old order was a bulwark against communism. Visuals from the time show that such propaganda appeared constantly in school classrooms, reminding the nation's children of the injustice of the partitions made by the Treaty of Trianon. In many of these photos, the American mission was linked with this call by association. The field of transnational child relief was appropriated for political lobbying. In line with Hoover's strong anti-communism, the Americans preferred a close tie with a firmly conservative government under Horthy than risk a return to a regime like Béla Kun's. Thus, Hungary was successful in gaining international support for its revisionist aims. Likewise, child destitution and relief turned into a projection screen to gain international recognition of how territorial loss had damaged Hungary and the need for redress. Although revisionist ideas circulated both locally and internationally, many of the agents involved had very individual interpretations of and attitudes toward Hungary's lost territories. "Revisionism was far from uniform or all-encompassing: some people were indifferent, others opportunistic, and still others tried to use it for their own ends."[26]

Official reporters evaluating the work of the ARC in Hungary used bodily imagery to describe the geopolitical situation of the country: "Hungary looks like an agonizing human being, not wishing to die, but unable to live."[27] Following this logic, rescuing children's bodies meant rescuing the impaired, truncated national body of Hungary itself. In part, it was due to this analogy that the US representatives joined in the revisionist rhetoric; according to Horthy, the Treaty of Trianon should be revoked and Greater Hungary be restored.[28] Support for Hungary's revisionist politics was perceived by revisionists and some observers alike as a necessary means to bring about political and economic stability in the country and wider region. Problematic implications were rarely considered. Michael Geyer and Johannes Paulmann have pointed out how "internationalizing an issue" can "strengthen the collective identity of a social group" and "further ... national interests."[29] Internationalizing knowledge about the suffering of Budapest's children enabled postwar Hungary to pursue its nationalizing project. The social issue of starving children provided highly useful ammunition in this cause.

Thanks to the massive reach of photography, Hungary's plight could be made known throughout Europe and in the United States. Visual material from both the ARA and the Save the Children International Union (the SCIU, fig. 7.2 and the cover image of this book) show Greater Hungary propaganda in documentation for children's relief programs. The implication was that the food crisis had been caused through the loss of Hungary's ceded territories. It seems that some international relief workers were themselves highly critical of the peace treaty and thought so, too. The spaces and places of children's food relief were used to advocate for the recovery of Hungary's next generation and of its territorial integrity. Even movies were used to convey the local revisionist propaganda. In an International Committee of the Red Cross film from 1921, the camera pans out to the outer wall of a relief workroom (described in the final chapter of this book) at one of the city's housing barracks for

Fig. 7.2. Recruiting scene: Examination of a tubercular child, ARA Hungary. Unknown photographer, American Relief Administration European Operational Records, Box 851, Folder J, HILA.

the impoverished. The scene not only shows the "working" children but also captures two posters of pre-Trianon Hungary with the *"Nem! Nem! Soha!"* caption on the right and an image of a Hungarian peasant in the national Hungarian dress on the left. These visuals advocated for territorial revision. As Geneva and the League of Nations were the place to appeal against the peace treaty, an ICRC movie was an ideal means to gain the broadest possible audience for Hungary's postwar territorial claims.[30] Hungary, who had joined the League of Nations in 1922, used the League for the sole purpose of lobbying for the revision of the peace treaty. Hungary did not share the "underlying assumptions of the international organization," as Zoltán Peterecz argues, nor did it "believe in the brotherhood of countries" or the "power of world opinion."[31] It just joined this international endeavor due to the "sheer power of its interests," which resulted in a "short-term internationalism pursuant to long-term anti-internationalism."[32] Yet for that period, Hungary used the international forum to lobby for its territorial revision.

And indeed, this project was politically successful. The United States never ratified the Treaty of Trianon. In December 1919, Ulysses Grant-Smith was sent as the US commissioner to Hungary. An American legation followed on December 26 of the same year.³³ On August 29, 1921, Grant-Smith, as the representative of the United States, and Count Nicholas Bánffy, the Hungarian minister of foreign affairs, signed in Budapest their own "U.S.-Hungarian Peace Treaty" with Miklós Horthy, establishing "friendly relations."³⁴ The treaty fueled Hungarian hopes of a possible revision of Trianon. A propaganda war continued to attempt "to win the favor of public opinion" internationally. Revisionists denounced violations of minority treaties (requiring neighboring countries to treat minority populations well), especially the unfair treatment of Romania's Hungarian and Jewish minorities.³⁵ Hungary's starving children were actively used to support the nationalist victim narrative. A 1923 ARC report by Elsie Graves Benedict, assistant director of the European Junior Red Cross (JRC), noted it was "practically impossible" to receive letters from Hungarian children without bitter references to the "unfortunate results" of Trianon.³⁶ And the spirit of bitterness and resentment was catching. When Dutch reporters interviewed some Hungarian children that had been sent to Holland, probably in 1920, they were amazed at "how deep this feeling" of revenge and revisionism was: the children all wanted to become army officers "to recapture the lost territories."³⁷

Meanwhile in Paris, the Hungarian Territorial Integrity League, among other lobbying groups, pressed for the restoration of Hungary's "territorial integrity," using children as part of its appeal.³⁸ This was a prolongation of the campaigning that had been ongoing since the appeals prepared for the Paris Peace Conference in 1919, which had raised fears of "the consequence of the division of Hungary from the standpoint of eugenics"—that Hungary would no longer be able to "raise enough children and would to a great extent soon become extinct."³⁹ Another fear was that the injustice of the peace treaty would bequeath "to future generations a legacy of hatred, unrest and permanent militarism."⁴⁰

Nationalism and Patriotism through Internationalism

Hungarian nationalism and American patriotism, together, were fundamental driving forces behind transatlantic and internationalist relief efforts in Budapest. Paradoxically, each one aided the other. Beyond the revisionist plight, the transnational encounter of international aid yielded other opportunities for the promotion of the Hungarian national(istic) project. In postwar relief, Julia Irwin points out, "the emergence and development of modern humanitarianism coincided with surging nationalism."⁴¹ The two were entangled and remained so. While themselves acting beyond the nation, Patricia Clavin explains, the "transnational networks and epistemic communities need coherent nations and intergovernmental cooperation to have [their] biggest impact."[42] Glenda Sluga has argued the same case, exposing the widespread belief that nationalism and internationalism were "antithetical or even agonistic" as false. In reality, "the national and international remained entwined as ways of thinking about the self and society."[43] To trace the "genealogy of internationalism," as Karen Gram Skjoldager and her coauthors point out, one needs to understand how certain internationalist "beliefs and practices that sought to promote a more peaceful, secure international order through the strengthening of international mechanisms and institutions" were propagated and employed "without questioning the notion of nation states and national sovereignty as building blocks of the international order."[44]

The "history of internationalism," in Sluga's understanding, "maps profoundly onto the genealogy of nations and nationalism."[45] The "acceleration and intensification of global flows of people, goods, commodities and ideas," Steffi Marung, Matthias Middell, and Uwe Müller note, enabled the East Central European countries receiving aid to "pursue their own political, economic and cultural ambitions" just as much as donor countries like the United States.[46] Hungary comprehensively used the international relief endeavor and the discourse over famished children to advance its nationalist and revisionist ideas. Hungary was not alone in using its starving children to press for a revision of the peace treaty; hoping to "win foreign sympathies," Germany also did so. Yet, in contrast to Germany's failure to gain support through a "diplomacy of pity," Hungary's stories of its starving children and displaced middle class won considerable sympathy in the United States.[47]

A difficulty for Hungary lay in the fact that it had to convince the international community and the donor nations of its own destitution while at the same time demonstrating its strong national merits and worthiness for aid. Vera Hajtó observes, in the case of Hungarian children in Belgium, that the propaganda was only successful if the children symbolized both their country's misery and the community of "proud people with a glorious past and an old tradition" behind them.[48] Activity in the field of humanitarian relief enabled Hungarians to manifest national and patriotic sentiments. These did not stand "in opposition to transnationalism"; rather, the international nature of the relief mission was "an essential element in shaping the phenomenon."[49] One report from Pattie Day Miller, the field director of the American Junior Red Cross in Hungary, recalls a concert series organized by the Hungarian JRC. She was moved when the concert closed "with the national hymn or prayer called 'My Creed,'" which was "sung everywhere in Hungary since the partition of the old empire." She found it touching that "the eyes of even the smallest children fill[ed] with tears" when they sang:

> I believe in God.
> I believe in my country.
> I believe in one divine eternal truth.
> I believe in the regeneration of Hungary. Amen.

The prayer poses Hungary's victimhood as an element of Christian morality. Miller felt that Budapest children were "consciously dedicating themselves" with their performance "to the regeneration of their beloved country."[50] Here we have direct evidence of Hungarian national and revisionist sentiments, staged by Hungary's children, being publicly appreciated by international relief workers. Nationalism and internationalism were closely intertwined.

Many of the women activists who played a role in the drive to protect children and ensure their welfare were traditionalists in their politics, contributing further dimensions to the Hungarian politics behind relief aid. "Gender issues appeared in the context of the defeated nation's desperate efforts to regain what was lost during the war," notes Judit Acsády.[51] Efforts to reassert traditional gender roles not only "played an integral part in re-establishing the social hierarchy and legal order" in postwar Hungary;[52] they also helped to legitimize Horthy's government, including many of its more unpleasant aspects. Judith Szapor has stressed the significant "contribution of right-wing women activists . . . to the regime's radical nationalist, illiberal, antisemitic ideology."[53] The field of child protection was particularly suitable for urging a restoration of the old social order. A postwar political program aimed at "re-educating" the population "in a Christian and national spirit" to erase any memories of the "communism, cosmopolitanism [and] liberalism" that had briefly surfaced.[54] Again, children, the prototypical recipients of education and the future of the nation, were ideal targets for this program.

Some of the deeply conservative women activists were instrumental in helping "construct a strong nationalist, chauvinist discourse" that could serve as "a background to irredentist (i.e. revisionist) policies."[55] In particular, Magdolna Purgly, Regent Horthy's wife and thus a representative of the Hungarian nation, figured extensively in photographs of national child welfare activities. She injected her husband's conservative politics into these social endeavors. Purgly had reportedly enrolled herself in the relief endeavors of the American Red Cross as early as 1921. Knitting side by side "with thousands of other women from all classes of society," she offered the ARC her help

Fig. 7.3. István Horthy greets his mother, Mrs. Horthy. Unknown photographer, May 1941, Signature 78.855, Hungarian National Museum, Budapest.

and her conservative reputation.[56] Over the next two decades, she appeared extensively at national child welfare activities. As late as 1941, Purgly supported the Hungarian National Child Protection League, raising funds for destitute children of another war. In figure 7.3, she is shown being greeted by her son, István Horthy, as he passes by one of the league's fundraising stands. Figure 7.4 shows Christmas packages being distributed by the American Red Cross to children during World War I, with Purgly in attendance. The packages prominently display her name. This illustrates the shift of relief from the international to the national, or nationalist, realm. The children's happy faces suggest heartfelt thanks for the national relief efforts, enabling them to receive their Christmas gift. Magdolna Purgly inscribed herself, quite literally, into this beneficence.

Photographs like this had the double purpose of raising additional funds for the country's children and of propagating, nationally and internationally, the humanitarian deeds undertaken by Hungary's political and financial elite. Oblivious of women's new social standing in the larger postwar world, the women depicted here are "wives"—the wives of politically active, economically prosperous husbands. Both the children and the benefactresses mirror the restoration of class hierarchy and traditional gender roles after the war.

Fig. 7.4. Christmas celebration in 1941: Children receive a Christmas package from the wife of Miklós Horthy. Unknown photographer, Signature 2066-1962, Hungarian National Museum, Budapest.

When the ARA's relief work came to an end in 1922, "Admiral Horthy expressed the thanks of the entire nation" to Captain Pedlow, the American representative, "for feeding Hungary's children, and conferred a decoration upon his guest."[57] After that, food relief converted from an international project to a more local endeavor. Russell W. Bell, a worker for the ARA, saw this as indicative of the Hungarians' "willingness to meet their obligations."[58] A so-called Horthy Action ran for five more months, through the winter of 1922.

In much the same way that Hungarians pursued national aims in the context of international relief, so, too, did the Americans. While the Hungarian state pursued revisionist and nationalistic politics, the American relief organizations cared much more about winning the hearts of children and promoting American patriotism. As European children entered the American feeding stations, they were welcomed at a table "spread with American food." As a "service" for "protection to your children and to my children," Hoover told Americans, the American nation should "plant . . . the American flag in the hearts of these fifteen million children." Hoover referred to the "American heart," the "American conscience," and "American generosity" behind the relief mission.[59]

Creating an association between food and the American flag in every child's mind was a strategic move to win the hearts of a future generation in East Central Europe. Certain foods were especially used to win children's sympathy for the United States. In the kindergartens and milk kitchens, children received not only typical Hungarian dishes but also iconic American food products like American cocoa and condensed milk, novelties at the time.[60] Such foodstuffs helped to win over the public as well as the children. The Unites States even involved its own youngsters to forge a connection between the young in both countries. In 1923, the "Juniors of America" (American Junior Red Cross), sent two hundred Christmas gift boxes, because they "believed in making childhood happy, the world over." Although not richly filled with material gifts, the boxes would remind the Hungarian children that "each American boy and girl enclosed a bit of love." A report describes "impatient fingers" "prying the boxes" open and notes that the children were filled with "excitement" when encountering "fascinating" jumping jacks, balls, and fluffy dolls; it was the "greatest joy" to them to "receive a toy all of [their] . . . very own." At a ceremony of appreciation, Buda's children performed a Hungarian national folk dance, a csárdás, shown in figure 7.5, and sang Hungarian national songs for the ARC representative and donors.[61] National sentiments were played out on both ends of this humanitarian endeavor.

Through donations and relief, the United States projected the image of a selfless, altruistic nation, at the same time expanding its influence and securing its own political interests in the region.[62] It is widely believed that humanitarianism is impartial, neutral, and independent from politics,[63] but humanitarian activities and political ideologies can easily be conflated. As a "concept in motion," Michael Barnett observes, humanitarianism can exhibit a "commitment to emancipation [able to] justify forms of domination."[64] As the very embodiment of economic and social dependence, the child was an especially easy target for domination.[65] The sick or destitute child was even easier to control and dominate. According to Tara Zahra, the mentality of domination was even more deeply rooted. Together with "American values and anti-Communism," she maintains, the American relief workers brought "unspoken prejudices to Eastern and Central Europe, depicting the region and its people as inherently backward, violent, and corrupt—in imagined opposition to American modernity and efficiency."[66] Davide Rodogno takes a similar view: by implementing modern relief programs, the Americans "paternalistically demonstrated their superiority, and intended to teach

Fig. 7.5. Celebration in the workrooms. Unknown photographer. CH AEG AP 92 105.81 (2).

'half-civilized' Central, Eastern, and South-Eastern Europeans the path to peace and prosperity. Through relief, social and political inequalities could be sustained, maintaining impressions of the region's 'backwardness.'"[67]

Appreciation for the United States was publicly demonstrated in relief circles. When US president Warren G. Harding was inaugurated on March 4, 1921, the Hungarian government, the capital city, and various American charities in Budapest held a celebratory ceremony that was attended by officials and representatives of the US mission, including Pedlow and the former US consul. The city's schoolchildren, as seen in figure 7.6, joined the celebration in the garden of the Hungarian national museum, richly decorated with American star flags, Hungarian tricolors, and the flags of the capital.

Both nations used this celebration to manifest their respective national sentiments, while expressing Hungary's appreciation of and ongoing dependence on American relief. A Hungarian source from that day stated, "Today ... all peoples and nations are celebrating America's great presidents. Let's ... look at America with love and a childlike spirit.... The soul of Hungarian children, broken through destitution, speaks to America: our father and our mother are unhappy, we are destitute, you are the president of a free home, make

Fig. 7.6. Thanksgiving of Budapest's children on the day of the inauguration of Harding. *Az Érdekes Újság* 9, no. 9 (March 3, 1921): cover.

the peoples and nations happy and look to us in the future as you have done so far."[68]

"Proving" the Success of the Relief Initiative

The various parties involved in relief all craved signs of success for their constituencies on both sides of the Atlantic. Donors, doctors, aid officials, local politicians, and parents alike all sought evidence of positive outcomes. The forms of proof they favored are diverse, providing a mix of scientific, visual, and written evidence. Before-and-after pictures were staged to demonstrate the success of the relief measures in far-off Europe to the American public. The images were aimed especially at possible future donors. A 1919 three-part drawing, "The Feeding Class of the American Mission," shown in figure 7.7,

Fig. 7.7. The feeding class of the American Mission. Drawing by Károly Mühlbeck, *Új Idők* 25, no. 25 (December 17, 1919): 477.

portrayed the physical transformation of young children benefiting from donated food.[69] On the left-hand side of the image, three emaciated children in torn, patched clothes arrive at the schoolroom where they will receive their daily meal. In the center, they are among children seated on benches and eating food that a woman is serving. On the right, the three children leave the scene, entirely transformed. They are healthy and well dressed in socks, coats, and hats, and the little boy has a full belly. Thanks to the American mission, the picture suggests, the poor children have been newly clothed and saved from starvation.

The quantities of relief food and milk consumed provided an easy, objective measure of the extent of humanitarian aid.[70] Increased weights among the children were taken as proof of the mission's overall success. However, despite the massive distribution of milk and meals, a report by János Bókay in 1921 on "The Result of the Hungarian Mission from a Medical Point of View" indicated that "52 per cent of the 8,870 children fed showed an actual loss of weight, which circumstance is simply another proof of the difficult living conditions in the city of Budapest." Nevertheless, the ARA was "glad to report that the extensive action of the enthusiastic and magnanimous philanthropists of the United States of America was closed with satisfactory results."[71]

Such reports were published to document the success of the American and British relief actions. In the *New York Times* of October 19, 1919, a British observer acknowledged that the work of American relief in Hungary "created immense joy among all classes." On behalf of the Hungarian government, he was to "convey grateful thanks to the American nation," because poverty in Hungary was "terrible and the need immense." Therefore, Americans and Hungarians alike should continue "this work of humanity," which would result in the "gratitude of millions."[72] As for the British child relief effort, even

Pope Pius XI was moved to write a letter to Eglantyne Jebb, expressing his gratitude to her: "His Holiness accords whole-hearted approval to the generous and timely undertaking." "With deep tenderness," he recalled "the sublime words of the Savior whose love for children was so great: 'Whoso shall receive one such little child in My name receiveth me' (Matthew xxviii 5)."[73] Enjoying recognition of their valuable work from such distinguished leaders as the pope, international humanitarians saw themselves as rescuers.

In many of the relief reports, the reactions and voices of children themselves were used to relay the success of and appreciation for the relief effort. In 1921, Count Reding-Biberegg, accompanied by representatives of the international relief organizations and a number of journalists from Switzerland, arranged for a small "party" to visit children, who, he reported, "received us with songs and flags." In one school facility where food was distributed, a little girl presented the journalists "with flowers" and "cordially thanked" them for having come to "see their meal," begging them to "convey through their journals the deepest gratitude of the Hungarian children to all generous donors."[74]

Sometimes children were asked to write or draw about their experiences at the relief kitchens and workrooms. In 1929, a girl drew a picture (see fig. 7.8) of her experience of getting food, titling it *Vive l'Union Internationale de Secours aux Enfants* (Long Live the Save the Children International Union). Relief organizations frequently used the voices of children and images created by them to prove children's neediness and their agency's efficiency. It would be inaccurate to present this picture as a little girl's spontaneous expression. The relief organization concerned had asked the schoolchildren to write accounts or make illustrations that could be used to convey thanks or gain publicity. Thus, the young artist was following the SCIU's agenda rather than acting entirely on her own agency. Because the image was exhibited and archived, we can surmise that it fit with the self-image and self-presentation of the Save the Children organizers.

The published reports of the American Red Cross in Hungary consistently emphasized the donors' amazing generosity to people in need. James Pedlow reported in 1922 that the past year, donors "had given out large quantities of material and wool in August and September and many of the made-up articles were kept for Christmas distribution." This enabled the ARC "to close up in a blaze of glory and [have] a fitting end to [their] work in that line."[75] One report went so far as to state that "the recognition and gratitude of the Hungarian nation for the help of the ARC was unparalleled. . . . The

Fig. 7.8. Child drawing of feeding at a Save the Children workroom. Unknown child artist, Budapest December 1, 1929, tenth anniversary of the SCIU, CH AEG AP 92.3.62.

commissioner of the ARC was the most popular man in the country in the last three years."[76] Both donors and recipients publicly announced their satisfaction with the relief program. Hungarian politicians were happy to join in with these plaudits, because doing so guaranteed financial support. They extolled the United States as the savior of their children and their country: "It is not only for the lives and health of our children that Hungary is thankful to America, but for the resultant effort in political and economic stability and social improvement."[77] The United States was succeeding in its quest to use postwar relief to gain international political power.

Reenacting Children's Hunger and Satisfactory Self-Congratulation

At the same time, American humanitarian relief in impoverished and starving Central and Eastern Europe was instrumental in affecting public opinion and domestic politics back in the United States. It showed the American public that their donations were not simply draining away in faraway Europe but were reaching their targets, achieving their original purpose, and helping to strengthen and spread America's good name.[78] Through its humanitarian intervention in former enemy countries, American relief organizations simultaneously succeeded in providing relief to the stricken and in meeting the foreign-policy aspirations of the US government. When American relief officers left Europe in 1923, the "legacies of their Great War–era humanitarian intervention endured," Julia Irwin claims, because the United States had realized the "strategic importance of aid" and invested in expanding its global humanitarian role.[79]

In a bid to raise donations and support for the relief effort, Hoover arranged big publicity events all over America. These included formal dinners and fundraising functions. He invited people to balls, for instance, at which the standard daily meal of the starving children in Europe (cocoa, rice, and dry bread) would be served as the sole refreshment. On December 29, 1920, at 7:30 p.m., he personally invited over a thousand prospective donors from New York to a dinner of the European Relief Council for "The Invisible Guest" in the grand ballroom of the Commodore Hotel in New York City. The invitees were key sponsors and representatives of important relief organizations who had donated money or raised funds for the relief of a minimum of one hundred children in Central and Eastern Europe. When Hoover sent a personalized invitation to John D. Rockefeller asking him to be one of the distinguished honorary guests, he explained that every table at the dinner would represent on hundred "saved" children, who would be present in spirit. Hence, in total, 350,000 children would be "invisible guests" at the event. Their symbolic presence helped to "visualize to the American people and to the people of Europe the sum of effort" New York's donors were generously accomplishing.[80] Through this dinner Hoover was stage-managing a bodily act of compassion. The event made real for the attendees the experience of minimal nutrition and children's daily hardship. Hoover's reference to the exact number of consumed calories reflects the contemporary scientific approach to nutrition. As the *New York Times* reported, many wept at the dinner when confronted, once again, with shocking images of starving children.[81] Such emotional reactions among attendees were expected at fundraising functions.

Beyond letting the donors physically feel the hunger of the starving child, the events were meant to remind attendees of the greater horrors of the war. During the dinner, General John J. Pershing spoke. "As we contemplate the causes of the World War," he said, "and realize its horrors, every right-thinking man and woman must feel like demanding that some steps be taken to prevent its recurrence." "The world does not seem to learn from experience," he continued. "It would appear that the lessons of the past six years should be enough to convince everybody of the danger of nations striding

Fig. 7.9. Long live the great and powerful American nation. Unknown photographer, 1920s, Signature 1455-1952, Hungarian National Museum, Budapest.

up and down the earth armed to the teeth."[82] Forced identification with the enemy's suffering served to generate antiwar sentiment as well as feelings of solidarity with Europe's victims. By 1921, the United States itself was in the midst of a depression, with high unemployment rates and spreading "anxiety" among the economic elite, necessitating "hype" to secure donations.[83] In return, "New York"—meaning its rich donors—wanted public "acknowledgement" and "good human interest stories" from the sites of relief, as a message from the ARA's Children's Fund to M. M. Mitchell makes clear. Letters and expressions of appreciation were expected to serve as evidence of the actual need and the proper administration of relief. Above all, they were supposed to show deep appreciation for all donations. Thanks were also expected from "leading scholars, educators, thinkers and chiefs of state."[84]

As "saviors" of Europe's children, the American relief organizations hoped to nurture long-term appreciation among the civilian populations of Europe. Images such as the one shown in figure 7.9 were accompanied by patriotic slogans. Public acknowledgment of the debt to the United States for Hungary's recovery flattered Americans, happy to have the self-image of belonging to a benevolent and humanitarian nation. The sentiment of "Long live the great and powerful American Nation" in the poster might also have conveyed hopes of a long-term continuation of American relief efforts in Hungary.

To Vernon Kellogg and Alonzo Taylor, two of Hoover's most important nutritionists, US involvement in World War I was "a time of rare and glorious opportunity; a time in which prosaic business and industry may be lifted up to the high plane of national service." They were impressed by an editor of a miller's journal who said that everyone in the United States "who grinds a barrel of flour or makes a loaf of bread to the glory and the good of the nation, forgetful of self, performs his duty in a spirit of devotion equal in its way to that of him who goes forth to actual fighting."[85] This understanding of national duty did not cease with the war's end. János Bókay, administrative president of the ARA in Budapest, concluded his medical report on the feeding of children in Hungary with these words: "We . . . take a patriotic pride in stating that the great action of the magnanimous American donors was closed by us with satisfactory results, and that we have promoted the effective improvement of the physical condition of our children."[86]

When the American food mission in Hungary wrapped up, Americans expressed their pride in fulsome tones. "The completion of this task is indeed the completion of a great chapter in our national history," Hoover proclaimed, "a chapter for which our children will remember our generation with gratitude." The "abandonment of this mass of children" would have compromised American "national honor abroad" and disappointed all "who believe in the ideals of the American people." America did not abandon the children. And, Hoover went on, "I would rather have the American flag implanted in the hearts of these fifteen million children than flying from any citadel in Europe."[87] A Red Cross article of 1920 dwelt on the same theme. A lot of people had shrugged the war off as a distant affair that a "lot of foolish people in Europe had started." They had felt it was not "our war" and that the United States need not be involved. But neither during nor after the war, the author contended, could the nation simply keep out of the conflict and the misery. "You cannot have one-half of the world starving and the other half eating." America was right to "put Europe on its feet"; otherwise it would become part of Europe's misery.[88] An expanded global political presence for the United States was a significant aspect of these endeavors.

Embodying America: James Pedlow in Budapest

Key American figures became "humanitarian celebrities" in Budapest. The most notable of them was Captain James Pedlow, the representative of the

Fig. 7.10. Statue of James Pedlow. Unknown photographer, *Új Idők* 28, no. 6 (February 5, 1922): 121.

American Red Cross in Hungary. The chairman of a meeting of foreign relief missions in Budapest welcomed Pedlow on behalf of the metropolis on March 1, 1921.[89] Embodying US economic, military, and political power, yet dedicated to the plight of children, Pedlow figured prominently in the contemporary print media. The capital city's appreciation was literally carved in stone, as shown in figure 7.10, when a bust of Pedlow was erected in Budapest City Park.

"The first European statue to a living American has been erected by Hungary," the *New York Times* reported about the official May 11, 1922, ceremony. The Hungarian government wanted to thank Pedlow for his work and his "humanity." In a speech at the unveiling ceremony, Count Albert Apponyi, the Hungarian revisionist politician who had headed the Hungarian peace delegation in Paris, declared "the Americans are the only real pacifists in the world who are showing a spirit of reconciliation in their generous charity toward the vanquished." He noted that "thousands of children in gala dress paraded in front of the statue and heaped flowers around it."[90] Throughout the city of Budapest, Pedlow was very well known. When he appeared on the street, according to a 1921 Red Cross report, "all the policemen salute him," "the postmen take off their hats," and even the "officers of the Hungarian army stop in the streets and click their heels together in the snappiest salute you ever saw." "Best of all," the report continued, "the ragged men and women and the children simply adore him." He had "everyone in town doing something to help" and had even asked prisoners in the jails to help his relief work by "making Christmas presents of cradles and children's beds from the packing-cases in which wool was shipped."[91]

Before Pedlow left Hungary on July 1, 1922, after two and a half years of relief work, he was hosted for lunch by Regent Horthy at his "country castle" in Gödöllő, where "Horthy expressed the thanks of the entire nation for feeding Hungary's children and conferred a decoration upon his guest." Room 75 of the third floor in the Hotel Ritz, the headquarters of the American relief mission, was "besieged by children bringing toys and flowers and weeping bitterly" as Pedlow left. "Crowds of children escorted him to the ship, where a bareheaded multitude sang the American and Hungarian national anthems."[92] The Council of the City of Budapest also made a point of offering him thanks. It issued a special publication, personally dedicated Pedlow. In a picture on the cover, shown in figure 7.11, Pedlow's name was written into the cityscape.

Pedlow's role as a bridge between the United States, the Swiss organizations, and the city of Budapest was conveyed by a joint arrangement of the American flag, a Red Cross flag, and the flag of the city. A palm branch, symbol of peace, acknowledged that Pedlow's was a true mission of peace to the city. The text of the publication, written like a public speech or even a hagiography, was endorsed at a meeting of the council on June 28, 1922. Pedlow had "not forgotten" the "hospitals, charitable institutes, poor-houses, orphanages and refuges" of the metropolis. He had not followed the dictates of the peace treaty but instead the "noble dictates of [his] own heart"—apparent in his "genuine good-will," his "devoted affection," and his "sympathy for the Hungarian nation." "Inspired by true love of mankind," "true philanthropy," and "nobleness of sentiment," he had provided constant help to Hungary's distressed population. Above all, he had given unparalleled assistance to the most innocent—the capital's children "on whom the distress caused by the war has weighed, and still weighs, most heavily." The council was more than happy to express "lasting gratitude" and thanks to Pedlow and asked of him one final favor: to convey "our heart-felt gratitude to the noble American people" and beg for the continuation of donations. With "genuine warm affection" the author closed, wishing Pedlow the "Blessing of the Almighty."[93]

(Inter)Nationalism | 233

Fig. 7.11. Cover of *Captain James Pedlow, Commissioner of the American Red Cross Society in Budapest*. Unknown artist, Budapest 1922, Collection of the Metropolitan Ervin Szabó Library.

In 1925, after Pedlow had already left Hungary, an appeal was published in an American Hungarian newspaper, the *Magyar Tribune*, dedicated to him. Recounting his deeds on behalf of the Hungarian nation, the author doubted there was ever "a stranger of another nationality among our Hungarian people, who [was as] well-known and respected by all of us" as Pedlow, a "man who [did] not understand our language, who [was] not of our kind, and yet [who] stood by us in good faith" and who "has been mentioned by Hungarians in prayer . . . many times." Pedlow, this text says, did not "ask what nationality" any recipient of relief was, but provided relief "without asking any questions." And now, years after the relief action was brought to a close, Pedlow was still appealing to American Hungarians to "brighten the sorrowful

Hungarian Christmas." Everyone who had compassion for Hungarians and "some dollars available" should "pack up a bundle" and send it to "Captain Pedlow's Relief Center at Union Square in New York."[94] His work had a lasting impact on Hungarian-American relations. As late as 1931, after the Great Depression had hit the United States and there was a worldwide economic crisis, Pedlow again publicly appealed on behalf of the "unfortunate people of Hungary," who had "suffered more than others." Every Hungarian American, who had "someone in Hungary, father, mother, brother or other relatives," should send something. As he himself "love[d] the Magyar people," he wished "to aid them."[95]

Back in the early 1920s, Pedlow was not the only one to be held up for praise; other humanitarians were rewarded with carefully orchestrated appreciation.[96] Public demonstrations of the country's gratitude displayed the unequal relationship between the donor and recipient countries. Hungarians stated that the ARA "had helped us more than any former enemy or friend," and, with "deepest gratitude," they had come to have "faith in America." They considered Hoover to be the "greatest American."[97] At the time of the official closure of the ARA offices, János Bókay thanked Hoover personally for the "noble humanitarian work" carried out in Hungary. In a note, he conveyed the "undying gratitude" of this "suffering nation" for American help "in our hours of need" and expressed his "highest personal esteem" for Hoover himself and his organization. The United States would continue to have Hungary's eternal loyalty.[98] Pedlow may not have been a politician per se, and Herbert Hoover had not yet risen to the US presidency, but both men's high-profile roles in the relief efforts made them figures of tremendous importance in transatlantic politics.

The Power of Things: Material Donations

Many published written sources and photographs described and depicted the abundant material generosity of the American humanitarian intervention. Figure 7.12 shows Mrs. Thomson, head of the American cotton initiative, dwarfed by a massive load of donated raw cotton, duly decorated with two American flags and flags of the ARC. The display is a striking demonstration of the economic and material power the United States could flaunt. American wealth was manifested here in the vast mass of cotton that had crossed national borders and had entered destitute Budapest, where it would be stored, processed, and manufactured into garments for the children. American raw materials and capitalist goods were being used to fulfill local Hungarian

Fig. 7.12. "Mrs. Thomson, the Head of the American Cotton Initiative." Photo by Mór Eiser, *Az Érdekes Újság* 9, no. 7 (February 17, 1921): 4.

needs and cultural expectations. Relief in the form of material objects was an important part of the humanitarian mission in postwar Budapest and a tool in relief work's international political aims.

As humanitarian relief, American cotton crossed the Atlantic to a former enemy country and changed in significance in the process. As Arjun Appadurai aptly defined them in *The Social Life of Things*, "commodities [are] objects of economic value" that are exchanged.[99] But this was a new kind of exchange. In the past, cotton had led "to an explosion both of slavery and wage labor" and had been the embodiment of global inequality. However, in its distribution among "the needy" in Hungary, it acquired a changed moral value. Sven Beckert's *Empire of Cotton* argues that cotton "spanned the globe unlike any other industry," "wove continents together," and came to play a key role in the foundation of a postwar system of transatlantic humanism.[100] Thomson "distributed more than 150 wagons full of cotton," not among the long-term poor but the newly impoverished Hungarian middle class. The donations were meant to relieve those families from the former Austro-Hungarian Empire who had been uprooted by the change of borders. But there was further distribution, too. The American Red Cross organized workshops where hundreds

Fig. 7.13. "Clothes Exhibition." Unknown photographer, 1920s, Signature 2139-2139-1954, Hungarian National Museum, Budapest.

of women made garments for the children from "over a hundred thousand pounds of wool" sent to Budapest between July 1 and December 20, 1920, by fifty thousand women engaged in knitting and sewing.[101]

These "humanitarian" garments were often exhibited in select public places. The *Red Cross Bulletin* describes one such display as "the largest exhibition of knitted woolen articles ever held in Central Europe." On American Thanksgiving Day in 1920, forty thousand garments "knitted by Hungarian women of American wool" were put on display.[102] A great mass of women's clothes at another exhibition is shown in figure 7.13.[103]

Usually, national flags and symbols, floral decorations, and large posters and images of important political figures were displayed as well to make a public demonstration of nationalism and patriotism. In this pictured exhibition, a massive American flag in the center is flanked on either side by Hungarian flags. A poster in front of the American flag identifies the donated clothing as both a "gift of the Americane [sic] nation" and as the "work of the grateful Hungarian ladies"; below, surrounded by a floral wreath, is a large portrait of George Washington, the first US president. Thus, the display is a simultaneous, coordinated demonstration of Hungarian and American nationalism. Though acknowledging economic dependence on the great donor nation, the relief workers of Budapest have arranged the exhibition in a way that pays tribute to the people of Hungary. There is gender fairness, too. The male figure of Washington personifies the United States, while the Hungarians acknowledge women and their work. Especially on festive occasions such as Christmas and Easter, Americans demonstrated their material generosity with considerable showmanship. And Hungary's material dependence on US donations was pressed home by the ubiquitous presence of American flags.

Reports often recorded children's reactions on receiving donations of clothes. One of these related the story of a war orphan named Ilona Balogh, who turned into "a happy little girl the day American clothing was given out at her school." Arriving in a "veritable bunch of rags . . . from head to foot," she pushed forward to a big table full of clothes, "on which lay the realization of her dreams." Among the many overcoats, shoes, and stockings, she discovered "a complete outfit for her," rushing home with her prize.[104]

Individual donations were targeted for the immediate relief of newborn infants. On January 1, 1920, the ARC provided a "baby outfit" to all 183 babies born on that day in Budapest, consisting of "one layette," "two cans of condensed milk," two bars of laundry soap, "six linen handkerchiefs," a nightgown for the mother, and one hundred kronen for the family. The most important item among these gifts was a new bedroll for the baby's cradle. This carried the words, "The American Red Cross Cradle Roll for Budapest, January First, 1920," together with the names of the parents and the child, the address, and the hour of birth.[105] While the bedroll fulfilled its practical function of securing sound, safe sleep for the infant, the inscription reflected the appropriation of this material everyday object by the ARC. The ARC was inscribing itself into the item for self-advertisement and, in a figurative sense, was proclaiming that it was one of the child's key providers.

The meanings of things are, according to Appadurai, "inscribed in their forms, their uses, their trajectories." The inscription on bedding transformed this everyday object into an embodiment of humanitarian relief.

Through the individualization of the object, this thing gained importance and value. Furthermore, the words exemplified how the poverty and scarcities in Hungary had resulted in a shift in responsibility from the parents to the foreign relief organizations. Georg Simmel reminds us that "economy" is a "particular social form" that "consists not only in exchanging *values* but in the *exchange* of values."[106] The bedroll served to transmit American values to the recipient society. As a handmade object, of cotton, it linked the economic value of modern capitalism to the social value of the child and represented the internationalization of relief. These objects exemplify well that "the rise of humanitarianism is inseparable from the rise of capitalism and imperialism."[107]

Many images also emphasized the high value of the material donations. A report on the ARA's work in Hungary contained two pictures intended to illustrate how children's appearance changed through the donors' generosity. These before-and-after pictures were taken in Fóth, a small town north of Budapest, which later, in the 1950s, became known for its large children's orphanage, the Fóth Gyermekváros (Fóth Children's City) in the Károly Castle. In the first of two contrasting photos shown in figure 7.14, the children are depicted barefoot and wearing torn, ragged clothes; in the second photo, they are perfectly dressed and have proper boots on their feet.

The images are intended to demonstrate the efficacy of material things in changing lives. While the first image evokes associations of the children as little vagrants, whose physical appearance mirrors their economic and social decline, the second shows them as well-fed, warmly clothed, respectable young citizens. The images and their captions suggest that American donations had rescued the children from starvation and exposure as well as further social degeneration. Their clothes were made from military overcoats—wartime equipment now turned to peaceful ends.[108] The text that accompanies the pictures states that, "on the inside neckband of each of their coats, a little American flag has been sewn, with the inscription, *Amerika a Magyar gyermekeknek* (America to Hungarian Children)." The making of infants' clothing "from odds and ends of Red Cross army supplies by volunteers," an ARC report from 1921 recalled, was the first successful attempt of cooperation between the various social and relief agencies in the capital city. Americans appreciated the "ingenuity" of the Hungarian women relief workers in repurposing "war-stocks of surgical dressings, comfort bags, and trench-foot socks for the manufacture of children's clothing"—so much so that an exhibition of these innovative handmade items went on display at the Red Cross Museum in Washington, DC. From the scraps, Hungarian women even once

Fig. 7.14. "A Group of Boys at Fóth, Hungary, Before and After the Distribution of American Clothing." Unknown photographer, in *Final Report on the Work in Hungary*, 17.

manufactured a rug, given to the wife of the US president "as a mark of their appreciation of American aid."[109]

Both visual evidence like this and various hints found in reports suggest that international relief workers wished to strengthen the Hungarian middle class and even the former imperial elite. If their power could be restored, it was thought, Hungary would find itself on the path to modernity and progress. In a report on "Public Health Conditions in Hungary," the Rockefeller Foundation's Selskar M. Gunn stated that, under postwar conditions, the "Hungarians feel that they have their backs to the wall and are an inferior race." He thought this dangerous, because it would be "particularly galling to their pride," which dated back to their defense of Europe against the Turks in the Early Modern era. Gunn counted on the "intelligent brains" that could lead Hungary back to "the path of progress."[110] Others put forward similar arguments. Nutritionist Alonzo Taylor argued that it was of the greatest importance to revive the middle class, because it would be "upon the brains" of this group that the future of Hungary's industry, education, and public affairs would depend. And, most significantly, the middle class was politically dependable, "neither radical at the left nor reactionary at the right."[111] Providing the impoverished middle class with adequate relief was one way of shaping Hungary's political future.

Relief across the class spectrum posed problems, however. Material relief deepened the inequality between recipient and donor nations, making Central and Eastern European societies seem backward. Through "instinct of self-preservation," destitute individuals might accept relief, but "emotionally [they] resent[ed] it."[112] An ARC worker recognized that, in postwar Budapest, there were three classes of people requiring assistance: the poor, the middle class, and the aristocrats. The first were easily reached, since they would generally accept assistance. People of the second type, he judged, were "very difficult" to reach, and those of the third, "extremely so." As other relief workers had observed in the railcar settlements, people in the third category would rather "starve before they will beg." Yet the ARC did succeed in reaching these better-off classes through persistent persuasion "that the ARC [was] not a charity organization, but an emergency relief one, and that in coming to us for relief they were not begging or considered beggars by the American people."[113]

Underlying economic and social inequalities often set off emotional outbursts. Aladár Kaszab, a social worker in Budapest, recalled that once, when distributing some items, a "crying woman who had received shoes and clothes came angrily back and shouted at me: Why would I think she could wear black clothes and high-heels?" She made such a fuss about it that the police had to be called to remove her. In his account, Kaszab concluded that some relief recipients were "profiteers," ungrateful people who not only harmed the real poor but disappointed and disillusioned the donors.[114] The woman's reaction reflects the inherently problematic nature of transnational relief work. Any reaction that did not fit the donors' expectation was considered inappropriate. Conversely, the recipients might feel belittled by the evident paternalism of the intervention. A 1925 article about British support of workrooms in Budapest stated that, while appreciating all the international financial help that was given, "All donations are humiliating, even if given with any good heart."[115] Whatever the reticence, material relief provided vitally necessary item for thousands of children and families and were tangible products of American and Western political diplomacy.

Conclusion

In postwar Budapest, food relief figured importantly in the struggle for postwar economic, scientific, and moral hegemony. The power of food is always evident in global politics. As Helen Veit observes, the war made it clear that "world power in the new century would hinge on the ability to marshal and coordinate food resources, both within and without national borders."[116] The US relief organizations—as "saviors" of Budapest's children—used the relief intervention to display America's modernity and to expand its political influence felt in supposedly backward Hungary, and Europe more broadly. Food and material relief were supposed to be gratefully received, allowing donor societies like the United States and other nations to appear generous and "humanitarian." At the national and international levels, such feelings took on an enlarged form in the political economic and social spheres. Apart from figuring prominently in the struggle for postwar economic, scientific, and moral hegemony, the postwar Hungarian state also used the global awareness of Hungary's postwar destitution for its own postwar political agenda.

Children's relief served the nascent and postimperial Hungarian state as an arena in which to advocate for territorial revisionism. The icon of the starving Hungarian child drew international attention to Hungary's postwar condition, denouncing the social repercussions of the peace treaty on Hungary's national body. On the day the peace treaty was signed, a journalist compared the "lost" Hungarian cities in Transylvania, Banat, Vojvodina, Upper Hungary, Burgenland, and Transcarpathia to the country's own children: "Today they took from us our dazzling Hungarian cities: the treasure Cluj-Napoca, the Kassa of the Rákóczi family, the crowning city of Bratislava, the industrial Timisoara, the city of martyrs, Arad, and all the rest, as if these were our own raised children. They took away our dear, beautiful Hungarian centers." On this black Friday, when in Budapest "all parlors were closed, all trains and cars stopped, and all workers put down their tools for a minute," even the "girls and children came with the heads of their families, who had become homeless [refugees], to take part in this silent demonstration."[117]

For Hungary, a difficulty lay in the fact that it had to convince the international community and the donor nations of its own destitution while simultaneously demonstrating its strong national merits. But as the United

States was driven by strong anti-Bolshevism and openly favored Horthy's government over the short-lived Soviet-type republic, children's transnational relief offered Miklós Horthy a way to lobby for and consolidate his "counterrevolutionary Hungary" and the prewar social order. Hence, postwar politics on all ends of this relief endeavor could broadly profit from the giving and receiving of food.

Notes

1. Weinreb, *Modern Hungers*, 4; Veit, *Modern Food, Moral Food*; Langthaler, "Food and Nutrition"; Zweiniger-Bargielowska, Duffett, and Drouard, *Food and War*; Davis, *Home Fires Burning*; Barona Vilar, "International Organisations"; Jackson, Ward, and Russell, "Moral Economies of Food."
2. Martschukat and Simon, *Food, Power, and Agency*, 3.
3. Counihan, *The Anthropology of Food and Body*, 7.
4. On the value of "things" and "material turn," see Appadurai, *The Social Life of Things*; Bennett and Joyce, *Material Powers*; De Grazia and Furlough, *The Sex of Things*; Gerritsen and Riello, *Writing Material Culture History*; and Hicks and Beaudry, *Oxford Handbook of Material Culture Studies*. On consumption, see Cook, "Children's Consumption in History," and Michelle McDonald, "Transatlantic Consumption."
5. Pirquet, *An Outline of the Pirquet System*, 58.
6. Childfund to Mr. Quinn, cablegram, Budapest January 6, 1921.
7. Watenpaugh, *Bread from Stones*, 59.
8. Childfund to Mr. Walter Lyman Brown and Mr. Mitchell, cablegram, Budapest, December 1, 1920, American Relief Administration European Operational Records, Box 36, no. 2, R.57, HILA.
9. American Relief Administration European Children's Fund, *American Relief Administration European Children's Fund Mission to Poland: 1919–1922*, 22, 13.
10. Childfund to Mr. Walter Lyman Brown and Mr. Mitchell, cablegram, Budapest, April 10–11, 1921, American Relief Administration European Operational Records, Box 36, no. 2, R.57, HILA.
11. Westerman, "Touring Occupied Belgium," 44.
12. Childfund to Mr. Walter Lyman Brown, cablegram, Budapest, February 23, 1921, American Relief Administration European Operational Records, Box 36, no. 2, R.57, HILA.
13. Magyarics, "American-Hungarian Relations," 169.
14. The following personnel had a military background: James Pedlow (Captain, USA), Cardner Richardson (Captain Infantry, USA), Carleton G. Bowden (1st Lieutenant FA, USA), Carlisle M. Davidson (1st Lieutenant, SC, USA), John J. Sutton, (Regt. Sgt. Major, 48th CAC), Emily Friedland (American Ambulance Field Service), Wallace B. Johnson (Ensign USNRF) (October 23, 1919–March 15, 1920).
15. Childfund to Mr. Walter Lyman Brown, cablegram, Budapest, February 23, 1921, American Relief Administration European Operational Records, Box 36, Folder 2, Reel 57, HILA.
16. Clements, *The Life of Herbert Hoover*, 3.
17. Also, the American Child Welfare mission relied on soldiers, including Carleton G. Bowden. See Glant, "Herbert Hoover and Hungary," 98.
18. Adlgasser, *American Individualism Abroad*, 14.

19. Childfund to Mr. Brown and Mr. Quinn, cablegram, Budapest, December 5, 1920, American Relief Administration European Operational Records, Box 36, Folder 2, Reel 57, HILA.

20. Ibid.

21. Childfund to Mr. Brown, cablegram, Budapest, November 13, 1920, American Relief Administration European Operational Records, Box 36, Folder 3, Reel 57, HILA.

22. American Relief Administration European Children's Fund, *Final Report*, 10.

23. Childfund to Mr. Gay, cablegram, Budapest, February 2, 1921, American Relief Administration European Operational Records, Box 36, Folder 2, R57, HILA.

24. American Relief Administration (W. L. Brown) to Childfund, cablegram, December 20, 1920, American Relief Administration European Operational Records, Box 36, Folder 3, Reel 57, HILA.

25. "Képek az amerikai gyermeksegélyző akcióról," 4.

26. Jeszenszky, review of *Trianon arcai*.

27. Andrew Cherna, "Report to the American Red Cross on Investigation in Austria and Hungary," September 1923, 5, RG 200 Records of the American National Red Cross 1917–1934, 953.08, Box 878, NARA.

28. On the US approach to Hungary, see McElroy, *Morality and American Foreign Policy*, 63.

29. Geyer and Paulmann, *The Mechanics of Internationalism*, 5.

30. International Committee of the Red Cross, "Organisation of Help in Favor of the Hungarian Children in Budapest" (*Actions de secours en faveur des enfants hongrois á Budapest*), Budapest 1921, Minute 8:43, ICRC Archive.

31. Peterecz, "Hungary and the League of Nations," 165.

32. Ibid.

33. "Key Dates in Hungarian-American Diplomatic Relations," Embassy of Hungary, Washington, accessed January 10, 2022, https://washington.mfa.gov.hu/eng/page/fontos-datumok.

34. "US Peace Treaty with Hungary."

35. Motta, *Less than Nations*, 180.

36. Elsie Graves Benedict, "Report on Hungary," March 9, 1923, 1–4. RG 200, Records of the American National Red Cross 1917–1934, 953.11/08, Box 878, NARA.

37. "To the Rescue! Being the Impressions Collected by Five Dutch-Men during a Fortnight's Stay in Hungary," CH AEG AP 92.21.3.

38. Glant, "Herbert Hoover and Hungary."

39. Hungarian Territorial Integrity League, *The Consequences of the Division of Hungary*, 2.

40. Apponyi, *The American Peace and Hungary*, 1.

41. Irwin, "Taming Total War," 137.

42. Clavin, "Introduction," 5.

43. Sluga, *Internationalism in the Age of Nationalism*, 12, 150.

44. Gram-Skjoldager, Ikonomou, and Kahlert, "Introduction," 3.

45. Sluga, *Internationalism in the Age of Nationalism*, 157.

46. Marung, Middell, and Müller, "Territorialisierung in Ostmitteleuropa," 129.

47. Piller, "German Child Distress," 460.

48. Hajtó, *Milk Sauce and Paprika*, 68.

49. Clavin, "Introduction," 3.

50. Pattie Day Miller to Mr. R. P. Lane, European Director of the Junior Red Cross, Report for October, 1–6, 1. 953.11/08, NARA.

51. Acsády, "Diverse Constructions," 311.

52. Ablovatski, "Between Red Army and White Guard," 88.

53. Szapor, *Hungarian Women's Activism*, 88.
54. Vari, "Re-territorializing the 'Guilty City,'" 709.
55. Acsády, "Diverse Constructions," 312.
56. "The American Red Cross in Hungary," 1921, Sheet 1–5, Sheet 2. RG 200. Records of the American National Red Cross 1917–1934, 953.08, Box 878, NARA.
57. "Magyar Children Cry as 'Uncle Pedlow' Goes," 7.
58. Bell, "Hungary Initiates the 'Horthy Action,'" 72.
59. Hoover, "Central European Relief," 110.
60. "A fővárosi óvodákban amerikai cacaot reggeliznek a gyermekek," 23.
61. Pattie Day Miller, Field Director, to R. P. Lane, European Director, Junior American Red Cross, report, January 1923, 2–3, RG 200. Records of the American National Red Cross 1917–1934, 953.11/08, Box 878, NARA.
62. Irwin, *Making the World Safe*, 72.
63. Skinner and Lester, "Humanitarianism and Empire," 730.
64. Barnett, *Empire of Humanity*, 21.
65. Murdoch, *Imagined Orphans*, 17.
66. Zahra, *The Lost Children*, 40.
67. Rodogno, "The American Red Cross," 84.
68. "Ne legyen többé nélkülöző magyar," 2.
69. Mühlbeck, "Az amerikai misszió táplálkoztatási póttanfolyama," 477.
70. Marshall, "Children's Rights and Children's Action," 357.
71. Bókay, "The Result of the Hungarian Mission," 14.
72. Haan, "Hungary Thanks America."
73. "Save the Children's Fund," 8.
74. "Le Délégué de la croix-rouge de Genève a Szekszárd," and Rodophe de Reding-Biberegg, Delegate of the CIRCR, to the SCIU, June 3, 1921, CH AEG AP 92.21.3.
75. J. G. Pedlow to Ernest P. Bicknell, Budapest, January 27, 1922, RG 200, Records of the American National Red Cross 1917–34, 953.08, Box 989, NARA.
76. "The American Red Cross in Hungary," Sheet 6.
77. Nándor Bernolák to Herbert Hoover, November 1922, printed in Hoover, *An American Epic*, 429–30.
78. Adlgasser, *American Individualism Abroad*, 181.
79. Irwin, "Taming Total War," 136. For US aid after World War II, see Wieters, *The NGO Care and Food Aid*.
80. Herbert Hoover to John D. Rockefeller Jr., December 18, 1920, Collection RFAM, Record Group RG-2 OMR, Series Q: World Affairs, Box 41, Folder 361, Rockefeller Archive Center, Sleepy Hollow, NY.
81. "Many Weep at Hoover War Dinner," 8.
82. "A Statement by General Pershing at the Invisible Guest Dinner, 29 December 1920," 2.
83. Hoover, "Central European Relief," 108.
84. M. M. Mitchell to Childfund, cablegram, Budapest, June 29, 1920, American Relief Administration European Operational Records, Box 36, Folder 3, Reel 57, HILA.
85. Kellogg and Taylor, *The Food Problem*, 211.
86. Bókay, "The Result of the 1921 Feeding," 47.
87. Hoover, "The Children Must Be Saved," 2.
88. "Mr. Davison on the Situation in Europe," 5.
89. "Protocol of the Meeting of the Foreign Missions and Home Institutions. March 1, 1921," CH AEG AP. 92.21.3.
90. "Hungarians Erect Monument to American Red Cross Chief," 1.

91. "Everyone Helps in Work," 6.
92. "Magyar Children Cry as 'Uncle Pedlow' Goes," 7.
93. *Captain James Pedlow.*
94. "An American Name in a Hungarian Prayer."
95. "Captain Pedlow's Plea to the American-Hungarians."
96. Dauphinée, "The Politics of the Body"; Scarry, *The Body in Pain.*
97. Richardson to Mr. Brown, cablegram, Budapest, April 19, 1920, American Relief Administration European Operational Records, Box 36, Folder 4, Reel 56, HILA.
98. Vinchild to Mrs. Lutress, cablegram, Budapest, February 24, 1922, American Relief Administration European Operational Records, Box 36, Folder 1, Reel 56, HILA.
99. Appadurai, *The Social Life of Things*, 3.
100. Beckert, *Empire of Cotton*, xviii.
101. "Hungary Faces Severe Season," 5.
102. "Hungary Celebrated the American Thanksgiving," 8.
103. "Clothes Exhibition," 1920, Collection of the Hungarian National Museum, Budapest, Signature 2139.
104. American Relief Administration European Children's Fund, *Final Report*, 13.
105. Lt. Colonel Samuel Moffat, "Report of the American Red Cross Commission," 3, ACICR B. Mis.4.5/585–4.5/639, 1131–250, Archive of the ICRC.
106. Georg Simmel, cited in Appadurai, "Introduction: Commodities and the Politics of Value," 4.
107. Baughan, *Saving the Children*, 22.
108. American Relief Administration European Children's Fund, *Final Report*, 16.
109. "The American Red Cross in Hungary," Sheets 4, 2.
110. Selskar M. Gunn, "Public Health Conditions in Hungary, March 20–March 23, 1922," 1–42, 40. Collection RF, Series 100, Box 57, Folder 567, Rockefeller Archive Center, Sleepy Hollow.
111. Alonzo Taylor, "The Situation of the Intellectual Class in Central Europe," 1–2, Commonwealth Fund, Series 18 Grants, Box 12, Folder 119, Rockefeller Archive Center, Sleepy Hollow.
112. Cherna, "Report to the American Red Cross," 17–18.
113. Robert Davis, "Report of Buda-Peste Unit," American Red Cross, February–June 1920, Sheet 1, RG 200 Records of the American National Red Cross, 953.108, Box 878, NARA.
114. Kaszab, "A zsidó jótékonyság," 9.
115. "Magyar gyerekek munkája Londonban," 10.
116. Veit, *Modern Food, Moral Food*, 3.
117. "Aláírták a békeszerződést," 1.

8

DISPLACEMENT

The Ambiguity of the Children's Trains

Food relief in Budapest guaranteed children one warm meal per day, whereas more comprehensive international child protection initiatives addressed children's temporary or long-term displacement. In Hungary, "a movement got going to arrange long-term summer placements in the healthy Hungarian countryside for an 'army of children' who had been weakened through deprivation."[1] Thousands of children were sent away from the city for summer vacations or short- or medium-term residence with foreign families. The so-called children's trains, or King Charles / Károly Király Summer Holiday Action, relocated starving and destitute urban children to better-off regions in the countryside. More extensively, in the immediate postwar years, some sixty thousand children were dispatched to foster families abroad. Engaging with children's voluntary evacuation, this chapter argues that such dislocation, while indeed helping secure improved nutrition and forging transnational social ties, also led to a new level of public interference into the lives of families and children. Relying on printed and visual sources as well as subjective accounts of a handful of former children who participated in the children's trains and whom I interviewed, the chapter demonstrates the long-term biographical implications of this relief endeavor on the children's lives and family relationships. In doing so, it tests the assumption that, even a hundred years later, the displaced children's "lives and actions have meanings in and relevance to present societies."[2]

The Rural Temptation: Summer Vacations

Already during the war, starving and destitute children were sent to better-supplied regions. From 1917 on, the Budapest Welfare Center helped organize summer activities that were run by the Association of Children's Holiday

Placements (Szünidei Gyermektelep Egyesület). Established in 1884, this association saw to the temporary placement of selected "anemic and weak children" from the city, giving them respite in the better-off countryside during school holidays.[3] Already in the late nineteenth century, "scientific" methods were being applied: children were weighed and examined to determine whether they qualified for the scheme.[4] When they went on these organized holidays, the majority of the children were sent together to institutions, in so-called colonies (*telepek*). In 1918, for instance, around twenty thousand poor children were sent to Abbázia (Opatija, in present-day Croatia) for a summer vacation. Others went individually to foster families that were willing to take a child or two for a few weeks. Placements in this latter arrangement were matched according to the foster parents' "language, religious belief, age," and preference for the kind of child they would accept.[5] Sometimes a mansion or small castle would be offered by an aristocratic family. In 1906–7, the Hungarian National Child Protection League reported that it ran summer boarding programs for children who were "physically exhausted from the bad urban dwellings."[6]

The Welfare Center worked closely with the Child Proection League during the war and arranged in the summer of 1917 the placement of 182 children in Switzerland, in two six-week stints. The costs were covered by a financial collection organized by the wife of the Swiss military attaché. The selectors chose "children of judges and state officials," targeting families of the newly impoverished urban middle and upper classes. Less generous holiday placements were made for war orphans, who were sent to prosperous farms. The Welfare Center also supported summer vacations for German and Austrian children in the Hungarian countryside in 1917 and 1918. It was hoped that a "mutual summer exchange program would develop" with these wartime allies. On a much larger scale, in 1917, the Workers' Children's Friends Association (Munkások Gyermekbarát Egyesület) joined the Welfare Center in sending twenty-four hundred children from the capital and its suburbs to the Hungarian countryside. In 1918, this initiative was enlarged into a "mass holiday" (*tömegnyaraltatás*). In the framework of the Emperor Charles Children's Summer Action (*Károly király gyermeknyaraltatási akció*), approximately nine thousand children were sent to the imperial Austrian seashore. As Hugó Csergő pointed out in 1919, an endeavor like this required considerable institutional and professional backing.[7]

Another state-organized evacuation scheme for impoverished Hungarian children's "summer vacations" had been initiated by the Imperial Kaiser Karl Wohlfahrtswerk in Vienna. The Wohlfahrtswerk, named after the last Habsburg emperor as Charles I and king of Hungary as Charles IV, offer limited and selective relief to impoverished children during the last years of the war.[8] Relief was to go to "the poorest children of the population," among whom "war orphans" were included.[9] Besides feeding hungry children, providing medical care, and placing orphaned children in foster families or state asylums, the Wohlfahrtswerk had the idea of sending children away en masse for respite and recuperation on healing summer breaks. During the war's last two summers—the final years of the Austro-Hungarian monarchy—urban children in need were sent to rural or coastal areas to recover from the strains of war. The imperial response to the problem of emerging child poverty were the Kinder aufs Land (Children in the Countryside) and Kind zu Gast (Guest Child) schemes. In mutual exchanges across the empire, thousands of urban children were sent on holiday.[10]

In competition with the domestic imperial summer-away programs, the Austro-Hungarian People's Nutrition Office organized a program of holidays outside the national borders. The aim of the Children to Switzerland program was to give the children access to better food and fresh air. Because of its neutrality, Switzerland was not hard to reach. Parties of children went there throughout 1917 and early 1918, but the Swiss printed media were antagonistic. According to the popular press, Switzerland should not waste its remaining resources on foreigners. In 1918, the Foreign Ministry of Austria-Hungary cited an article that had appeared in the *Neue Züricher Zeitung* and had asked, "What if all the surrounding countries were to send their needy children to Switzerland?" According to the article, the daily bread "of our own people" was in short supply and "should not be reduced any further. Facing [shortages in] our food and firewood supplies, we have far too many foreign people in the country anyway." Unwilling to strain diplomatic relations with Switzerland, the imperial authorities put pressure on the nutrition office to discontinue the scheme for the war's duration.[11]

The squabble over Switzerland did not stop the Wohlfahrtswerk's summer holiday project from going ahead. The child relief scheme was designed to assist middle-class children whose families had become impoverished during the war and whose bodies showed signs of starvation and neglect. Emperor Charles (King Charles IV), though exhibiting genuine concern for the children, had evident imperial aims behind the summer holiday initiative. His correspondence with the Wohlfahrtswerk indicates that he hoped to strengthen the bonds between the disconnected crown lands and bolster a severely weakened monarchy. Associating imperial power with building up the next generation of Hungarians, whose fate the war had threatened, was good propaganda to drum up support for himself and his empress-queen

Fig. 8.1. "Long live the King! First group of children leaving from Eastern Railway Station." Unknown photographer, *Az Érdekes Újság* 6, no. 28 (July 18, 1918): cover.

among the people. Images of the children's relief he was sponsoring portrayed Charles as the people's champion. An image of two enthusiastic children in one of the first arranged holidays at the Adriatic seaside, seen in figure 8.1, uses their expressions of happiness and gratitude to emphasize the ruler's benevolence. They carry a sign identifying them as participants in the "Emperor Charles Summer Vacation Program," and the image is captioned "Long Live the King!" The children's visages served as an appeal for the maintenance of the imperial order.

For a while, the status quo held. However, by the late summer of 1918, friction between the various national groups involved in the children's holidays was becoming apparent. Observers criticized the accommodation and feeding Hungarian children received on the Austrian Adriatic coast. The *Pesti Hírlap* of August 4, 1918, reproached the Austrians for their poor organization and seemingly unfair implementation of the "child holidays." "A minor incident disturbed this showcase holiday, and the lousiness of the whole arrangement was laid bare: they [the Austrians] had given no thought to [proper] accommodation or feeding."[12] Prejudices and stereotypes were becoming

Fig. 8.2. "Hungarian Children on the Abbázia Pier." Unknown photographer, *Az Érdekes Újság* 6, no. 31 (August 8, 1918): 2.

more entrenched. News articles reported the interethnic conflicts that surfaced when Hungarian, Austrian, and Croatian children holidayed together in Abbázia (today Opatija in Croatia), as shown in figure 8.2.

The goal was for these children and their leaders from different parts of the empire to learn to get along with one another, but the program did "not happen without any inconveniences."[13] Politically, it was a failure. Though it was conceded that the Hungarian authorities committed mistakes, there was ill feeling over the reactions from "the Croatian and Austrians," who "did not express their greatest sympathy" with the Hungarians with whom they were partnering.[14] A month later, and just a few weeks before the war's end and the defeat of the Central powers, the *Pesti Hírlap* printed a photo of some of the Hungarian children returning from abroad (see fig. 8.3), titled "Home Is Best" (*Legjobb otthon*).

At home in Hungary, the children were sheltered from the national rivalries exacerbated by the war and the festering animosities. The attempt to achieve interethnic rapprochement within the Austro-Hungarian Empire through the schemes for children's holidays had failed. Not even among children was there agreement. The child relief holiday initiative hinted at the shift from empire to embittered nation that was to come. Yet the children were to have a summer holiday and a little escape from their hungry lives in the destitute capital city.

Fig. 8.3. "Home Is Best." Photo by János Müllner, *Az Érdekes Újság* 1, no. 35 (September 5, 1918): 4.

Once Hungary had lost a major part of its prewar territory in 1920, the new Hungarian state realized the need to relieve the suffering of the arriving refugee families and their children. Efforts were made to save the economically and socially "valuable" migration group from too much social decline. In 1920, the Hungarian Refugee Office placed 646 children with relatively prosperous farmers in different parts of the country. In 1921, with support from the American Relief Administration, the refugee office sent 485 children with forty-two refugee officers to the Prohászka Ottó Orphanage in Martonvásár and to Balatonkenese for recuperative holidays (see fig. 8.4).

Many groups of children were placed with farming families in the counties of Győr, Veszprém, and Békés as well as in child sanitaria in smaller cities. In Balatonkenes, a little village by Lake Balaton, Count István Bethlen—the prime minister of the Kingdom of Hungary since 1921—"set up a camp under his name, in which 200 children could be received." Because Bethlen came from a noble Transylvanian family, he had a special empathy with the refugees from his home region.[15]

These holidays generally were met with appreciation. They also had great symbolic potential. In a report, Petrichevich-Horváth stressed the impact of

Fig. 8.4. "Bathing at the Beach. The Summer Camp of Refugee Children in Balatonkenese." Unknown photographer, in Karsai, *Jelentés az Országos Gyermekvédő Liga 1906-7 évi működéséről*, 28.

geographical displacement on refugee children's health and bodies and the happiness a holiday brought. "How much these children's trains were needed!" The children's bodies had been "atrophied" through the cramped, unhealthy life in the rail wagons and mass accommodation; nothing proved the success of the holidays better than the fact that "those children, who participated in the cure, came back from the holiday with a large gain in weight." And later, due to their participation, the children "survived the winter and schooling without sickness." The Hungarian Refugee Office continued to provide children with amusements on a smaller scale once they returned to Budapest. In addition to taking them "every year for a free boat tour to Visegrád," the office arranged excursions to the zoo, to the circus, and to an English garden; and every Christmas there were "Christmas tree celebrations."[16] Alongside food relief and supplies, children needed these opportunities to be children.

In 1920, with the war over, Julia Vajkai lobbied for the Swiss summer vacations to start up again. In a letter to the Save the Children International Union written in April 1920, she drew attention to the fact that the Swiss seemed willing to welcome Czech and Serbian children but not children from Hungary.[17] The resistance came not from Swiss families but from the Swiss state. Could the SCIU not "involve Hungarian children" in the program? She pleaded especially for Catholic Hungarian children—not "because of my own creed" but because Budapest had a Catholic majority and most of the children who had gone to Holland were Protestants and she wished to avoid any kind of "injustice."[18] Like other forms of relief, summer holidays for needy children had both domestic and international aspects.

Into the House of the Enemy: Transnational Children's Trains

Thousands of impoverished and starving children from Budapest were sent out of Hungary to improve their physical well-being. The practice of sending trains of children to foreign countries was partly a reaction to the disastrous economic situation in Hungary and partly due to the fact that, after the Treaty of Trianon, Hungary had lost access to the Adriatic Sea and to the Transylvania mountains, where children had previously been sent. International children's trains offered an alternative. In addition to sending clothes and food supplies to Hungary, neutral countries rushed to "help local Hungarian charity organizations to arrange for the children summer vacations abroad."[19] From 1920 on, international child relief agencies, in cooperation with national relief agencies, sent around sixty thousand needy Hungarian children to foster families in the Netherlands, Switzerland, Britain, and Sweden, with Belgium joining the list in 1923.[20] The activity was financially and bureaucratically supported by the Save the Children Fund and the International Committee of the Red Cross and organized in Hungary by the National Child Protection League. The National Child Protection League selected the children who were to be sent away and paired them with foster families. To qualify, the children had to be malnourished, severely underweight, or sick. Visual images, including drawings, photographs, posters, and everyday objects, were used to justify, illustrate, and document children's suffering and their geographic displacement.

As well as physical examinations and weighing, which were done the same way as in the American feeding stations, children were also subjected to a close social examination. A "question sheet for children's aftercare committee" from 1922 asked about the financial and social condition of the child's birth family. A question sheet filled out with information about eleven-year-old Endre Brück recommends another stay in Britain because he was "anemic and rather underfed" and also because he came from a "poor home, mother a widow humpback, most deserving, struggling hard to bring up her two boys." Additionally, his mother suffered from a stomach disease and could not properly care for her children. The concluding remark judged that "it is a sad case, they really deserve help."[21] Half orphans like Endre Brück and full orphans were considered good candidates to participate in the children's

Fig. 8.5. "Foreign Countries for Hungarian Children." Drawing by Károly Mühlbeck, *Új Idők* 26, no. 11 (April 24, 1920): 27.

trains. Yet these children were also vulnerable to a permanent placement abroad and the resulting alienation from their home country.

Many impoverished and physically impaired parents, often those displaced by the war or Hungary's territorial losses, gained the opportunity to send their children abroad for a certain amount of time. Placing poor Hungarian children into better-off foster families abroad was perceived as a sensible act of relieving their suffering. Yet there were some critical voices. A report by five Dutch investigators assessing Hungary's economic situation concluded that the system of sending children abroad entailed "great expense" and only relieved the suffering of a "limited number of children." Moreover, the "difference[s] of language and race" they encountered in these international placements gave rise to "exceptional difficulties."[22] A 1936 report of the National Child Protection League reviewing the children's trains drew a very different conclusion; it claimed that this mass action had been "the most interesting chapter . . . in the entire life history" of the league, because it had not only "recovered children's strength and health" but also "contributed to better understanding between the nations" and had an impact on Hungary's international tourism and economy.[23]

In a hand drawing made in 1920 by Károly Mühlbeck for *Új Idők* (New Times) titled "Foreign Countries for Hungarian Children" (shown in fig. 8.5), stereotypically dressed foster parents from other lands are depicted at the moment of the children's arrival to stay with them.[24] Presenting four hosting foster parents from four different countries all in one scene, the picture captures the internationalist character of the postwar children's relief holidays. On the left-hand side is a typical Dutch farmer's wife; to the right of her is a (possibly) Swedish foster mother; farther right still is a British gentleman with a checkered suit and a pipe; and on the far right, a Swiss woman walks hand in hand with the children—all leading the children in their care away to some warm home. The children are thin but well dressed, and they carry their own luggage. The four foster parents lead the children in various directions, indicating the broad international character of the holiday scheme. This picture (like the scheme itself) aptly conveys the powerful idea of internationalism and the use of all kinds of print and visual media for its propagation. The image, and the program of sending children abroad, must have evoked ambivalent feelings and thoughts in families. The children were taken away because of the economic and material destitution affecting their homes, not because of any parental unwillingness to show love and care.

Being sent abroad could be a challenging experience, for both the children and the host families. Ibolya, a former foster girl in the program I interviewed in 2012, recalled arriving in Roermond after a three-day train journey and being welcomed by three Dutch women who had asked for a ten-year-old foster girl. The little numbered sign around her neck matched the number the women had. Although Ibolya was three and not ten, as had been communicated in advance, they felt obliged to take the girl home despite her young age.[25] István, whom I interviewed in Budapest in 2012 and who had had been sent to Belgium as five-year-old, recalled similar number matching: "When the numbers matched, one picked the child out of the crowd and brought it home." He was duly picked. His Flemish foster parents were very happy, he remembered, that "they had their Hungarian child they'd been waiting for." In the evening, they prepared a real feast, to which they invited all their village acquaintances. István remembers feeling happy, as "everyone favored him." Yet, retrospectively, he wondered, "What could I actually [have understood] about what [was happening] to me?"

If the placement went well, transnational social ties between families could ensue, and even develop into international goodwill. Often the foster parents and their families were invited to Hungary to visit their former foster children years later. In 1926, a group of Belgian foster parents went to visit their former Hungarian foster children in Budapest. They were invited by the Austrian archduchess Izabella of Croÿ-Dülmen, who had married in Belgium, to join her for five o'clock tea. On another occasion in 1926, Swiss foster parents were invited by the archbishop János Csernoch to visit the Roman Catholic archdiocese in Esztergom.[26] Such international reunions and the participation of high-ranking aristocrats, Catholic dignitaries, and politicians was meant to strengthen the conservative and restorative ties between Hungary and Belgium.

In other acts of rapprochement, diplomatic representatives of the countries hosting children were publicly thanked by the Hungarian government in ceremonies that put the children center stage. The ceremonies were closely

Fig. 8.6. "Twenty Thousand Children from Budapest Parade in Front of the Flat of the Dutch Consul in Budapest." Unknown photographer, *Új Idők* 26, no. 13 (May 10, 1920): 257.

reported in the contemporary Hungarian media, again with pictures. On one occasion, twenty thousand children from Budapest, all in Hungarian national dress, paraded before the apartment of Clinge Fledderus, the Dutch consul, and his wife, shown in figure 8.6, to express their thanks to the Dutch nation. Children thus strengthened international cooperation and intercultural understanding. Even today, on the house where the Fledderuses lived, a plaque reminds visitors of the consul's relief work after World War I.

It was especially when the children were sent abroad and began to learn a foreign language that intercultural rapprochement became real. Before leaving for placements, Hungarian children were provided with a one-page pocket aid—a "daily-life dictionary for children sent to Britain" for example—so they could communicate their basic needs to the foster parents. These phrase sheets, like the one shown in figure 8.7, included general vocabulary for everyday items, along with a pronunciation guide (because most of the children had little knowledge of the host language before departing). Words relating to food and to pain—pain in the throat, hand, foot, belly, heart, and back, and also dizziness—were a primary focus of these guides. Many of other words and phrases were useful especially at mealtimes. These translation sheets reveal the underlying objective of the relocation schemes—to foster peace between civilian populations of the former enemy countries. Yet, at a very concrete, everyday level, they show the centrality of food and some awareness of the problems involved in cultural displacement.

Piroska, the girl mentioned in this book's introduction, was seven years old when she was sent in spring 1922 to Holland for a few months. In my

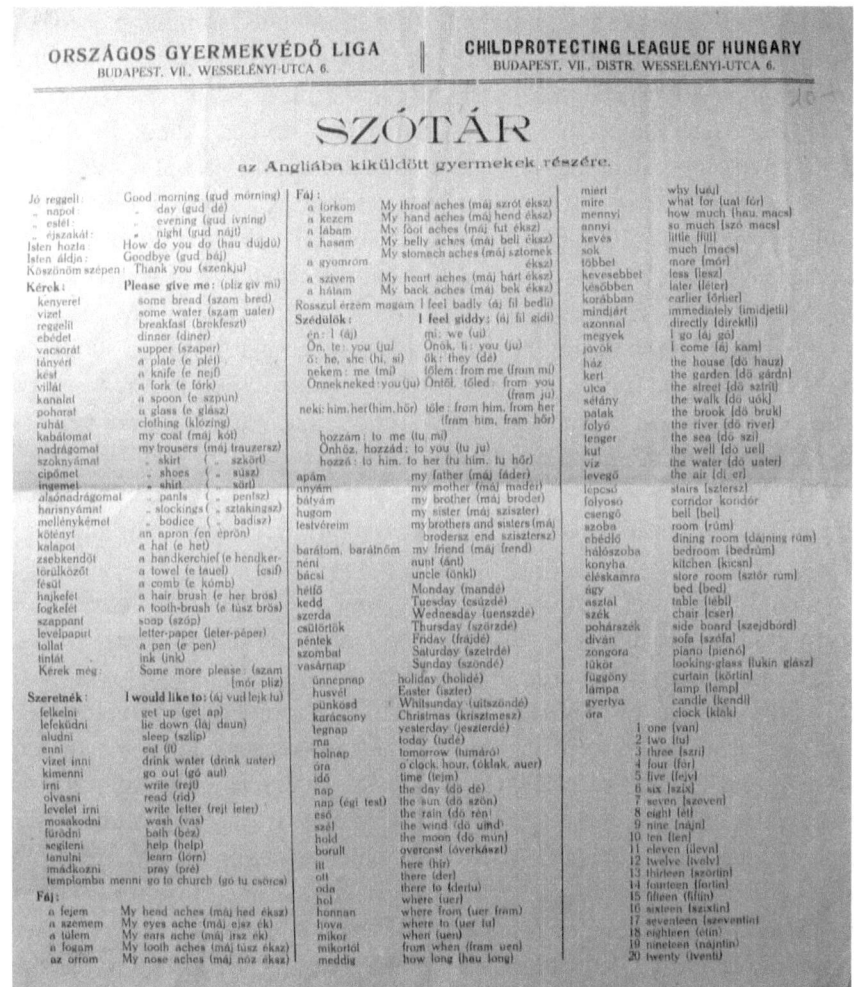

Fig. 8.7. "Dictionary of the National Child Protection League." Unknown author, Signature 73.63.1, Hungarian Pedagogical Library and Museum, Budapest.

interview with her ninety years later, she recalled various memories of food and eating.[27] Because her mother suffered from a stomach disease, Piroska was institutionalized at age four in a nunnery in Óbuda in 1918, where "the children were hungry." She recalled the evening of Saint Nicholas Day, December 6, when her father brought her some sweets; by the next morning she had finished them, "evidently not because of gluttony" but sheer hunger. "What happened to the child who didn't receive anything?" she wondered. Many children's parents were not in a position to provide extra food on festive days. Yet she was poor enough to qualify for an extended summer placement abroad, from late spring to early fall, though many of the placements during the war happened for a few weeks only in the summer.

On her arrival in Holland, Piroska ("Priszka" to her Dutch hosts) was fed cod liver oil because she was so thin. She did not like it, but it was effective. Prominent among her memories was celebrating Easter with her foster family. "I woke up on Easter Day, and on my bedside table was a rabbit.... It was made of paper, but stood on four legs, and attached to its two sides were two chocolate eggs. It was so nice, I'll never forget it in all my life.... This was the most beautiful thing." Piroska also recalled her first food shopping experience with the foster parents. For the first time in her life she visited a confectioner's, where they ate several pieces of cake. After that, the parents took her by the hand and they went home. "Even today," she recalled, "I can feel their hands, how they led me along ... as if they were my parents." These moments of her foster parents' emotional and physical affection are fixed in her memory.

Though her foster family in Holland lived a "simple Dutch life," there were occasions, she remembered, when the foreign children were all invited to the home of an aristocratic Dutch widow. "Just as [Dutch] Queen Wilhelmina opened the gates of her country" to Hungary's children, so, too, this dowager opened the doors of her house to them on weekends. In groups of ten to twenty, the children received lunch. Piroska remembered that they always had a "cocoa and milk break." What she loved most were "these round rusks on those blue-white porcelain plates over which they poured hot milk." As well as getting meals at the aristocrat's house, Piroska and the other children were invited to go shopping with her, and Piroska ended up with the two pockets of her apron filled with sweets. When recalling how she fit in with the new family, Piroska stressed how easy it was to communicate with the foster parents and the other children, even though they spoke a different language. She learned the language fast, because "I was the only Hungarian child [in the village] which is why I spoke Dutch in an instant."

To illustrate this (speaking in and out of the present tense), she recalled a particular day when she came home early, sweating and feeling very hot. "I run into the room, almost fall into the woman's apron, and say in Hungarian: 'Melegem van! Melegem van!' ('I'm hot! I'm hot!') She then takes my hand and leads me into the room, where, in one corner, milk was always kept in a Delftware jug, and she thought that I wanted to drink milk. And I told her in Hungarian, 'No! I'm hot!' Then she knew right away that *meleg* in Hungarian means 'hot' and she knew that it was not the milk." With this recollection,

Piroska conveys her past sense of the initial difficulties in communicating with her foster family. Yet through such moments of intercultural miscommunication, her foster mother learned some Hungarian words, and Piroska also felt that she learned Dutch "incredibly fast." Learning a new language had some impact on her mother tongue as well. She recalled that she was forgetting Hungarian rather quickly: "When I was lying upstairs trying to recall my memories in words, I often didn't find Hungarian equivalents for the Dutch words." Learning the language, Piroska thought, was a proof of her successful assimilation. While learning the new language helped her abroad, it also mirrored her separation from her home. Letter writing was the most important, and often also the sole, means for the evacuated children to maintain contact to their birth families. As such, the loss of their mother tongue, causing children's inability to write letters, affected their relationships. At the same time, letter writing also helped children to continue practicing their mother tongue and share their everyday experiences abroad with their birth families.[28]

The displaced children had to navigate between their former and their new lives. When Piroska first arrived in Holland, she felt "like a bird that had fallen out if its nest, not caring where they placed it, simply going where it was told." But this feeling of not-belonging was not triggered by her departure for Holland but by her early childhood experiences—her mother's absences due to severe lung disease, her father's difficulties raising four children alone, along with moving between various accommodations. In Holland, she felt loved by her foster mother, who "accepted" her "fully" and whose "motherly love is still in me," she later remembered. Piroska concluded that, "because as a child I had such a torn-apart life, this was a first nesting." She felt that her experience in Holland "gave her . . . a backbone for life." This "zest for life," she recalled, "I first felt in Holland and lost when I arrived back in Budapest." Agreeing with the official discourse about children's relief, Piroska believed the holiday program "returned a whole generation to Hungary which had been bled dry." She expressed a particular feeling of thankfulness to Queen Wilhelmina for supporting the relief mission. Piroska believed that the queen's experience as a mother influenced her compassion for Hungary—a country that Piroska maintained had been ruined by "the Trianon peace, the so-called peace (it is an insult that this was thought of as a peace)."

Ibolya judged her stay abroad differently.[29] As a child, she also had been placed in Holland, though hers was a longer stay. She was with a foster family in Roermond for nine years, from 1926 to 1935. Her return to Hungary was more difficult than her departure, because she left for Holland when she was three and rapidly acclimated to her foster family and to Dutch customs. She quickly forgot her own parents and even asked her foster parents to take their photograph off the wall because they no longer meant anything to her. Instead of perceiving her displacement in Holland as traumatic, the event that shook her emotionally was when a relative came to her foster parents' home to take her back to Budapest. She hid to avoid going, but afterward a letter arrived demanding her return within a year. At age twelve, she went back to Hungary. When her train arrived in Budapest, she recalled, some "people, the age of my parents," came to the window of her compartment and called out, "Ibi!" She replied: "No, I am Bolya!" (the name she had been known by in Holland.) She did not even recognize her birth mother and had to have an interpreter ask who she was. When they arrived home, the interpreter left and Ibolya realized that she "did not know a word of Hungarian." Her parents hired a tutor so she could relearn the language. Ibolya's Dutch foster mother once came to visit her in Budapest, and Ibolya shared that she wanted to return to Roermund. But her father refused, and so she remained. One day she found out she had a sister she had never known, because this girl, too, had been sent abroad, to Antwerp in Belgium. On her return, the girls felt very distant, but they soon became very close. They shared a common bond: both of them had spent years in foster care abroad to be fed, sparing them from hunger but saddling them with other lasting consequences.

Looking back on her life, Ibolya recollected that, with the foster parents in Holland, she felt like "one of their own children." In her upbringing there, she had been "loved by many, but not as a mother can love." When she came back from Holland, she was loved again by her birth mother, "but not like a real mother" because the crucial experience of a shared "childhood up to the age of 12 was missing." Despite these experiences of personal and cultural displacement, she maintained, in retrospect, that she was not depressed when abroad, nor unwell when back in Hungary. She had "become . . . a person who could assimilate." She did not keep longing for a different life. Yet her narrative suggests that she resented her forced return to Budapest and yearned for her life in Holland, at least for a time. In the end, Ibolya succeeded in integrating her fragmented experiences into a meaningful life story. Her decision to become a translator enabled her to create coherence between her past memories and her life as an adult.

In addition to hunger, illnesses in destitute families were special push factors that might determine whether children were sent away. The authorities did not want children to be exposed to tuberculosis, influenza, or other postwar diseases. "If a parent got tuberculosis," István remembers, "they divided up the children" and "solved the problem that way." His own mother was sick with a lung infection, so István and his siblings were all removed from the home. While his younger sister was packed off to stay with her grandparents "in relatively better living conditions," István was sent by the Child Protection League and the Franciscan Order to Belgium. Though children were sent abroad if their parents were sick, children who themselves had diseases were seldom allowed to travel. "Sick children," István recalled, "were not sent abroad." Children sent to Britain under the so-called hospitality scheme were only allowed to enter "under stringent medical precautions prescribed by the Ministry of Health." To "prevent the introduction of disease," an examination of every child evacuee was "carried out by one of the ministry's representatives."

Most of the children's placements abroad were closely linked to church institutions. Taking a poor Hungarian child into the home was often an act of religious compassion. "In Holland it was different, as the Dutch were richer," István remembered, but they accommodated Hungarian children as "they were good Catholics who had compassion and pity." Frida Victor, a Hungarian teacher who accompanied children traveling to Holland in the early 1920s, recalled (writing in 1928) how "deep religiosity warmed the peaceful, orderly and healthy Dutch family life."[30] Institutional reports and accounts by individuals are full of detailed descriptions of the host families' overall national characteristics, but the issue of religion figures the most prominently. Vera Hajtó observed that local publicity in Belgium on receiving Hungarian children was heavily interwoven with a sense of "apostolic" mission. Catholic foster parents there were called on to save not only the children's bodies but also their souls, lest they stray to other denominations.[31] The Catholic Church was the driving force behind placements in Flanders, the Catholic part of Belgium. Nuns accompanied the children during the train journeys and taught their classes.

In Switzerland and Holland, the Reformed Church dominated children's placements. Irénke Márton, a Hungarian supervisor who went with children to Switzerland, remarked that the Swiss were "religious; in the family, I found a Bible next to almost every bed."[32] Despite the grave economic situation in Switzerland, the Center for Swiss Aid to Hungarian Children (Zentralstelle der schweizerischen Hilfsaktion für ungarische Kinder) invited more than sixteen thousand Hungarian children for respite stays. This Swiss mission had been founded by Rev. Carl Irlet. In a 1921 letter to Eglantyne Jebb, Irlet explained his great desire to "continue the blessed work of Christian charity." There was little money to spare, so Irlet was (again) asking the SCF "to quickly provide help."³³ Any "blessed Christian charity" had to rely on financial support from organizations like theirs. Because Irlet's Swiss scheme was largely funded through the Save the Children Fund, it is not surprising that most of the reports the organization received were positive.

Regardless of religion or sense of duty, foster parents and Hungarian child guests often formed bonds of affection. Many reports referred to the successful cultural integration of foster children and their ability to engage with their foster parents emotionally. The hosts "right away fell in love with the children and could easily enchant the direct, attached, intelligent, and easily adaptable Hungarian children, who after the deprivations at home accepted with greatest joy the smallest gifts and who could cheer up the mood of the hosts' children."³⁴

Foster parents might want to keep in contact after the foster children had returned to Hungary. On December 20, 1920, a Mr. Bohlen wrote a letter to Lord Weardale, the chairman of the executive committee of the Save the Children Fund, appreciating the fact that the Hungarian "children sent to England under the 'Hospitality Scheme' were so carefully chosen that in their case the scheme proved an entire success unlike those sent from Vienna."³⁵ Indeed, the relief effort went so well that foster parents sent letters to the SCF asking how they could maintain contact with their former foster children.³⁶ Sometimes stays abroad could be repeated if the birth parents were still in need of support and foster parents were willing to host the child a second time. The success of the children's placements was assessed after the foster period ended and took into consideration the conditions the children returned to.³⁷

The children's stays abroad were originally meant to provide short-term relief for periods not exceeding six months. But sometimes there were longer-term placements with foster families, or even stays of many years. István, who was sent to Belgium at age five, became "for two years a Flemish farmer's child." Around 5–10 percent of the Hungarian children sent to Belgium never returned to Hungary.³⁸ This also happened elsewhere. Whether children returned often depended on the circumstances of the children's birth families. The greater the economic gulf between the birth family and the foster family, the more likely it became that children would not return home. István recalled that, when he was allowed to return to Hungary, he had a lot of problems, because there was still "great poverty" at home. However, because his father had been employed for a while, his parents "could demand my return." His foster parents had no children of their own and did not want him to leave. They hoped that István could become the "successor" to his foster father. This led to considerable conflict between his birth and foster parents.

The National Child Protection League distributed declarations that provided for cases in which parents might want to allow their children to remain with the foster families once the "international holiday" came to an end.[39] The lists of the children's trains often show blank spaces in the column for the children's return. Some former child evacuees report many cases in which children remained abroad longer or even remained in the foreign country for good. The number is unknown. Some of the cases can still be traced through personal letters exchanged between the National Child Protection League and the involved families. The Hungarian tax office documented the case of two children who remained abroad for twenty years. After the death of their father, Lajos Tamás, in 1920, Irén (born 1907) and Zsófia (born 1912) were sent to Dordrecht in the Netherlands, where their foster parents "started to love them, raise them and care for their future." Their mother's death in 1932 made them full orphans and prevented reintegration into their birth families in Hungary. "Nobody belongs to them [in Hungary and] they have forgotten their mother tongue entirely." If Irén and her sister had to return to Hungary, a letter from October 1939 stated, "they would be forced to return from their good placement there to a home which would be completely foreign to them, where the greatest misery and deprivation would await them, [those] who do not know Hungarian and who—without any relatives and support—would be in dire need."[40] To prevent such highly problematic relocations, confirmation of the children's identity and citizenship was needed from the Hungarian authorities so that they would not be expelled from Dutch territory.

The children who did return after long stays frequently encountered reintegration problems. István, for instance, had "serious troubles," because he could not "speak a single Hungarian word." Flemish had come to him "absolutely natural[ly]," and "perhaps already on the next day or on the third or fourth day," he could "speak to the girls and everyone." He recalled: "I had no problems at all to speak or communicate with them, almost from the first minute onwards." However, he relearned his native language quickly. In his interview, he stressed that it was far harder to relearn Hungarian than it had been to learn the language of his foster family in Belgium.

In the wider perspective, sending children to families in former enemy countries only a few years after the brutal conflict between the Allied and Central powers appears almost incomprehensible. It was so soon to expect transnational reconciliation. "Although we [Belgians and Hungarians] had been enemies," István recalled, "these Flemish Catholics were very welcoming . . . and even accommodated Hungarian children," despite the fact that they "were not that well-off."[41] The innocent children were able to bring about a personal rapprochement between the former enemy populations. As Vera Hajtó observes, the Hungarian child relief project was crucial in restoring understanding between Belgium and Hungary and in raising "sympathy in the international community" with the "victims" of Trianon.[42] There could be no more drastic and invasive measure than to place an "enemy" child into the everyday life of a foreign family.

The Ambiguities of Children's Displacement to Foreign Countries

A welfare agency of the state permitted local welfare agents to "save" children who were considered to be in physical or moral danger by removing them from their home. This new understanding of welfare and relief "stressed the importance" and ignored the possible dangers "of separating child and parent."[43] The impressions put out by the organizations that arranged for the children's trains rarely touched on intimate problems for the uprooted children. In their publicity, these organizations chose to portray idyllic childhood experiences abroad, full of innocence, purity, humanity, and solidarity. This brought out the "humanitarian" character of the relief endeavors, but the distinct identities of the individual girls and boys participating dropped out of the picture and were subsumed in a vague collective image of the healed child. Seeing the alleviation of the children's suffering through temporary relocation spurred the public to donate to this cause. Many of the photographs published of children's trains capture the scale, and the political and ideological importance, of the transnational endeavor. Hungary's new generation has been saved, many visuals seem to suggest, by the helping hands of organizers and donors. Possibly because Hungarians had been the "enemy" in the war, the children represented salvation, and their reception abroad signified restoration in the international community.

The primary interest of the relief organizations was children's physical well-being. They took no account of the children's wishes, and little was said about any undermining of the integrity of the birth family that might occur when foster parents became part of the picture. Another drawing by the famous Hungarian caricaturist Károly Mühlbeck titled "Here are the Dutch fathers and mothers" (fig. 8.8) depicts the moment when Dutch foster parents come bouncing in on a visit to their foster children in Hungary. The well-fed Dutch mothers, with packages and presents for the children, are welcomed by the children as proper parents. The birth parents are sidelined to the picture's edges. On the far right, a Dutch foster mother embraces a skinny

Fig. 8.8. "Here Are the Dutch Fathers and Mothers." Drawing by Károly Mühlbeck, *Új Idők* 30, no. 23 (June 1, 1924): 435.

Fig. 8.9. "Movie Recording of Children Returning from Holland." Unknown photographer, *Új Idők* 30, no. 31 (July 28, 1924): 87.

woman who appears to be one of the children's true mothers. A visually stark contrast is drawn between the bodily constitutions of the two. The depiction of the well-fed Dutch mother in her national dress is detailed, whereas the figure of the Hungarian birth mother is drawn as only a silhouette, emphasizing the physical destitution of her body. The image almost suggests that the Dutch foster parents, with their prosperity, high spirits, and good health, are better suited to care for Hungary's children than the children's own families in that moment.

Figure 8.9 shows the return of a large group of Hungarian children and youngsters who had been in Holland. This scene was captured for a contemporary

Fig. 8.10. "A Child's Return from Holland." Unknown artist, *Az Érdekes Újság* 9, no. 10 (March 10, 1921): cover.

movie about the children's trains. While this photo features the great masses of arriving child evacuees, the movie *The Dutch Heart* (*A Holland Szív*),[44] made by Alfred Deésy, centers on the destiny of a girl named Marika, from her departure to Holland to her return to Budapest and the visit by her Dutch foster parents. Various images portray impressive weight gain in the children as they return to Hungary with abundant gifts from their foster families. One cover picture that adorned *Az Érdekes Újság* (The interesting journal), shown in figure 8.10, shows a young girl arriving back from Holland at the Eastern Railway Station in Budapest. The girl is accompanied by a well-dressed, well-fed middle-class woman, probably the official supervisor during the journey. The girl is well nourished, a little overweight even, with a hint of a double chin. She is smartly dressed and has a trolley full of large parcels beside her. All this stands in stark contrast to the people depicted in the background, who have old clothes and emaciated, haggard faces. The picture's caption identifies her as one of many "showered with so many humanitarian

Fig. 8.11. "Home from Holland." Unknown photographer, *Új Idők* 18 (October 22, 1922): 293.

gifts they cannot carry them home." Interviewee Piroska also remembered that she came home with "a large package, a suitcase full of chocolate, and a suitcase full of new clothes."⁴⁵ Carrying the gifts from one country to another, as the image "Home from Holland" (fig. 8.11), documents, underlines the material relationship as well as dependency between the involved children, families, and countries.

Even once they were back in Budapest, deserving children received presents from Holland. The birthday of the Dutch princess Juliana, on April 30, 1920, was used to highlight and stage the new Dutch-Hungarian friendship. Visuals were taken to depict the moment when on that very same day that "twenty-four girls in Budapest who were born on the same day as the princess receive[d] a gift in the Dutch consulate."⁴⁶ But transnational gifts were not only one-sided; Hungary also sent gifts to Holland. Again, the birthday of the Dutch princess was used as an occasion to exhibit Hungary's appreciation of the help the country's children had received. On that day, some Budapest schoolchildren, shown in figure 8.12, sent a Transylvanian dollhouse, a highly symbolic item, as a birthday present to the Dutch princess.

Using the birthday of a royal descendant to celebrate the Dutch-Hungarian friendship in a time when the Austro-Hungarian monarchy had ended

Iskolás gyermekek kalotaszegi babaszobát küldenek születésnapi ajándékul Juliánna hollandiai királykisasszonynak. Eiser fényképe

Fig. 8.12. "School Children Are Sending a Transylvanian Doll House to the Dutch Princess Juliana." Photo by Mór Eiser, *Új Idők* 26, no. 13 (May 10, 1920): 295.

appears to be an attempt to remind the European nations of Hungary's royal heritage. That the Hungarian children sent a Transylvanian dollhouse to Holland in April 1920, when at the Paris Peace Conference the future of the Hungarian territory was decided, seems more than coincidental. Children were highly instrumental in making a statement about international politics at the time.

As the war and its aftereffects had resulted in large-scale devastation and poverty, the relocation of children offered a symbolic counterimage to the general misery. Through the images in various publications of rescued children, readers and donors could identify themselves as heroic child saviors, or at least as witnesses of child-saving activities. The "prevailing functions of humanitarian images remain largely consistent," we are told.[47] So dichotomist images of suffering and its alleviation appeared over and over again. Foster families who aided Hungarian children through motivations of religious belief must have felt assured of their place in heaven.

Yet among Hungarians—children, parents, the press, and officials alike—the outcomes of the children's trains did not always align with the relief organizations' positive representations. As my interviews with people who were fostered in the 1920s made clear, memories of the pain of alienation from birth families was sometimes longer lasting for the children than memories of the precious gifts abroad. The act of relocating children involved a high degree of public interference in their lives and those of their families. Humanitarian groups prioritized children's physical well-being, but their emotional well-being was naturally strained by being wrenched from home and placed under the care of strangers. As Emily Baughan observes, while humanitarian relief organizations in the post–World War I period often employed notions of the ideal family to call on donors, they "tended to overlook the children's existing families" and "viewed children as emotive objects, rather than emotional subjects."[48] Children's physical needs were often prioritized over their emotional well-being. The fine intentions of child relief activities were not always mirrored in the actual impact on children's lives. In "The Black Outlook in Europe," a British reporter dared to question the appropriateness of the child relief undertaking. While praising the charity of the Dutch and Swiss host families, the writer raised the problem of the separation of children from their families: "I doubt if as a child I should have liked to be sent among perfect strangers not one of whom could understand what I said, and the majority of whom would regard me, and probably treat me, as a little enemy."[49]

Gyula Krúdy's children's book *Liga Gida Kalandjai Hollandiában es a Világ Egyéb Tájain* (*The Adventures of Liga Gida in Holland and in Other Parts of the World*) was commissioned by the National Child Protection League and published in 1923. It recounts how a boy called Gida, the main character, initially hopes to fail the dreaded medical examination the relief doctors intend to make, because he does not want to leave his family and go abroad. "I know a grass in the old Rácvárosi cemetery," he says to himself, "with which I can rub my face and my hands so that they turn yellow [and] the doctor will lose his interest in the . . . examination."[50] But in the eight chapters of the book, Gida goes through an emotional transformation. The fear and reluctance he feels at the prospect of leaving for Holland is matched by his later sadness and unwillingness to return to Hungary. The book was intended to prepare children for what they would experience if, in the future, they were fostered abroad. The whole story is narrated in the first person, following Gida's thoughts and conversations with others, and describes the entire process of traveling away and staying with a foster family in a foreign land. In contrast to the many reports aimed at drawing national and international attention to this massive relief undertaking, Krúdy's story is one of the few writings that center on the child's agency.

The practice of sending children abroad was meant both to improve their physical constitution and to forge transnational links between Hungary and the host countries, but little thought was given to how the children felt. They often did not have a say in the initial decision about whether to go and subsequent decisions about which family to go to, how long to stay, and the whole matter of returning. As in many of the other relief initiatives, the child had little room for maneuver. Krúdy's children's book, on the other hand, enabled young readers to envision their own travel and prepare themselves for temporary displacement. Overall, however, despite good intentions, that displacement was done with a disregard for the family-child relationship and marked an even greater shift toward institutional intrusion into children's care and upbringing after the war.

Conclusion

Children's temporary and long-term displacement was one of the humanitarian relief endeavors that altered children's lives the most profoundly. The residencies in the countryside, at the imperial seashore, and at Lake Balaton were meant to secure improved nutrition for malnourished children and enhance their physical health. These imperial holiday programs intended to not only improve children's well-being but also advance imperial aims by strengthening bonds with the increasingly disconnected crown lands and helping prop up the tottering monarchy. To evacuate children after the war's end to temporary placements in foreign countries was a clearly internationalist initiative with an even greater impact. These cross-border displacements forged transnational social ties between the children and the foreign foster families. In this way, the relief initiative was a useful means to counter postwar nationalism and isolation, encouraging moves to secure wider cooperation and a pacifist postwar order.

Yet, at the same time, the children's trains allowed the involved relief organizations and the guest/foster families to take over the care of the destitute children. Responsibilities shifted from the birth family to the guest family, from the country of origin to the recipient society. While most children returned from their summer holidays, many who were evacuated to another country remained—and sometimes even lost contact with their birth country and family. Others returned but faced immense difficulties when attempting to reintegrate into their birth families, their former schools, and their social environment. Learning the language of their foster families played a crucial role in determining children's ability to integrate and feel at home in their foster families and society. Relearning their native language often affected the children's reintegration into their country of origin. The length and the quality of children's displacement determined the life paths of the concerned children. Many of the descendants of child transport children, are still—a hundred years later—seeking information about the lives of their parents or grandparents and wanting to find others with similar experiences. Hence, transnational displacement had such a long-term impact on children's identity that even generations later this child relief endeavor shapes today's families in Europe.

Notes

1. Petrichevich-Horváth, *Jelentés az Országos*, 27.
2. Piattoeva, Silova, and Millei, "Remembering Childhoods," 5.
3. Kun, *A fiatalkorúak támogatására hivatott*, 148.
4. For example, "Szegény gyermekek nyaralása," *Budapesti Hírlap* 10, no. 178 (June 30, 1890): 30; "Szegény gyermekek nyaralása," *Budapesti Hírlap* 23, no. 132 (May 15, 1903): 10.
5. "Egyesületek," 10–11.
6. Karsai, *Jelentés az Országos Gyermekvédő Liga*, 13.
7. Csergő, *A Budapesti Nyomor Vöröskönyve*, 122–23, 126.
8. Hämmerle, *Kindheit im Ersten Weltkrieg*, 333.
9. Expositur des k. ung. Regierungskommissar für das unter aller höchster Schirmherrschaft stehende König-Karl Wohlfahrtswerk "Kinder aufs Land" an den löblichen Gemeindevorstand, 1918/07/01, Državni Arhiv u Rijeci [Staatsarchiv Rijeka], HR-DARI-29 (Glavarstvo općine Volosko-Opatija), Opći spis 1588/18.
10. "Ungarische Blätter über die Kinderaktion," *Pesti Hírlap*, "Kaiser Karl Wohlfahrtswerk Der König für die Kinder," Vienna, HHStA Kabinettsarchiv Korrespondenzakten 1918, 291.
11. K.u.K. Ministerium des Äussern, "Wiener Kinder in der Schweiz," Vienna, 1918/01/07, Österreichisches Staatsarchiv/Archiv der Republik, Bundesministerium für soziale Verwaltung, Jugendfürsorge, 1918, 903.
12. "Magyar gyerekek nyaraltatása," 1.
13. Ibid., 2.
14. Ibid.
15. Petrichevich-Horváth, *Jelentés az Országos Menekültügyi Hivatal*, 27.
16. Ibid., 29.
17. Julia Vajkai to the Executive Committee of the SCIU, Mission de la Croix Rouge Hongroise en Suisse, April 20, 1920, 1–2, 1, CH AEG AP 92.21.2 (1).
18. Julia Vajkai to Mr. MacKenzie, Mission de la Croix-Rouge Hongrois, Geneva, April 15, 1920, CH AEG AP 92.21.3.

19. Petrichevich-Horváth, *Jelentés az Országos Menekültügyi Hivatal*, 27.
20. Hajtó, "The 'Wanted' Children," 206; Gergely, *A Magyar Gyermekvédelem Története*, 32.
21. Child Protection League: Questionnaire, Eglantyne Jebb Papers, Hungary, EJ 149–66, A0407, SCF Archive.
22. "To the Rescue! Being the Impressions Collected by Five Dutch-Men during a Fortnight's Stay in Hungary," CH AEG AP 92.21.3.
23. Rottenbiller, *Az Országos Gyermekvédő Liga Harminc Évi Működése*, 27.
24. Mühlbeck, "A Külföld a Magyar Gyermekekért," 217.
25. Ibolya, narrative interview with the author, Budapest, November 21, 2012.
26. "Az Országos Gyermekvédő Liga," 304.
27. Piroska, narrative interview with the author, Budapest, November 23, 2012.
28. See, for instance, the collection of letters of a girl sent to Britain in 1920, published by Petneki, and Petrich, *Gyermekvonat Angliába*.
29. Ibolya, narrative interview with the author, Budapest, November 21, 2012.
30. "A magyar gyermek—a nagyvilágban," 4.
31. Hajtó, *Milk Sauce and Paprika*, 59.
32. "A magyar gyermek—a nagyvilágban," 5.
33. Zentralstelle der schweizerischen Hilfsaktion für ungarische Kinder, Baden, Schweiz, October 14, 1921, addressed to the International Save the Children Fund in Geneva, Eglantyne Jebb Papers Hungary, A 0407, EJ 149–66, SCF Archive.
34. Pettkó-Szandtner, *A Huszonötéves*, 312.
35. Mr. Bohlen to Lord Weardale, December 20, 1920, Eglantyne Jebb Papers Hungary, A 0407, EJ 149–66, SCF Archive.
36. Allocations Department to Julia Vajkai, March 1, 1922, Eglantyne Jebb Papers Hungary, A 0407, EJ 149–66, SCF Archive.
37. "Child's Protection League: Question-sheet for the Children's [After Care] Hospitality Committee," 1922, Eglantyne Jebb Papers Hungary, A 0407, EJ 151 Hungary, SCF Archive.
38. Hajtó, "The 'Wanted' Children," 209.
39. "Nyilatkozat," March 31, 1928, MNL-OL, K 319-19-1941-23, 4 cs.
40. Magyar Kir. Titkos Tanácsos Üv. Elnök to Elöljárósághoz Szalkszentmárton, Budapest, 1938/11/21, MNL-OL, K 319-19-1941-23, 4 cs.
41. István, narrative interview with the author, Budapest, November 30, 2012.
42. Hajtó, *Milk Sauce and Paprika*, 41, 50.
43. Starkey, review of *Child, Nation, Race and Empire*.
44. Deésy, *The Dutch Heart*.
45. Piroska, narrative interview with the author, Budapest, November 15, 2018.
46. "Huszonnégy budapesti kislány, aki egy napon született, Juliána kisasszonnya, ajandokat kap a hollandi konsulatuson," 261.
47. Kennedy, "Selling the Distant Other."
48. Baughan, *Saving the Children*, 32.
49. Nevinson, "The Black Outlook in Europe," 14.
50. Krúdy, *Liga Gida Kalandjai*, 3.

9

EDUCATION

Workrooms to Teach the Children

In this chapter I conclude the story of Budapest's postwar children by recounting an initiative that went beyond immediate relief to emphasize children's long-term recovery. Because international relief organizations could not economically provide long-term relief to Budapest, it was important to strengthen local agencies and agents so that they could become self-sustaining. I tell the story of Budapest's workrooms or "work schools"—training workshops that were set up by Julia Vajkai with the financial help of the British Save the Children Fund (SCF) in the capital's impoverished areas. The initiative aimed at empowering the city's most disadvantaged children, especially those who had been displaced, orphaned, or neglected and were beyond school age. In the workrooms, these children were provided with an elementary education and training in a handicraft. This initiative fundamentally altered the approach to "saving" destitute children. When, by the mid-1920s, it became clear that the situation in Hungary's capital city was not going to improve quickly, Vajkai felt that the SCF's focus should be shifted from "gratuitous feeding" to education.[1] She was convinced that mere "donations" had an undesirable effect on the children's morale and wanted to promote an active role they could take in their own relief and long-term recovery. By 1922, she found herself "in a country which cannot count any more on foreign help and is entirely unable to help itself."[2] Providing education, she believed, would help children help and sustain themselves. The children of Budapest were to become the subjects of an educational experiment, which, it was hoped, would then be transferable to other European or global areas.

Children's Workrooms in the Capital City

Vajkai thought Hungary was an ideal site for a new kind of undertaking for industrial and educational institutions: the country was "near the East" but "on a Western level." She authored a report on "The Activity of Save the Children in Hungary" in November 1926, explaining why it was a good laboratory. The nation's children were judged to have "many characteristic features of Eastern races," while the postwar economic problems that beset them were practically the "same as in Western cities." Therefore, she thought, the knowledge to be gained from a relief experiment focusing on children's education could be of interest "to any big town of Western Europe" and for other "parts of the earth."[3] To prevent older children from falling into criminality or becoming socially "conspicuous," the SCF aimed to keep them "busy" in the most literal way—through the "learning of a craft."[4] SCF envisioned a program that would not only "meet the immediate physical needs of children" but also prepare them properly for adulthood; with this new mission and trust in children as capable beings, SCF "broke with the tradition of child welfare which saw children as vulnerable and dependent." Here the vision of the Budapest child relief projects and the larger vision of SCF were ideally interwoven. This may be the reason Hungarian work rooms represented one of the most successful and long-lasting projects of the SCF abroad.[5]

The plan for the workrooms was to involve children in a combination of educational training and labor. Because school attendance in the years after World War I was compulsory only to age twelve, children above that age missed out on proper education until they could begin to learn a trade at fourteen. In the interim, some slipped into criminality. Vajkai later recalled that her initial motivation to install the workrooms was to "prevent the serious danger of hundreds of adolescents multiplying the ranks of criminals because their forced inaction would force them into depravity." On behalf of the League of Nations, she and other child relief workers in Europe studied the impact of unemployment on juveniles in the 1920s and 1930s. They concluded that unemployment, or rather inactivity, of adolescents was far more severe than in adults or the elderly. The adolescents were "disrupted by spiritual inaction, apathy, disintegration and even exclusion from the community of workers." Production work, Vajkai believed, was the most effective educational tool for adolescents with a practical inclination and ability.[6]

Motivated to rescue adolescents, beginning in October 1920, Vajkai invested much energy in establishing fourteen workrooms in the poorer quarters of Budapest, such as the Mária Valéria settlement on the southeastern edge of Pest, to provide children with the opportunity to learn a useful craft.[7] Nine of the workrooms were founded and largely financed by the Save the Children Fund; between 1919 and 1928, the SCF spent more than £100,000 on Hungarian child protective initiatives.[8] In the workrooms, there was "no selection of any kind" for children's admission; the school's policy sought "to give every child the opportunity to develop his or her abilities as fully as possible."[9] Vajkai "did not see any harm" if children joined the workrooms, even if they "had not yet reached a state of dire misery." Still, among the participants, there was "not one child among them who enjoys comfort."[10]

Vajkai and Eglantyne Jebb were particularly drawn to the rescue of children from previously "quite well-to-do families" before the war. One girl remembered: "My parents were well-off. We had a house and a fine garden. My parents lived a happy family life and were very fond of us." But when the war broke out, "the struggle to live began," as the girl's father had to sell the house and enlist, leaving her mother with the family of eleven. Once the war was over, she had hoped that things would improve, "but the struggle had really only begun." The girl's recollections were similarly haunted by "visions of prewar days, as of a Golden Age," contrasted by harsh reality once the war broke out: "When I was quite a tiny little girl, the world was entirely different from what it is now. In that time, it was possible to buy anything you wanted. I had shoes, now I have none, sometimes I get some old rags. Now the world is such that one could not even dream of buying shoes or dresses."[11] This is why many of these children had to start contributing to the family income. Witnessing the large-scale displacement and impoverishment of middle-class families and the further social decline of the workers' children, Vajkai aimed to recuperate what had been lost of prewar family life and childhood. In 1919, she informed a large audience of women in Zürich why Budapest's population "was deprived, freezing, starving in the once happy and flourishing Hungary." It was "the war, the Károlyi government and communism" that had brought poverty and destitution to the country.[12] Raising funds for Hungary's children, would, Vajkai hoped, have a stabilizing effect on society more broadly.

Romantic notions of an ideal childhood were met with the reality of children's lives. Child relief workers drew attention to children's losses. In 1920, a group of child relief workers visited a barrack to recruit a skinny, ill-developed twelve-year-old orphan for the workrooms. A report describes "a small room crowded with old, good furniture. Needlework, embroidered knots. Dummy, sewing machine, with which you're now looking for your bread. On the wall some sacred images and a series of tasteful prints of atmospheric landscapes that were so loved by bourgeois families."[13] This girl, whose family had lost its social status, was considered an ideal candidate; she was not entitled to further education and had no opportunity to play with other children. The relief workers identified this moment as the poor girl's unfortunate departure from "the joys of her childhood" to an "unknown, scary life." Just before her final departure from one of the workrooms, a fourteen-year-old girl, as reported by a journalist in 1925, looked nostalgically back to the two years she had spent there, hoping that, once she had left to a sewing workshop, her younger sister could also attend the same training. The journalist filtered from these remarks "bitter accusation" and drew the conclusion that "Trianon kidnapped the Hungarian child's carefree, happy childhood!"[14]

The manufacturing techniques the children were taught in the workrooms were all practical crafts such as lacemaking, shoemaking, dressmaking, sewing, basketmaking, embroidery, and toy making (including dolls). Due to the financial support provided by the SCF (about fifty million crowns per month on wages and twenty-five million on food),[15] they were often called the British Save the Children Fund's workrooms.[16] Vajkai wanted to open more workrooms in every district of Budapest. By February 1921, four hundred children were employed in the workrooms, with the goal of increasing the number to one thousand children by that autumn.[17] During the 1920s, the number of youngsters thus employed amounted to several thousand. In a setup similar to that of the American feeding stations, Vajkai created a physical infrastructure with in the urban landscape of Budapest. On a contemporary map of the city, shown in figure 9.1, ten workrooms are identified with addresses and roman numerals.[18] The spaces for the SCF workrooms were provided for free by the Hungarian government. Workrooms were usually housed in either abandoned wartime medical huts for the wounded or decommissioned feeding kitchens. Although underwhelming venues, they were nevertheless, Vajkai claimed, better than the "dens and caves" in which many of the children lived.[19]

Asking her dear friend Eglantyne Jebb for financial help, Vajkai explained how she wished to provide relief to the children in the Mária Valéria settlement, with its "wooden, or cement sheds," which were largely the "remainder of a big war hospital" where several hundreds of refugees had taken shelter before being transferred to the railcars described in an earlier chapter. After making a survey of the area and visiting people there, Vajkai concluded that relief facilities should be installed in this slum quarter. She had seen with her own eyes what misery the people were in, yet they did not seek help by "begging"—something she was anxious to prevent—as did some in the Angyalföld district of Budapest. Vajkai thought of this quarter of Budapest as as new territory and a particularly needy area, which had simply "grown out of the earth under the pressure of the need" prevailing since the end of the war. It was "bare of any" comforts,[20] but a workroom might help.

All workrooms were coordinated from the headquarters of the British SCF in Budapest, which was located at 10 Balaton Street, near the parliament

Fig. 9.1. Addresses of children's workrooms. Unknown author, Eglantyne Jebb Papers 156 21/1, Save the Children Fund Archive, Birmingham.

building. When they were able, the municipal authorities covered fuel and lighting expenses, while the Hungarian government provided most of the staff and teachers.[21] The state delegated dozens of women refugees from the displaced middle class from the ceded territories as teachers to the workrooms, after they had been trained through the fund in a Hungarian handcraft.[22] In June 1922, when the government was "forced to reduce the staff of its employees" and dismissed all refugees who had not been appointed directly by the minister of public instruction, the workrooms were in danger of losing their staff. Vajkai managed in the end to keep the trained refugees among her teachers. The Ministry of Justice acknowledged that these teachers should continue to be employed, because they and the workrooms helped "reduce the expenses of correction-houses."[23]

The workrooms were not run by the Save the Children Fund alone but in close collaboration with the American Red Cross and the Junior Red Cross. The National Child Protection League and the International Committee of the Red Cross also figure in reports about the workrooms' everyday functioning. Armstrong Smith, who was the chief organizer of the SCF's initiatives on the European continent, functioned as the supervisor of Vajkai's work. Vajkai also had a close working relationship with Count Reding-Biberegg of the ICRC in Hungary. Whenever Vajkai invited important international visitors to the workrooms—for example, on June 1, 1921, Regent Horthy's wife, Magdolna Purgly, came to the Népház.[24] Vajkai would not have been able to accomplish much without this external financial support. The SCF therefore supported Vajkai's workrooms.

When publicly propagating its child relief work in impoverished postwar Europe, the SCF presented a radical critique of capitalism, urging members of the British public to share their wealth with the less privileged. "When we are disgusted" or even "hopeless," facing "the waste of money in the world," "the money poured out for national pomp," or the money "let slip for laziness, or lavished for fashion or the externals of things," SCF's Ethel Sidgwick proclaimed, it should be encouraging to see how "comparatively little money" Vajkai actually needed to implement her child relief work in Hungary. This comparison should, Sidgwick believed, spur the British people to donate more to the fund, because, when given to such a cause, the money would take on a new dimension; it would turn into the "very seed of life."[25]

The support of the Catholic Church, which was, in Hungary, a key actor in child protection work, was equally vital for the workrooms. Vajkai described in a 1921 letter "the most touching little feast" in a church where the children received their first communion. The Vatican's apostolic nuncio to Hungary,

Monsignor Lorenzo Schioppa, distributed among the children "the Holy *Hostia*," while James Pedlow of the American Red Cross gave "white dresses to all the poor children." During the ceremony, Schioppa told Vajkai that there was no work in Budapest that he appreciated as much as hers. He even invited Vajkai to visit the nunciatore, because he wanted to gift some material "for trousers for my shoe-maker boys."[26] From the gifts the workrooms received from Rome and the Catholic Church, the children were crafting "layettes" for the "Holy Father" in Rome.[27]

The children admitted to the workrooms were between ages twelve and fourteen—beyond the compulsory schooling age but not yet adults. Vajkai believed that errant children's "first collision with the law" was most likely to occur once children left school. "The bigger the child, the more acutely does it suffer," she concluded. The fund's greatest and most difficult task was to "prepare the child for an adult's life."[28] The workrooms targeted the children of the working class and the city's poorest families, especially in deprived areas such as the Mária Valéria settlement. Many of these children were the children of impoverished and displaced refugees, who had previously belonged, as an earlier chapter has shown, to the middle class.[29] Targeting the children from the slums and the refugee barracks was, Vajkai believed, a "possible solution" to one of the most important problems in the field of child welfare: "the education of the poorest children." Their education was seen to be of major social importance because they would otherwise turn into a "dull bestial mass" of unskilled proletarians, "ready prey for every kind of revolution." Education was the way to improve the conditions of children's lives and turn this "bulk of the nation" into useful citizens.[30]

In April 1922, a questionnaire was circulating in the various workrooms to identify children's condition and background. Almost half the children (303 out of 678) had not finished the six years of compulsory schooling. Children's forced displacement was among the main causes of children's absence from school. Refugees would "pass months being driven from one place to another, waiting to be settled somewhere, and in the meantime the children grow up to working age and are driven by misery to accept any job they can find." Another reason for truancy was the absence of fathers who had become prisoners of war and whose wives were obliged to earn their living and "had no time to see that their children attend school."[31] A girl named Anna recalled, "One evening father came home and said that he must go to war and I did not understand what he meant, but as mammy cried, I cried too, . . . with this day my life changed for the worse, because we were deprived of everything." Another girl remembered, "My father was obliged to march away, I was a little girl then. At this time, we were totally ruined." Another girl remembered that her "dear Daddy had to leave us for a long time" when the war broke out and "he marched off"; "at home, life became more and more difficult." Jebb was convinced that "the chief significance of the war for the children was the loss of the family breadwinner."[32]

On a visit to the workrooms in June 1922, Dr. Armstrong Smith, the SCF delegate who administered Budapest's workrooms, assessed the social condition of the parents, the number of children in each family, the children's state of health, and their living conditions. Out of 665 children seen in June 1922, 255 were the children of industrial workers, 107 were children of workers in state service, 115 were fatherless and supported only by their mothers, and nine were full orphans. The workrooms made particular effort to reach children who had lost a parent during the war or whose fathers had been "crippled," making the children the main breadwinners for their families. Half of the children came from families with five to eight siblings; 125 had contracted tuberculosis, and another ninety-five were living with tubercular relatives. The majority—360 children—lived with their families (typically seven people) in a one-room apartment. Another 120, also from families of seven, had no more than a "kitchen" to live in; and nine large families made do in a "cellar."[33] The SCF considered a child in such conditions "an emergency case." They "must earn their living" through work, but the SCF wished to remain faithful to its humanitarian principles and provide relief.[34]

Aside from the very young breadwinners with wounded fathers, all children above age twelve were regarded as "no longer a burden but a supporter of the household" and were expected to work.[35] To persuade parents to allow their children attend the workrooms, the SCF promised to educate the children in the manufacturing arts or basic craftwork. Because the items the children made were for sale, they would contribute to the family income.[36] Thus, the workrooms were financially self-sustainable, gaining more from the sale of the handmade items than they needed to keep the facilities going and train the children.[37] With the remainder, the pupils received wages. Once they had completed six weeks of training and had repaid any debts (such as advances for tram tickets, clothing, or shoes), the children were paid for each piece they manufactured or repaired.[38] Clothing was a particularly pressing problem. Anne explained, "My underclothes are torn, I have no winter coat. My shoes are full of holes. My dear father is a railway official. He cannot afford to buy any clothes out of his small wages, although even our bed-linen is already torn." For that reason, she stated, "we children are learning in the needlework school, kept up by kind English people, . . . dreaming of a better and nicer future." Another boy stated, "I have no clothes and no boots: I attend the class for basket-making, where I make doormats. Cooking is done there well enough. I like best cocoa and rice."[39] The workrooms replaced a number of social functions that the families could not adequately fulfill at the time, including proper clothing, regular food, and further education. By the late 1930s, the workrooms also offered evening courses and provided a certain degree of higher education. Vajkai judged the subject of "industrial history" and the "history of the fatherland" most important.[40]

Education to Forestall "Moral Degeneration"

The timetable the workrooms maintained for the children resembled the work plan of an adult institution more than that of a school. A weekly attendance of forty-six hours was required, meaning that the children were there on weekdays from 8:00 a.m. to 5:00 p.m. and on Saturdays from 8:00 a.m. to 3:00 p.m. They spent twenty-six hours a week on handiwork (for example, learning "the different embroidery stitches in use in Hungary"). Eleven hours were reserved for "theoretical work" and nine hours to "sundry lessons," including drawing, singing, games, cookery, religious education, and "two hours a fortnight for the baths."[41] The workrooms resembled real schools, where theoretical education was the priority. Vajkai drew up rules and regulations for everything: punctuality, cleanliness, order, precision, diligence, care with equipment, cooperation among the pupils, and so on. Access to food was based on children's punctuality. If they wanted to get the daily meal, they had to be at the workroom on time. Pupils who missed a day forfeited their cocoa the next day.[42] Even the breaks were regimented and supervised, with a fifteen-minute break in the morning, an hour at midday, and another break in the afternoon. The breaks were followed by "breathing exercises" conducted according to the "American system."[43] Vajkai believed that "bread and work are not sufficient" and that the children must have "some pleasure" to "grow to be strong and good in their minds."[44]

The pupils at the workrooms were not only learning a practical craft and contributing to the family income but also receiving regular meals. Local welfare organizations made efforts to persuade parents that "children over 12 have the same claim to be fed as their younger sisters and brothers."[45] In the larger workrooms, there was a distribution of "mass food," which Vajkai rated far inferior to that prepared in the SCF kitchens and was not given to children who did not need it.[46] Nevertheless, among the children in the workrooms, the need for food was great. Even many years later, in 1939, a questionnaire asked children about their daily food consumption at home. One girl responded: "I get soup every morning because my mom is never hungry in the evening and she puts her soup on me for breakfast." Yet that same girl complained about her mother's emotional neglect; she apparently "didn't like her, never kissed her, never said a good word to her." The girl did not understand it was because her mother lay down hungry every night.[47] The social needs for food access and a workroom education continued to overlap for many years after the war ended.

In the 1920s, the money for workroom meals came through SCF-organized financial "adoptions" made by donors from Britain to sponsor each child. In December 1920, the SCF reported sponsoring two thousand Hungarian "godchildren" at the workrooms, of which many had been displaced and were now rescued through the SCF. While a few of the workroom children lived in Buda, the majority came from across the Danube River in Pest, where "the overcrowding from the influx of refugees made many houses little more than dens, while many families must shelter as best they can in old railway carriages."[48] Many were also orphans, who were sent from the city's orphanages to attend the workrooms. The adoption and training were judged socially valuable, as the children were "not only fed but also really saved, for they are taught useful work and are prevented from gliding into an abyss of crime as most of them do in the absence of food and guidance."[49] Once adopted and paid for through individual British donors, the children received food parcels and breakfast. In addition, Armstrong Smith managed to obtain extremely scarce flour through the food ministry. Thus, the workrooms were able to provide children a breakfast of a roll and cocoa.[50]

At this time of serious food shortages and questionable food safety, the supervisors in the kitchens had to make sure that the food served and distributed at the workrooms was up to certain minimum standards. Vajkai personally inspected fats, some of which smelled "very strongly" as a result of the "awful heat."[51] Because the "material substance and form of foodstuffs" such as milk or fat profoundly affected the ways in which they were "produced, transported, sold, consumed, regulated and policed," Peter Atkinson explains, relief deliveries required continuous control.[52] If the materials abruptly changed and quality standards could not be certified, food relief could not be provided. In the case of the rancid fat, Vajkai asked the official chemist to determine whether it was fit for the children.[53] At other times, Vajkai herself sampled the food in the various workrooms; she often found it "quite excellent" and "just as good" as what the Americans were offering.[54] Before every meal, one of the teachers tasted the food, and only then could it be served or distributed to the children. If the teacher was dissatisfied, she complained to the head of the kitchen to have the problem fixed.[55]

Then there were the children's personal tastes to cope with. If the food was judged edible but a child refused to eat, then the child was required to leave the workroom.[56] In a report of 1922, Vajkai explained how the workrooms strove to prevent food waste by following the example set by the American Relief Administration's feeding stations. At the ARA, it had been noticed that, on days "when rice in milk or sweet pastry was provided," masses of children turned up; on other days, when the food was less to their liking, they kept away. This was why the SCF adopted its strict rule that children who did not eat their allotted portion would be "crossed off the luncheon list."[57] The rule was backed by a moral argument: British donors had been "working hard" to raise the money for their kind gift. Children who left the food on their plates were both "abusing the charity" and preventing "one of [their] unlucky fellow-creatures to profit from it."[58] In being banned from the workrooms, pupils who did not comply with the feeding regime also lost access to the training and education.

To involve children in the feeding regime at the workrooms, the children participated in the preparation of food, assisting a paid cook. This arrangement, Vajkai believed, had two advantages: first, the children learned to prepare simple, well-made food; second, the cook would not steal anything, because the assistants would call him or her out.[59] When it came to the allocation of cooked food, only children who worked the whole day received dinner; the others got breakfast only.[60] Vajkai's theory was that the combination of education and regular feeding constituted the ideal means of preventing children from falling into delinquency during their most critical age.[61] She hoped the children would find pleasure in their labors, which would improve their motivation and help create a permanent "correlation between work and satisfaction." Only if the focus remained on education could the program reach the children "who are compelled to earn their bread if they do not wish to starve."[62]

The creation of the workrooms had been driven by the fear that destitute children who were no longer eligible to be educated and controlled in school were likely to fall into "moral degeneration" or become vagrants like the "*type d'enfant vagabond*" (type of vagrant child) shown in figure 9.2. Vajkai encouraged children to "learn to appreciate work" and to make use of their hands.[63] The workrooms were an "experiment in education and social work," concerned simultaneously with both of these goals.[64] She saw that the state education system was in a sorry condition and feared for "the whole nation right

Fig. 9.2. "Type of Vagrant Child." Photo by Sándor Strelisky, CH AEG AP 92.105.76 (1).

from the top to the depths." That is why she felt the need to invest in children's education.[65] She had at first concentrated on child relief work, but education gradually "won its way." Vajkai always had to keep financial motivators in mind, but eventually "money-making retreated into the background" of the SCF's workroom program, and by 1926 the organization felt strong enough to challenge the parents' fixation on getting their children to contribute to family expenses. Vajkai did not want to erode the authority of parents,[66] but eventually "earnings as an object of work were thrown overboard" and no longer part of the plan.[67]

Vajkai considered education and diligence especially important in the postwar period, when severe privation "affected the nervous system of the children" and impaired their physical development.[68] She often spoke about the risk of "moral decline." At a meeting of the foreign missions in 1921, she linked the benefits of work to the improvement of the children's mental and moral states. The children, she said, "not only got used to work" but "even do it with enthusiasm." She believed this showed that both their physical state and their morale had been uplifted.[69] She hoped to shape the children's characters so that once they had finished their training, they would be able to "earn an honest living."[70] In short, she believed she was engaged in "pioneer work" for the rehabilitation of the entire country.[71] In 1926, the general secretary of the Save the Children Fund, L. B. Golden, noted that the workrooms were having a "wonderful effect on making slum children into good citizens." By that time, two thousand children had passed through the workrooms' training and were considered "morally, mentally and physically" better.[72]

Vajkai's close friend Eglantyne Jebb shared her hope in the promise of investment in the education of Europe's young people. In her collected series of autobiographies of the Hungarian workroom children, Jebb concluded that these life stories were not that sad after all. From children's concluding remarks, such as "I pray to god he may disperse the heavy clouds from over all good Hungarians, make mankind happy again, and bestow happiness on me too," Jebb gathered the impression of an "indomitable courage and buoyant hopefulness of youth." Devoted to the Church of England, Jebb related to the faith-based hopes of some of the children: "Now I and my sister struggle together for our future. For we believe in God and we believe that our fate will take a turn for the better with the whole world's fate." Jebb used children's sad but uplifting life stories, which showed a "merciful blotting out of tragic memories," to "infect" Europe's adults with children's optimism.[73] She and Vajkai saw it as their duty to educate the children in a practical craft and reeducate Europe's postwar populations toward European peace and transnational reconciliation.

Vajkai's vision was that, by engaging in the work and adhering to her strict disciplinary environment in the workrooms, children would become better socially adjusted to postwar economic, social, and political circumstances. The wider aim was to prepare them to become "responsible and capable member[s] of human society."[74] This same idea appeared in 1924 as the last article of the Geneva Declaration of the Rights of the Child, which asserted the right to an upbringing based on the premise that future "talents must be devoted to the service of its fellow men."[75] This declaration reflected postwar concern over the "crucial question of peace and civilization" and how far it was possible, Vajkai asked, to "extend the circle in which the collective spirit of the individual works."[76] The recent experience of violent conflict and war led her to search for ways to foster compassion, cooperation, and self-help.

A document titled "Request Addressed to Our Pupils" reminds the workroom children that they were to become "honest people" who would "earn their living with their proper work." Vajkai insisted that they show gratitude to the generous people abroad who had provided the places where they trained and "good, nutritious food." They "had been our enemies," but now, instead of donating mere charity "as the by-passer to the beggar," they were giving far more. They were "helping you to become one of their own kind, respectable working people" as if you were "brothers and sisters." Because of all that they have received, the children should themselves "feel for each other," be "indulgent towards the faults of the others," and forgive any adversaries. "We live in the hardest times that ever any Hungarian lived in," she explained. After the destruction of war, life had become "utterly bad and heavy." But as the country's future generation, the children should show kindness toward one another "in words and in deeds." "Be Kind to Each Other," she concluded, was the main injunction. That the children should keep it was "the one and only wish" of those who were offering them their charity.[77]

The workrooms aspired to be places of "self-government" and "leadership."[78] Vajkai was interested in seeing the "brighter children work together with the duller, the advanced ones with the backward," but she took care that the more capable children were not forced into a slower pace and that the weaker ones were in no danger of developing a feeling of inferiority. This equal treatment, she felt, was "imperative," because all the young workers were being prepared for a "life in industry." In the factories where they would work in the future, they might need to work well in groups, "where their own profits depend upon the performance of fellow-workers who are possibly much less competent than themselves."[79] Vajkai knew that factories expected from the "trained factory girl" not only dexterity but also cleanliness and good behavior. Because Vajkai was convinced that "the talkative girl is not liked in factories," there was a "quiet lesson," during which pupils were not allowed to speak for a full hour.[80] Day-to-day activities in the workrooms were founded on democratic, if not socialist, principles of self-government; children served as foremen or forewomen and were elected monthly by secret ballot.[81]

An observer judged the workrooms to be "soul rescuers" (*lélekmentők*), where "children are no longer only responsible for themselves, but for each other." As "cursed little lives," they were welcome at the workrooms, where they had a duty and a vocation. Many rules in the school were made by the children and were tested for efficacy before becoming the official rules of the workrooms.[82] The children evaluated their accomplished work products in the group, giving each other feedback. Some children opened up about challenging circumstances at home that impacted their work performance. Wiping away tears, one girl told her peers that she struggled because her family had been expelled from their emergency apartment. Her father had died, her mother and her seven brothers had not earned any money, and now that her older brother had a seasonal job, they no longer qualified for the apartment. Their family was scattered throughout the city, which distracted and distressed her all day.[83] Such moments reflect the social function of the workrooms—integrating the children into a community of peers and comforting adults while learning a craft that would prevent them from social decline.

The workrooms were largely managed and supervised by volunteers from the Hungarian Junior Red Cross (JRC). These volunteers also provided services, including "cleaning, laundry work, cookery and heating."[84] They were encouraged to participate in the higher management through their own elected committee, though under Vajkai's supervision. She thought that such participation was "an invaluable method of teaching children consideration for their elders and each other" and would help with "health propaganda."[85] Together with the workroom leader, the JRC volunteer staff who managed many of the workrooms were authorized to punish misconduct.

Vajkai's vision could sometimes become overzealous. Children who failed to keep the workroom's rules or standards were collectively and publicly shamed. Their "garlands of laurels" were taken down from the wall and a point was put next to their names on a board in the dining hall. Children were punished in this way for unsatisfactory production, laziness, nonobservance of silent hours, misconduct, and theft.[86] However, there is little mention of theft in the sources. As Vajkai explained, nothing could be stolen, because she knew the whereabouts of "every little bit of lace" being used, and she registered everything the children did in her mind so that nothing could be sold without permission.[87] Indeed, Vajkai was somewhat obsessed with strict order. Even during her holidays, she drew up details for developing her system.[88] Techniques of control "make it possible to adjust the multiplicity of men," as Foucault put it, and improve "production (and this means not only 'production' in the strict sense, but also the production of knowledge and skills in the school."[89] Children's cleanliness and hygiene were strictly supervised by the JRC volunteers and health inspectors, who also kept an eye on the children's general health.[90] Children's physical appearance and cleanliness was seen as key to children's development into proper future citizens.

The SCF believed it was important to train native social workers who could, in turn, train others: "All relief work should be organized so that as much as possible of the actual work should be done by Hungarians themselves, under supervision and control."[91] In addition to the volunteers from the JRC, adult social workers and teachers were part of the "educational

Fig. 9.3. "The Fashion and Sewing Studio of the SCIU in Budapest." Unknown photographer, CH AEG AP 92 105 80 (2).

experiment" of the workrooms.[92] Thus, Hungarian volunteers played an important part in training children in crafts; many possessed the knowledge to teach specifically Hungarian crafts, such as local motifs of embroidery.[93] In the Eighth District, one of Budapest's poor industrial neighborhoods, with the help of the "best children," Vajkai even opened a workroom that functioned as a *salon de mode*, or fashion studio, seen in figure 9.3. This enterprise was very successful, as it gave "poor middle-class women" who had to "go out to work to gain their living" the opportunity "to get their dresses made cheaply and in good style." It was appreciated as "good relief work for the middle-classes," but this was just an extra benefit, because the main focus was on the children's industrial training.[94]

The Social Value of Industrial Training

Hungary was a largely agricultural country in the 1920s, but some hoped that it would join the industrial age both economically and in modern social values. Some of the more ambitious factory owners perceived a remedy-in-the-making

Fig. 9.4. Budapest workroom. Unknown photographer, CH AEG AP 92.105.83 (1).

in the workrooms. With children being trained for specific types of work, perhaps industry could thrive in the postwar era. Vajkai's workrooms slowly drew attention from industrial representatives, such as the secretary of the Hungarian Chamber of Commerce and Industry, who wished to know more about the actual training and material output at the workrooms and schools. Vajkai took great pains to publicize the work scheme and its accomplishments, giving public lectures in schools, at parents' meetings, and at meetings of social organizations such as the Red Cross and the Feminist Association for the Protection of Mothers and Children. Despite growing local interest, she was continually disappointed that "foreign countries" took interest much earlier than Hungarian entities did. She had high hopes that Hungary would realize the great potential of the workrooms' industrial education, believing it could save thousands of children from hunger and raise "the future of the bulk of the next generation" and thus do much for society at large.[95]

The making of the various products was documented at the time in many photographs. The workrooms enforced the gender norms the relief organizations sought to further. The boys' workrooms would teach basket weaving, for example, while the girls would be trained in lacemaking or sewing, as shown in figure 9.4.

Fig. 9.5. Save the Children flag. Unknown photographer, CH AEG AP 02.105.80 (3).

Both groups might equally be involved in the making of flags and banners. In the workrooms, the core principles were self-help and education, and these became embodied in ensigns. Handcrafted by the children and displaying the emblem of the Save the Children International Union, these flags (see fig. 9.5) showcased children's intellectual and material contributions. Jebb's concern about and "frustration with ethnic-nationalism" led her to invest in the making of transnational humanitarian symbols and an institutional identity, which found expression in such items.[96]

While rejecting wartime nationalism, the relief facilities became sites to perform, exhibit, and thus strengthen children's national belonging and identity. Because children were considered an ideal "material" from which to build the new Hungarian nation, the workrooms involved children in the

Fig. 9.6. Works from the workrooms. Unknown photographer, CH AEG AP 92.21.5.

production of typical Hungarian crafts, such as Hungarian national embroidery. Their embroideries were exhibited and sold, as seen in figure 9.6.

Children's relief activities thus served to exhibit and propagate Hungarian national sentiments in an international environment. Altogether, the crafts that came out of the workrooms conveyed three messages: first, that education was the way to fight children's poverty and starvation; second, that knowledge and self-help would be the means by which Hungary could liberate itself from economic dependency on international relief organizations; and third, that Hungarian handicrafts would convey national sentiments to its future citizens and strengthen their Hungarian identity. Children's international relief illustrates well the intertwined relationship between internationalism and nationalism at the time.

Beyond the immediate impact on the children trained in the workrooms, Vajkai envisioned a larger social project: to present the workrooms as models for the improvement of the working conditions young people experienced in factories generally. A contemporary journalist saw the material items themselves as the perfect embodiment of the workrooms' overall success. "The beautiful result achieved proves that the situation of children who were thrown as prey to misery and sin can be radically improved not by providing alms, but by providing employment opportunities," the writer explained.[97] Vajkai tried to persuade factory owners that good working conditions would create increased efficiency, and she pleaded for the implementation of the recommendations of the 1919 International Labour Conference, which prohibited work in factories by children under age twelve. Protecting children from labor exploitation found its most refined expression in the Geneva Declaration of the Rights of the Child in 1924. Every act of child relief in the workrooms was thought of as a way to help "the words of the Declaration . . . become reality."[98] This was intended as a signal to the factory owners of Budapest that they should comply with the declaration's Fourth Article: "The child must be put in a position to earn a livelihood, and must be protected against every form of exploitation."[99]

Although children could only enter proper trade apprenticeships at age fourteen, factories and workshops could employ children as young as twelve, and many employed them even younger in defiance of the law. An eyewitness recalled in 1925, "Unfortunately I saw 'small things' of 9–10 years right next to large machines."[100] The workrooms opposed exploitative child labor and instead wanted to train the children to be employable and well-paid in factories later on. By 1936, Vajkai observed, Budapest's factories were "realizing the significance of this initiative and more recently they are also establishing similar institutions."[101] Contemporaries judged Vajkai's initiative to have been of "great social and educational importance" in "this century of the machine." The dedication to and unparalleled knowledge of the profession was thought to have made workers' lives "more hopeful and more and more human."[102]

The 1924 Congress of the SCIU, which took place in Vienna, advocated adherence to the Declaration of the Rights of the Child, and subconferences were held in Budapest.[103] With the arrival of many international child relief workers in the city, Hungarian journals such as *Tolnai Világlapja* published photographs of Budapest's child relief facilities to mark the occasion.[104] The workrooms were showcased as one of the most groundbreaking relief endeavors, with a lasting impact on local welfare and the children themselves.

Vajkai was vocally critical of the industrial revolution and children's place in it.[105] At the third biennial conference of the World Federation of Education Associations in Geneva in 1929, Vajkai spoke on "Practical Education for Life," expressing her skepticism about any progress being made while children served as "cog[s] in the machine." She warned listeners about the negative effect of mechanized work on a child of fourteen, who "slowly, but unavoidably" was likely to slide down "into the grey, irresponsible mass" of a deprived and brutalized proletariat. She wished to "call the attention of the world" to the enormous challenges confronting children's education because of "the recent evolution of industry." She demanded that working hours be reduced, conditions improved, appropriate recreation provided, and unnecessary exhaustion prevented for laborers. She also hoped that the psychology of labor would be developed into an established science. In the workrooms, she aimed to help the children develop their own personalities, so that in their future lives as workers they could withstand the strains put on them by modern industrial conditions. Without a capacity for resilience, the children would become victims of the labor system. They would then become impoverished and resentful, and not even the new "protective measures that legislation and welfare work may lavish upon [them]" could prevent them from becoming a "danger to that same society."[106]

Exhibiting Children's Work in Budapest and Abroad

The best way to gain support for the workrooms was to exhibit their output. One such exhibition was opened in Budapest on December 9, 1922, by the British minister T. B. Hohler and Captain Domaille. Five hundred people of economic and political standing were invited. Among the attendees were Magdolna Purgly; the archduchesses Izabella, Auguszta, and Baronne Seefried of Austria; Minister Vass from the Hungarian Ministry of Public Welfare; most of the foreign legations; and the papal nuncio, alongside the heads of the Catholic and Protestant Churches. The exhibition was staged by sculptor Géza Maróti, who had also staged all the workroom exhibitions abroad. Not only were handcrafted items amounting to 230,000 kronen sold on the spot, but there were orders for more—enough to occupy workroom children for years to come.[107] The exhibition was reported in the press as a success.[108] To show the efficiency and productiveness of the workrooms and to increase the publicity of such exhibitions, photographs were taken, as shown in figure 9.7, several of which also found their way to the pages of the SCIU's journal.

On June 17, 1923, a "National Children's Maternity Exhibition 'For the Child'" opened at the Palace of Art (Műcsarnok). Children's handcrafted items were on display to show "the triumphant culture of truncated Hungary" and of "everything that can influence the lives of present and future generations." The exhibition centered on scientific and pedagogical knowledge about children's proper upbringing. All presented objects were intended to highlight "the child, our most feared, most precious treasure." If properly

Fig. 9.7. The crew of the Save the Children Junior Red Cross Workrooms. Unknown photographer, CH AEG AP 92 105.83 (3).

"brought healthily to life, cared for, nurtured, dressed, and fed," children would "become the glory of any great state in the world." Vajkai brought handicraft objects from four hundred children to this exhibition, the largest of its kind. The event was opened by Horthy and the minister of culture[109] and captures well the phenomenal value placed on children at this time of political rupture, geopolitical reconfigurations, and destitution. It both mirrors and strengthens the close connection between local initiatives of child protection, such as the workrooms, the scientific study of childhood, and postwar politics. The workrooms ideally advanced this relationship.

Some handcrafted objects even reached Geneva, the European center of humanitarian child relief. On March 30, 1921, and August 29, 1923, congresses of the ICRC were held there, and they exhibited handmade items from Budapest's workrooms. In February 1921, along with Rodolphe Redding Biberegg, the local representative of the ICRC in Budapest, Vajkai sent a box with "things from the work-rooms" with one of the children's trains to Switzerland. These items included "specimens of basketwork, some garments from the sewing-room, a pair of repaired shoes, laces and handkerchiefs." Every item was labeled, in English and in French, with the name of the workroom, the age of the child who had made it, and the years of training needed to make the article. Vajkai herself asked William Andrew MacKenzie at the SCIU in Geneva to do his best to ensure that "the Hungarian children get a good place." And the children of the workrooms were to be visually present; their photos were displayed among the things they had made.[110]

The children's workroom products went on display in other venues as well. On one of her lecture tours in Britain, Vajkai brought a "case full of the exhibition stuff" so that she could display the crafted items at each place she went.[111] Producing crafts that were to be exhibited abroad aroused pride in the children and piqued their interest in other countries. A girl in one of the workrooms explained how the exhibiting and sale of her work abroad affected her way of thinking. She felt highly motivated in her work, because it was the "real thing." She was confident that the workrooms were providing her with a comprehensive and useful education. The "nice, useful things" she made were going "to other countries to be sold." This sparked her curiosity in geography, so she could know where the items were sent, and developed an appreciation of the mathematics of price calculation.[112]

Many of the expenses of the workrooms were recouped through the sale of handcrafted products that were shipped to and sold in Britain. The result was that "the English baby is dressed in a Somogy-cut dress," while the "tea table of many English families is decorated with a patterned tablecloth from Vojvodina and Sárköz." While the children back in Budapest were impoverished, their handmade objects were considered of such high quality that they were found in the private homes of middle- and upper-class British families and dressed the bodies of their young. Referencing here the English appreciation for handcrafted items from a former Hungarian region and town, by then annexed by Serbia and Romania, was meant to evoke compassion for the territorial and cultural losses. The author even claimed that "Hungarian cultural supremacy" would be proudly exhibited "by the abundance of valuable domestic work" from Hungary that would be regularly sold at London shops and could thus be turned into "bread for the most innocent victims of the war." These children's handicrafts were intended to alter the friend-versus-foe mentality of the British toward Hungary as the former enemy country. Furthermore, the material circulation of these very Hungarian items abroad established transnational ties that were based on shared middle-class values of children's proper upbringing, the importance of family traditions, and the appreciation of traditional handcrafts. The workrooms were so successful that, by 1925, the entire initiative continued under the supervision of the Ministry of Culture.[113]

Whereas the impact of the emergency feeding stations in Budapest was short-term, the workrooms persisted throughout the 1930s, continuing to accommodate the most impoverished and disadvantaged children. Gréte Harsányi, a Hungarian reporter, witnessed the everyday conditions at the girls' workrooms in the Mária Valéria settlement, which she called "the City of Girls." She called on Budapest's citizens to go to see for themselves the misery of the girls: "You have to go there and watch. It's as interesting as a movie show." During her visit, she saw girls whose parents had lost their homes, suffered from unemployment, and whose souls were so hardened that they could not be rescued. Many of the girls were orphans or half orphans and were the children of divorced parents, alcoholics, and people with severe depression. Because they were too great a burden at home, these girls ended up on the street. Harsányi judged it to be a wonder if these girls, whose "hand nobody held," were not lost for good. Having had such difficult start in life, they made a very good impression once they started to work in the workrooms, and could even teach visitors something about self-discipline, self-criticism, confidence, inner strength, and faith.[114] They were offered as ideal proof of the best way to rescue the most disadvantaged from permanent and lasting social decline.

Just before Christmas in 1937, "hundreds and hundreds of handicrafts and small objects" were exhibited at the third public Christmas exhibition of the workrooms in Webster Hall on Vörösmarty Street. The wife of Budapest's then mayor, Mrs. Károly Szendy, opened the exhibition, which was attended by the British, French, and Austrian ambassadors. Mrs. Gascoigne, the wife of the British chargé d'affaires, expressed her appreciation of how "docile, resourceful and skillful" Hungarian children were, which is why their products were successful in Budapest and also in Manchester. Vajkai also used the opportunity to strengthen and maintain diplomatic ties with Britain, noting that, through British aid, the "poorest daughters of Budapest" could study, work, and receive an education so long after the first postwar emergency workrooms had been established.[115]

Beyond Budapest: Transnational Learning

For all the initiatives that Vajkai—supported by the SCF and the Save the Children International Union—initiated and supervised over the years, she gained a robust local and international reputation, praised again and again for everything she did for Budapest's children. Sentiments of international appreciation for her work were expressed within the SCIU—especially by William Andrew MacKenzie, who between 1921 and 1936 was headquartered in Geneva.[116] MacKenzie had a deep appreciation for Vajkai's work, as he made clear in several letters. In one, he wrote that "everybody" in London "agreed to award the first prize" to Vajkai for her children's work. It should be a "gold medal," but "nowadays one no longer encounters gold in Britain." He wanted to offer his "deepest friendship" and "deep appreciation."[117] Vajkai, for her part, made her gratitude to MacKenzie clear in every letter she wrote to him. She was thankful "for all that you are doing for them [the children] and me" and for "all the trouble, which you are taking." Sometimes she sent him gifts from the workrooms, such as "2 yards from the laces" and she assured him of the good wishes of her "mother, sister and brother," who fondly remembered his visits and hoped to see him again.[118] Similar feelings were expressed by the SCF's general secretary. "The results achieved by Mme. Vajkai up to the present," Lewish Bernard Golden extolled, had "a wonderful effect on making slum children into good citizens." The SCF was enthusiastic about future prospects. There was "no reason why Mme. Vajkai's devotion should not, with the support of the SCF, achieve even greater results," he continued.[119] Among the "greater results" he had in mind were the children's vital role as future citizens, an aspect that was being increasingly recognized. Strengthening the local relief organizations to create a solidly reliable new generation was developing into a new strategy espoused by politicians as well as child philanthropists through their support for Vajkai's work.

Local relief workers like Vajkai had to rely on their international partners to accomplish their work. Because these international partners figured not only in the public discourse but also showed up regularly in the city, local recipients of aid became aware of the origin of the relief donations. Sometimes families who had been helped by the SCF's relief activities wrote personal thank-you letters to the organization, or even to Eglantyne Jebb herself. In one of these letters, the Horak family, which had suffered greatly in the war, attested that they had been rescued through the funding and housing provided by the Save the Children Fund: "We are always thinking gratefully of those who helped to get homes for us poor war invalids and widows with our families. May you be as happy as you have made us.... We beg the Almighty to pour his blessing on you.... This will be our prayer on this holy Christmas Eve."[120] These words of mutual appreciation reflect the transnational entanglements that resulted from the relief.

The cooperation between professional women was central to international relief work and domestic implementation in Hungary. The correspondence between Jebb and Vajkai is evidence that these two women had a close, while professional, relationship. As a result of such personal contacts and their professional cooperation, relief workers temporarily serving in Hungary realized their home countries could learn from Hungarian relief workers. In 1927, British novelist Ethel Sidgwick expressed the SFC's wish to "introduce the personality of Madame Vajkai to the English public." This was not only because donations from Britain had made much of the relief work in Hungary possible; Vajkai's "own words" from her hardscrabble experience were needed in England, because she was now recognized as an international expert on children's relief and welfare. Between 1920 and 1927, the joint efforts of Jebb and Vajkai had brought about a "far-reaching reform" in the field of international child welfare, and the model developed in Budapest deserved to "stretch beyond the limits of Hungary."[121]

Jebb was determined that Vajkai's work should inspire British relief workers. Vajkai was accordingly invited to Britain to study and report on the state of British child relief. In *Through Hungarian Eyes: Impressions of Juvenile Social Work in England*, Vajkai reported her observations on the British child welfare institutions of the time. In the foreword to Vajkai's report, Rev. John Christian Pringle, secretary of the British Charity Organization Society, marveled at Vajkai's "capacity to grasp the essentials of work in a foreign country communicated to her in a foreign language." He acknowledged that several gaps and deficiencies had been found in the British child welfare system and that it had "not kept up with the march of progress." He hoped that the governmental and voluntary child welfare institutions would heed the outside perspective offered by Vajkai and remedy any deficiencies she had identified. Vajkai had had the courage to "criticize severely" aspects of the country's welfare system and its "attitude, or lack of attitude, towards our problems." The East-West relationship was being turned upside down.[122] Inviting welfare workers from Central Europe and thus acknowledging local expertise exemplified the ways in which "Britain imported as well as exported child welfare practices."[123] During a short visit to Budapest and Vienna, Reverend Pringle marveled that, even in the time of the emperor Joseph II, this area had initiated child welfare institutions "on a grand scale," "considerably earlier than we had anything corresponding in importance here." Hungary's people had been "naturally ahead of us" and "had been engaged upon these services longer than we had." Acknowledging the immense challenge faced in Hungary of rebuilding "innumerable wrecked families" and reestablishing ordinary life after the chaos of war and mass migration, Pringle extolled Vajkai's children's work and questioned where the British welfare system would "be now" if England had been through such a dreadful time. Despite all challenges and lack of financial resources, and relying on a "touching simplicity of equipment," Vajkai had succeeded in implementing ideas of "self-government," "seriousness," and devotion in her facilities for training children in Budapest.[124]

When Vajkai, on the other hand, evaluated the British welfare system, she spoke of her envy of the "economic facilities" available to British child welfare institutions, while in Budapest the sandy courtyards, cold rooms with cement floors, and lack of space made everything a challenge. Yet she would not change these conditions even if she could, because it would be dangerous to provide better conditions than the children would have in their future lives. Nevertheless, comparing the British and Hungarian childcare facilities, she acknowledged that it was hard for her to see the British "laundries and playgrounds, the experts . . . , the charming rooms for the staff" when she remembered the privations in Hungary. Vajkai also encountered the paid professional social worker. From her observations in Britain, she believed that there was no danger that the spirit of voluntary work would be lost; the "paid workers of to-day" were, after all, "the descendants of voluntary workers of previous generations." The long-term tradition of responsibility for fellow human beings could not be destroyed. The profession of social work required a great amount of study and training as well as a "full physical and mental effort," "spirit," "responsibility," and "self-sacrifice"—qualities she admired.[125] The interactions of emergency child relief in Central and Eastern Europe after the war strengthened the international community of humanitarian works, not only allowing the West to help the impoverished East but also providing opportunities for transnational relief workers, increasingly professional, to learn from one another.

Conclusion

This final chapter examines an initiative that invested in children's futures. Activist Julia Vajkai shared Eglantyne's Jebb's wish to go beyond the classical humanitarian relationship and espouse "the contemporary behaviourist emphasis on training the child in the habits of self-reliance and good citizenship" as a provision for years to come.[126] To this end, workrooms Hungary's capital city taught neglected and disadvantaged children a craft. This initiative fundamentally altered the approach to "saving" the destitute children. These efforts went beyond immediate relief, shifting to emphasize children's longer-term welfare through educational and work initiatives. This local development mirrored the larger reformulation of children's protection in Europe. The motto of Save the Children changed from providing in the immediate postwar years "life-saving first aid in food and clothing" to saving the child's whole life and soul through education.[127] Education and training offered children a new strategy to contribute to their families' incomes in the short term and provided them with marketable skills, which could be translated into future jobs. This new approach to children's protection and welfare was reflected in the 1924 Geneva Declaration of the Rights of the Child. The workrooms fundamentally altered the humanitarian relationship between the donor and recipient countries as well as between the relief organization and Budapest's children. They helped lay the foundation for common discourses and practices of children's care and protection, which had reciprocal effects on the local welfare systems of those countries involved. Child protection through education was becoming not only an integral part of the international community's agenda but also one of the new nation-state's core responsibilities.

Notes

1. Julia Vajkai, "Notes on the Budapest Work-Schools of the S.C.F.," 1935, Mme Julia Vajkai (Reports and Memos), Eglantyne Jebb Papers, Hungary, Poland EJ 167–82, A0408, SCF Archive.
2. "Statistics Concerning the Children Who Receive Assistance in the Work-Rooms of the Save the Children Fund in Budapest," May 19, 1922, 3, British Save the Children Fund's Work-Rooms, Eglantyne Jebb Papers, Hungary, Poland, EJ 167–82, A0408, SCF Archive.
3. "Report on the Activity of the SCF in Hungary, November 1926," 2, Eglantyne Jebb Papers, EJ 166-4/1, SCF Archive.
4. "Statistics Concerning the Children," 3.
5. Selick, "Responding to Children," 46.
6. Julia Vajkai, "The Problem of Idle Adolescents," 92.
7. Julia Vajkai, *Child Saving and Child Training*, 1.
8. "Népnevelés a gép században," 3.
9. Julia Vajkai, "The Problem of Idle Adolescents," 92.
10. "Statistics Concerning the Children," 3.
11. Jebb, "Life Stories of Hungarian Children," 28.
12. "Külföldi anyák magyar gyermekekért," 4.
13. "A barakok világából," 3.
14. "Magyar gyerekek munkája Londonban," 10.
15. Ibid.
16. Mrs. Julia Vajkai to Mr. MacKenzie, June 6, 1921, CH AEG AP 92.21.2 (1).
17. "Protocol of the Meeting of the Foreign Missions and Home Institutions, February 15, 1921," Sheet 1, CH AEG AP 92.21.2.
18. The workrooms are visually indicated on a map of 1913: Kogutowicz, *Budapest Kis Közlekedési Térképe A Legújabb Villamos Jelzésekkel*.
19. Julia Vajkai, *Child Saving and Child Training*, 9.
20. Julia Vajkai to Eglantyne Jebb, Budapest, September 2, 1921, 1–2, 1, CH AEG AP 92.21.2.
21. Julia Vajkai, *Child Saving and Child Training*, 9.
22. "Magyar gyerekek munkája Londonban," 10.

23. Julia Vajkai, "Report on the Save the Children Fund's Work-Rooms in Budapest," September 27, 1922, 1–15, 1, Eglantyne Jebb Papers Hungary, A 0407, EJ 149–66, EJ 166, SCF Archives.

24. Julia Vajkai to Mr. MacKenzie, May 31, 1921; Mrs. Julia Vajkai to Mr. MacKenzie, June 6, 1921, CH AEG AP 92.21.2.

25. Sidgwick, "Foreword," v.

26. Mrs. Julia Vajkai to Mr. MacKenzie, 6 June 1921, CH AEG AP 92.21.2.

27. Letter to Mrs. Jebb, May 31, 1921, CH AEG AP 92.21.2.

28. Julia Vajkai, *Education for Life*, 2, 11; Julia Vajkai, *Child Saving and Child Training*, 3.

29. Armstrong Smith, "Report on Visit to Budapest in June 1922," Reports and Correspondences, From 1 June 1921, EJ 156-21/1 Section II/3, SCF Archive.

30. "Report on the Activity of the Save the Children Fund in Hungary," November 1926, Budapest, EJ 166 4/1, SCF Archive.

31. "Statistics Concerning the Children."

32. Jebb, "Life Stories of Hungarian Children," 28–29.

33. Armstrong Smith, "Report on Visit to Budapest."

34. Julia Vajkai, *Child Saving and Child Training*, 39.

35. Ibid., 4.

36. Julia Vajkai, *Education for Life*, 2.

37. Julia Vajkai to Eglantyne Jebb, Budapest, September 2, 1921, 2.

38. "Wages," CH AEG AP 92.21.2.

39. Jebb, "Life Stories of Hungarian Children," 27.

40. "Népnevelés a gép században," 3.

41. Julia Vajkai, *Education for Life*, 4.

42. "Rules of the Sewing-Room," CH AEG AP 92.21.2.

43. Julia Vajkai, *Education for Life*, 4.

44. Julia Vajkai to Mr. MacKenzie, Budapest, February 15, 1921, 2, CH AEG AP 92.21.2.

45. Julia Vajkai, *Child Saving and Child Training*, 1, 5.

46. Armstrong Smith, "Report on Visit to Budapest."

47. Harsányi, "Lányok városa," 67.

48. "'Our' Godchildren," 45.

49. "Hungary," 43.

50. Julia Vajkai to Mr. MacKenzie, Budapest, February 15, 1921, 1–2.

51. Julia Vajkai to Eglantyne Jebb, Budapest, September 2, 1921, 1.

52. Atkins, *Liquid Materialities*.

53. Julia Vajkai to Eglantyne Jebb, Budapest, September 2, 1921, 1.

54. Julia Vajkai to Mr. MacKenzie, Budapest, January 26, 1921, AP 92.21.2, Secours à la Hongrie, Correspondance et rapports de Mme J. E. Vajkai, CH AEG.

55. "Rules Concerning the Meals," AP 92.21.2, Secours à la Hongrie, Correspondance et rapports de Mme J. E. Vajkai, CH AEG.

56. Ibid.

57. "Statistics Concerning the Children."

58. "Rules Concerning the Meals."

59. Julia Vajkai, *Child Saving and Child Training*, 12.

60. Julia Vajkai to Eglantyne Jebb, Budapest, September 2, 1921, 2.

61. Julia Vajkai, *Child Saving and Child Training*, 4.

62. Julia Vajkai, "The Budapest Work-Schools," 160.

63. "In Budapest: Making Life Better for the Children," 142.

64. L. B. Golden, "Report to the Council of the SCF and the Executive Committee of the UISE on the SCF and UISE Work in Central Europe and the Balkans," Geneva, 1926/03, 14 pages, 3, Eglantyne Jebb Papers Hungary, A 0407, EJ 149–66, EJ 166 Hungary, Folder 2, 1920–21, SCF Archive.

65. Armstrong Smith, "Report on Visit to Budapest."

66. Julia Vajkai, "Report on the Budapest Work," Budapest, 10 July 1924, Reports and Correspondences, From 1 June 1921, EJ 156-21/1 Section II/3, SCF Archive.

67. Julia Vajkai, *Education for Life*, 2.

68. Julia Vajkai, *Child Saving and Child Training*, 39.

69. "Protocol of the Meeting of the Foreign Missions and Home Institutions," Sheet 2.

70. Julia Vajkai, "Report on the Budapest Work."

71. Julia Vajkai, "Report on the Activity of the SCF in Hungary, November 25, 1925," 1–3, 1, Reports and Correspondences, From 1 June 1921, EJ 156-21/1 Section II/3, SCF Archive.

72. Golden, "Report to the Council of the SCF," 3.

73. Jebb, "Life Stories of Hungarian Children," 29.

74. Julia Vajkai, "Talk on 'Practical Education for Life,'" Third Biennial Conference of the World Federation of Education Associations, Geneva Switzerland, July 20, 1929, 9, Mme Julia Vajkai (Reports and Memos), Eglantyne Jebb Papers, Hungary, Poland EJ 167–82, EJ 169 16/14, A0408, SCF Archive.

75. United Nations, *Geneva Declaration of the Rights of the Child*.

76. Julia Vajkai, "Notes on the Budapest Work-Schools of the SCF," 1935, 1–8, 7, Mme Julia Vajkai (Reports and Memos), Eglantyne Jebb Papers, Hungary, Poland EJ 167–82, A0408, SCF Archive.

77. "Request Addressed to Our Pupils," 1–2, CH AEG AP 92.21.2.

78. "Second Study on Leadership in the Experimental Workschools of the Save the Children Fund in Budapest," Mme Julia Vajkai (Reports and Memos), Eglantyne Jebb Papers, Hungary, Poland EJ 167–82, A0408, SCF Archive.

79. Julia Vajkai, *Social Adjustment through the Junior Red Cross*, 1.

80. Szendy, "Egy nagy angol jótékonyság szervezet Budapesti munkaiskoláinak kiállitása," 6.

81. Julia Vajkai, "Talk on 'Practical Education for Life,'" 6.

82. Miskolczy, "Lélekmentés," 11.

83. Harsányi, "Lányok városa," 67.

84. Julia Vajkai, "Scope and Method of the Save the Children Fund's Workschools in Budapest," October 1931, 1–5, 3, Eglantyne Jebb Papers, Hungary, Poland EJ 167–82, A0408, SCF Archive.

85. Golden, "Report to the Council of the SCF," 3.

86. Julia Vajkai, "Scope and Method," 3–4.

87. Julia Vajkai, "The British Save the Children Fund's Work-Rooms," Budapest, 26 September 1922, 1–15, 9, Western Aid and the Global Economy, Series 1: SCF Archive, London, Reels 15–35, EJ 149, Hungary I/1: General: Reports on Conditions in Budapest Etc., 1921–22, Microfilm, Rare Book and Manuscript Library Columbia University.

88. Vajkai, "The British Save the Children Fund's Work-Rooms," 9.

89. Rabinov, *The Michel Foucault Reader*, 208.

90. Vajkai, "Scope and Method," 4.

91. "Mademoiselle Ferrieré's Report," 24 September 1920, Eglantyne Jebb Papers Hungary, A 0407, EJ 149–66, EJ 155 Hungary, Folder 2, 1920–21, International Commissioners Reports and Correspondence, SCF Archive.

92. "Report on the Activity of the SCF in Hungary," November 1926, 2.

93. Julia Vajkai, *Child Saving and Child Training*, 9.
94. Armstrong Smith, "Report on Visit to Budapest."
95. Julia Vajkai, "Report on the Activity of the SCF in Hungary," November 25, 1925, 2–3.
96. Gill, *Calculating Compassion*, 205.
97. "Magyar gyerekek munkája Londonban," 10.
98. "Hungary," and "Report on the Activity of the SCF in Hungary," November 1926, 1–8, 2, Reports and Correspondences, From 1 June 1921, Section II/3, SCF Archives.
99. United Nations, *Geneva Declaration of the Rights of the Child*.
100. "Magyar gyerekek munkája Londonban," 10.
101. Miskolczy, "Lelekmentés," 11.
102. "Népnevelés a gép században," 3.
103. Mulley, *The Woman Who Saved the Children*, 311–12; Jebb, *The Geneva Congress on Child Welfare*.
104. *Tolnai Világlapja* 16, no. 23 (October 29, 1924): 5.
105. Julia Vajkai, *Népnevelés a gép századában*.
106. Julia Vajkai, "Talk on 'Practical Education for Life,'" 2, 9.
107. "In Budapest: Making Life Better," 142.
108. Julia Vajkai to Mr. Golden, December 15, 1922, Western Aid and the Global Economy, Series 1: SCF Archive, London, Reels 15–35, EJ 149, Hungary I/1: General: Reports on Conditions in Budapest Etc., 1921–22, Microfilm, Rare Book and Manuscript Library Columbia University.
109. "Holnap megnyílik az Országos Gyermekügyi kiallitás," 3.
110. Julia Vajkai to Mr. MacKenzie, Budapest, February 15, 1921, 1.
111. Julia Vajkai to Mr. Golden, Budapest, April 29, 1922, 1–3, 1, Western Aid and the Global Economy, Series 1: SCF Archive, London, Reels 15–35, EJ 149, Hungary I/1: General: Reports on Conditions in Budapest Etc., 1921–22, Microfilm, Rare Book and Manuscript Library Columbia University.
112. Julia Vajkai, "Talk on 'Practical Education for Life,'" 4.
113. "Magyar Gyerekek Munkája Londonban," 10.
114. Harsányi, "Lányok városa," 66.
115. Szendy, "Egy nagy angol jótékonyság szervezet Budapesti munkaiskoláinak kiállitása," 6.
116. Save the Children International Union, League of Nations Search Engine, http://www.lonsea.de/pub/org/380.
117. Mr. W. A. MacKenzie to Julia Vajkai, January 31, 1922, CH AEG AP 92.21.2.
118. Julia Vajkai to Mr. MacKenzie, Budapest, February 15, 1921, 2.
119. Golden, "Report to the Council of the SCF," 3.
120. Letter to Save the Children Fund, Christmas 1922, Eglantyne Jebb Papers, Hungary, A 0407, EJ 149–66, SCF Archive.
121. Sidgwick, "Foreword," 5.
122. Pringle, "Foreword," 7. See also Pringle, *British Social Services*.
123. Baughan, *Saving the Children. Humanitarianism*, 29.
124. Pringle, "Foreword," 8–9.
125. Julia Vajkai, *Through Hungarian Eyes*, 43, 47.
126. Gill, *Calculating Compassion*, 206.
127. "Népnevelés a gép században," 3.

CONCLUSION

Transformation: From Aid to Self-Help

WHEN CONINGSBY DAWSON, AN ANGLO-AMERICAN NOVELIST, TRAVELED to Budapest in 1921, he was deeply concerned about children's destitution and the capital's overall suffering that he witnessed. He reminded his English readers that Hungary "used to lead the world in its legislation for child-conservation." Before the war, Hungary's "modern" child protection system was celebrated as "particularly human"; if a parent failed to take care of a child, "the state automatically became the parent," and if an "unprotected woman" was about to become a mother, "the state undertook a man's responsibilities," both "for the woman and the life unborn."[1] Three years after the war had ended, however, Dawson witnessed an overwhelmed child protection system, material scarcity, and children's physical "degeneration." Hence, he appealed to the moral sentiments of his readers for help. Dawson's eyewitness report was just one of many transnationally circulating narratives that used starving children in Budapest to publicize Central Europe's miserable postwar condition. As *Budapest's Children* has demonstrated, the war and its aftermath had wide-ranging negative repercussions on children's lives. Hunger, severe malnutrition, displacement, and epidemic diseases struck everywhere throughout the war. But in Hungary, and especially in Budapest, these conditions affected children's lives far more severely as they raged for months and years following the Armistice of November 1918, a Bolshevist revolution in March 1919, Romanian occupation in the summer of 1919, and the Treaty of Trianon in 1920.

The children's suffering did not go unnoticed. It gained immense public attention among local child protection organizations, representatives of the Hungarian government, and international relief organizations. The children's challenges and deprivation were debated in Hungary, Great Britain, the United States, and in the international city of Geneva and fed into a new awareness of children's vulnerability in times of political turmoil and economic distress. Significantly, reactions to children's destitution also substantially changed family-state dynamics. *Budapest's Children* has shown how attempts to cope with postwar conditions resulted in a partial, and sometimes complete, transfer of children's care from the private sphere to the public domain. This began with a temporary shift of responsibility for children's relief and care from the family to local and international relief organizations. In the long run, this move altered conceptions and practices of children's welfare altogether.

At this time of crisis, Budapest's hungry, destitute, and often displaced children depended on local assistance and help from abroad. With their plight widely publicized by eyewitnesses such as Dawson and other relief activists, the cause was embraced by postwar Western society, which rallied to a humanitarian—hence, morally "good"—relief mission. This enabled former combatant states to push for a new era of peace and rapprochement. Humanitarian reporting on Budapest's suffering children reflected a new, outspoken criticism of the impact of war and its aftermath on civilians. This extended to protests about the dissolution of the empires and the peace treaties' new arrangement of Europe, which had radical effects on the region's most vulnerable subjects. Children, viewed as innocent victims of the war, came to be seen as entitled to international reflief: middle-class ideals of childhood were based on "economic dependence, purity, and innocence," as Lydia Murdoch notes.[2] The fate of Budapest's children shocked those with these middle-class sensibilities; they feared "moral decline" and vagabondage among this new generation. Humanitarian child relief organizations stepped in to prevent children's social, moral, and physiological "degeneration," attending first to their hunger and then to their broader needs.

It is no surprise, then, that Herbert Hoover of the American Relief Administration and various other international humanitarian relief organizations such as the American Red Cross, the Save the Children Fund, the Save the Children International Union, the Jewish Joint Distribution Committee, and the International Committee of the Red Cross focused primarily on feeding and relieving this new generation. Their investment in the younger generation hoped to create a renovated society for the future and open new avenues to shape the social outlook of Europe. The children were the ideal subjects to project onto the political screen, and humanitarian organizations were able to raise a new moral consciousness throughout Europe and the United States. The deep-rooted war mentality that had prevailed during the preceding years was radically questioned by a new rhetoric of humanitarian compassion pressing the imperative to reduce suffering.

The everyday cooperation between local and international relief workers, aimed at children's rescue, produced new social ties that spanned borders and even the Atlantic Ocean. *Budapest's Children* has demonstrated how relief evolved into a truly glocal undertaking, relying on international intervention while using local infrastructures and personnel who had been active in children's protection for decades. Examining the ways in which Budapest's children were helped reveals the politics of humanitarian relief, especially the politics of the high-profile American food mission. Whether feeding malnourished children, evacuating children to foreign countries, or establishing workrooms where children learned a skill, postwar relief fundamentally altered the approach to "saving" children in need. Humanitarian thinking and actions shifted away from the idea of "just giving" to empowering local institutions and even children to directly sustain and help themselves. With the shift from relief to education, Budapest's children gained some of their agency back, equipped with resources or skills that could enable them to ease their destitution.

The relief efforts had other long-term implications as well. Child protection became an integral part of the international community's agenda and one of modern nation-states' core responsibilities. While prewar welfare had been shaped primarily by religious and philanthropic charity, wartime and postwar initiatives exemplified the emergence of a more comprehensive public welfare regime. When the activities of international organizations in Budapest slowed in the mid-1920s, key national figures and domestic state authorities assumed greater responsibility in child welfare. "Humanitarian projects, of both domestic and international origin," whether in the field of child relief or health care, "catalyzed the state's welfare objectives and became part of its governance structures."[3] Relief practices were turning into welfare practices. In Hungary and elsewhere, governments successfully appropriated parts of the former international relief organizations' practices.

While in the immediate postwar period Hungary and its neighbors had been perceived, treated, and publicized as a mere recipient of relief, donations, and Western expertise, by the late 1920s attitudes were changing. Hungary could build on its former reputation as a model in child protection practices. Hungarian activist and child relief worker Julia Vajkai was sought out to assess and improve other welfare systems. Her knowledge and experience were translated to and applied in Britain, altering the dependency balance to a more even relationship and one where mutual influence was possible.[4] Even thirty years after the end of World War I, in 1948, Vajkai was still active in children's rescue. In the aftermath of World War II, an international conflict that brought displacement, orphanhood, destitution, and death to a far greater number of children than had World War I, Vajkai again gained international recognition for her initiatives to rescue and reeducate Hungarian children. The French magazine *Sauvegarde* described how Vajkai had gathered twenty-four orphaned girls between ages twelve and fifteen in a rural

Hungarian castle to educate them on the principles of self-government and to teach them to become model members of society by "awakening in them the idea of community." It was hoped that such initiatives would become widespread and that "from now on no member of this future generation will be left unattended." In Europe's second postwar period, most relief work was directed toward the broader psychological, rather than narrowly physical, recovery of the war's child victims.[5]

Budapest's particularly distressing condition after World War I made for a situation in which international humanitarian agencies felt compelled to alter both the children's individual and collective bodies. The need for close medical control and observation turned the spaces of health care and child relief into "space[s] of surveillance" under the eyes of the international social worker.[6] Health care and relief officers were keen to exhibit new professional medical methods, standards, and trained personnel to the public. In particular, the American Red Cross aimed to take advantage of children's relief as a means "to bring the next generation of European citizens into line with American medical and social ideals."[7] This book has detailed the procedures used in the medical examinations and administration of relief measures, presenting a large number of documentary photographs, statistical tables, reports, and testimonies.

Throughout this transformation process, visual documentation was a powerful tool. It induced viewers to engage emotionally with Budapest's suffering children and their rehabilitation. The ubiquity of humanitarian visuals at the time reflects public uneasiness about the unforeseen but highly visible social consequences of war (coerced migration, hunger, poverty) and the postwar transformations. As James Vernon has pointed out, the hungry only became figures of humanitarian concern "when novel forms of news reporting" connected other people emotionally to their suffering. In postwar Budapest, the hungry were no longer perceived as "lazy, morally inadequate human beings" to be ignored.[8] Instead, the visual imagery of starving children mobilized compassion—even from afar—and produced voluntary gestures of charity from the populations of the victorious nations toward impoverished Eastern Europe. Humanitarian imagery and the "potentially educative possibilities of images" often managed to "nurture dispositions of action towards human vulnerability."[9] The images generated a new "social sympathy" and encouraged social change.[10]

While they did indeed save the lives of hundreds of thousands of Hungarian children, transnational and transatlantic humanitarian relief efforts served various local and international agendas with specific political, ideological, social, and scientific objectives. Food relief represented the most iconic materialization of humanitarianism, but it was a materialization of capitalism as well. Internationally donated food not only relieved starving children; it also elicited outward appreciation toward individual relief workers and donor nations. Donated bread and milk, "material objects," guaranteed children's survival and gained a new meaning and social function: they created symbolic linkages between the donor societies and distant Central and Eastern Europe. Through its food operations, international relief organizations—and the American relief program in particular—gained unprecedented access to foreign economies and health systems. And the United States could present itself not only as a winner of the war but also as a generous victor in a new humanitarian "war against hunger." Food relief gave US relief workers the opportunity to display America's modernity and make its influence felt in supposedly backward Central Europe. "Hunger, feeding the hungry and famine" evolved into a "central locus of action" that could drive "social and political stability, change and modernization."[11] At times, transatlantic humanitarian relief turned into an ostentatious display of unequal power relations.

The pattern of giving and receiving relief in this postwar Central European "laboratory" initially followed a paternalist logic. The West gave generously to its former enemies; the vanquished and stricken countries were thought of as passive recipients. Humanitarian "politics of compassion" are always a "politics of inequality," as Didier Fassin reminds us.[12] The children's relief program in Budapest was characterized by a social and economic gap between the donors and recipients, with a marked lack of reciprocity. The international relief endeavor in Budapest was also deeply embedded in nation-building processes on both sides. It mirrored the global competition for economic, moral, and social hegemony taking place in the recently pacified world.

In this way, the relief program in impoverished Central Europe reinforced perceptions of social and economic inequalities and deepened the asymmetric power relations between "destitute" Central Europe and the "benevolent" United States. Saving and healing Budapest's children in need—through food, material donations, and care—provided Western humanitarian organizations with a unique opportunity to apply aid to a distant and destitute population. It was openly said that the "most desirable compensation, which America received for her generosity" was "admiration for American social conscience" and "moral influence."[13] The relief of Budapest's children thus laid the foundation for a new long-term postwar constellation.

Budapest's Children has also shown how, although born out of a wish to overcome the animosities of the war, internationalism was closely intertwined with postwar nationalism. This entangled yet paradoxical relationship—between the "imaginings of nationalism and of internationalism"—figured heavily in the relief action in Budapest.[14] While "empire remained a powerful reference point and model for international humanitarianism," and organizations such as the League of Nations were considered by some "to secure imperial . . . interests," the concept of the nation was paramount only when the imperial project had failed.[15] Humanitarian appeals to the international community to rescue Budapest's children were deeply embedded in postwar conceptions of nationalism and national sovereignty. All states and organizations used their involvement in this humanitarian undertaking to pursue their own notions of nationalism or internationalism.

For the postimperial and nascent Hungarian nation-state, it was politically and ideologically expedient to win the moral support of the United States and international humanitarian organizations, both for relief and for broader political purposes. If, in 1918, Hungary was still seen as an enemy state, the discourse over the suffering and rescue of Budapest's children was crucial for regaining an international image and reputation. International humanitarian relief helped Hungary break out of its international isolation, opening up "a social 'dialogue' between its people and other European countries."[16] Hungary could reshape its international image from enemy country to victim nation, thereby codifying a nationalistic sense of identity and revisionist claims that still reverberate today. Contemporary humanitarian discourse, though focused on Budapest's children, went beyond individual victims to lament Hungary's suffering collectively. Each child's suffering was taken as a symbol of the suffering of the new nation-state as a whole. The discourse over Budapest's destitute children mirrored the psychological condition of one of Europe's "still-born democrac[ies]." Robert Gerwarth characterizes postimperial states as "impoverished, aggressively insecure, and populated by large, unloved minorities," leading to violence beyond 1918.[17] As Keith Watenpaugh has observed of relief programs in the Middle East, the concept of suffering encompasses "forms of social, legal, political, and . . . cultural suffering."[18] Budapest's children thus gained agency that went far beyond getting help for their own plight. They drew international attention to Hungary's cultural and national suffering in this postwar period.

Budapest's children can be seen as an important catalyst for the "evolving myth of Hungarian national martyrdom" as the nation experienced Bolshevist revolution and had to accept major territorial losses and massive displacement of its population.[19] Out of compassion toward the new and troubled nation-state and its iconic starving children, some transatlantic and international relief organizations tuned into Hungary's national(istic) quest for a revision of the Treaty of Trianon and the return of its lost territories. Many international relief workers were united in their belief that great damage would be done to the Hungarian people if the treaty were to be ratified and supported or sympathized with territorial revisionism. It was not lost on them that the city had absorbed thousands of refugee families migrating to the capital from neighboring states when new borders had been drawn between them. Organizations such as the International Committee of the Red Cross and the Save the Children International Union expressed special compassion toward the masses of displaced Hungarians and their children. This compassion helped institutionalize the rhetoric of Hungary's victimhood.

At the same time, through their presence and their reports, relief workers in Budapest created an international "humanitarian space" where they advocated for the relief of Budapest's destitute children and for Hungary's national interests. The idea of a common humanity that should be extended to the losers of the war influenced much of their work, but it embraced pleas for national self-determination, too, and hence reflected a "pronounced nationalist turn" at the time.[20] Fear of political chaos and Bolshevism were among the motives guiding international, and especially American, relief organizations. Hungary's desperation following the fall of the short-lived Bolshevist government provided Herbert Hoover and other relief donors with ideal timing and means to counter the further spread of Bolshevism in Central Europe. American and British relief organizations were eager to cooperate with Regent Miklós Horthy and his firmly conservative government. Popular ideas of national recovery were "based on equating the nation with a specific territory"—the territory of prewar Hungary.[21] In this way, the humanitarians helped legitimize Horthy's revisionist claims, as this book has argued. Thus, humanitarian relief in Budapest had an unequivocal political effect: it helped to consolidate and legitimate "counterrevolutionary Hungary."

Reestablishing social hierarchy and order in Hungary also involved the reaffirmation of the value of childhood and the family and the supremacy of a middle-class and conservative value system. The discourse and practices of the relief operation for the displaced, and especially for the impoverished middle-class, were instrumental in helping stabilize Horthy's postrevolutionary regime. The tribulations of displaced middle-class families, often civil service employees and professionals, from Hungary's lost territories, and especially of their disadvantaged and uprooted children, drew extra attention and sympathy. Appeals featuring children's vulnerability and innocence played nicely into the effort to suppress social unrest and reforge ties with other nations. This enforcement of stability reasserted Hungary's old imperial elites and much of the prerevolutionary social setup. Postwar "reeducation" in the country, done "in a Christian and national spirit," was aimed at erasing all traces of the city's "communism, cosmopolitanism [and] liberalism."[22] The transnational field of child relief helped Hungary achieve this—but only by helping restore the old political and social order, dominated by middle- and upper-class elites with a revisionist outlook.

Hungary failed to gain sufficient international support to prevent territorial revisions, but the nation made good use of its impoverished and starving children to rewrite its role in the international community. *Budapest's Children* has revealed the comprehensive use and usefulness of children's destitution in the new Hungarian state—an uncomfortable corollary to their malnutrition and suffering. The immediate postwar period was critical in generating a nationalistic mentality that shaped Hungarian identity and that still reverberates today. These postwar years were essential in laying the ideological foundations for Hungary's interwar political agenda, which was driven by a shift toward right-wing nationalism and political extremism. They solidified contemporary aspirations to appropriate and exhibit a victim identity centering on the recovery of the nation. The story of Budapest's children also demonstrates how difficult it was and still is for Hungary to recover from this "infinite mourning or interminable mourning" that was caused by the postwar distress.[23] Strongly anchored feelings of loss are still (mis)used in collective and commemorative ceremonies and new memorial sites today, such as that on the hundredth anniversary of the Treaty of Trianon in June 2020.[24]

Hungary's wartime children themselves remember and reinforce these narratives of loss almost a century later. But their memories are not undistorted recollections of the past; even if reshaped, distorted, and adapted to the present, children's narrated stories show how their memories in past and present were embedded in their time and social contexts. Hence, children's recollections are valuable because they demonstrate how children responded to the dominant postwar mentality at the time and how they embedded their experiences and memories in their milieus of family, neighborhood, school, and social life. Furthermore, their memories exhibit "what aspects remained in their consciousness"[25] and what details they thought worth remembering and telling.

I conclude this book with the exemplary narratives of three Hungarian children who figured throughout the book and who participated in the international children's trains. Their life courses demonstrate how some Hungarian children remembered and interpreted their own postwar destitution and how their collective longing for territorial revision at the time shaped their past and future identities. Their stories showcase how their own experiences of destitution and relief were closely intertwined with collective narratives about territorial loss and the hope to regain what had been lost. Their life trajectories and their political identities mirror how Hungary's postwar trauma was used and useful in shaping their own identities as children of the time.

When Ibolya returned from her stay in Holland, Hungary "got Transylvania back" in the Second Vienna Arbitration on August 30, 1940, because "the Germans helped the Hungarians, not because they wanted to but because they had to." Her school initiated a personal letter exchange with Hungarian children in Transylvania, which she took part in. Ibolya picked a letter from a girl her age out of the "big bag with letters." Through her pen pal in Transylvania, Ibolya met her future husband, whom she married in 1943 and with whom she went to work in industry during World War II. Ibolya's involvement in the international children's trains abroad as well as in school exchanges in Hungary's regained territories exemplifies how instrumental children were in consolidating specific postwar identities.[26]

Another child from the children's trains, Piroska, would be drawn as a young woman to become a teacher in Transylvania. In 1938, Piroska moved to the southern Hungarian town of Sándorfalva, close to the Serbian and Romanian border. As Hungary had just regained some territories from Czechoslovakia under the First Vienna Arbitration, she sensed "this Hungarian national feeling that it might be possible to revise Trianon," fueling "a national boom in handicrafts." A mass of "embroidered clothes even appeared on film," she recalled. A grant was advertised to teach Hungarian folk art in elementary school; she won the grant and started teaching embroidery. Piroska was invited once to lecture about folk art, traveling with all her pupils to Budapest. "I made a huge [embroidered] map of greater Hungary, you know, not just of truncated Hungary, which showed these different folk art centers in Kalócsa, Matyó, Sárközi." After her talk, the wife of a minister invited her to teach embroidery in Transylvania, where Hungarian folk art had a long tradition. Piroska immediately accepted and went to Bánffyhunyad. Although the area was initially in Romania, Hungary's new borders would soon move with her: "When the troops marched into Transylvania, I was already there." She stayed in Transylvania until 1944, when the Soviet Army entered and she had to flee with her baby in her arms.[27]

Another interviewee, István, argued that the postwar experience with poverty, unemployment, and destitution after the Great War was instrumental in forming the basis for the widespread support of right-wing politics he observed in the 1930s and 1940s. He remembered Budapest's poverty and high unemployment rate. His father, who was a skilled worker, was precariously employed at the Ganz factory. Similar underemployment in Germany, István asserts, "unfortunately contributed to Hitler being able to come to power," or was at least "one of the reasons." In Hungary, "there was high unemployment and there existed great social differences between people." "I don't want to politicize," he demurred regarding political issues. He had appreciated Albert Apponyi's "beautiful speech in Paris" in 1920 to help Hungary retain territories populated by Hungarians, explaining that "the peace treaty happened under the worst conditions." He did not think particularly highly of Horthy but appreciated his efforts to right that injustice.[28] István's testimony reveals that retrospective interpretations of childhood are worth exploring to understand how children's subjectivities and political identities are made.

Beyond the political implications of the postwar endeavor on children's future identities, children's relief was also a humanitarian project that centered on children's collective and individual well-being. Above all, the relief program affected the children in intimate, personal, and long-lasting ways. Thousands of children were helped close to home, while others were sent abroad—for a single summer or even several years—not only sparing them from starvation but shaping their individual identities fundamentally and their future paths in life. This is clearly demonstrated in Piroska's recollections of her stay in Holland. In the Dutch community, she was renamed Priszka, which she considered a sign of local acceptance rather than alienating. "I felt so much home" there, she remembered. Her time in Holland fundamentally altered the course of her life and her ways of thinking. She became a teacher and was invested in the care of disadvantaged children in rural areas. Even eighty years later, she thought fondly of her "bundle of Dutch experiences, the pure pleasure of simply being, which gives the child a base of life, because of which it jumps around and feels good, because it is one with the world of beings."[29]

Through these individual recollections of relief, we can better understand how these postwar relief efforts shaped the child recipients' life courses. Children gained a new social role and social agency in being recognized as particularly deserving of societal support. In postwar Hungary, children's well-being reached a new level of local and international attention that translated into modern expanded welfare regimes.

Notes

1. Dawson, *It Might Have Happened to You*, 71.
2. Murdoch, *Imagined Orphans*, 17.

3. Silverstein, "Reinventing International Health in East Central Europe," 85.
4. Pringle, "Foreword," 7.
5. Dévai, "World Organization for Lost Souls," 2. Some of these programs came together in 1948 in the Pestalozzi children's village in Trogen, Switzerland, to form a UNESCO-sponsored International Federation for Children's Communities.
6. Foucault, *Abnormal: Lectures at the Collège de France, 1974–1975*, 245.
7. Irwin, "Sauvons les Bébés," 53.
8. Vernon, *Hunger*, 19.
9. Chouliaraki and Blaagaard, "The Ethics of Images," 253.
10. Wilkinson, "The Provocation of the Humanitarian Social Imaginary," 267.
11. Barona Vilar, "International Organisations," 131.
12. Fassin, *Humanitarian Reason*, 3.
13. Andrew Cherna, "Report to the American Red Cross on Investigation in Austria and Hungary," September 1923, 5, Records of the American National Red Cross 1917–1934, 953.08, Hungary, NARA.
14. Jerónimo and Monteiro, *Internationalism, Imperialism*, 13.
15. Skinner and Lester, *Humanitarianism and Empire*, 738.
16. Hajtó, *Milk Sauce and Paprika*, 40.
17. Gerwarth, "1918 and the End," 37.
18. Watenpaugh, *Bread from Stones*, 59.
19. Ablovatski, "Between Red Army and White Guard," 74.
20. Betts, "Universalism and Its Discontents," 55.
21. Haynes, "Hungarian Identity," 91.
22. Vari, "Re-territorializing the 'Guilty City,'" 709.
23. Audoin-Rouzeau and Becker, *1914–1918*, 9.
24. "Trianoni emlékmű."
25. Sachs, "Children Remember," 17–18, 27.
26. Iboly, narrative interview with the author, Budapest, November 21, 2012.
27. Piroska, narrative interview with the author, Budapest, November 23, 2012.
28. István, narrative interview with the author, Budapest, November 30, 2012.
29. Piroska, narrative interview, Budapest, November 23, 2012.

BIBLIOGRAPHY

Archival Collections

Austria

Austrian State Archives, Vienna
- Archive der Republik, Vienna, K.u.K. Ministerium für soziale Fürsorge, Bundesministerium für soziale Verwaltung, Jugendfürsorge, 1918
- Haus-, Hof- und Staatsarchiv, Vienna, Kabinettsarchiv Korrespondenzakten, 1918

Britain

The National Archives, Kew
- Foreign Office 608, Peace Conference (British Delegation)
- Foreign Office 371, Political Central General
- W 3, F10 Austria-Hungary

National Library, London
Save the Children Fund Archives, Cadbury Research Library, Special Collections, University of Birmingham (referenced as SCF Archive)
- Eglantyne Jebb Papers, Hungary, A 0407, EJ 149–66
- Eglantyne Jebb Papers, Austria, A 0407, EJ 33–43
- Save the Children, A 0680, A 860

Hungary

Archive of the Reformed Church, Budapest
Budapest History Museum, Budapest
Hungarian Central Statistical Office, Budapest
Hungarian Jewish Museum and Archives, Budapest
Hungarian National Museum, Budapest
Hungarian Pedagogical Museum and Library, Budapest
Institute of Political History, Budapest
Kiscelli Museum, Budapest
Metropolitan Ervin Szabó Library, Budapest
Museum of Ethnography, Budapest
National Archives of Hungary, State Archive, Budapest/Óbuda
- P 999 Anya- és Gyermekvédelem Bizottság (Feministák Egyesülete), 20 d: 18–20 t
- K 150 Belügyminisztériumi Levéltár, Általános Íratok 4365, Gyermekvédelem
- K 26 ME 1922-XL III
- K 150, 1933-89910
- K 319-19-1913-23
- Z 1610, MÁV

Semmelweis Library and Museum, Budapest
National Széchényi Library, Budapest

Switzerland

Archive of the International Committee of the Red Cross, Geneva (referenced as Archive of the ICRC)
- ACICR, B MIS 4, Budapest
- ACICR, B MIS 7, Hungary
- ACICR, B UISE 3, Budapest

Archive of the League of Nations, Geneva
- R1669/41/17190, Jewish Minorities in Hungary
- R1685/41/27356, Public Education in Hungary
- R642, International Eugenics

State Archives of Geneva (Archives d'Etat de Genève, referenced as CH AEG)
- Archives Privées de la Union International de Secours aux Enfants (referenced as AP)

United States

Hoover Institution Library & Archives, Stanford (referenced as HILA)
- United States Food Administration Records, 1909–57
- American Relief Administration European Operational Records, 1919–23
  - European Children's Fund, 1911–38
  - London Office Cable and Telegram File, 1919–23
  - London Office Correspondence, 1919–23
  - Paris Office Countries File, 1918–30
  - Paris Office Subject File, 1914–37
  - Photographs, 1921–24

Jewish Joint Distribution Committee Archives, New York, NY
- New York Headquarters Records, 1919–21

National Archives and Records Administration (NARA), College Park, MD
- RG 59, Department of State, Decimal File, 1910–29
- RG 200, Records of the American National Red Cross, 1917–34

Rare Book and Manuscript Library, Columbia University, New York
- Western Aid and the Global Economy, Series One: The Save the Children Fund Archive, London, Reels 15–35, EJ 151

Rockefeller Archive Center, Sleepy Hollow, NY
- RG 1.1, Projects, Series 100N (International, War Relief)
- RG 6.1, Paris Field Office, Series 1.1 (Prewar Correspondence)
- RG 1.1, Projects, Series 750 (Hungary)
- RG 2, Office of the Messrs. Rockefeller, Series Q (World Affairs)
- Commonwealth Fund, Series 18.1 (Grants)

Narrative Interviews with the Author

Ibolya, Budapest, November 21, 2012
István, Budapest, November 30, 2012

Piroska, Budapest, November 23, 2012, and November 15, 2018
All audio files and transcripts are in the author's records.

Bibliography

"A barakok világából." *Népszava* 48, no. 218 (September 15, 1920): 3.
Abbott, Grace. *From Relief to Social Security: The Development of the New Public Welfare Services and Their Administration*. Chicago: University of Chicago Press, 1941.
Ablonczy, Balázs. "Menni vagy maradni? Az 1918 utáni távozás és a helyben maradás motívumai az emlékiratokban." *Pro Minoritate* (2018): 77–99.
Ablovatski, Eliza. "Between Red Army and White Guard." In *Gender and War in Twentieth-Century Eastern Europe*, edited by Nancy M. Wingfield and Maria Bucur, 70–79. Bloomington: Indiana University Press, 2006.
———. *Revolution and Political Violence in Central Europe: The Deluge of 1919*. Cambridge: Cambridge University Press, 2021.
Acsády, Judit. "Diverse Constructions: Feminist and Conservative Women's Movements and Their Contribution to the (Re-)Construction of Gender Relations in Hungary after the First World War." In *Aftermaths of War: Women's Movements and Female Activists, 1918-1923*, edited by Ingrid Sharp and Matthew Stibbe, 309–31. Leiden: Brill, 2011.
Adlgasser, Franz. *American Individualism Abroad: Herbert Hoover, die American Relief Administration und Österreich, 1919–1923*. Vienna: Verband Wissenschaftlicher Gesellschaften Österreichs, 1993.
"A fővárosi ovdákban amerikai cacaot reggeliznek a gyermekek." *Az Érdekes Újság* 7, no. 35 (September 1919): 23.
"Agonising Deaths of Children at Easter-Tide." *Manchester Guardian*, March 29, 1921, 7.
"A hatóság és a társadalom együttműködéséről és a Népjóléti Központról." *Fővárosi Közlöny* 27, no. 37 (July 7, 1916): 69–77.
Ahlbäck, Anders. *Manhood and the Making of the Military: Conscription, Military Service and Masculinity in Finland 1917–1939*. Farnham, UK: Ashgate, 2014.
"A 'kincses' város inségben." *8 Órai Ujság* 4, no. 202 (August 30, 1918): 3.
"A Kis Csaba Ferenc temetése." *Népszava* 45, no. 82 (March 25, 1917): 8.
"Alairták a békeszerződést." *Pesti Napló* 71, no. 134 (June 5, 1920): 1.
Allen, Keith. "Food and the German Home Front: Evidence from Berlin." In *Evidence, History and the Great War: Historians and the Impact of 1914-1918*, edited by Gail Braybon, 172–97. New York: Berghahn Books, 2004.
"A magyar gyermek—a nagyvilágban." *Család és Gyermek* 1, no. 5–6 (September 1928): 4.
"A magyar gyermekvédelem kettős jubileuma." *Budapesti Hírlap* 47, no. 147 (July 2, 1927): 95–96.
A Magyar Kir. Központi Statisztikai Hivatal. *Magyar Statisztikai Évkönyv. Új Folyam. XIV, XV, XVI. 1916, 1917, 1918*. Budapest: Athenaeum R. Társulat Könyvnyomdája, 1924.
———. *Magyar Statisztikai Évkönyv. Új Folyam. XXVII, XXVIII, XXIX, XXX. 1919, 1920, 1921, 1922*. Budapest: Athenaeum, 1925.
"A menekültek szállásán." *Világ* 10, no. 143 (November 25, 1919).
"An American Name in a Hungarian Prayer." *Magyar Tribune*, October 2, 1925.
"American Relief Administration European Children's Fund." *Világ* 10, no. 128 (November 7, 1919): 5.
American Relief Administration. *A Sketch of the Child-Feeding Operations of the A.R.A. Mission to Czecho-Slovakia, 1919–1921: The American Relief Administration in Czecho-Slovakia*. New York: American Relief Administration, 1922.

American Relief Administration European Children's Fund. *American Relief Administration European Children's Fund Mission to Poland: 1919–1922.* Warsaw: Galewski and Dau, 1922.

———. *Final Report of the Work in Hungary.* Budapest: ARA, 1920.

American Society of International Law. "Treaty between the Principal Allied and Associated Powers and Roumania." *American Journal of International Law* 14, no. 4 (1920): 324–32.

"Amerika a pesti gyermekekért." *8 Órai Újság* 7, no. 67 (March 30, 1921): 6.

"A miniszterelnök beszéde a jóvátételi bizottság előtt." *Pesti Hírlap* 45, no. 102 (May 6, 1923): 1.

Anastasiadou, Irene. *Constructing Iron Europe: Transnationalism and Railways in the Interbellum.* Amsterdam: Amsterdam University Press, 2011.

Appadurai, Arjun. "Introduction: Commodities and the Politics of Value." In *The Social Life of Things: Commodities in Cultural Perspective*, edited by Arjun Appadurai, 3–63. Cambridge: Cambridge University Press, 1986.

———, ed. *The Social Life of Things: Commodities in Cultural Perspective.* Cambridge: Cambridge University Press, 1986.

Apponyi, Albert. *The American Peace and Hungary, 1919.* Budapest: Hungarian Territorial Integrity League, 1919.

Arendt, Hannah. *The Origins of Totalitarianism.* New York: Harcourt Brace Jovanovich, 1973.

Arsan, Andrew, Su Lin Lewis, and Anne-Isabelle Richard. "Editorial—The Roots of Global Civil Society and the Interwar Moment." *Journal of Global History* 7, no. 2 (July 2012): 157–65.

"A magyar gyermek—a nagyvilágban," *Család és gyermek* 1, no. 5–6 (September 1928): 3–6.

"A spanyol járvány." *Budapesti Hírlap* 38, no. 236 (October 9, 1918): 6.

"A Stefánia-Liga az anyák és csecsemők védelmére." *Fővárosi Közlöny* 25, no. 71 (October 30, 1914): 1–3.

Atkins, Peter. *Liquid Materialities: A History of Milk, Science and the Law.* Farnham, UK: Ashgate, 2010.

Audoin-Rouzeau, Stéphane. *La guerre des enfants, 1914–1918. Essai d'histoire culturelle.* Paris: Armand Colin, 2004.

———. *L'enfant de l'ennemi 1914–1918: Viol, avortement, infanticide pendant la Grande Guerre.* Paris: Aubier, 2009.

Audoin-Rouzeau, Stéphane, and Annette Becker. *1914–1918: Understanding the Great War.* London: Profile, 2002.

"A vagonlakók és menekültek lakásügye." *Pesti Hírlap* 44, no. 29 (February 5, 1922): 2.

"Az amerikai vöröskeresztes misszió." *Az Érdekes Újság* 9, no. 3 (January 20, 1921): 23.

"Az Országos Gyermekvédő Liga." *A Pesti Hírlap 1926 évi Nagy Naptára* 35 (1926): 304.

Baader, Meike. "Tracing and Contextualising Childhood Agency and Generational Order from Historical and Systemic Perspectives." In *Reconceptualising Agency and Childhood: New Perspectives in Childhood Studies*, 135–150, edited by Florian Esser, Meike Baader, Tanja Betz, and Beatrice Hungerland. New York: Routledge, 2016.

Badenoch, Alexander, and Andreas Fickers, eds. *Materializing Europe: Transnational Infrastructures and the Project of Europe.* New York: Palgrave Macmillan, 2010.

Bálint, Angelika. "Nyomor az utcán—A budapesti hajléktalanokról alkotott kép a századfordulón." *Valóság* 57, no. 7 (2014): 89.

Bandholtz, Harry H., and Fritz-Konrad Krüger. *An Undiplomatic Diary.* New York: Columbia University Press, 1933.

Bane, Suda Lorena, and Ralph Haswell Lutz, eds. *Organization of American Relief in Europe 1918–1919.* Stanford, CA: Stanford University Press, 1943.

Bárczy, István. "A főváros segítő munkája." *Budapest Központi Segítő Bizottság Közleményei: A Fővárosi Közlöny Melléklete.* Budapest, September 25, 1914, 1–10.

Barnett, Michael. *Empire of Humanity: A History of Humanitarianism*. Ithaca, NY: Cornell University Press, 2013.
Baron, Nick, ed. *Displaced Children in Russia and Eastern Europe, 1915–1953: Ideologies, Identities, Experiences*. Leiden: Brill, 2017.
Barona Vilar, Josep L. "International Organisations and the Development of a Physiology of Nutrition during the 1930s." *Food and History* 6, no. 1 (2008): 120–62.
Barth, William Kurt. *On Cultural Rights: The Equality of Nations and the Minority Legal Tradition*. Leiden: Johanneshov, 2008.
Baughan, Emily. "'Every Citizen of Empire Implored to Save the Children!' Empire, Internationalism and the Save the Children Fund in Interwar Britain." *Historical Research* 86, no. 231 (2013): 116–37.
———. "The Imperial War Relief Fund and the All British Appeal: Commonwealth, Conflict and Conservatism within the British Humanitarian Movement, 1920–25." *Journal of Imperial and Commonwealth History* 40, no. 5 (2012): 845–61.
———. *Saving the Children: Humanitarianism, Internationals and Empire*. Oakland: University of California Press, 2021.
Becker, Peter, and Natasha Wheatley. "Introduction: Central Europe and the New International Order." In *Remaking Central Europe: The League of Nations and the Former Habsburg Lands*, edited by Peter Becker and Natasha Wheatley, 1–17. Oxford: Oxford University Press, 2020.
Beckert, Sven. *Empire of Cotton: A Global History*. New York: Vintage, 2015.
Behrends, Jan C., and Martin Kohlrausch, eds. *Races to Modernity: Metropolitan Aspirations in Eastern Europe, 1890–1940*. Budapest: Central European University Press, 2014.
"Békés forradalom." *Új Idők* 52, no. 34 (September 28, 1946): 565.
Bell, Russell W. "Final Inspection Trip to Budapest." *American Relief Administration Bulletin* 2, no. 29 (October 1922): 54.
———. "Hungary Initiates the 'Horthy Action.'" *American Relief Administration Bulletin* 2, no. 31 (December 1922): 72–73.
Bender, Thomas, and Carl E. Schorske, eds. *Budapest and New York: Studies in Metropolitan Transformation 1870–1930*. New York: Russel Sage Foundation, 1994.
Bennett, Tony, and Patrick Joyce, eds. *Material Powers: Cultural Studies, History and the Material Turn*. London: Routledge, 2010.
Bernolák, Nándor. "Agreement between the Royal Hungarian Government and the American Relief Administration." *American Relief Administration Bulletin* 2, no. 21 (February 1922): 28–29.
Betts, Paul. "Universalism and Its Discontents: Humanity as a Twentieth-Century Concept." In *Humanity: A History of European Concepts in Practice from the Sixteenth Century to the Present*, edited by Fabian Klose and Mirjam Thulin, 51–72. Göttingen, Germany: Vandenhoeck & Ruprecht, 2016.
Bihari, Péter. *1914: A nagy háború száz éve*. Budapest: Pesti Kalligram, 2014.
Bókay, János. "The Result of the Hungarian Mission from a Medical Point of View." *American Relief Administration Bulletin* 2, no. 10 (March 1, 1921): 10–19.
———. "The Result of the 1921 Feeding from a Medical Standpoint." *American Relief Administration Bulletin* 2, no. 23 (April 1922): 44–48.
Bonzon, Thierry, and Belinda Davis. "Feeding the Cities." In *Capital Cities at War: Paris, London, Berlin 1914–1919*, edited by Jay Winter and Jean-Louis Robert, 305–41. Cambridge: Cambridge University Press, 1997.
Borsányi, György. *Kun Béla, egy politikai életrajz*. Budapest: Kossuth Kiadó, 1979.

Bösch, Frank, and Manuel Borutta. "Medien und Emotionen in der Moderne: Historische Perspektive." In *Die Massen bewegen: Medien und Emotionen in der Moderne*, 13–42. Frankfurt: Campus, 2006.

Bourke, Anna. *Dismembering the Male: Men's Bodies, Britain and the Great War*. London: Reaktion Books, 1999.

Bowden, Carleton G. "Economic Conditions and Relief in Hungary, 1920–21." *American Relief Administration Bulletin* 2, no. 12 (May 1, 1921): 10–17.

Breen, Rodney. "Saving Enemy Children: Save the Children's Russian Relief Organisation, 1921–1923." *Disasters: The Journal of Disaster Studies and Management* 18, no. 3 (1994): 221–37.

Brubaker, Rogers. "Aftermaths of Empire and the Unmixing of Peoples." In *After Empire: Multiethnic Societies and Nation-Building; The Soviet Union and the Russian, Ottoman, and Habsburg Empires*, edited by Karen Barkley and Mark von Hagen, 154–80. Boulder, CO: Westview, 1997.

———. "Nationalizing States in the Old 'New Europe' and the New." *Ethnic and Racial Studies* 19, no. 2 (February 1996): 411–37.

Brubaker, Rogers, Margit Feischmidt, Jon Fox, and Liana Grancea. *Nationalist Politics and Everyday Ethnicity in a Transylvanian Town*. Princeton, NJ: Princeton University Press, 2006.

Burman, Erica. "Innocents Abroad: Western Fantasies of Childhood and the Iconography of Emergencies." *Disasters: The Journal of Disaster Studies and Management* 18, no. 3 (1994): 238–53.

Burrin, Michael. "Clemens Pirquet: Early Twentieth-Century Scientific Networks, the Austrian Hunger Crisis, and the Making of the International Food Expert." In *Remaking Central Europe: The League of Nations and the Former Habsburg Lands*, edited by Peter Becker and Natasha Wheatley, 39–70. Oxford: Oxford University Press, 2020.

Butler, Judith. "Foucault and the Paradox of Bodily Inscriptions." *Journal of Philosophy* 86, no. 11 (1989): 601–7.

Buxton, Charles R., and Dorothy F. Buxton. *The World after the War*. London: Allen & Unwin, 1920.

Cabanes, Bruno. *The Great War and the Origins of Humanitarianism, 1918–1924*. Cambridge: Cambridge University Press, 2014.

Canning, Kathleen. "The Body as Method? Reflections on the Place of the Body in Gender History." *Gender and History* 11 (1999): 499–513.

———. "Feminist History after the Linguistic Turn: Historicizing Discourse and Experience." *Signs* 19 (1994): 368–404.

Captain James Pedlow, Commissioner of the American Red Cross Society in Budapest. Budapest: Printing Office of the Metropolis of Budapest, 1922.

"Captain Pedlow's Plea to the American-Hungarians." *Otthon*, September 6, 1931.

Carden-Coyne, Ana. *Reconstructing the Body: Classicism, Modernism and the First World War*. Oxford: Oxford University Press, 2009.

Case, Holly. *The Age of Questions, Or, A First Attempt at an Aggregate History of the Eastern, Social, Woman, American, Jewish, Polish, Bullion, Tuberculosis, and Many Other Questions of the Nineteenth Century, and Beyond*. Princeton, NJ: Princeton University Press, 2018.

———. *Between States: The Transylvanian Question and the European Idea during World War II*. Stanford, CA: Stanford University Press, 2009.

"Central Powers' Greatest Battle Being Won on Farms of Empires, Writes American Correspondent." *Washington Post*, August 10, 1916, 3.

Charpy, Manuel. "How Things Shape Us: Material Culture and Identity in the Industrial Age." In *Writing Material Culture History*, edited by Anne Gerritsen and Geiorgio Riello, 199–221. London: Bloomsbury, 2015.
Chenery, William L. "Starving Budapest, Capital of Human Misery." *New York Times*, May 30, 1920, 2.
Chouliaraki, Lilie. "The Humanity of War: Iconic Photojournalism of the Battlefield, 1914–2012." *Visual Communication* 12, no. 3 (2013): 315–40.
Chouliaraki, Lilie, and Bolette B. Blaagaard. "The Ethics of Images." *Visual Communication* 12, no. 3 (2013): 253–59.
Clavin, Patricia. "The Austrian Hunger Crisis and the Genesis of International Organization after the First World War." *International Affairs* 90, no. 2 (2014): 265–78.
———. "Introduction: Conceptualising Internationalism between the Two World Wars." In *Internationalism Reconfigured: Transnational Ideas and Movements between the World Wars*, edited by Daniel Laqua, 1–14. London: I. B. Tauris, 2011.
———. *Securing the World Economy: The Reinvention of the League of Nations, 1920–1946*. Oxford: Oxford University Press, 2013.
Clements, Kendrick A. *The Life of Herbert Hoover: Imperfect Visionary, 1918–1928*. New York: Palgrave Macmillan, 2010.
Clouzot, Étienne. "Secours aux enfants en Hongrie." *Revue Internationale de la Croix-Rouge* 3, no. 26 (February 15, 1921): 137–43.
Collingham, Lizzie. *The Taste of War: World War Two and the Battle for Food*. New York: Penguin Books, 2012.
Colpus, Eve. *Female Philanthropy in the Interwar World: Between Self and Other*. New York: Bloomsbury, 2018.
Conklin, William E. *Statelessness: The Enigma of the International Community*. Oxford: Hart, 2014.
Cook, Daniel Thomas. "Children's Consumption in History." In *The Oxford Handbook of the History of Consumption*, edited by Frank Trentmann, 585–600. Oxford: Oxford University Press, 2012.
Cornwall, Mark, and John Paul Neumann. *Sacrifice and Rebirth: The Legacy of the Last Habsburg War*. New York: Berghahn Books, 2016.
Counihan, Carole. *The Anthropology of Food and Body: Gender, Meaning, and Power*. New York: Routledge, 1999.
Cox, Mary Elisabeth. "Hunger Games: Or How the Allied Blockade in the First World War Deprived German Children of Nutrition, and Allied Food Aid Subsequently Saved Them." *Economic History Review* 68, no. 2 (2014): 600–31.
———. *Hunger in War and Peace: Women and Children in Germany, 1914–1924*. Oxford: Oxford University Press, 2019.
Csergő, Hugó. *A budapesti nyomor vöröskönyve*. Budapest: Népjóléti Központ, 1919.
Csóti, Csaba. "Vagonlakók, barakklakók, menekültek." *Rubicon Történelmi Magazin*, no. 4–5 (2010): 54–59.
Cullather, Nick. "The Foreign Policy of the Calorie." *American Historical Review* 112, no. 2 (2007): 337–65.
Curti, Merle. *American Philanthropy Abroad: A History*. New Brunswick, NJ: Rutgers University Press, 1963.
Dauphinée, Elizabeth. "The Politics of the Body in Pain: Reading the Ethics of Imagery." *Security Dialogue* 38, no. 2 (2007): 139–55.
Davis, Belinda. *Home Fires Burning: Food, Politics, and Everyday Life in World War I*. Chapel Hill: University of North Carolina Press, 2000.

Dawes, James. *That the World May Know: Bearing Witness to Atrocity*. Cambridge, MA: Harvard University Press, 2007.

Dawson, Coningsby. *It Might Have Happened to You: A Contemporary Portrait of Central and Eastern Europe*. New York: John Lane, 1921.

Deák, Francis. "The Rumanian-Hungarian Dispute before the Council of the League of Nations." *California Law Review* 16, no. 2 (1928): 120–33.

Deák, István. "Budapest and the Hungarian Revolutions of 1918–1919." *Slavonic and East European Review* 46, no. 106 (1968): 129–40.

———. "The Habsburg Empire." In *After Empire: Multiethnic Societies and Nation-Building; The Soviet Union and the Russian, Ottoman, and Habsburg Empires*, edited by Karen Barkley and Mark von Hagen, 129–41. Boulder, CO: Westview, 1997.

———. "Strangers at Home." *New York Review of Books*, July 20, 2000. https://www.nybooks.com/articles/2000/07/20/strangers-at-home/.

Deésy, Alfred, dir. *The Dutch Heart*. Budapest: Magyar-Holland Kultúrgazdasági Rt., 1924. http://mandarchiv.hu/tart/jatekfilm?name=jatekfilm&action=film&id=290019258.

De Grazia, Victoria, and Ellen Furlough, eds. *The Sex of Things: Gender and Consumption in Historical Perspective*. Berkeley: University of California Press, 1996.

Dékány, István. "Csonka Vágányon." Budapest, 2014. https://www.youtube.com/watch?v=WwvFd53VueU.

Derix, Simone, Benno Gammerl, Christiane Reinecke, and Nina Verheyen. "Der Wert der Dinge: Zur Wirtschafts- und Sozialgeschichte der Materialitäten." *Zeithistorische Forschungen* 3 (2016): 387–403.

"Dér Zoltán diákkori emlékei a háborús évekből." *A Nagy Háború írásban és képben* (blog). May 4, 2015. http://nagyhaboru.blog.hu/2015/05/04/repatrialas.

Dévai, Erzsébet. "Világszervezet a kallódó lelkekért," *Magyar Nemzet* 4, no. 183 (August 11, 1948).

de Waal, Alex. *Mass Starvation: The History and Future of Famine*. Cambridge: Wiley, 2018.

"Distribution of Food to Poles, Czechs, Austrians and Germans Spurred." *New York Times*, February 9, 1920, 8.

Donson, Andrew. "Children and Youth." In *1914–1918 Online: International Encyclopedia of the First World War*, edited by Ute Daniel, Peter Gatrell, Oliver Janz, Heather Jones, Jennifer Keene, Alan Kramer, and Bill Nasson. Berlin: Freie Universität Berlin, 2016. https://doi.org/10.15463/ie1418.10265.

Dragoman, Dragos. "Linguistic Pluralism and Citizenship in Romania." In *Language Rights Revisited: The Challenge of Global Migration and Communication*, edited by Dagmar Richter, Ingo Richter, Reetta Toivanen, and Iryna Ulasiuk, 287–99. Berlin: BWV Berliner, 2012.

Droux, Joëlle. "Life during Wartime: The Save the Children International Union and the Dilemmas of Warfare Relief, 1919–47." In *Dilemmas of Humanitarian Aid in the Twentieth Century*, edited by Johannes Paulmann, 185–206. Oxford: Oxford University Press, 2016.

Druelle, Clotilde. *Feeding Occupied France during World War I: Herbert Hoover and the Blockade*. Cham, Switzerland: Springer International, 2019.

Duerden, Timothy J., and Lewis Hine. *Photographer and American Progressive*. Jefferson, NC: McFarland, 2018.

Dwork, Deborah. *War Is Good for Babies and Young Children: A History of the Infant and Child Welfare Movement in England, 1898–1918*. London: Tavistock, 1978.

Egry, Gábor. *Etnicitás, identitás, politika: Magyar kisebbségek nacionalizmus és regionalizmus között Romániában és Csehszlovákiában, 1918–1944*. Budapest: Napvilág Kiadó, 2015.

"Egyesületek." *Budapesti Hírlap* 18, no. 61 (March 2, 1898): 10–11.

Eichenberg, Julia, and John Paul Newman, eds. *The Great War and Veterans' Internationalism.* New York: Palgrave Macmillan, 2013.
"Europe's Need: Save the Children Fund." *Record of the Save the Children Fund* 1, no. 3 (December 1920): 41.
"Everyone Helps in Work." *Bulletin of the Red Cross*, January 10, 1921, 6.
"Famine, Freezing and Bolshevism Menace Existence." *Los Angeles Times*, January 5, 1919, I1.
"Famine in Hungary While Women Riot." *New York Times*, October 16, 1916, 2.
Fass, Paula S. "Introduction: Is There a Story in the History of Childhood?" In *The Routledge History of Childhood in the Western World*, 1–14. Milton Park, UK: Routledge, 2013.
Fassin, Didier. "Humanitarianism as a Politics of Life." *Public Culture* 19, no. 3 (2007): 499–520.
———. *Humanitarian Reason: A Moral History of the Present.* Berkeley: University of California Press, 2012.
Federico, Giovanni. *Feeding the World: An Economic History of Agriculture, 1800–2000.* Princeton, NJ: Princeton University Press, 2005.
Fehrenbach, Heide. "From Aid to Intimacy: The Humanitarian Origins and Media Culture of International Adoption." In *Dilemmas of Humanitarian Aid in the Twentieth Century*, edited by Johannes Paulmann, 207–34. Oxford: Oxford University Press, 2016.
Fehrenbach, Heide, and Davide Rodogno, eds. *Humanitarian Photography: A History.* Cambridge: Cambridge University Press, 2015.
———. "Introduction: The Morality of Sight; Humanitarian Photography in History." In *Humanitarian Photography: A History*, 1–22. Cambridge: Cambridge University Press, 2015.
Feldberg, Georgina D. *Disease and Class: Tuberculosis and the Shaping of Modern North American Society.* New Brunswick, NJ: Rutgers University Press, 1995.
"First Steps to the Real Settlement: Raise the Blockade." *Observer*, May 18, 1919, 10.
Fischer, Harold H. *The Famine in Soviet Russia, 1919–1923: The Operations of the American Relief Administration.* Stanford, CA: Stanford University Press, 1927.
"Food and Bolshevism." *Washington Post*, December 20, 1919, 6.
"Food for Europe by Personal Gifts; American Relief Administration Arranges a Warrant System for Shipments." *New York Times*, December 15, 1919, 12.
Foucault, Michel. *Abnormal: Lectures at the Collège de France, 1974–1975.* Edited by Valerio Marchetti and Antonella Salomon; translated by Graham Burchell, 231–62. New York: Verso, 2003.
———. *The Birth of Biopolitics: Lectures at the Collège de France, 1978–1979.* Basingstoke, UK: Palgrave Macmillan, 2008.
———, ed. *Discipline and Punish: The Birth of the Prison.* New York: Vintage Books, 1995.
———. *Society Must Be Defended: Lectures at the Collège de France, 1975–76.* New York: Picador, 2003.
"400,000 Czech Youths Fed." *New York Times*, August 28, 1919, 28.
Freedman, Russell. *Kids at Work: Lewis Hine and the Crusade against Child Labor.* New York: Clarion Books, 1994.
Gal, Csilla V. "Borrowing Ideas: The Changing Form of Metropolitan Housing in Budapest." Fifteenth International Planning History Society Conference, Sao Paolo, Brazil, July 2012. https://www.researchgate.net/publication/309208702_Borrowing_ideas_The_changing_form_of_metropolitan_housing_in_Budapest/citations.
Gammerl, Benno. *Untertanen, Staatsbürger, Untertanen und Andere: der Umgang mit ethnischer Heterogenität im Britischen Weltreich und im Habsburgerreich, 1867–1918.* Göttingen, Germany: Vandenhoeck & Ruprecht, 2010.
Gardner, Agnes. "American Red Cross Work in Serbia." *American Journal of Nursing* 16, no. 1 (1915): 36–40.

Gatrell, Peter. *The Making of the Modern Refugee*. Oxford: Oxford University Press, 2013.
———. *A Whole Empire Walking: Refugees in Russia during World War I*. Bloomington: Indiana University Press, 1999.
Gatrell, Peter, and Liubov Zhvanko, eds. *Europe on the Move: Refugees in the Era of the Great War*. Manchester: Manchester University Press, 2017.
Géra, Eleonóra. "A spanyolnátha Budapesten." *Budapesti Negyed* 64 (2009): 208–32.
Gergely, Ferenc. *A magyar gyermekvédelem története (1867–1991)*. Budapest: Püski, 1997.
Gerritsen, Anne, and Giorgio Riello, eds. *Writing Material Culture History*. London: Bloomsbury, 2015.
Gerwarth, Robert. "1918 and the End of Europe's Land Empires." In *The Oxford Handbook of the Ends of Empire*, edited by Martin Thomas and Andrew S. Thompson, 27–42. Oxford: Oxford University Press, 2018.
———. *The Vanquished: Why the First World War Failed to End, 1917–1923*. Oxford: Oxford University Press, 2016.
Geyer, Martin H., and Johannes Paulmann, eds. *The Mechanics of Internationalism: Culture, Society, and Politics from the 1840s to the First World War*. Oxford: Oxford University Press, 2001.
"Ghastly Tragedy of Europe's Children." *Manchester Guardian*, April 8, 1920, 3.
Gill, Rebecca. *Calculating Compassion: Humanity and Relief in War, Britain, 1870–1914*. Manchester: Manchester University Press, 2013.
Givoni, Michal. *The Care of the Witness: A Contemporary History of Testimony in Crises*. Cambridge: Cambridge University Press, 2016.
Glant, Tibor. "Herbert Hoover and Hungary, 1918–1923." *Hungarian Journal of English and American Studies* 8, no. 2 (2002): 95–109.
Glover, Jonathan. *Humanity: A Moral History of the Twentieth Century*. New Haven, CT: Pimlico, 2001.
Godby, Michael. "Confronting Horror: Emily Hobhouse and the Concentration Camp Photographs of the South African War." *Kronos: Southern African Histories* 32 (2006): 34–48.
Goebel, Stefan, and Derek Keene. "Towards a Metropolitan History of Total War: An Introduction." In *Cities into Battlefields: Metropolitan Scenarios, Experiences and Commemorations of Total War*, 1–46, edited by Stefan Goebel and Derek Keene. Farnham, UK: Ashgate, 2011.
Gram-Skjoldager, Karen, Haakon A. Ikonomou, and Torsten Kahlert. "Introduction." In *Organizing the 20th-Century World: International Organization and the Emergence of International Public Administration, 1920–60*, edited by Karen Gram-Skjoldager, Haakon A. Ikonomou, and Torsten Kahlert, 1–12. London: Bloomsbury Academic, 2020.
Granick, Jaclyn. *International Jewish Humanitarianism in the Age of the Great War*. Cambridge: Cambridge University Press, 2021.
Gratze, Walter. *Terrors of the Table: The Curious History of Nutrition*. Oxford: Oxford University Press, 2005.
Graupner, Rudolf. "Statelessness as a Consequence of the Change of Sovereignty over Territory after the Last War." In *The Problem of Statelessness*, edited by Paul Weis and Rudolf Graupner, 27–40. London: British Section of the World Jewish Congress, 1944.
Guest, Haden. "Starvation and Misery in Hungary." *Manchester Guardian*, October 13, 1919, 6.
Gyuris, Géza, ed. *Az amerikai gyermeksegélyző akció étkeztető helyei Magyarországon: American Relief Administration European Children's Fund; List of Child Feeding Stations in Hungary, 1919–1920*. Budapest: American Relief Administration, 1920.

Haan, R. M. "Hungary Thanks America: Relief Committee and Grateful Recognition of Aid for Children." *New York Times*, October 19, 1919, 21.
Hajdú, Tibor. *Az 1918-as magyarországi polgári demokratikus forradalom*. Budapest: Kossuth Könyvkiadó, 1968.
Hajtó, Vera. *Milk Sauce and Paprika: Migration, Childhood and Memories of the Interwar Belgian-Hungarian Child Relief Project*. Leuven, Belgium: Leuven University Press, 2016.
———. "The 'Wanted' Children: Experiences of Hungarian Children in Belgian Foster Families during the Interwar Period." *History of the Family* 14, no. 2 (2009): 203–16.
Halttunen, Karen. "Humanitarianism and the Pornography of Pain in Anglo-American Culture." *American Historical Review* 100, no. 2 (1995): 303–34.
Hämmerle, Christa, ed. *Kindheit im Ersten Weltkrieg*. Vienna: Böhlau, 1993.
Hanák, Péter. *Zsidókérdés, asszimiláció, antiszemitizmus: Tanulmányok a zsidókérdésről a huszadik századi Magyarországon*. Budapest: Gondolat, 1984.
Hansen, E. F. "Third Distribution of Food Packages Donated by the Commonwealth Fund to the Intelligentsia of Hungary." *American Relief Administration Bulletin* 2, no. 119 (December 1921): 39–41.
Hansen, Jason D. *Mapping the Germans: Statistical Science, Cartography and the Visualization of the German Nation, 1848–1914*. Oxford: Oxford University Press, 2015.
Harsányi, Gréte. "Lányok városa." *Új Idők* 45, no. 28 (July 9, 1939).
Haskell, Thomas L. "Capitalism and the Origins of the Humanitarian Sensibility." Pts. 1 and 2. *American Historical Review* 90, no. 2 (1985): 339–61; no. 3 (1985): 547–66.
Haupt, Heinz-Gerhard, and Jürgen Kocka. *Comparative and Transnational History: Central European Approaches and New Perspectives*. New York: Berghahn Books, 2012.
Haynes, Rebecca Ann. "Hungarian National Identity: Definition and Redefinition." In *Contemporary Nationalism in East Central Europe*, edited by Gavin Sullivan, 87–105. London: Macmillan, 1995.
Healy, Maureen. "Civilizing the Soldier in Postwar Austria." In *Gender and War in Twentieth-Century Eastern Europe*, edited by Nancy M. Wingfield and Maria Bucur, 47–69. Bloomington: Indiana University Press, 2006.
———. *Vienna and the Fall of the Habsburg Empire: Total War and Everyday Life in World War I*. Cambridge: Cambridge University Press, 2004.
Hegedűs, Judit. "Kleinkinderpflege- und Kinderschutzbewegung während der k.u.k. Monarchie." In *Pädagogische und kulturelle Strömungen in der k.u.k. Monarchie: Lebensreform, Herbartianismus und reformpädagogische Bewegungen*, edited by Johanna Hopfner and András Németh, 185–98. Frankfurt am Main: Peter Lang, 2008.
Hertog, Johan den. "The Commission for Relief in Belgium and the Political Diplomatic History of the First World War." *Diplomacy and Statecraft* 21, no. 4 (2010): 593–613.
Herwig, Holger H. *The First World War: Germany and Austria-Hungary, 1914–1918*. London: Arnold, 1997.
Hicks, Dan, and Mary C. Beaudry, eds. *The Oxford Handbook of Material Culture Studies*. Oxford: Oxford University Press, 2010.
"Holnap megnyílik az Országos Gyermekügyi kiallitás." *Budapesti Hírlap* 43, no. 134 (June 16, 1923): 3.
Hoover, Herbert. *An American Epic: Famine in Forty-Five Nations: The Battle on the Front Line. 1914–1923*. Washington, DC: Henry Regnary, 1959.
———. "Central European Relief. Address by Herbert Hoover, Delivered in Boston, Massachusetts, January 13, 1921." *International Conciliation* 160 (March 1921): 107–10.
———. "Child Life in Central Europe and the Need of Cooperation in Relief." *American Relief Administration Bulletin* 2, no. 1 (October 1, 1920): 1–3.

———. "The Children Must Be Saved," *American Relief Administration Bulletin* 2, no. 9 (February 1, 1921): 2.

———. "Children's Relief and Democracy." *American Relief Administration Bulletin* 2, no. 15 (August 1, 1921): 1.

———. *The Memoirs of Herbert Hoover: Years of Adventure 1874–1920*. New York: Macmillan, 1951.

———. "Relief for Europe." *International Conciliation* 160 (March 1921): 111–12.

———. "What Peace Has Done to Europe." *New York Times*, March 27, 1921, BRM 1.

"Hoover Made Head of American Relief." *New York Times*, March 3, 1919, 18.

"Hoover Wants 1,000,000." *New York Times*, January 18, 1920, N1.

Hóman, Bálint. *Művelődéspolitika*. Budapest: Magyar Történelmi Társaság, 1938.

"Hungarians Erect Monument to American Red Cross Chief." *New York Times*, May 11, 1922, 1.

Hungarian Territorial Integrity League. *The Consequences of the Division of Hungary from the Standpoint of Eugenics*. Budapest: Hungarian Territorial Integrity League, 1919.

"Hungary." *Record of the Save the Children Fund* 1, no. 3 (December 1920): 43.

"Hungary Celebrated the American Thanksgiving." *Red Cross Bulletin*, January 3, 1921, 8.

"Hungary Faces Severe Season." *Red Cross Bulletin*, December 20, 1920, 5.

"The Hungry Sheep." *Review of Reviews* 59, no. 352 (April 1919): 251.

Hunt, Karen. "Gender and Everyday Life." In *Gender and the Great War*, edited by Susan R. Grayzel and Tammy M. Proctor, 149–68. Oxford: Oxford University Press, 2017.

"Hús, tej, zsír." *Az Est* 10, no. 44 (February 20, 1919): cover.

"Huszonnégy budapesti kislány, aki egy napon született, Juliána kisasszonnya, ajandokat kap a hollandi konsulatuson." *Új Idők* 26, no. 13 (May 10, 1920): 261.

"Igy redezkedett be vaggonban levő lakásán egy erdélyi menekült család." *Az Érdekes Újság* 7, no. 48 (December 25, 1919): 48.

"In Budapest: Making Life Better for the Children." *Record of the Save the Children Fund* 2, no. 8 (January 15, 1922): 142.

"Inured to War, Vienna Crowds Theaters, Cafes." *Chicago Daily Tribune*, July 23, 1917, 7.

Irwin, Julia. *Making the World Safe: The American Red Cross and a Nation's Humanitarian Awakening*. Oxford: Oxford University Press, 2013.

———. "Nurses without Borders: The History of Nursing as U.S. International History." *Nursing History Review* 19 (2011): 78–102.

———. "Sauvons les Bébés: Child Health and U.S. Humanitarian Aid in the First World War Era." *Bulletin of the History of Medicine* 86, no. 1 (2012): 37–65.

———. "Taming Total War: Great War–Era American Humanitarianism and Its Legacies." In *Beyond 1917: The United States and the Global Legacies of the Great War*, edited by Thomas W. Zeiler, David K. Ekbladh, and Benjamin C. Montoya, 122–39. Oxford: Oxford University Press, 2017.

Jackson, Peter, Neil Ward, and Polly Russell. "Moral Economies of Food and Geographies of Responsibility." *Transactions of the Institute of British Geographers* 34, no. 1 (2009): 12–24.

Janicki, David A. "The British Blockade during World War I: The Weapon of Deprivation." *Inquiries Journal/Student Pulse* 6, no. 6 (2014). http://www.inquiriesjournal.com/articles/899/the-british-blockade-during-world-war-i-the-weapon-of-deprivation.

Jászi, Oscar. "Dismembered Hungary and Peace in Central Europe." *Foreign Affairs* 2, no. 1 (January 1, 1923): 276.

Jebb, Eglantyne. "Cheap Publicity." *Record of the Save the Children Fund* 2, no. 5 (November 15, 1921): 67–69.

———. "Life Stories of Hungarian Children." *Record of the Save the Children Fund* 3, no. 1 (1922): 27–32.

Jerónimó, Miguel Bandeira, and José Pedro Monteiro, eds. *Internationalism, Imperialism, and the Formation of the Contemporary World: The Pasts of the Present.* Cham, Switzerland: Palgrave Macmillan, 2018.
Jeszenszky, Géza. Review of *Trianon arcai: Naplók, visszaemlékezések, levelek*, by Gergely Kunt, L. Balogh Béni, and Anikó Schmidt. *Századok* 153, no. 4 (2019): 837–38.
Jones, Heather. "International or Transnational? Humanitarian Action during the First World War." *European Review of History* 16, no. 5 (2009): 697–713.
Judson, Pieter M. *The Habsburg Empire: A New History.* Cambridge, MA: Harvard University Press, 2016.
Kádár, Béla, and Vilmos Sárbó, ed. *A nagy vihar hajótöröttei: Hivatalos feljegyzések, tanulmányok és más irások a háború és a pusztitó béke idejéről.* Budapest: Wodianer, 1927.
Kallio, Kirsti P. "The Body as a Battlefield: Approaching Children's Politics." *Geografiska Annaler* 90, no. 3 (2008): 285–97.
Karlinksy, Nahum. "Jewish Philanthropy and Jewish Credit Cooperatives in Eastern Europe and Palestine up to 1939." *Journal of Israeli History* 27 no. 2 (2008): 149–70.
Karsai, Sándor. *Jelentés az Országos Gyermekvédő Liga 1906-7 évi működéséről.* Budapest: Thalia Nyomda, 1907.
Kasianov, Georgiy, and Philip Ther, eds. *A Laboratory of Transnational History: Ukraine and Recent Ukrainian Historiography.* Budapest: Central European University Press, 2008.
Kaszab, Aladár. "A zsidó jótékonyság hibái és tévedései." *Egyenlőség*, April 16, 1927, 9.
Kelety, Dénes. *A megcsokontított államvasutak.* Budapest: Németh József Könyvkereskedés, 1921.
Keller, Lajos. "A magyar anyavédelem." *Anya- és Csecsemővédelem* 1, no. 1 (1928): 3–11.
———. *Annual Report on the Activities of the Stephania National Association for 1927.* Budapest: Egyesült Nyomda, 1927.
———. *Országos Stefánia Szövetség 10 éves működése: 1915. Június 13–1925. December 31.* Budapest: Egyesült Könyvnyomda, 1926.
———. *Report on the Activities of the Stefánia National Association for 1928.* Budapest: Egyesült Nyomda, 1928.
Kelley, Victoria. "Time, Wear and Maintenance: The Afterlife of Things." In *Writing Material Culture History*, edited by Anne Gerritsen and Geiorgio Riello, 191–97. London: Bloomsbury, 2015.
Kellogg, Vernon. "Paderewski, Pilsudski, and Poland." *World's Work* 38 (May 1919).
———. "In Budapest and Vienna." *New York Times*, March 28, 1920, 2.
Kellogg, Vernon, and Alonzo E. Taylor. *The Food Problem.* New York: Macmillan, 1917.
Kelly, Catriona. *Children's World: Growing Up in Russia, 1890–1991.* New Haven, CT: Yale University Press, 2007.
Kennedy, Denis. "Selling the Distant Other: Humanitarianism and Imagery—Ethical Dilemmas of Humanitarian Action." *Journal of Humanitarian Assistance* 18 (February 28, 2009): 1–25.
"Képek az amerikai gyermeksegélyző akcióról." *Az Érdekes Újság* 9, no. 5 (1921): 4.
Kienitz, Sabine. *Beschädigte Helden: Kriegsinvalidität und Körperbilder, 1914–1923.* Paderborn, Germany: Ferdinand Schöningh, 2008.
Kind-Kovács, Friederike. "Compassion for the Distant Other: Children's Hunger and Humanitarian Relief in Budapest in the Aftermath of WWI." In *Rescuing the Vulnerable: Poverty, Welfare and Social Ties in Nineteenth- and Twentieth-Century Europe*, edited by Beate Althammer, Lutz Raphael, and Tamara Stazic-Wendt, 129–59. New York: Berghahn Books, 2016.

---. "The Great War, the Child's Body and the American Red Cross." *European Review of History* 23, no. 1–2 (2016): 33–62.
---. "The Heroes' Children: Rescuing the Great War's Orphans." *Journal of Modern European History* 19, no. 2 (2021): 183–205. https://journals.sagepub.com/doi/full/10.1177/1611894421992688.
---. "The 'Other' Child Transports: World War I and the Temporary Displacement of Needy Children from Central Europe." *La Revue d'histoire de l'enfance "irrégulière"* 15 (2013): 75–95.
---. "Transatlantic Humanitarianism: Jewish Child Relief in Post-WWI Budapest." In *From the Midwife's Bag to the Patient's File: Public Health in Eastern Europe*, edited by Heike Karge, Friederike Kind-Kovács, and Sara Bernasconi, 125–72. Budapest: Central European University Press, 2017.
Kind-Kovács, Friederike, and Machteld Venken. "Childhood in Times of Political Transformation: An Introduction." *Journal of Modern European History* 19, no. 2 (2021), 1–11. https://journals.sagepub.com/doi/metrics/10.1177/1611894421994710.
Kiss, László. "Egészség és politika—az egészségügyi prevenció Magyarországon a 20. század első felében." *Korall* 17 (2004): 107–37.
Klose, Fabian, ed. *The Emergence of Humanitarian Intervention: Ideas and Practice from the Nineteenth Century to the Present*. Cambridge: Cambridge University Press, 2016.
Klose, Fabian, and Mirjam Thulin, eds. *Humanity: A History of European Concepts in Practice from the Sixteenth Century to the Present*. Göttingen, Germany: Vandenhoeck & Ruprecht, 2016.
Knoch, Habbo, and Benjamin Möckel. "Moral im 20. Jahrhundert. Prolegomena einer zeithistorischen 'Moral History.'" *Zeithistorische Forschungen* 1 (2017): 93–111.
Kogutowicz, Károly. *Budapest kis közlekedési térképe a legújabb villamos jelzésekkel*. Budapest: Magyar Földrajzi Intézet, 1913.
Königin Zita Anstalt. Zentrale für Mutter- und Säuglingsschutz in Ungarn. Budapest: Königin Zita Anstalt, 1918.
Koven, Seth. "Remembering and Dismemberment: Crippled Children, Wounded Soldiers, and the Great War in Great Britain." *American Historical Review* 99, no. 4 (1994): 1167–202.
---. *Slumming: Sexual and Social Politics in Victorian London*. Princeton, NJ: Princeton University Press, 2004.
Krúdy, Gyula. *Liga Gida kalandjai, Hollandiában és a világ egyéb tájain*. Budapest: Országos Gyermekvédő Liga, 1923.
Kučera, Rudolf. *Rationed Life: Science, Everyday Life, and Working-Class Politics in the Bohemian Lands, 1914–1918*. New York: Berghahn Books, 2016.
"Külföldi anyák magyar gyermekekért." *Új Nemzedék* 1, no. 66 (December 16, 1919): 4.
Kun, Béla. *A fiatalkorúak támogatására hivatott jótékonycélú intézmények Magyarországon*. Budapest: Wodianer F. és Fiai Könyvnyomda Műintézete, 1911.
---. *Hadiárvák érdekében szükséges tennivalókról*. Budapest: Országos Gyermekvédő Liga, 1915.
Kurasawa, Fuyuki. "The Making of Humanitarian Visual Icons: On the 1922–1923 Russian Famine as Foundational Event." In *Iconic Power: Materiality and Meaning in Social Life*, edited by Jeffrey C. Alexander, Bernhard Giesen, and Dominik Bartmański, 67–84. Basingstoke, UK: Palgrave Macmillan, 2012.
Kürti, László. *The Remote Borderland: Transylvania in the Hungarian Imagination*. Albany: State University of New York Press, 2014.

Kuzmics, Helmut, and Sabine A. Haring. *Emotion, Habitus und Erster Weltkrieg: soziologische Studien zum militärischen Untergang der Habsburger Monarchie*. Göttingen, Germany: Vandenhoeck & Ruprecht Unipress, 2013.
Ladd-Taylor, Molly. *Mother-Work: Women, Child Welfare, and the State, 1890-1930*. Urbana: University of Illinois Press, 1995.
Lammers, Anna. *Fotografie und Medizin: Von der Glasplatte zur Simulation*. Marburg, Germany: Jonas, 2015.
Langthaler, Ernst. "Food and Nutrition (Austria-Hungary)." In *1914-1918 Online: International Encyclopedia of the First World War*, edited by Ute Daniel, Peter Gatrell, Oliver Janz, Heather Jones, Jennifer Keene, Alan Kramer, and Bill Nasson. Berlin: Freie Universität Berlin, 2016. https://doi.org/10.15463/ie1418.10265.
Last, Murray. "Putting Children First." *Disasters: The Journal of Disaster Studies and Management* 18, no. 3 (1994): 192-202.
Lazaroms, Ilse. "Marked by Violence: Hungarian Jewish Histories in the Wake of the White Terror, 1919-1922." *Zutot: Perspectives on Jewish Culture* 11 (2014): 39-48.
"Legnagyobb öröme." *Budapesti Hírlap* 34, no. 121 (May 24, 1914): 22.
Leikam, Susanne. "Visualizing Hunger in a 'City of Plenty': Bread Line Iconographies in the Aftermath of the 1906 San Francisco Earthquake and Fire." *Amerikastudien/American Studies* 58, no. 4 (2013): 583-606.
Lévai, Ödön. "Az elhanyagolt gyermekegészség." *Budapesti Hírlap* 38, no. 153 (July 4, 1918): 8.
Liber, Endre. "Budapest a menekültügy szolgálatában." In *A nagy vihar hajótöröttei: Hivatalos feljegyzések, tanulmányok és más írások a háború és a pusztitó béke idejéről*, edited by Béla Kádár and Vilmos Sarbó, 13-130. Budapest: Wodianer, 1927.
Lukács, Sarolta. "Az Amerkai Vöröskereszt anya- és csecsemővédelem akciójának szociális munkássága." In *Az Amerikai Vöröskereszt anya- és csecsemővédő akciója Magyarországon. Oktober a. 1921-Június 30-1922*, edited by János Bókay, 41-42. Budapest: American Red Cross Action for Protection of Mothers and Babies, 1923.
Lydon, Jane. *Photography, Humanitarianism, Empire*. London: Bloomsbury, 2016.
MacMillan, Margaret. *Paris 1919: Six Months That Changed the World*. New York: Random House, 2003.
Macrae, Norman. *John Von Neumann: The Scientific Genius Who Pioneered the Modern Computer, Game Theory, Nuclear Deterrence, and Much More*. New York: Pantheon Books, 1992.
Madzsar, József. *Az anya- és csecsemővédelem országos szervezése: a Stefánia Szövetség programjának és alapszabályainak tervezete*. Budapest: Székesfővárosi Házinyomda, 1915.
———. *Mit akar a Stefánia-Szövetség?* Budapest: Pfeiffer, 1916.
"Magyar Children Cry as 'Uncle Pedlow' Goes." *New York Times*, July 2, 1922, 7.
"Magyar gyerekek munkája Londonban." *Magyarság* 6, no. 158 (July 17, 1925): 10.
"Magyar gyerekek nyaraltatása." *Pesti Hírlap* 11, no. 180 (August 4, 1918): 1.
"Magyar gyermekek nyaraltatása a tengerparton." *Az Érdekes Újság* 6, no. 31 (August 8, 1918): 2.
Magyarics, Tamás. "American-Hungarian Relations in the 1920s." *Hungarian Studies* 9, no. 1-2 (1994): 163-71.
Mahood, Linda. *Feminism and Voluntary Action: Eglantyne Jebb and Save the Children 1876-1928*. New York: Palgrave Macmillan, 2009.
Mahood, Linda, and Vic Satzewich. "The Save the Children Fund and the Russian Famine of 1921-23: Claims and Counter-Claims about Feeding 'Bolshevik' Children." *Journal of Historical Sociology* 22 (2009): 55-83.
Malkki, Liisa H. "Refugees and Exile: From 'Refugee Studies' to the National Order of Things." *Annual Review of Anthropology* 24 (1995): 495-523.

Mann, Leon. "Queue Culture: The Waiting Line as a Social System." *American Journal of Sociology* 75, no. 3 (1969): 340–54.
"Many Weep at Hoover War Dinner." *New York Times*, December 30, 1920, 8.
Marien, Mary Warner. *Photography: A Cultural History*. London: Laurence King, 2010.
Markowska-Kuźma, Sylwia. "From 'Drop of Milk' to 'Bureaus for Mothers': Infant Care and Visions of Medical Motherhood in the Early 20th Century Polish Part of the Habsburg Empire." In *Medicine within and between the Habsburg and Ottoman Empires, 18th–19th Centuries*, edited by Teodora Daniela Sechel, 131–47. Bochum, Germany: Dr. Dieter Winkler, 2011.
Marshall, Dominique. "Children's Rights and Children's Action in International Relief and Domestic Welfare: The Work of Herbert Hoover between 1914 and 1950." *Journal of the History of Childhood and Youth* 1, no. 3 (2008): 351–88.
———. "Humanitarian Sympathy for Children in Times of War and the History of Children's Rights, 1919–1959." In *Children and War: A Historical Anthology*, edited by James Allen Marten, 184–200. New York: New York University Press, 2002.
Marten, James, ed. *Children and War: A Historical Anthology*. New York: New York University Press, 2002.
———. "Children and War." In *The Routledge History of Childhood in the Western World*, ed. Paula S. Fass, 142–57. Milton Park, UK: Routledge, 2013.
Marten, James, and Mischa Honeck. "More Than Victims: Framing the History of Modern Childhood and War." In *War and Childhood in the Era of the Two World Wars*, edited by Mischa Honeck and James Marten, 1–14. Cambridge: Cambridge University Press (Publications of the German Historical Institute), 2019.
Martschukat, Jürgen, and Bryant Simon, eds. *Food, Power, and Agency*. London: Bloomsbury, 2017.
Marung, Steffi, Matthias Middell, and Uwe Müller. "Territorialisierung in Ostmitteleuropa bis zum Ersten Weltkrieg." In *Handbuch einer transnationalen Geschichte Ostmitteleuropas*, edited by Frank Hadler and Matthias Middell, 37–130. Göttingen, Germany: Vandenhoeck & Ruprecht, 2017.
Matauschek, Isabella. *Lokales Leid-Globale Herausforderung: Die Verschickung österreichischer Kinder nach Dänemark und in die Niederland im Anschluss an den Ersten Weltkrieg*. Vienna: Böhlau, 2018.
Maza, Sarah. "The Kids Aren't All Right: Historians and the Problem of Childhood." *American Historical Review* 125, no. 4 (2020): 1261–85.
McCagg, William O. *A History of Habsburg Jews, 1670–1918*. Bloomington: Indiana University Press, 1989.
McDonald, Hortense. "Generation in Peril: 2,500,000 Children in Central Europe Starving or Underfed, Require Prompt Aid." *New York Times*, October 31, 1920, XX8.
McDonald, Michelle Craig. "Transatlantic Consumption." In *The Oxford Handbook of the History of Consumption*, edited by Frank Trentmann, 111–26. Oxford: Oxford University Press, 2012.
McElroy, Robert W. *Morality and American Foreign Policy: The Role of Ethics in International Affairs*. Princeton, NJ: Princeton Legacy Library, 1992.
McSorley, Kevin. *War and the Body: Militarization, Practice and Experience*. London: Routledge, 2012.
Meckel, Richard A. *Urban Schools and the Protection and Promotion of Child Health, 1870–1930*. New Brunswick, NJ: Rutgers University Press, 2013.
Members of the American Child Welfare Mission in Hungary. "Child Feeding in Hungary." *American Relief Administration Bulletin* 2, no. 5 (December 1, 1920): 31–33.

"Menekültek asztala." *Budapesti Hírlap* 36, no. 273 (October 1, 1916): 18.
"Miért olyan sok a vagonlakó Csonkamagyarországon?" *Melléklet az Erdélyi Hírek* 1, no. 41 (November 14, 1920).
Minka, Czóbel. "A hontalan," *Új Idők* 28 (April 16, 1922): 307.
"Misery Tales from Europe." *New York Times*, October 17, 1920, 1.
Miskolczy, Erle. "Lélekmentés." *Budapesti Hírlap* 56, no. 274 (November 29, 1936): 11 1–12.
Mócsy, István. *The Effects of World War I: The Uprooted: Hungarian Refugees and Their Impact on Hungary's Domestic Politics, 1918–1921*. New York: Columbia University Press, 1983.
Motta, Guiseppe. *Less Than Nations: Central-Eastern European Minorities after WWI*. Cambridge: Cambridge Scholars, 2013.
"Mr. Davison on the Situation in Europe." *Red Cross Bulletin*, April 26, 1920, 5.
Muckle, James. "Saving the Russian Children: Materials in the Archive of the Save the Children Fund Relating to Eastern Europe in 1920–1923." *Slavonic and East European Review* 68, no. 3 (1990): 507–11.
Mühlbeck, Károly. "Az amerikai misszió táplálkoztatási póttanfolyama." *Új Idők* 25, no. 25 (December 17, 1919), 477.
———. "A külföld a magyar gyermekekért." *Új Idők* 26, no. 11 (1920): 217.
Mulley, Clare. *The Woman Who Saved the Children: A Biography of Eglantyne Jebb*. Oxford: One World, 2009.
Murdoch, Lydia. *Imagined Orphans: Poor Families, Child Welfare, and Contested Citizenship in London*. New Brunswick, NJ: Rutgers University Press, 2007.
"Napihírek: Temesvárról kiutasított magyar családok." *Budapesti Hírlap* 40, no. 22 (January 25, 1920): 1.
"The National Collection of the European Relief Council." *American Relief Administration Bulletin* 2, no. 15 (August 1, 1921): 10.
National "Hands Off Russia" Committee. *Russian Famine: Mr. Hoover's Sinister Role in Hungary*. London: National "Hands Off Russia" Committee, 1921.
Naumann, Katja. "Verflechtung durch Internationalisierung: Die ostmitteleuropäische Partizipation an Inernationalen Organisationen." In *Handbuch einer transnationalen Geschichte Ostmitteleuropas: Band I. Von der Mitte des 19. Jhd. Bis zum Ersten Weltkrieg*, edited by Frank Hadler and Matthias Middell, 325–402. Göttingen, Germany: Vandenhoeck & Ruprecht, 2017.
"Ne legyen többé nélkülöző magyar, ne legyen többé megnyomoritott Magyarország." *Magyarország* 28, no. 48 (March 5, 1921): 2.
"Népjólét." *Pesti Hírlap* 39, no. 159 (June 24, 1917): 1.
"Népjóléti Központba szervezik Budapest jótékonysági akcióját." *Az Est* 7, no. 160 (June 9, 1916): 4.
"Népjóléti miniszterium." *Jogtudományi Közlöny* 23 (June 10, 1917): 218.
"Népnevelés a gép században." *Budapesti Hírlap* 58, no. 18 (January 23, 1938): 3.
"Nestlé gyermekliszt." *Budapesti Hírlap* 36, no. 257 (September 15, 1916): 14.
Neugebauer, Vilmos. *Az Országos Gyermekvédő Liga alapszabályai*. Budapest: Egyesült Könyv. és Kiadó, 1926.
Nevinson, Henry Wood. "The Black Outlook in Europe." *Manchester Guardian*, March 8, 1920, 14.
"1920. Június 14-én Budapest különböző pályaudvarain marhakocsikban tengetik életük." *A Melléklet az Erdélyi Hírek*, June 19, 1920.
Nolan, Mary. *The Transatlantic Century: Europe and America, 1890–2010*. Cambridge: Cambridge University Press, 2012.

O'Connor, Kaori. "Anthropology, Archaeology, History and the Material Culture of Lyra." In *Writing Material Culture History*, edited by Anne Gerritsen and Geiorgio Riello, 73–92. London: Bloomsbury, 2015.
"1,000,000 Children Saved by America." *New York Times*, November 16, 1919, 20.
Orgad, Shani. "Visualizers of Solidarity: Organizations Politics in Humanitarian and International Development NGOs." *Visual Communication* 12 (2013): 295–314.
"Országos kenyérjegy-rendszer." *Budapesti Hírlap* 35, no. 349 (December 15, 1915): 11.
Országos Stefánia Szövetség. *Jelentés a Stefánia-Szövetség működéséről, Jun. 13 1915–Jun. 15 1917*. Budapest: Pfeifer Ferdinánd bizománya, 1917.
"'Our' Godchildren: Who They Are and Where They Live." *Record of the Save the Children Fund* 1, no. 3 (December 1920): 45.
Panyai, Panikos, and Virdee Pippa. *Refugees and the End of Empire: Imperial Collapse and Forced Migration in the Twentieth Century*. Basingstoke, UK: Macmillan, 2011.
Pastor, Peter. "Hungary in World War I: The End of Historical Hungary." *Hungarian Studies Review* 28, no. 1–2 (2001): 163–84.
Patenaude, Bertrand M. *The Big Show in Bololand: The American Relief Expedition to Soviet Russia in the Famine of 1921*. Stanford, CA: Stanford University Press, 2002.
Pathé, Anne-Marie, and Fabien Théofilakis, eds. *Wartime Captivity in the 20th Century: Archives, Stories, Memories*. New York: Berghahn Books, 2016.
Paul, Vincent C. *The Politics of Hunger: Allied Blockade of Germany, 1915–1919*. Columbus: Ohio University Press, 1985.
Paulmann, Johannes, ed. *Humanitarianism and Media: 1900 to the Present*. New York: Berghahn Books, 2018.
Pearson, Raymond. "Hungary: A State Partitioned, a Nation Dismembered." In *Europe and Ethnicity: The First World War and Contemporary Ethnic Conflict*, edited by Seamus Dunn and T. G. Fraser, 85–106. London: Routledge, 1996.
Perényi, Roland. "Urban Places, Criminal Spaces: Police and Crime in Fin de Siècle Budapest." *Hungarian Historical Review* 1, no. 1–2 (2012): 134–65.
Peterecz, Zoltán. "Hungary and the League of Nations: A Forced Marriage." In *Remaking Central Europe: The League of Nations and the Former Habsburg Lands*, edited by Peter Becker and Natasha Wheatley, 145–165. Oxford: Oxford University Press, 2020.
Petneki, Katalin, and Kató Petrich. *Gyermekvonat Angliába. Egy budai kislány leveli (1920-1921)*. Budapest: Európa Könyvkiadó, 2019.
Petrichevich Horváth, Emil. *Jelentés az Országos Menekültügyi Hivatal négy évi működéséről*. Budapest: Pesti Nyomda, 1924.
Pettkó-Szandtner, Aladár. *A huszonötéves állami gyermekvédelem emlékkönyve*. Budapest: Népjóléti Minisztérium, 1928.
———. "Anya- és csecsemővédelem." *Anya- és csecsemővédelem* 1, no. 1 (January 16, 1928): 1–2.
———. *Child Protection by the Royal Hungarian State*. Budapest: Magyar Királyi Népjóléti és Munkaügyi Minisztérium, 1926.
Piana, Francesca. "The Dangers of 'Going Native': George Montandon in Siberia and the International Committee of the Red Cross, 1919–1922." *Contemporary European History* 25, no. 2 (2016): 254–74.
———."Dr. Ruth A. Parmelee: Witnessing the Armenian Genocide and (Re)negotiating the Self." *Papiers d'actualité* 5 (June 2005): 1–6.
Piattoeva, Nelli, Iveta Silova, and Zsuzsa Millei. "Remembering Childhoods, Rewriting (Post) Socialist Lives." In *Childhood and Schooling in (Post)Socialist Societies: Memories of Everyday Life*, edited by Iveta Silova, Nelli Piattoeva, Zsuzsa Millei, 1–18. Cham, Switzerland: Palgrave Macmillan, 2017.

Piller, Elisabeth. "German Child Distress, US Humanitarian Aid and Revisionist Politics, 1918–1924." *Journal of Contemporary History* 51, no. 3 (2016): 453–86.
Pirquet, Clemens Peter. *An Outline of the Pirquet System of Nutrition.* Philadelphia: Saunders, 1922.
"Plan Found to Save Starving Children, Million-Dollar Drive on Behalf of 100,000 Suffering Little Ones in Hungary." *New York Times,* September 30, 1919, 16.
Porter, Theodore. *The Rise of Statistical Thinking, 1820–1900.* Princeton, NJ: Princeton University Press, 1986.
Pottle, Emery, and Dana Durand. "Conditions in Hungary." *American Relief Administration Bulletin* 19 (July 25, 1919): 29–35.
Pringle, J. C. *British Social Services: The Nation's Appeal to the Housewife and Her Response.* London: Longmans, Green, 1933.
———. "Foreword." In *Through Hungarian Eyes: Impressions of Juvenile Social Work in England,* edited by Julia Eva Vajkai, 7–9. London: Weardale, 1929.
Proctor, Tammy M. "An American Enterprise? British Participation in US Food Relief Programmes (1914–1923)." *First World War Studies* 5, no. 1 (2014): 29–42.
———. *Civilians in a World at War, 1914–1918.* New York: New York University Press, 2010.
Prohászka, Ottokár. *Az Országos Gyermekvédő Liga, 14 évi Április hó 26-án tartott évi közgyűlésen és Az 1914-ik évi gyermeknap alkalmából segédkező hölgyek névsora.* Budapest: Márkus Samu Könyvnyomdája, 1914.
Puskás, Tünde, and Aleksandra Ålund. "Ethnicity: The Complexity of Boundary Creation and Social Differentiation." In *International Migration and Ethnic Relations: Critical Perspectives,* edited by Magnus Dahlstedt and Anders Neergaard, 13–37. New York: Routledge, 2015.
"Pusztit a spanyol járvány." *Pesti Napló* 69, no. 227 (September 27, 1918): 5.
Rabinov, Paul, ed. *The Michel Foucault Reader.* New York: Pantheon Books, 1984.
Rachamimov, Alon. "'Female Generals' and 'Siberial Angels': Aristocratic Nurses and the Austro-Hungarian POW Relief." In *Gender and War in Twentieth-Century Eastern Europe,* edited by Nancy M. Wingfield and Maria Bucur, 23–46. Bloomington: Indiana University Press, 2006.
Ramsbrock, Annelie, Annette Vowinkel, and Malte Zierenberg. "Bildagenten und Bildformate: Ordnungen fotografischer Sichtbarkeit." In *Fotografien im 20. Jahrhundert. Verbreitung und Vermittlung,* edited by Annelie Ramsbrock, Annette Vowinckel, and Malte Zierenberg, 7–20. Göttingen, Germany: Wallstein, 2013.
Rappaport, Helen. "Eglantyne Jebb." In *Encyclopedia of Women Reformers.* Vol. 1. Santa Barbara, CA: ABC-Clio, 2001.
"Relief Problems in Hungary, First Reports on Work Being Done by Red Cross in Cooperation with Other American Agencies." *Red Cross Bulletin* IV (February 8, 1920): 7.
"Revolt in Budapest; Bela Kun Shot At." *New York Times,* June 28, 1919, 2.
Riis, Jacob A. *How the Other Half Lives.* New York: Scribner, 1890.
Ripka, Ferenc. "Emlékezés." In *A nagy vihar hajótöröttei: Hivatalos feljegyzések, tanulmányok és más irások a háború és a pusztitó béke idejéről,* edited by Béla Kádár and Vilmos Szabó, 8–9. Budapest: Wodianer Nyomda, 1927.
Rivière, Antoine. "'Special Decisions' Children Born as the Result of German Rape and Handed Over to Public Assistance during the Great War (1914–1918)." In *Rape in Wartime,* edited by Raphaelle Branche and Fabrice Virgili, 189–206. Basingstoke, UK: Palgrave Macmillan, 2012.
Rodogno, Davide. *Against Massacre: Humanitarian Interventions in the Ottoman Empire.* Princeton, NJ: Princeton University Press, 2011.

———. "The American Red Cross and the International Committee of the Red Cross: Humanitarian Politics and Policies in Asia Minor and Greece (1922–1923)." *First World War Studies* 5, no. 1 (2014): 83–99.

Roehrkohl, Anne. *Hungerblockade und Heimatfront: die kommunale Lebensmittelversorgung in Westfalen während des Ersten Weltkrieges*. Stuttgart: F. Steiner, 1991.

Romsics, Ignác. *Hungary in the Twentieth Century*. 2nd ed. Budapest: Corvina kiadó, 2010.

Rooke, Patricia T., and Rudy L. Schnell. "Uncramping Child Life: International Children's Organizations, 1914–1939." In *International Health Organizations and Movements*, edited by Paul Weindling, 176–202. Cambridge: Cambridge University Press, 1995.

Roszkowski, Wojciech, and Jan Kofman, eds. *Biographical Dictionary of Central and Eastern Europe in the Twentieth Century*. London: Routledge, 2008.

Rothschild, Joseph. *East Central Europe between the Two World Wars*. Seattle: University of Washington Press, 1974.

Rottenbiller, Fülöp. *Az Országos Gyermekvédő Liga harminc évi működése, 1906–1936*. Budapest: Fővárosi Nyomda Rt., 1936.

Rubinek, Gyula. *Magyarország gazdasági térképekben*. Budapest: Pallas Nyomda, 1920.

Rürüp, Miriam. "Lives in Limbo: Statelessness after Two World Wars." *Bulletin of the German Historical Institute* 49 (Fall 2011): 113–34.

Sachs, Miranda. "Children Remember the German Occupation of Northern France." In *France in an Era of Global War, 1914–1945*, edited by Alison Carrol and Ludivine Broch, 13–30. New York: Palgrave Macmillan, 2014.

Sargent, Thomas J. "The Ends of Four Big Inflations." In *Inflation: Causes and Effects*, edited by Robert E. Hall, 41–98. Chicago: University of Chicago Press, 1982.

Sasson, Tehila. "From Empire to Humanity: The Russian Famine and the Imperial Origins of International Humanitarianism." *Journal of British Studies* 55 (July 2016): 519–37.

"Save the Children's Fund: The Pope's Letter." *New York Times*, September 24, 1919, 8.

Sayward, Amy L. "Food and Nutrition: Expertise across International Epistemic Communities and Organizations, 1919–63." In *Organizing the 20th-Century World: International Organization and the Emergence of International Public Administration, 1920–60*, edited by Karen Gram-Skjoldager, Haakon A. Ikonomou, and Torsten Kahlert, 109–25. London: Bloomsbury, 2020.

Scaglia, Ilaria. *The Emotions of Internationalism: Feeling International Cooperation in the Alps in the Interwar Period*. Oxford: Oxford University Press, 2020.

Scarry, Elaine. *Austria-Hungary: The Polyglot Empire*. New York: Frederick A. Stokes, 1917.

———. *The Body in Pain: The Making and Unmaking of the World*. New York: Oxford University Press, 1985.

Schierbrand, Wolf von. "The Food Situation in Austria-Hungary." *North American Review* 205, no. 734 (1917): 46–52.

Schulte, Dagmar. "Conclusions, Reflections and Outlooks: Case Studies and Their Contribution to a Holistic History of Social Work." In *Need and Care—Glimpses into the Beginnings of Eastern Europe's Professional Welfare*, edited by Kurt Schilde and Dagmar Schulte, 257–92. Opladen, Germany: Barbara Budrich, 2005.

Schultheiss, Katrin. *Bodies and Souls: Politics and the Professionalization of Nursing in France, 1880–1922*. Cambridge, MA: Harvard University Press, 2001.

Schwartz, Agatha, ed. *Gender and Modernity in Central Europe: The Austro-Hungarian Monarchy and Its Legacy*. Ottawa, Canada: University of Ottawa Press, 2010.

———. *Shifting Voices: Feminist Thought and Women's Writing in Fin-de-Siècle Austria and Hungary*. Québec: McGill-Queens University Press, 2008.

Selick, Patricia. "Responding to Children Affected by Armed Conflict: A Case Study of Save the Children Fund (1919–1999)." PhD diss., University of Bradford, 2001.
"Serious Food Situation in Hungary: Ill Treatment of Jews." *Manchester Guardian*, August 11, 1919, 8.
Sharp, Ingrid, and Matthew Stibbe, eds. *Aftermaths of War: Women's Movements and Female Activists, 1918–1923*. Leiden: Brill, 2011.
Sidgwick, Ethel. "Foreword." In *Education for Life: The Training of the Girl Worker*, edited by Julia Eva Vajkai, v. London: Weardale, 1927.
Siklós, András. *A Habsburg birodalom felbomlása, 1918*. Budapest: Kossuth, 1987.
Silverstein, Sara. "Reinventing International Health in East Central Europe: The League of Nations, State Sovereignty, and Universal Health." In *Remaking Central Europe: The League of Nations and the Former Habsburg Lands*, edited by Peter Becker and Natasha Wheatley, 71–98. Oxford: Oxford University Press, 2020.
Singer, Hedwig. "Mothers' and Babies' Breakfast Action in Hungary." *American Relief Administration Bulletin* 2, no. 19 (December 1921): 34–38.
Skinner, Rob, and Alan Lester. "Humanitarianism and Empire: New Research Agendas." *Journal of Imperial and Commonwealth History* 40, no. 5 (2012): 729–47.
Slim, Hugo. "Editorial: Disasters." *Disasters: The Journal of Disaster Studies and Management* 18, no. 3 (1994): 189–99.
———. "Relief Agencies and Moral Standing in War: Principles of Humanity, Neutrality, Impartiality and Solidarity." *Development in Practice* 7, no. 4 (1997): 342–52.
Sluga, Glenda. *Internationalism in the Age of Nationalism*. Philadelphia: University of Pennsylvania Press, 2013.
Sluga, Glenda, and Patricia Clavin, eds. *Internationalisms: A Twentieth-Century History*. Cambridge: Cambridge University Press, 2016.
Smith, Armstrong. "Budapest Revisited." *Record of the Save the Children Fund* 1, no. 17 (July 15, 1921): 264.
Smith, Leonard, Stéphane Audoin-Rouzeau, and Annette Becker. *France and the Great War, 1914–1918*. Cambridge: Cambridge University Press, 2003.
Sömjén, László. "Az állampolgarsági opció." *Budapesti Hírlap* 42, no. 132 (June 11, 1922): 8.
Sontag, Susan. "Looking at War." *New Yorker*, December 9, 2002.
———. "On Photography." In *Communication in History: Technology, Culture, and Society*, edited by David J. Crowley and Paul Heyer, 174–78. New York: Longman, 1999.
———. *Regarding the Pain of Others*. New York: Farrar, Straus and Giroux, 2003.
Starkey, Pat. Review of *Child, Nation, Race and Empire: Child Rescue Discourse, England, Canada and Australia, 1850–1915*, by Shurlee Swain and Margot Hillel. *Reviews in History*, review no. 1033 (February 2011). http://www.history.ac.uk/reviews/review/1033.
"Starvation Seen in Film." *New York Times*, January 10, 1920, 0.
"The Starving Children of Hungary, Babies Dying by Hundreds." *Continental Times*, June 23, 1919.
"A Statement by General Pershing at the Invisible Guest Dinner, 29 December 1920." *American Relief Administration Bulletin* 2, no. 8 (January 15, 1921): 2.
Stearns, Peter. "The Emotional Life of Children." In *The Routledge History of Childhood in the Western World*, edited by Paula S. Fass, 158–73. Milton Park, UK: Routledge, 2013.
Stefánia Szövetség az Anyák és Csecsemők Védelmére. *Országos Magyar anya- és csecsemővédelem központi intézet szervezeti szabályzata*. Budapest: Pesti Könyvnyomda Részvénytársaság, 1917.
Stöhr, Hermann. *So half Amerika: Die Auslandshilfe der Vereinigten Staaten 1812–1930*. Stettin, Prussia: Ökumenischer Verlag, 1936.

Straka, Donald E. "Peace and Reform: The Attempts of the Meinl Group to Preserve the Habsburg Monarchy, 1917–1918." Master's thesis, Rice University, 1968.
Szana, Sándor. "A gyermekkor közegészségügyének bajai." *Orvosi Hetilap* 61, no. 15 (April 15, 1917): 206–8.
"Szegény gyermekek nyaralása." *Budapesti Hírlap* 10, no. 178 (June 30, 1890): 30.
"Szegény gyermekek nyaralása," *Budapesti Hírlap* 23, no. 132 (May 15, 1903): 10.
"Szegénység és jótékonyság." *Pesti Napló* 54 (May 27, 1903): 11.
Szénásy, József. "Országos Stefánia Szövetség (1915–1941)." *Orvosi Hetilap* 135, no. 6–9 (February 1994): 415–17.
Szendy, Károly. "Egy nagy angol jótékonyság szervezet Budapesti munkaiskoláinak kiállitása." *Pesti Hírlap* 59, no. 274 (December 2, 1937): 6.
Surface, Frank M., and Raymond L. Bland. *American Food in the World War and Reconstruction Period: Operations of the Organizations under the Direction of Herbert Hoover, 1914 to 1924*. Stanford, CA: Stanford University Press, 1931.
Szapor, Judith. *Hungarian Women's Activism in the Wake of the First World War: From Rights to Revanche*. London: Bloomsbury, 2017.
Szűts, István Gergely. "Optálási jegyzőkönyvek mint a trianoni menekültkérdés forrásai." *Századok* 6 (2018): 1236–60.
———. "Vasutas vagonlakók és a MÁV menekültpolitikája, 1918–1924." *Múltunk* 4, no. 194 (2012): 89–112.
Tábori, Kornél. *Egy halálraítélt ország borzalmaiból*. Budapest: Kultúra, 1920.
———. *Háborús album: a világháború történelme képekben*. Budapest: Pesti Napló, 1915.
"Tájékoztató a magyar anya- és csecsemővédelem országos szervezetéről." *Anya- és csecsemővédelem* 1, no. 1 (January 16, 1928): 33–34.
Tanielian, S. Melanie. *The Charity of War: Famine, Humanitarian Aid, and World War I in the Middle East*. Stanford, CA: Stanford University Press, 2017.
"Terjed a spanyol influenza." *Pesti Napló* 69, no. 221 (September 21, 1918): 7.
Terry, Prentiss N. "Hungary in the Third Peace Winter." *American Relief Administration Bulletin* 2, no. 11 (April 1, 1921): 40–42.
Teuteberg, Hans-Jürgen. "Food Provisioning on the German Home Front, 1914–1918." In *Food and War in Twentieth Century Europe*, edited by Ina Zweiniger-Bargielowska, Rachel Duffett, and Alain Drouard, 59–72. Burlington, VT: Ashgate, 2011.
Thomas, T. Nigel, and Dusan Babac. *Armies in the Balkans 1914–18*. London: Osprey, 2012.
Thompson, T. Jack. *Light on Darkness? Missionary Photography of Africa in the Nineteenth and Early Twentieth Centuries*. Grand Rapids, MI: Eerdmans, 2012.
Thoms, Ulrike. "Hunger—ein Bedürfnis zwischen Politik, Physiologie und persönlicher Erfahrung (Deutschland, 19. und 20. Jahrhundert)." *Body Politics: Zeitschrift für Körpergeschichte* 3, no. 5 (2015): 167–68.
Thorpe, Julie. "Displacing Empire: Refugee Welfare, National Activism and State Legitimacy in Austria-Hungary in the First World War." In *Refugees and the End of Empire: Imperial Collapse and Forced Migration in the Twentieth Century*, edited by Panikos Panyai and Pippa Virdee, 102–26. Basingstoke, UK: Palgrave Macmillan, 2011.
"To Aid 2,500,000 Children." *New York Times*, September 23, 1920, 7.
Tomsics, Emőke. "Tábori Kornél és a szociofotó," *Fotóművészet* 49, no. 3–4 (2006).
Tooze, Adam. *The Deluge: The Great War and the Remaking of Global Order 1916–1931*. New York: Penguin Books, 2014.
Treitel, Corinna. "Max Rubner and the Biopolitics of Rational Nutrition." *Central European History* 41, no. 1 (2008): 1–25.

"Trianoni emlékmű: avatás huszadikán," *Magyar Nemzet*, August 5, 2020, https://magyarnemzet.hu/belfold/trianoni-emlekmu-avatas-huszadikan-8475969/.
"Tüdővész és egyéb nyavalyák pusztitják a kurzus állami menhelybe jutott protetárgyermekeket." *Új Előre* 18, no. 3645 (September 6, 1922): 6.
Turda, Marius. *Eugenics and Nation in Early 20th Century Hungary*. New York: Palgrave Macmillan, 2014.
———, ed. *The History of East-Central European Eugenics, 1900–1945: Sources and Commentaries*. London: Bloomsbury, 2015.
"The Typhus Epidemic in Central Europe." *International Conciliation* no. 160 (March 1921): 117–19.
Udvarhelyi, Éva Tessza. "'You People Would Keep on Dwelling': Twentieth-Century State Responses to Homelessness in Hungary from Above and Below." *Journal of Urban History* 41, no. 4 (July 2015): 693–710.
Umbrai, Laura. "A hatósági kislakás-építés története Budapesten (1870–1948)." PhD diss., Eötvös Loránd University, 2007.
"Unheated, Wet and Dreary: 'Hungary.'" *Record of the Save the Children Fund* 1, no. 7 (March 1, 1921), 121.
United Nations. *Geneva Declaration of the Rights of the Child*. Adapted by the Fifth Assembly of the League of Nations, Geneva, September 26, 1924, http://www.un-documents.net/gdrc1924.htm.
"US Peace Treaty with Hungary." Budapest, August 29, 1921. World War I Document Archive. Last modified May 20, 2009. https://wwi.lib.byu.edu/index.php/US_Peace_Treaty_with_Hungary.
Vajkai, Julia. "The Budapest Work-Schools: Some Secondary Results." *The World's Children* 5, no. 9 (June 1925), 159–60.
———. *Child Saving and Child Training: The Budapest Scheme*. London: World's Children, 1926.
———. *Education for Life: The Training of the Girl Worker*. London: Weardale, 1927.
———. *Népnevelés a gép századában*. Budapest: Studium Főbizománya, 1938.
———. *Social Adjustment through the Junior Red Cross*. Geneva: Save the Children Union, 1929.
———. "A tétlen serdülők problémája." *Budapesti Hírlap* 58, no. 18 (January 23, 1938), 92–93.
———. *Through Hungarian Eyes: Impressions of Juvenile Social Work in England*. London: Weardale, 1929.
Vajkai, Rozsi. "In the Slums of Budapest. Saving the Children." *The World's Children* 7, no. 9 (June 1927): 131–33.
Vari, Alexander. "Re-territorializing the 'Guilty City': Nationalist and Right-Wing Attempts to Nationalize Budapest during the Interwar Period." *Journal of Contemporary History* 47 no. 4 (2012): 709–33.
Vay, Gáborné, and Márta Zichy. *Az Országos Gyermekvédő Liga ismertetése*. Budapest: Magyarországi Nőegyesületek Szövetsége, 1911.
Veit, Helen Zoe. *Modern Food, Moral Food: Self-Control, Science, and the Rise of Modern American Eating in the Early Twentieth Century*. Chapel Hill: University of North Carolina Press, 2013.
Vernon, James. *Hunger: A Modern History*. Cambridge, MA: Harvard University Press, 2007.
Vittachi, Varindra T. *Between the Guns: Children as a Zone of Peace*. London: Hodder and Stoughton, 1993.
Vowinkel, Annette. *Agenten der Bilder: Fotografisches Handeln im 20. Jahrhundert*. Göttingen, Germany: Wallstein, 2016.
Wank, Solomon. "The Habsburg Empire." In *After Empire: Multiethnic Societies and Nation-Building: The Soviet Union and the Russian, Ottoman, and Habsburg Empires*, edited by Karen Barkley and Mark von Hagen, 45–57. Boulder, CO: Westview, 1997.

Wargelin, Clifford F. "A High Price for Bread: The First Treaty of Brest-Litovsk and the Break-up of Austria-Hungary, 1917–1918." *International History Review* 19, no. 4 (1997): 757–88.

Watenpaugh, Keith David. *Bread from Stones: The Middle East and the Making of Modern Humanitarianism*. Oakland: University of California Press, 2015.

———. "The League of Nations' Rescue of Armenian Genocide Survivors and the Making of Modern Humanitarianism, 1920–1927." *American Historical Review* 115, no. 5 (2010): 1315–39.

Watson, Alexander. *Ring of Steel: Germany and Austria-Hungary in World War I*. New York: Basic Books, 2014.

Watson, Cameron J. "Ethnic Conflict and the League of Nations." *Hungarian Studies* 9, no. 1–2 (1994): 173–80.

Weardale, Lord. "The To-Morrow of Society." *Record of the Save the Children Fund* 1, no. 3 (December 1920): 33–36.

Weindling, Paul. "From Sentiment to Science—Children's Relief Organizations and the Problem of Malnutrition in Interwar Europe." *Disasters: The Journal of Disaster Studies and Management* 18, no. 3 (1994): 203–12.

———. *Healthcare in Private and Public from the Early Modern Period to 2000*. New York: Routledge, 2015.

———, ed. *International Health Organisations and Movements, 1918–1939*. Cambridge: Cambridge University Press, 1995.

Weinreb, Alice A. "Embodying German Suffering: Rethinking Popular Hunger during the Hunger Years (1945–1949)." *Body Politics: Zeitschrift für Körpergeschichte* 2, no. 4 (2014): 468–88.

———. *Modern Hungers: Food and Power in Twentieth-Century Germany*. Oxford: Oxford University Press, 2017.

Weir, Lorna. *Pregnancy, Risk and Biopolitics: On the Threshold of the Living Subject*. New York: Routledge, 2006.

Wells, Karen. "The Melodrama of Being a Child: NGO Representations of Poverty." *Visual Communication* 12, no. 3 (2013): 277–93.

Wendland, Anna Veronika. "Ostmitteleuropäische Städte als Arenen der Verhandlung nationaler, imperialer und lokaler Projekte." In *Vergessene Vielfalt: Territorialität und Internationalisierung in Ostmitteleuropa seit der Mitte des 19. Jahrhunderts*, edited by Steffi Marung and Katja Naumann, 108–35. Göttingen, Germany: Vandenhoeck & Ruprecht, 2014.

Westerman, Thomas D. "Touring Occupied Belgium: American Humanitarians at 'Work' and 'Leisure' (1914–1917)." *First World War Studies* 5, no. 1 (2014): 43–53.

Wiegand, Karl H. von. "Exodus from Hungary: 100,000 Refugees Fleeing from Roumanian Border," *Washington Post*, September 5, 1916, 1.

Wieters, Heike. *The NGO Care and Food Aid from America, 1945–1980: "Showered with Kindness"?* Manchester: Manchester University Press, 2017.

Wilkinson, Iain. "The Provocation of the Humanitarian Social Imaginary." *Visual Communication* 12, no. 3 (2013): 261–76.

Wingfield, Nancy, and Maria Bucur, eds. *Gender and War in Twentieth-Century Eastern Europe*. Bloomington: Indiana University Press, 2006.

Winkler, Martina. *Kindheitsgeschichte. Eine Einführung*. Göttingen, Germany: Vandenhoeck & Ruprecht, 2017.

Winter, Jay. "Introduction: The Practices of Metropolitan Life in Wartime." In *Capital Cities at War: Paris, London, Berlin 1914–1919*. Vol. 2, edited by Jay Winter and Jean-Louis Robert, 1–20. Cambridge: Cambridge University Press, 1997.

———. "Paris, London, Berlin 1914–1919: Capital Cities at War." In *Capital Cities at War: Paris, London, Berlin 1914–1919.* Vol. 1, edited by Jay Winter and Jean-Louis Robert, 3–24. Cambridge: Cambridge University Press, 1997.
Winter, Jay, and Jean-Louis Robert, eds. *Capital Cities at War: Paris, London, Berlin 1914–1919.* Cambridge: Cambridge University Press, 1997.
Wróbel, Piotr J. "Foreshadowing the Holocaust: The Wars of 1914–1921 and Anti-Jewish Violence in Central and Eastern Europe." In *Legacies of Violence: Eastern Europe's First World War,* edited by Jochen Böhler, Wlodzimierz Borodziej, and Joachim von Puttkamer, 169–209. Munich: Oldenburg, 2014.
Yochelson, Bonnie, and Daniel Czitrom. *Rediscovering Jacob Riis: Exposure Journalism and Photography in Turn-of-the-Century New York.* Chicago: University of Chicago Press, 2007.
Youde, Jeremy. *Biopolitical Surveillance and Public Health in International Politics.* Basingstoke, UK: Palgrave Macmillan, 2010.
Zahra, Tara. "Each Nation Only Cares for Its Own: Empire, Nation, and Child Welfare Activism in the Bohemian Lands, 1900–1918." *American Historical Review* 111, no. 5 (2006): 1378–1402.
———. *The Great Departure: Mass Migration from Eastern Europe and the Making of the Free World.* New York: W.W. Norton, 2017.
———. *Kidnapped Souls: National Indifference and the Battle for Children in the Bohemian Lands, 1900–1948.* Ithaca, NY: Cornell University Press, 2008.
———. *The Lost Children: Reconstructing Europe's Families After World War I.* Cambridge, MA: Harvard University Press, 2011.
———. "'The Psychological Marshall Plan': Displacement, Gender, and Human Rights after World War II." *Central European History* 44, no. 1 (2011): 37–62.
———. "Reclaiming Children for the Nation: Germanization, National Ascription, and Democracy in the Bohemian Lands, 1900–1945." *Central European History* 37, no. 4 (2004): 250–65.
Zeidler, Miklós. *A magyar irredenta kultusz a két világháború között.* Budapest: Teleki László Alapítvány, 2002.
———. *Ideas on Territorial Revision in Hungary, 1920—1945.* Boulder, CO: Social Science Monographs, 2007.
Zelizer, Viviana A. *Pricing the Priceless Child: The Changing Social Value of Children.* Princeton, NJ: Princeton University Press, 1985.
Zimmer, Oliver. "Nationalism in Europe, 1918–1945." In *The Oxford Handbook of the History of Nationalism,* edited by John Breuilly, 414–34. Oxford: Oxford University Press, 2013.
Zimmermann, Susan. *Divide, Provide, and Rule: An Integrative History of Poverty Policy, Social Policy, and Social Reform in Hungary under the Habsburg Monarchy.* Budapest: Central European University Press, 2011.
———. *Prächtige Armut: Fürsorge, Kinderschutz und Sozialreform in Budapest. Das sozialpolitische Laboratorium der Doppelmonarchie im Vergleich zu Wien, 1873–1914.* Mainz, Germany: Jan Thorbecke, 1997.
Zimmermann, Susan, and Gerhard Melinz. *Gyermeksorsok és gyermekvédelem: Budapest a Monarchia idején.* Budapest: Fővárosi Szabó Ervin Könyvtár, 1996.
"Zsolnai Kálmán tragédia." *8 Órai Újság* 4, no. 228 (September 9, 1918): 5.
Zweiniger-Bargielowska, Ina. "Introduction." In *Food and War in Twentieth Century Europe,* edited by Ina Zweiniger-Bargielowska, Rachel Duffett, and Alain Drouard, 1–10. Burlington, VT: Ashgate, 2011.
Zweiniger-Bargielowska, Ina, Rachel Duffett, and Alain Drouard, eds. *Food and War in Twentieth Century Europe.* Burlington, VT: Ashgate, 2011.

INDEX

Allied Reparation Commission, 35, 84
American Commission to Negotiate Peace, 71
American Commonwealth Fund, 44–45
American Red Cross, 10, 101, 146, 163–64, 170–72, 175–77, 218, 222, 226–27, 231–32, 237, 278, 287, 289, 307
American Relief Administration, 18–20, 85, 136, 154–74, 185–86, 195–99, 204–5, 211–13, 234, 283
American Relief Committee for Hungarian Sufferers, 102, 115
anti-Bolshevism. See Hungarian Soviet Republic
Apponyi, Albert, 140, 231
Austria, 6, 18, 62–63, 74–75, 79, 155
Austro-Hungarian Empire, 5, 26, 30, 32, 60–61, 64, 78–79, 86, 235, 250

Bandholz, Harry, 83
Bárczy, István, 106, 137
Bärtle, Theodor, 38–39
Belgium, 153–54, 212, 218, 253–55, 260–64
Bethlen, István, 35, 251
blockade, 60–61, 66–69, 81–83
bodies, childrens', 7, 15–16, 91–93, 103, 184–98, 284
Bókay, János, 213, 225, 230, 234
Bolshevist government in Hungary. See Soviet Republic, Hungarian
Bowden, Carleton G., 185
bread, 47, 51, 53, 62–63, 66, 73–79, 83, 160–61, 173, 186, 195, 198–200, 228, 230, 248, 275, 295, 308
breastfeeding, 137, 139–41, 144, 198–99, 201
Budapest Central Aid Committee, 137–39
Buxton, Dorothy, 16, 103

calories, 64, 73, 79, 155–56, 195, 197, 228
Charles I/IV, 80, 144–45, 246–49
Children's Day, 127–28
Christmas, 12–13, 213, 220–22, 226, 232–34, 237, 252, 296–97
class dynamics, 27, 34–35, 40, 54, 80, 124–25, 133, 174, 240, 288, 310

clothing, 52, 73, 138–39, 174–75, 235–39, 275, 280–81
coal, 70–71
countryside, 5, 63, 77–83, 246–48
Csergő, Hugó, 137, 247
Czechoslovakia, 27, 70–71, 131, 157, 160, 173, 312

daycare, 96, 124, 137–39, 141, 145
Declaration of the Rights of the Child, 14, 285, 292, 300
diseases, 94–99, 260–61, 280

Edelsheim-Gyulai, Lipót, 123, 126–27
education, 52–53, 124–26, 129–30, 194, 219, 274–300
emotions, 6–9, 32, 35, 61, 65, 101–3, 111–12, 133, 169, 171, 218, 228, 240, 258–62, 269, 279, 292, 307
European Children's Fund, 160, 212–13
European Famine Bill, 18
European Relief Council, 168–69, 173, 228
exhibitions, 145, 191, 236–38, 293–96

fathers and war, 3, 6, 44, 75, 95–96, 129, 192–95, 280
films, 46, 215–16, 265–66
First World War. See World War I
foster placements, international, 270

gender and relief work, 124–25, 133–37, 173, 219–20
Geneva, 14, 16–17, 37–38, 135, 153, 172, 178, 189, 216, 292–96
grain/flour, 5, 61–62, 69–70, 78, 83, 164, 173–74
Grant-Smith, Ulysses, 213, 216–17
Gunn, Selskar M., 157, 239

Harding, Warren G., 223–4
Hine, Lewis, 43
Holland, 19, 217, 256–70

341

Hoover, Herbert, 15, 67, 71, 82–85, 104, 113, 153–54, 159–61, 167, 195, 201, 212, 227–28, 305, 310
Horthy, Miklós, 5, 213–15, 219–21, 232, 242, 294, 310
housing conditions, 3–4, 8, 34, 106–8, 280
Hungarian Soviet Republic, 15, 28, 79–84, 159–60

infant mortality, 3, 7, 49, 62–63, 67, 96–98, 140–44
infant relief, 67, 93, 135–46, 155, 173–77, 191–92, 198–201, 204–6, 237
inflation, 73–74, 133,
influenza, 95–97
Inter-Allied Food Council 154–55
Inter-Allied Trade Commission, 83
International Committee of the Red Cross, 65, 135, 169–72, 216, 253, 276, 294
internationalism, 11–13, 19–21, 61, 113, 171–72, 216–19, 255, 308–9

Jebb, Eglantyne, 13, 16, 43–44, 102, 111, 113, 124, 130, 276, 285, 290, 297–98
Jewish children and refugees, 14, 26, 31
Jewish Joint Distribution Committee, 18, 168, 186, 305
Juliana of the Netherlands, 267–68

Kaiser Karl Wohlfahrtswerk, 247–50
Kellogg, Vernon, 154, 203
kindergartens, 161–62, 194–95, 222, 306
Koestler, Arthur, 82
Kun, Béla, 5, 20, 30, 81–84, 159, 215

League of Nations, 14, 55, 114, 169, 216, 309
Lévai, Ödön, 25, 93–95
London, 102–3, 203, 211–13, 297

MacKenzie, William Andrew, 38, 294–97
Madzsar, József, 137, 143–44
malnutrition, 16, 73, 86, 91–95, 114, 121, 156, 161, 184, 187, 190–92, 199, 304
Mária Valéria settlement, 46, 95, 274, 279, 296
MÁV (Hungarian State Railway), 33, 72, 74
Meinl, Julius, 74–75
midwifery, 139–46
milk, 62–63, 69, 71, 139–41, 144, 164, 174, 198–201, 204

milk kitchens, 18, 141, 144–45, 153, 178, 184, 198–205
milk powder, 139, 198, 205
Ministry of Labor and Social Welfare, 145
minority treatment, 29–31, 55
mortality, 49, 62, 98, 123, 137, 140, 142, 143–44, 148, 200
mothers, 6, 44, 54, 65–67, 77, 96–98, 104–5, 124, 134–48, 175–77, 186, 198–205, 265
Müllner, János, 251, 254

National Child Protection League, 121–29, 135, 170, 176, 204–5, 220, 247, 253–54, 263, 278
nationalism, 11, 19–21, 172, 200, 210, 217–19, 237, 290–91, 309–11
National Stefánia Association for the Protection of Mothers and Infants, 135–36, 140–46, 172, 175, 198, 204
Neugebauer, Vilmos, 135–36, 170
New York, 102, 111, 228–29
nursing and nurses, 133–35, 172, 177

orphanages, 18, 124, 130–31, 137, 139, 148, 161, 195, 232, 282

Paris Peace Conference. *See* Treaty of Trianon
Pedlow, James, 17, 132, 171–75, 212, 221, 223, 230–34
Pirquet, Clemens von, 155–56, 162, 195, 211
Poland, 69, 94, 157, 172–73
prisoners of war, 65–66, 81–82
Prohászka, Ottokár, 172–73
Purgly, Magdolna, 219–20, 278, 293

queuing, 76–77, 200

Rädda Barnen, 169, 171
rationing, 75–77, 82
Reding-Biberegg, Rodolphe de, 170, 178, 278
refugees, Transylvanian, 26–36, 40, 44, 53–54, 174
relief kitchens, 161–62, 195, 213, 226
religious organizations, 125–27, 168–73, 195, 213, 252–55, 261–63, 278–79, 293, 298
Richardson, George, 163, 212
rickets, 99, 155, 170, 190, 198, 203

Riis, Jacob, 43
Rockefeller Foundation, 18, 157
Rockefeller, John D., 228
Romania, 26–31, 36, 70–71, 82–83, 131, 157, 295, 213

Save the Children Fund, 16, 44, 104, 113, 124, 130, 135, 171, 253, 274–300
Save the Children International Union, 16, 130, 169–71, 191, 226, 252, 290, 292–93
Schioppa, Lorenzo, 279
school attendance and truancy, 52–53, 77, 96
schools, feeding at, 76, 137–39, 161–62, 170, 186, 194–95
Second Vienna Arbitration, 312
self-help, 176, 179, 285, 290–91, 304
Singer, Hedwig, 136, 198
slumming, 37, 43
Smith, Armstrong, 114, 278, 280, 282
Spanish flu. *See* influenza
statelessness, 28–31, 35
statistics, 70, 192, 197, 200, 206, 307
Sweden, 174, 253
Switzerland, summer children's trains to, 248, 252
Széchényi, László, 132–33
Széll, Kálmán, 126

Tábori, Kornél, 6, 38, 47–48, 104
Taylor, Alonzo, 154, 230, 240
Teleki, Pál, 36
territorial loss, 4, 27, 36, 54, 69, 130–31, 217, 241, 312–13

territorial revisionism, 27, 37, 54, 92, 214–19, 241
Terry, Prentiss M., 51, 53, 97–98
transnationalization of aid, 11, 16–21, 172–79, 218, 306
Transylvanians. *See* refugees, Transylvanian.
Treaty of Trianon, 26, 29–31, 36, 54, 215–17, 276, 310
tuberculosis, 94–99, 126, 135, 155, 260, 280

unemployment, 71, 82, 287, 313
United States Food Administration, 18, 154, 156, 212

vagrants, 51, 238, 283
Vajkai, Julia, 2, 17, 38–43, 130, 135–36, 171, 178, 252, 274–300, 306–7
Vajkai, Rose, 41, 130, 135–36, 171
Vienna. See Austria.
visuals, role of, 8–9, 12, 48–49, 99–105, 108–10, 113, 191, 204, 215
vulnerability, 3, 7, 85, 91–94, 113, 304, 307, 310

Weardale, Lord, 113, 262
weight, 67, 156, 185, 188, 192–93, 197, 201, 204, 225, 252–53, 266
White Cross Hospital, 97, 191, 204
White Terror, 5
workrooms, Save the Children, 19, 43, 223, 226, 240, 273–303
World War I, 4, 13, 26, 64–65

YMCA/YWCA, 168

FRIEDERIKE KIND-KOVÁCS is a contemporary historian and Senior Researcher at the Hannah Arendt Institute for Totalitarianism Studies at TU Dresden. She is author of *Written Here, Published There: How Underground Literature Crossed the Iron Curtain*, which won the University of Southern California Book Prize in Cultural and Literary Studies in 2015. She is editor (with Machteld Venken) of the double special issue "Childhood in Times of Political Transformation in the 20th Century" of the *Journal of Modern European History*; (with Heike Karge and Sara Bernasconi) of *From the Midwife's Bag to the Patient's File: Public Health in Eastern Europe*; and (with Jessie Labov) of *Samizdat, Tamizdat, and Beyond: Transnational Media during and after Socialism*.

www.ingramcontent.com/pod-product-compliance
Lightning Source LLC
Chambersburg PA
CBHW031704230426
43668CB00006B/104